IMPROV NONSENSE:
ALL THE POSTS

MARCH 2010-JUNE 2016

WILL HINES

Copyright © 2016 by Will Hines

All rights reserved. No part of this publication may be reproduced, distributed or transmitted in any form or by any means, including photocopying, recording, or other electronic or mechanical methods, without the prior written permission of the publisher, except in the case of brief quotations embodied in critical reviews and certain other noncommercial uses permitted by copyright law.

Will Hines/Pretty Great Publishing
Los Angeles, California
www.improvnonsense.com

Book Layout © 2016 by Nick Jaramillo
Cover Lettering: Erica Sera

Improv Nonsense: All The Posts/ Will Hines. —1st ed.
ISBN 978-0-9826257-4-3

To my brothers Kevin and Brian being friends with me even when I do silly things like write about improv for 500 pages.

CONTENTS

Introduction	1
2010	**5**
Mission Statement	6
New Harold Team Members	6
Brothers Hines Thanks	7
Two Kinds of Listening	9
Third Beats: Try Initiating Without a Connection in Mind	11
Team Brooklyn: In Defense of Fast Screamy Improv Sets	13
RIP John Ward ("Dr. Wimpy")	15
Painting of Achilles	16
People People's Standing Ovation	16
It's Okay to Ask Questions	17
Stumbling on a Great Show	18
Physical Matching at the Top	19
Young Improvisers Fighting	23
Fighting, Lying, Being Stupid	24
Know Everything	25
Dwell on Good Scenes, Not Bad Ones	26
Q: Old Days	27
Q: Improv Changed Since You Started?	28
Billy Merritt's Improv Party	29
Q: Underrated Improviser?	29
Q: Avoiding Break-Ups?	30
Q: Disagree with UCB Curriculum?	30
Q: Nervous about Cagematch?	31
Q: Too Funny?	31
Q: Favorite Structure?	31
Q: Venues?	32
Q: Negative Partner?	32

Q: Fantastic Scene?	32
Q: Avoid One-Dimensional Straight Man?	33
Q: Real Names?	33
Q: Favorite Bastian Member?	34
Q: Get Over Self-Doubt?	34
Q: Area You Wanted to Improve?	34
Q: Your Sense of Humor?	35
Q: Second-Favorite Member of Bastian?	35
Q: Blasphemous	36
Q: Burned Out	36
Q: Scared of Skeletons?	36
Q: Pre-Show Ritual?	37
Q: Favorite Stepfather?	37
Q: Harold Teams with More Women Than Men?	37
A Set of 2-Person Scenes to Bond Over	38
Act Like Life, Except…	39
Q: Archetypal Characters Boring	39
Q: Eternalism?	40
Q: How Long to Not Suck?	40
Q: Improv Hero?	41
Q: Overthinking	41
Q: Picking Scene Partners Mid-Show	41
Q: Not Ben Rodgers	42
Q: Best Shoves Show without Erik?	43
Q: Themed Harolds?	43
Q: Premise vs. Organic	43
Q: Always Getting Better?	44
Q: All-Star Team?	45
Q: Don't Want House Team	45

There Are Days When I Hate This	45
Tanouye and I Discuss Themes	46
Two Follow-Up Questions to Theme Discussion	50
My Vision Quest	51
The Hard Part Is Connecting to Someone Else's Idea	53
Try It Without Any Rules	55
Q: TJ and Dave	56
Q: Comedy or Theater?	57
Q: Big A-Ha moment?	57
Q: Character vs. Game	58
Q: Demise of Straight Man	58
Q: Blackout on Your Move?	59
Q: What Does Improv Mean to You?	59
You Should Want to Be Funny	59
Improvising Better	60
Conversation: Why Do Improv?	61
Q: Slump	64
Q: Too Crazy Too Soon	65
Q: Mental Rut	66
Q: iO vs UCB?	66
Q: No Way You'll Be a Smart Improviser	67
Q: Emotional Fights with Your Brother Over Improv?	68
Q: Invocation "Elementary?"	68
Q: San Fran Improv?	69
Q: Terrible Show	69
Q: Hate Sketch?	69
Q: Doubts	70
Q: Poop Object Work	72
Why I Do Improv	72

Q: Leaving a Team?	73
Q: Supportive Straight Man?	74
Q: How Far Love?	75
Q: Support vs. Upstaging	75
Q: Vonage Point?	76
Q: Improv Teams = Classic Bands	76
Q: UCB Generations?	77
Q: Besser Contradicts You?	78
Q: Improv in Existential Crisis	79
Q: Bad Mood = Better Show	80
Q: Most Epically Ridiculous Show?	80
Q: Improv Innovations	81
Q: Improv People Common Energy	82
Q: Clarify Terminology	82
More UCBTNY Generations Thoughts	83
Quick Thought on Openings	85
Doppelganger; Mullaney; Two-Person Improv	85
Maybe When Giving Notes	86
Stop Focusing on Individual Notes	87
Q: Improv Hat Trick	88
Q: Words of Wisdom that Stuck	88
Let the Exercise Do the Work	89

2011 — 91

Harold Night Shakeups and Bastian	92
Accepting Offers, Rich Specifics, Physicality and Commitment	93
Have an Opinion at All Times, to Everything	97
Two Types of Connecting	97
Chivalry	98
Stop Naming People "Jenkins"	101

Q: Labeling a Woman as a Man	101
Q: How do Improvisers Make a Living?	102
Q: Too Many Fuck-Arounds?	102
Q: Thinking About the Button	103
Q: justcraig: Ever Farted on the Back Line?	103
Things I Know About Only From Watching Improv	104
Placeholder Thought: Empathy	104
Better Conversations	104
Hey, Anthony King	108
Better Conversations Follow-Up	109
Yes (Pause) And	111
Q: Repeat (Pause) And	111
Accept Offers: Speak to the Topic Offered	112
Accept Offers: Accusations/Complaints	114
Accept Offers: Here's What's Funny	115
Accept Offers: After an Opening	119
Accept Offers: Agreement Before Reality	119
Accept Offers: Do It Casually, Easily	121
Accept Offers: When You're Not Expecting It	122
Accept Offers: Don't Break Game	123
Accept Offers: When It's Refused	124
Accept Offers: Conclusion	126
Q: More on Accepting Offers	127
Q: "Smart" Play	127
Q: Our Mutual Friend Robbie	128
YES Over AND	128
Practice vs. Chemistry	129
Q: Where Can I Put This Line?	129
Q: justcraig: What Percentage Wearing a Hat?	130

Something to Unpack	130
My Favorite Woody Allen Jokes	131
Maybe Every Game Is Just "Opposites"	132
Amy Poehler Quote	133
Walk-Ons vs. Tag-Outs	134
Q: Ad-Lib vs. Improv	135
Kitchen Rules	136
An Important Phase in Improv Students' Development	138
Stages	138
Q: Pimps vs. Weak Offers	139
The Danger of Clarity	139
Q: Good and Bad Justifying?	141
Q: Cut Down on Terminology, Improv Nerds	142
Q: Mick's Book	142
"Baby Got Back" Appears in 100% of Hot Spot Warm-Ups.	143
How Are You Supposed to Remember Stuff From the Opening? I Can Never Remember Stuff From the Opening! Do You Have Any Advice on Remembering Stuff from the Opening?	143
Best Recurring Character in Any Improv Team's History	144
Amy Poehler Quote	144
How to Say No	144
Yes and No	145

2012   **147**

Funny, Smart and No	148
Know Everything!	149
Play It Real? A Police State	152
Teaching Interviews: Chris Gethard, Part 1 of 2	153
Q: Improv Order of Operations?	161
Q: People Will Only Improviser with Each Other?	162

Q: Improv Specific to Its Home City?	162
Q: Should Everything Be Justified?	163
Q: justcraig: Silly or Goofy?	163
Improvy Moves in Movies	163
Q: Examples of Good Fights?	164
In Cagematch	165
Notes: December 22, 2000	166
Don't Ask Questions = Don't Be Surprised	168
Q: Improv Team of Historical Figures	169
Q: justcraig: Funniest Volume of Yelling?	170
Q: Improv Exercises for When You're Alone?	170
Q: Funniest Thing Erik Tanouye Has Done?	171
Triangle	171
Empathy	172
Condition	174
Like Minded People	174
Q: People Laugh When Names are Given	180
Q: justcraig: Funniest Food?	180
How Do I Get More Involved?	181
Ways I Felt Involved at UCB Theatre	182
Q: I wasn't invited to audition.	187
YouTube Commenting in Real Life	189
Getting Swept Up in It	189
Q: Is UCB/Improv a Cult?	192
Q: Is UCB Trying to be More Diverse?	192
Initiation Etiquette	193
Q: Coddling Timid Players?	194
Q: Why Not Rhyme?	195
Remember, Don't Invent	195

Q: Improv a Road to Nowhere?	196
Q: Should I Have Skipped Class?	199
Q: Exercises for Empathy?	199
Follow-Up to "Road to Nowhere"	200
Q: LA Improv Scene?	200
Q: TMBG Lyric?	201
Q: Pet Peeves?	201
Q: One Leading, Another Following?	202
Q: Popular Improv Names?	202
Q: Why Don't You Call Out Noah Forman?	203
Thank You	204
Quote	204
Q: Favorite Part of Playing with Convoy?	204
Q: Least Favorite Part of Playing with Convoy?	205
Q: When to Support?	205
The Music, Not the Lyrics	205
Q: One Person I Dislike?	206
Q: Gum Chewing?	207
Q: Nothing is Fun.	207
Q: justcraig: Is Sue Galloway Upset?	208
Q: Not Emotional Person	208
Q: Can You Tell if Someone Will Never Be Good?	209
Q: Finishing Move?	210
Q: Notes after Shows	210
Q: I'm Not Standing Out	211
Q: Do Improvisers Make Terrific Liars?	212
Q: Missing the Sense of "How Did They Do That?"	212
Q: Why 3 Years to Get Good?	213
Q: Have We Seen It All?	214

Q: What Teams Would You Bring Back?	215
Q: Worst Advice?	215
Q: Honesty the Best Policy?	215
Q: Why Not "Have Fun Out There?"	216
Q: Ian's "Worst Yes-And I've Ever Seen"	217
Something for Me	217
Q: Improv on Video vs. Just Audio?	219
Q: What Should I Do to Get Better for Advanced Study?	220
Q: Minimizing "Comparing Myself to Others?"	221
Q: Family Tree of House Teams?	221
Q: Best Way to Leave a Group?	222
Q: What Should Coach's Charge?	222
Q: Improvise with Anyone You've Never Met?	224
Q: Should Coaches Take Notes on Their Phones?	224
Q: Is Writing Sketch Part of the Transformation?	225
Q: Indie Teams Don't Care?	225
Q: I Won't be at Stepfathers.	226
Q: justcraig: Funniest Thing to Order?	226
Q: I'll be at Stepfathers.	226
Q: Harolds Not Making It 20 Minutes?	227
Q: Perplexed by Something New?	228
Q: Where's the Line at How Short Harolds Should Be?	228
Q: Why are Couples Always a Man and Woman?	229
Q: How Hard to Do an Impression?	230
Q: I Have Humped People in the Last Two Shows.	230
I'm Not Going To Yes-And You Shitting On Me	231
Q: You Attacked Me. Enjoy Your Hoodie.	232
Q: Ever play Mo'Nique?	233
Q: Chicago Harolds are Often 22-25 Minutes.	233

Q: You Were a Smug Arrogant Jerk.	233
Q: justcraig: Best Name for a Male Butler?	234
Hostile Characters	234
Q: Agreement Too Passive?	236
Q: Hostile Character Example Seemed Good.	236
Q: Why is There Bitterness Towards UCB?	237
How Do You All Deal with Improv Ruts?	240
Q: Choosing Characters Who Are Cool	240
Q: Racist Caricature?	241
Q: Can Someone Ask Why They Didn't Get into a Class?	241
Q: Initiation Etiquette Example	243
Q: Letting Someone Know I Felt Demeaned	244
Q: 10,000 Hours?	244
Q: Am I a Ninja, Pirate or Robot?	245
Q: Dealing With Harassers Outside the Theater.	245
Q: Should I Join a Team Run by Someone I Don't Respect?	246
Shows and Scenes I Like Remembering	247
Scenes I Saw in Class or Practices that Made Me Cry Laughing	251
The Messiness Makes It Real	254
Play Like a Great Team	254
Trying to Win the Scene	255
You Go to Them	256
You Must Appreciate the Good in What You Do	259
Q: Fictional Character Harold Team?	260

2013 — 263

Watching Zip Zap Zop	264
The Brave Choice	264
Q: Crush on a Teacher	265
Q: Why Do I Always Suggest a Food?	265

Follow the Follower	266
Lying, Meanness, Stupidity	266
The Rules	268
Know, Care, Say	269
Q: Game vs. Premise	271
Q: justcraig: Correct Name for Japanese Company?	272
Q: Second Game Move?	272
Q: Be the Bird or Just Flap my Arms?	273
Mini-Rut	273
Q: justcraig: Funnier bird?	274
Coaching Rates	275
Coaching Rates, Amended	275
Q: justcraig: Coaching Question	278
New Controversy	279
Q: Greg Rowan	279
How Can I Get Out of My Head?	279
You Will Never Figure This Out	284
"Good" Fighting?	285
Q: Can One Initiate with a Game?	286
Q: Stop Being Clever?	287
Q: Would You Blow Off Semantics Questions in Class?	288
Q: Why Do You Like Putting Limits on Scenes?	290
Q: justcraig: How Much Tongue?	290
Q: What Kind of Support When I See No Way to Help?	291
Q: Advice for a Show Tonight?	291
Rave	292
Q: Are Strong Acting Skills Necessary?	293
Small Men Drafts: Liberty Plaza	294
Small Men Drafts: Security Questions	301

"Relationship"	307
More Specific?	307
Small Men Drafts: Your Son's Band	307
Q: justcraig: Should You Speak in a Lower Voice When You're Someone's Father?	314
Q: What's Your Advice If No Game Is Found?	314
Undermine Yourself	315
Let Improv Be Small	315
UCB Comedy Improvisation Manual	316
Justification: Make Sure Someone's Home	322
Q: "That Guy" Question	323
Q: "That Guy" Question	323
Q: Difference Between "Raising the Stakes" and "Heightening?"	324
Q: The Group Missed the Best Idea.	324
Q: Why So Many "J" Names?	325
Over Emphasis	325
All Advice	326
New Workshop: Get in Your Head!	326
Conundrum	327
Change the Lyrics, Keep the Music	327
It's Yours	327
New Terms	328
Q: justcraig: When Someone Mentions Will Smith?	329
Things That Are Hard to Do in Long-Form Improv	329
The Judge vs. The Heart	330
Noting a Bad Habit	331
Q: Why Is It Good to Choose to Know Things That Have Been Confessed?	331
Yin and Yang	332
True and Important	333

Fights	334
Teams are Valuable but Overrated	335
Q: What Does "There Aren't Enough Spots" Mean?	336
Empathy Again	337
Territory	338
It's Not a Rule but for My Taste Don't Say the Suggestion in a Scene Kinda Ever but Certainly Once You're More Than Three Minutes in	338
Q: What if I Don't Like Being Funny in the First Line?	339
Practice	340
How Can I Get Better at Game?	341
Yeah, but Really, How Can I Get Better at Game?	345
I Can't Remember Anything from the Opening	348
Fighting Advice: Maybe This?	349
Future Talk and Past Talk	349
Brothers Hines	350
Q: How Can You Both Know Someone and Find Them Unusual?	351
Q: What If Only You Go to Them, and They Don't Go to You?	352
Made-Up Proper Noun Improv	352
Improv as Religion	353
Q: You Acted Like a Bully!	355
Q: Best Time to Reveal You're Not Dead?	356
Q: What About Being the "Real" Dead Body?	356
Q: What If the ACTOR Dies?	357
Q: INVENTORY	357
Office Workers Arguing	357
Go See Plays	359
Important Update	360
Q: Should One Start at iO then Go to UCB?	360
Q: How to "Be Playful?"	361
Q: How Come I've Never Seen You ONCE Play a Talking Bear?	362

2014 — 365

Saying "No" to Offensive Things	366
Q: When Is It Too Late to Make the Scene an Orgy?	369
Q: What About Teachers Who Say "Don't Make Jokes?	370
Accusations: Three Exercises	371
Q: justcraig: What's Funnier in a Subway Scene?	374
Pace	375
Q: Offensive Subject Matter?	376
Irony	378
Q: When Is It Appropriate to Have a Coach and When Not?	380
Irony: Exercises	381
Exercises for Better Improv	384
Improv As Practical Advice	385
Q: Have You Ever Had to Kick Someone Out?	386
Q: What About Low-Energy Bored Students?	387
Q: What About a Reluctant Person?	389
Q: What About People Who Want to Be "The Star?"	389
Q: Awkward / Uncomfortable Students?	390
Q: What About People Who Look to the Back Line for an Edit?	390
Q: I'm Confident in Class but Very Nervous in Shows.	391
Q: How About Jealousy / Anxiety Over Your Career?	392
Q: Advice on Playing Characters?	393
Q: When Someone Pimps You into an Accent?	393
Q: I'm Yessing and Not Anding.	393
Q: Object-Work a Walker or Use a Chair?	394
Q: What is "No Action" by Elvis Costello About?	394
Q: Should a Team Acknowledge a Show Was Bad?	395
How Do You Make a Living?	396
The Future Vanishes!	398

Q: Grey Area Between Offers and Denials?	400
Q: About "React Honestly?"	401
Q: justcraig: Eating Marijuana at DCM?	401
Q: How'd You Guys Come Up with the Beer Commercials Guys?	402
Some Suggestions for Level One Class Etiquette	403
You Already Know the Real "Why"	405
Q: Directing My First Improv Show.	406
Q: My Improv is Too Deferential.	407
Q: What If the House Team at Your Theater Sucks?	407
Defensiveness	409
Is It Coming from Fear?	413
Exercises: The Samurai	413
Exercises: You Wanted to See Me?	416
Q: Giving Too Many Heady Notes	418
Exercises: Words Slash Follow (Warmup)	420
Exercises: Who's Unusual?	421
Q: An Exercise for Focusing on the Other Character?	422
Q: How Useful to Note a Scene's Problems When It Went Well?	423
Q: Is the Pattern Game Good for a Performance?	424
Q: justcraig: Better to Lean Angrily in an Interrogation Scene?	426
Exercise: Compliment/Boast	426
Suggested Practices for Better Listening at Top of Scenes	428
Q: How to Get Rid of Fighting?	430
No Bullshit Harolds	431
Exercise: Object into POV	435
An Unfair List of Pet Peeves and Personal Preferences	436
Difficult People	438
Q: Can I Cherry Pick Who I Want to Form a Team with?	439
General Qualifier	441

Giving Positive Notes	442
Q: I'm in My Head in UCB 401	443
Q: How Do I Avoid "Me-First" Moves?	444
Jimmy and Will: Worrying about Being Smart Enough	446
Q: Does "Clever" Improv Lead to Ironic Detachment?	449

2015 — 451

RIP Jason Chin	452
Q: I Got Worse at the Things I Was "Good" at?	452
The Appalled Tone	454
Q: I Felt Bad Starting Out with our Characters Hating Each Other	455
Ask Jimmy, Ask Will: Short-Form Group Trying Long-Form	456
Phrases for Describing the Game of the Scene	458
Emotional Priorities	458
Exercise: The "Stations" Pattern Game	459
Shoulds	463
A Night I Remember from My Level 1 Practice Group	464
"Relationship" and "Game"	465
Q: Why are There Less Women on Harold Teams than Men?	466
Q: justcraig: Plopping down a Pile of Papers or Saying "Johnson Files?"	470
Would You Rather	470
Q: What About People Who Say "Gender/Race Shouldn't Even be Thought About?"	471
Ask Jimmy/Ask Will: Am I Funny Enough?	475
Improvising in Offices After Work	477
"Themes" Pattern Game	478
Q: I'm Self-Conscious Being Older than Everyone Else.	482
What Made the UCBT Work?	483
Ping Pong Table Metaphor	485

Q: Advice for Someone Going into College Who Wants to Pursue Comedy?	486
First Improv Classes	487
Q: What does It Mean for Your Character to Have a Philosophy?	487
Q: justcraig: What's Better? Re: Job interviews	488
Inbound Pass	488
Handshake	490
Q: Why Does Ironic Detachment Get Laughs?	490
Q: How Do You Feel about All the Bullying?	491
Q: MBTI Personality Types in Improv?	492
Q: Transphobic Jokes in Improv	492
Q: What about "That Guy" Who Gives Notes?	494
Q: How to Come Up with a Second Beat without Ignoring Current Scene?	495
Q: You Dropped a Quarter.	496
Q: How to Discuss Your Show with the Other Players?	496
Q: What if YOU are "That Guy?"	497
Q: How to Pick Where to Take Classes?	497
Witches	498
Q: I Can't Afford Classes.	498
Q: Is It Funny to Fart in a Scene?	500
Q: Can I Tell Someone to Chill Out in a Scene?	500
Some Notes I've Been Giving	501
Q: What if I Like to be Patient, but Everyone Keeps Doing Every Idea "Now?"	502
Consider Every Offer (Don't Accept Blindly)	503
Q: I'm Playing with a Bad Partner Who Likes to Call Out Everything	504
Q: How Many Questions Do You Get?	506
Q: You Get Labeled as Having an Accent but You Haven't Had One	507
Q: justcraig: When is Too Late to Put Up X-Rays?	507

Q: More Advice on How to Discuss Shows with Your Fellow Players?	508
How Does Your Team Talk to Each Other?	510
Q: Do you read Any New-Age Type Books That Correlate to Improv?	510
Q: Why is "Broad" Bad?	511
No One Here Wants to Be Funny?	511
Q: How Long Before You Stopped Bombing?	514
Be Unnecessarily Specific	514
Argue That the World Is Flat	515
Q: 2-3 years in, I'm Suddenly Anxious.	516
Give a Shit	517
Q: How to Improve Timidity?	517
Improv for People Not That Good	519
Q: Is It Crazy to Think Someone Should Be on a Lloyd Team Before Coaching?	520
Q: How Much Money Do You Make as a Working Actor?	521
Q: Have You Ever Quit a Duo Team?	522
Q: justcraig: In Improv…	523
Notes I Got	523

2016 — 529

Q: I'm Starting 101 in 2 Weeks and Feeling Antsy.	530
Q: "Wizard Fighting" vs. "Giving a Gift?"	530
Be a Great Straight Man	530
Q: Any A-to-C Exercises to Do Alone?	532
Q: How to Coach Someone's Aggressively Sexual Behavior?	533
LGBTQ Characters in Improv	538
Q: "Long Distance Runaround" by Yes or "Space Truckin" by Deep Purple?	542
Q: What Prompted You to Move to LA?	543
Q: My 201 Teacher is "Brutally" Honest.	545

Truthful at All Costs	545
"Is This About..."	547
Q: Most Humbling Experience?	549
Q: How to Make Your Partner Look Funny?	549
Q: What's the Best Way to Work on Justification/Philosophy?	550
Q: justcraig: "Yo, Yo, Yo, Yo"	552
Q: What Should My Practice Group Do About "That Guy?"	552
Q: "End the Group and Reform the Group" Sounds Childish	553
Q: How Much Stage Time Should an Improviser Really Want?	553
Q: My Team Is Too Quick with Initiating and Walking On	554
Q: I Find Myself Trying to "Fix" Very Bad Improv.	555
Q: How Do You Get a Team You're Directing to Listen More?	555
Code of Conduct for Classes, First Draft	556
Q: Any Tips for Getting Out of This Rut?	556
Q: My Classmate Is Not Great at Improv.	557
Q: My Partner Is a Real Problem, He Moved to LA.	557
Q: I Feel I Haven't Been Creative or Adding Lately.	558

Special Essays	**561**
How Can I Get Out of My Head?	562
What Do We Do About "That Guy?"	570
How Can I Get Better at Game?	576
Yeah, But Really, How Can I Get Better at Game?	580
How Do You Make a Living?	583

INTRODUCTION

This book is a collection of every post from my blog Improv Nonsense. Oh man, almost every noun in that sentence requires an explanation.

A blog is an online journal. Improv Nonsense is a blog about long-form improv comedy. Improv comedy is the art of making up comedic scenes with no script, on a stage. "Long form" is the subset of improv in which there is very little structure. This is to distinguish it from "short form," which has strictly defined games with clear rules.

Okay, phew.

I'm the sole author. My name is Will Hines, and I've been one of the senior teachers and performers at the Upright Citizens Brigade Theatre since the year 2000. In Improv Nonsense, I'd put my thoughts, memories and stories about improv. It ran from 2010 to 2016. At its peak it had 20,000 subscribers.

Improv Nonsense is retired now. Well, I don't know. Technically, it's still running. It's up at http://improvnonsense.tumblr.com/. I may post in it again, but for now it's retired.

A lot of the essays are very insightful and helpful, like a series in which I break down the phrase "accept offers." Others are clearly misguided and wrong, like when I scold improvisers that they should simply "know everything" in order to handle the many subjects that get referenced in a show.

I also fielded many questions from readers. Some of those questions were really interesting, like when someone asked why there were always more men than women on the house teams at the UCB Theatre. Other questions made me get very short and terse, like when someone said they thought the UCB cut off its improv shows too early. Still others were silly, like anything that Craig Rowin asked, including, "In improv, what's better: improv or improv?"

Many times students will come to up me and say, "Hey, I found your blog. It's really helpful." They'll also say, "It's hard to read a lot of the posts—I lose track of where I am." Or, "I wish it were printed out in a book."

Okay, only one person said that last one. His name was Scotty. But when he suggested it, I really liked the idea of making a book, both as a way to conveniently present all of the posts from the blog and also to document for myself all of the work I put into it.

This is a pretty faithful reproduction of the blog. I didn't correct the spelling or grammar. I didn't go back and change any of my old essays, which I sometimes disagree with. I didn't leave any posts out. This is the whole blog, as it ran.

If you were a fan of Improv Nonsense, or are a current improv nerd who wants to dive into six years—SIX YEARS—of improv-obsessed rants, or are just a strange completist who likes "complete" versions of ANYTHING... well, this is for you.

Thank you for taking a look.

Dear God, I had no idea this would be almost 600 pages.

Will Hines
September 2016
Los Angeles

2010

MARCH 23RD, 2010 at 2:51PM

MISSION STATEMENT

My plan is to indulge myself with improv ramblings, including my very one-sided overly generalized memories of show and groups past, thoughts of techniques and strategies—both for performing and teaching, and any other proclamations I usually save for when I'm in the corner booth of McManus at 2am after Harold Night. Follow or not, respond as you wish, but you have been warned!

MARCH 25TH, 2010 at 10:48PM

NEW HAROLD TEAM MEMBERS

Congrats to all the new UCBT Harold Members! You are all awesome. Thank you for caring about improv and for investing your time and energy in the UCBT improv world.

Some unsolicited advice (thx to Erik Tanouye and some others for help with this)

- When people tell you they liked your show, say "Thanks" even if you don't believe them. ESPECIALLY if you don't believe them.
- Don't try to make this group into something it's not. If you're looking to do a show with your eight best friends, call them and put a show together. These people MIGHT turn out to be your best friends, but you can't force that and it has less to do with how good your improv will be than you might think.
- No one will remember your first show or first entrance music in a few months. If you do a few shows and get great, everyone will remember you as a great team, so don't put too much pressure on the "first" any-thing. Five years from now, no one will say "Elastic Police was a great team that did amazing Harolds, but at their first show, they came out to a RUN DMC song which I didn't like."
- You're not getting paid enough to have a bad time.
- Don't blame the Harold night host or the audience if you have a bad show.

- You are not a better or worse person than you were one week ago.
- Dress well until you've earned the right to look like a slob.
- Watch other teams.
- Take your picture soon. You can always take a different one later.
- When you feel bad after a show, pick one specific thing to improve on and forgive yourself for everything else.
- Compliment your teammates honestly but generously.
- Know what warm-ups / openings / coaches you like and bring them up. But be cool with trying other people's stuff. And know that whatever opening you pick, one person will hate it and that person might be you.
- Instead of "Guys, I really hate this opening. It's really putting me in my head." try "When the time is right, I'd love to try a different opening."
- Most funny people are at least partly crazy, and you have to enjoy / tolerate / embrace that craziness to a certain degree.
- The name of your team will be the one that no one hates, not the one that anyone loves.

MARCH 25TH, 2010 at 11:07PM

BROTHERS HINES THANKS

Brothers Hines lost Cagematch tonight to a very cool and funny Reuben Williams show. We won 7 in a row, which we never would have expected and it was terrific fun!

I want to thank everyone who watched us and voted for us. It has been some of the most fun improv I've ever gotten to do. I feel like even though I've been doing this 10 years, that I learned a tremendous amount in the last 7 weeks—all by being able to do these long sets in front of a great, informed, supportive audience.

But most of all I want to thank my brother Kevin! I always knew he was good at this but I don't think I really appreciated HOW good until these sets where I've gotten to play with him for this long. It is the easiest thing in the world and it's not because we're brothers, but because Kevin Hines does not miss a trick. He hears everything and uses it. He understands everything. And he knows how to let a scene be the kind of scene it wants to be.

In these sets—for maybe the first time—I felt like I wasn't thinking, that the callbacks would show up without forcing them (er, not forcing them TOO much anyway), that I could drop just the tiniest feather of an unusual thing and it would grow into the spine of a scene, that it was better to be a smart character than a dumb one, that it was okay at almost every moment to express my opinions that I feeling at that moment—that it would fit. And that's because I got to play with an improviser who makes everything better. I knew he'd catch everything.

And he was big and brave before the show. I started getting greedy these past few shows and started requesting things. Let's do a Harold, I said. And he said yes and ten minutes later we're doing a sound and movement opening. Let's do a big slow scene up top. He said yes and I'm performing acupuncture. Let me just say whatever I want—I'm going to just have conversations that I like. He said yes and I'm listing the last ten vice-presidents of the losing political party. We had plans for a monoscene where neither of us left the stage, and for a Harold in the Dark but we didn't get to it. Still, even to have it on the table.

Three weeks ago we did a Harold, and although it wasn't a great one—it was illuminating in a huge way. Without the ability to think ahead those third beats felt very real in a way I've never felt them. They felt like true third acts, revelations and climaxes that were interesting to me as we did them. And it felt brave to do it at all. I think I learned more doing that one Harold than I've learned in the last 4 years.

Tonight, our last show, I got to do what was probably my favorite show we've done. It wasn't our most successful, but we both liked it. And I loved it. And that's because we were much quieter and slow than we usually are. I'm usually a wordy player, and shamelessly so. I like listing things, I like dropping rambling monologues about stupid shit I've read on wikipedia. I like philosophizing and being overdramatic.

So tonight I asked Kevin if I could do a scene where I'd start with some physicality, allowing that my object work is sloppy and unreadable, and that he should just wait and that I would initiate—he just had to wait. My brother of course said yes because Kevin Hines is scared of nothing on an improv stage.

So we did an acupuncture scene, and he could tell when I pushing hard even though I wasn't actually doing so. And we did a bakery scene where I dragged him into the oven. And we did a date in the old west where we rode a horse up to a table on a cliffside and a bald eagle landed on my arm. And we drove the slowest train in the west. The games were weak and slippery, but the scenes felt very real to me. And I felt like I could have kept them going forever. It was the most effortless I've felt in a long, long time. It's happening at the same time as some of my favorite Stepfathers shows ever, and it doesn't seem like a coincidence. I'm tempted to say that it's all my brother's doing. It certainly feels like it.

I'm not saying they were anywhere near as good, but it felt like the shows I used to see Delaney and Dave do, or that I see Adsit and Gausas do. I AM NOT SAYING THEY WERE THAT GOOD. I am saying I got to feel that feeling I get when I watch those shows. I got to be the player I want to be. In front of 200 people at the coolest comedy theater on the planet.

And that's because I was smart enough to get on stage with Kevin Hines!

A fantastic trip—thanks to Charlie Todd for booking us and everyone who voted for us. For realz, yo!

MARCH 25TH, 2010 at 11:53PM

TWO KINDS OF LISTENING

I gotta hit the sack but before I forget I wanted to write that in doing these shows with Kevin I became aware of two types of listening, both important.

One is the top of scene listening. The yes-and, pre-game listening. I felt with Kevin that I could say or do anything at the top and he would get what I meant. And once I was confident of that, I started to be a more interesting person at the top of my scenes. If I wanted to be a female character who was in in a bold mood, I could sit down on a chair, sort of cock my head to the side and half-grin, and he'd get it. Or something close. He'd see what I was trying to do and confirm it. I also felt like I could say anything, no matter how subtle and he'd understand it. Something simple like a man who hates his neighbor, or maybe something much more subtle, like a farmer who wants to use genetic seeds but resents what it implies about the weaknesses of nature.

Either Kevin would get it, or he would slow down and spend some time using yes-and to clarify what I meant, or what he meant. We would make sure we connected first at the top before doing anything else. Maybe it'd happen in one line, but it always always happened. No faking it and continuing. Connect and understand.

The second kind was a comedic listening—related but separate. Once we connected we could just chat and whoever dropped something unusual it would get noticed. Now that I think about it we'd miss this one sometimes. But we hit it enough that I felt confident that I could merely hint at something and he'd hear it. I remember we once did a scene of two people looking at a walrus, and at first we were just looking at the walrus and being chatty with it. As silly as that was, it didn't feel like that was the focus. But then I think I said "you're scary, aren't you?" and I knew that Kevin would notice that was slightly different, and he came back with something like "Yes, you're very dangerous aren't you Mr. walrus? You could rip our limbs off!" Once you know your scene partner will notice when you want something to be the focus, you get very relaxed. You know that the slightest push will create a scene.

I think they are different muscles, or at least they are the same muscle applied at different points in the scene. And it helps if you are only listening for one at time.

Step out—connect and listen for your starting point. Then and only then, start making work for the funny thing. If you can feel those things as separate steps, and you know when you have successfully done each one, you feel very very confident to step out and do the next scene.

MARCH 27TH, 2010 at 12:25PM

THIRD BEATS: TRY INITIATING WITHOUT A CONNECTION IN MIND

I've been coaching Harold teams this year and the third beat is something we talk about a lot. There's lots of Harolds that zip along quite well but never build into the big satisfying finishes that you need to blow the audience away.

One way to improve them is to initiate a third beat scene without a connection in mind and then aggressively yes-and until you find a connection by surprise.

In watching the third beats at Harold night over the past few months, it seems like most scenes are very short—people initiate with a connection in the first line, or something that's obviously meant to be alley ooped into a connection. I don't think that's bad, but those types of scenes HAVE to be short—they don't feel right to continue for that long. And if they are not super hilarious ideas the Harold feels a bit flat.

Another type of scene is to initiate something that was mentioned as an aside somewhere in the Harold. Someone makes an offhanded reference that they learned about proper applause techniques in school, and in the third beat someone will initiate as the teacher running that lesson. Those are fun, but they also don't often feel like they have legs.

Or teams will do a run, where they are trying to do a bunch short callback and connections from the show. Sometimes that works, but it feels too much like a high wire act to count on. It doesn't really build. (Though I do think teams should be cool with doing mini runs in a third beat and should recognize them when they start. They're fun, just kinda empty)

Then Kevin and I did a two man Harold in cagematch, and we got to our third beats with 10 minutes left. I remember noticing the clock and thinking "we're screwed!" But since we HAD to keep going, we started revisiting each scene, and we did not start with a connection. I think i wouldn't have been able to—I was having trouble remembering what the scenes had been. I'd run through the Harold in my brain and as soon as I remembered someone

I'd initiate it with no regard of how good a third beat it might be. I needed something and couldn't be picky.

First I initiated as a neighbor whose house had been vandalized by Kevin—Kevin's character had said that his yoga was making him more confident and aggressive. I remembered Kevin had described knocking a hole in his neighbor's house because it blocked his view of the sun. So I was going to be that neighbor. My initiation was to lean out of a window and yell at Kevin to stop putting holes in my house. Kevin recognized that I wanted him to be that yoga guy so he starts talking and acting like the yoga guy.

Normally someone would enter there probably with some character from another scene but Kevin and I were too busy doing the scene to think. So we yes-anded away from the game of aggressive yoga. We described the damage to the house and I talked about my character's job and how I could understand that we all need to be more aggressive. I had no idea what to do. Kevin said he was going to continue to do whatever he wanted. I couldn't think of anything that my character would say so I told him that I was going to call the police.

Then and only then did I remember that I had been the leader of a secret police in other scenes who wanted to stop being mean. Excited that we could have a connection I said again "I'm calling the police" hoping Kevin would notice. He did indeed notice and he returned to a scene that we had where the secret police had been refusing to answer the phone. Big reaction from the crowd. Big reaction from me—I was as surprised as anyone that we had found that. I certainly did not have that idea when I initiated the scene.

And that might be the way to improve third beats. Initiate away from a connection, yes-and a bunch of info until you find a connection that is a surprise even to you. And if it is a surprise to you it will be a surprise to the audience. The idea is to make the third beats big a-ha moments.

Your own lack of imagination will save you I think because even if your intention is to just yes-and arbitrarily you will naturally drive the scene toward things that happened earlier—you haven't had time to think of that many new topics.

I've started running this with the Harold teams and I think it's not even that hard (for seasoned improvisers). In fact it might be easier than a run or pressuring yourself to initiate with a connection. Or maybe this is the way we were always supposed to be doing them but we just got too good at seeing connections so we started with them?

I think ideally you should have a mix. Initiate with a connection and be ready to edit hard, then initiate with something that is not a connection and be ready to yes-and hard. Throw in a few moments that were mentioned as asides for fun.

It sounds right! I have no idea yet if it's actually going to make a difference.

MARCH 27TH, 2010 at 11:46PM

TEAM BROOKLYN: IN DEFENSE OF FAST SCREAMY IMPROV SETS

Any long-time long-form improviser should have a group or a show or something that lets them do loud screamy improv, where you and the other people are making playing it real the absolute lowest priority and you are just yelling most of the show and tagging out constantly. It is terrific fun. Don't let it become your default style but find a place to do it and enjoy it.

In December 2002 Kevin Mullaney put together "Team Brooklyn" which was any UCBT Harold Team person living in Williamsburg and had us do shows in Williamsburg. Every Tuesday there'd be three Harold teams and then us. It was Charlie Sanders, Brian Finkelstein, Will Becton, Mark Sam-Rosenthal, Jeff Cambpell and me. First show was in the back room of the (now moved or maybe just totally gone?) Galapagos—a big echoey room where the seats were spread out and far from the un-miked stage.

Three teams went up and were greeted with mostly silence. We stepped out and told each other "make sure to be loud, it's hard to hear" and then screamed the entire show. No scene lasted longer than 60 seconds. The pattern we kept calling back was one member of a scene falling forward on his face. Tag-outs occurred roughly every five seconds. It was the most fun

I'd had in months! Something about Charlie Sanders always made me hyper and silly. Three years later we'd be on 1985 together and I was right back to doing handstands on chairs and things.

Anyway, every time Team Brooklyn performed it was a "fun first" show. It was exciting and liberating. I was at a point in my improv career (3 years, I guess?) where the rules in my head were so oppressive. I didn't feel like a top improviser or anything, just a guy who had been doing it a little while and who maybe wasn't even noticed that much compared with his teammates. Harold Night felt difficult and a bit scary. Team Brooklyn was a chance to let it hang out. Instant reactions from everyone, big decisions being made early and often. Lots of screaming. Terrible acting. A complete lack of reality and subtlety.

Terrible play in a lot of ways. But it made me more fun, more brave, more commanding. TEAM BROOKLYN!

One scene involved Charlie as a police chief asking his two employees (Becton and I) about what we were doing with our 401Ks. The conversation continued in a normal non-jokey way except during the entire scene Sanders was hiking up both of his pant legs until they were bunched tightly around his thighs. Edit.

Another one was 4 guys talking about girls, but we'd cut to a group of 4 girls talking. Later in the show we were 4 dogs sitting on chairs, and we cut to 4 cats. All characters in all of those scenes were masturbating.

Another show we said before the set "We're going too blue too often—let's not go blue." That ended with Brian as Jesus—still nailed to a cross—giving a blow job to Charlie as Buddha.

Another show had all of its scenes begin with "could you step into my office?" where each office was located within the office of the previous scene. It was not as good as that makes it sound, but it was terrifically fun to do.

Another one I remember trying to be a tough high school kid that wanted to kick everyone's ass and Charlie endowed me as having been accepted into Sarah Lawrence college.

One show I initiated with something like "I would like to do a scene about FotoMats." And Mark-Sam said "And what is that?" and I said "It's a yellow building in parking lots where you'd drive up and drop off film to be developed." and he said "Okay." and got into position to be in a FotoMatt, and then said "May I have your film?" Edit.

A year later my brother formed Primal Bias, and we also went through a long phase of loud, screamy tag-out crazed sets, and I loved those shows too.

Those can all become terrible habits if you don't rein them in. But I think feeling the fun and recklessness of those types of shows is necessary. Have fun. This game's fun, right?

MARCH 28TH, 2010 at 10:36PM

RIP JOHN WARD ("DR. WIMPY")

Anthonyking: After Asssscat tonight, I received word that John Ward passed away this afternoon.

I didn't know John very well. I was only lucky enough to know him as a student, performer, and Improv Everywhere agent. But he always brought such a warm and happy energy to every interaction I ever had with him. And he made me laugh—hard—in so many unexpected ways.

The suddenness of this is pretty hard for me to wrap my head around. John was just at callbacks for Harold auditions on Tuesday—funny and energetic as ever. I'm very sad I won't get the chance to see him again.

Will Hines spoke to John's sister this evening. When he told her he was from UCBT, she said, "Everybody there made his life. He loved it. He just loved it. Before that, I mean, his wife died, he'd come down here sometimes. But when he found you guys that was out of this world. You made his life for the last several years and the whole family thanks everyone for everything you've done."

I'm so happy that John decided to be a part of this school, theatre, and community. He was a unique and wonderful part of the family.

You will be missed, Dr. Wimpy. Rest in peace.

Healywu: John was in my audition group last Saturday, he was so good in it—I knew he was going to get a callback. We got there first and chatted for awhile before the rest of the group arrived. It was his 10th time auditioning. I didn't know him well but I am reeling right now. Totally shocked.

Caitlintime: Terrible news. I often think of him in his role as Santa in the 2008 mixtape '98 Christmas show. He was hilarious. He will be missed.

A shy, sweet and smart man. He was a kindred spirit to anyone who loved improv enough to bravely throw himself into it and become really good at it. He was an earnest, smart actor who made shows better and more real. We miss you, John.

MARCH 29TH, 2010 at 1:45PM

PAINTING OF ACHILLES

Iamachilles: This is the chair (and the row of seats) I was talking about in [his blog]. Notice the milk crates propping up the first two seats.

Immortalized in paint by Chelsea Clarke!

Beautiful painting, and expresses a feeling that lots of UCBT students go through—and I love the theater at those moments before shows—exciting but quiet.

I'm proud that Achilles is teaching with us now.

MARCH 30TH, 2010 at 9:56PM

PEOPLE PEOPLE'S STANDING OVATION

People People did their last Harold tonight and the crowd gave them a standing ovation. The members of People People (the People People People, I guess?) have been on some of the greatest improv teams ever at UCBT—Mother, Dillinger, Creep—and are all great players. But that's all in the past, and the collective memory of the UCB Theater seems so short that I feared this Harold would end and no one would realize it was a big deal to us old timers. Erik Tanouye and Kevin Hines and I were going to say something in the introduction or maybe say something afterward—we wanted people to know: Hey, this is Tara Copeland from Mother, you philistines! This is Risa Sang-Urai, who was the center of that Harold that ended up taking place in her head and made everyone crap their pants for like two years! You clowns, we were going to shout, you don't know what you're looking at!

But we didn't do that. And People People did a great show. And then at the end the whole room stood up and bellowed cheers. They didn't need us to tell them. And Erik Tanouye ran up and gave Risa flowers. As touching (and deserved and lovely) as the John Ward tribute was, that standing ovation for People People is what made my night. Ah, I thought, someone remembers! How nice.

APRIL 1ST, 2010 at 3:10PM

IT'S OKAY TO ASK QUESTIONS

Of all the common rules we through at young improvisers the first one you can get rid of is "Don't ask questions." It's good for new people because lots of new people will do all kinds of things to not add info to the scene. But once you've had two improv classes you've probably settled down enough and are adding information. Questions can be good—they give the other player a chance to clarify, they express your position without muddying the issue. As long as you are in general adding information it's okay to ask questions.

Listening and reacting are way more important. Listen and if your reaction is a question, go ahead and ask.

As with all opinions presented on this blog, I will defer and back down at the slightest confrontation.

APRIL 2ND, 2010 at 10:57AM

STUMBLING ON A GREAT SHOW

I love when I see a great improv show when I wasn't necessarily expecting to. For example: one of my favorite improv sets I saw last year was by Alden Ford, Anna Rubanova, Steven Slate and Marielena Logsdon. They were up third at Alan Starzinski's Kaleidoscope show. I love Kaleidoscope—Alan picks 3 captains each week, and they each assemble an improv team. It's in the vein of Terry Jinn's various incarnations of The Project—fun and friends are the priority over high-stakes THIS MUST BE THE BEST EVER. There's a good vibe.

The sets there are often good, but they're also relaxed in a way that I'm not expecting a super-home-run show every time I go. It's for the good vibes and good players relaxing. Also when I'm there I'm usually nervous that I'm going to suck in front of a bunch of people that are in my classes. I'm a teacher, I've been doing improv longer than most of the people there, I should be good, right? I don't want to be one of these old dogs who can't bring the heat! So I'm not on the lookout to be blown away.

So I was sitting waiting to go up and sizing up the room. It was warm and stuffy as the Creek often is, and the room felt sleepy. I decided that I was going to be decisive and high-energy—start the scene with a definite MOVE—no languid discovering. My group was fourth so I figured the audience would be the most tired so we'd need to wake them up.

But then right before us went Anna, Steven, Marielena and Alden. And they did a patient, fun, smart set that was very hilarious. And what impressed me was they were a) natural and b) smart in a casual way. Their characters felt free to ask each other questions, and to point out things that didn't make sense. They moved their scenes forward but weren't in a hurry. It was the exact opposite of the energy I was looking to bring to my set, but it was clearly better.

The details of the show are fading to me—I just remember the tone. Shit, does anyone remember this show? I remember a scene where Alden was at a company and Anna and everyone was sort of ganging up on him as having screwed about something. It was funny, but Alden's response was this measured, polite "I really don't see what I did wrong" in a way that made the others giggle a bit and was very funny. It felt like honesty was a priority over blindly pushing a unusual thing, and it was a relief. It looked easy in the best way.

I remember thinking "Thank God I didn't go before this group, I'd look like a strutting ass." Then my group got up there, and there was a monologue from James Ferrarella which mentioned British music festivals. And I thought "i'm going to initiate with a character who is not an idiot, and I'll let someone else find what's funny." Andrew Mendillo and I stepped out, and I tried to be a woman at a travel agency booking a ticket to the Reading England Music festival. I messed up the name but Charlie Todd walked on to straighten it out. Mendillo wanted to not just see the show but move his entire life there, and so my character helped him book what he needed to move into the music festival permanently. It felt pretty good. Certainly I felt pleasantly un-desperate.

And I felt like a real actor! I chilled out, even though the room was sleepy and warm. I still think of that show now and then –the set before mine– to remember not to panic or feel like I have to switch up where I'm at because of the mood in the room.

APRIL 5TH, 2010 at 8:03AM

PHYSICAL MATCHING AT THE TOP

Kevin Hines and I debated via email.

Subject: PHYSICAL MATCHING AT THE TOP OF A SCENE

Will: When two people step out at the top of a scene and start matching each other physically I think "THIS SCENE WILL BE BORING FOR AT LEAST 60 SECONDS."

One person comes out and chops carrots. Then a second person, who probably stepped out just one fraction of a second later, starts chopping a separate pile of carrots right next to the first person. Then they both just chop carrots for five seconds. I feel like they're starting with less than nothing. Now they have to invent something fun that involves this mundane action. People seem to put making choices on hold for ten seconds or more when they have physically matched each other—zombieprov.

Kevin: Yeah, that sounds bad. But I think the alternative is worse! Someone steps out, starts chopping carrots, and the other person steps out and watches them. Maybe they are trying to figure out what the other person is doing. Are they chopping vegetables? Are they a chef? Are they using drumsticks? Maybe they don't want to step on that person's idea, so they are waiting for that first person to speak.

Now when someone does speak it comes from a place of indecision. I didn't choose to match, or do anything so my character isn't doing anything. I'm not a chef, I'm not helping make dinner, I'm lazy. That's not a choice. That's the absence of choice. In either case you need to make choices, but if you matched you are going to start stronger then if you just stood and watched for a noticeable amount of time.

Will: It might just be at what point you see someone in their development. Maybe at first younger students, like one two or three courses into their training –someone tells them to physically match first and make the choice second and it makes a big difference from just standing there because they relax and start making choices.

But then they settle into that too much! They get comfortable making that physical match and then STILL don't make a choice. They see the person chopping carrots and they start chopping carrots for a WHILE—like ten or fifteen seconds before the next line. It's really no better than doing nothing at that point. Even worse, they think they're making a decision—or at least they act like they've made a decision. But there I sit, fuming unfairly.

Ideally, you'd physically match and as you're doing it make a decision about what's happening and either say something or have your energy be affected by it.

Kevin: Matching is definitely more important for newer improvisers. But I still see it with experienced folks a lot.

Truthfully (and possibly off-topic) I think the first guy out should speak immediately If someone steps out and starts an action but doesn't speak,

I assume they have no idea. So I speak immediately. I label what they are doing, and I start doing something as well. That's my decision. I jump start the scene even though they stepped out first. Even more so if there is an opening. If you did a 3 minute opening and you're only idea is "cutting carrots" then we have a lot of work to do. We should have a game or something close. So I initiate something from the opening, ideally something inspired from the "cutting carrots" part of the opening.

The top of the show needs CHOICES. Keep making choices until we know what is going on. I am cutting carrots. I am also cutting carrots. We are in a restaurant. I am nervous about the amount of work we have. I am even more nervous. We are freaking out as the mountain of orders keeps increasing. Now we are getting somewhere. Until you reach that point, not adding (and more importantly ANDing) is boring. And you will sit in your seat angrily whether or not they matched.

So I like matching because it's a choice. An easy choice, sure. And not the final choice. But a choice. While watching and waiting is not a choice.

Will: We agree that you need choices. And I agree that compared to just standing and watching, that matching energy/physicality is much better. But I posit to you sir, that intermediate performers stay happy with that choice far far too long. They match and then wait upwards of 20 seconds.

I'm not so suspicious of silence at the top, but I don't see it so much so maybe I would. It IS cool when a wordless initiation gets things going. What if the opening had a big long thing about the repression of housewives in the 50s, and there's all these images suggested of sad angry housewives—and after THAT someone walked out and started chopping carrots? I bet the audience would laugh, because people would assume there's a simmering volcano behind that action. But that's because there's a lot more information associated with that simple action.

What I'm saying is: chopping carrots is hilarious! Always do it.

Kevin: Your example, of the repression of housewives leading to silently cutting carrots would be good. But I'd be surprised if for every 100 silent starting scenes any more than 5 were from anything other than not having an idea.

Again, if someone is not speaking and chopping carrots, but they are humming a song or looking super sullen or chopping angrily then I'd count that as making a choice, and maybe not feel the need to deliver a line of dialogue.

We are way off topic! We are now discussing silent starts: good or bad? I blame my half of the discussion.

Chopping carrots is a bad decision. Cut a chicken breast instead. It's different!

Will: How about after an opening? A group does a 3 minutes pattern game. One person comes out and stirs a pot, the second person matches. Are you furious?

Kevin: Furious? No. I am more even-tempered than you. But I would rather that first person spoke and initiated a game or idea from the opening, or something more than "cooking" or "kitchen" which is what it seems they came in with. Use that opening! If the scene goes on too long without talking and nothing but mindless stirring, I am disappointed in both performers for not adding information.

Here is what I believe: I think physical matching encourages you to make a quick decision. It shouldn't allow either performer to stop making early decisions. It should be the first of many for both performers.

I don't mind silence, to be honest, if it is a choice. I think it is generally used as a delaying tactic among many students. I think silence in the middle of the scene can be powerful, and it can work up top. Some of my favorite scenes I have ever seen were dialogue free. But they had numerous other non-talky decisions being made.

Stop being so furious.

Will: On reflection, I get more fidgety than furious.

Here's what I am asserting: I think improvisers learn that physical matching is a good thing, and for young improvisers it is. But for too long in their development they simply match and do not truly choose and add—the tops of scenes are much slower than they realize. That's what I see. They're not matching with a choice, they're matching with empty physical parroting and not backing it up with full reactions/choices.

I DO agree that standing and watching is worse.

I am not AS suspicious of silent beginnings but then again I don't see many so maybe I would be suspicious if I saw more that failed.

I also realized we never discussed the difference between "physical matching" and matching in general—where you're just trying to be someone with the same point of view and general experience at the top. Next time!

APRIL 9TH, 2010 at 9:57AM

YOUNG IMPROVISERS FIGHTING

One tragic thing about watching young improvisers fight: it's the first time they're acting naturally, even though they're ruining scenes.

Young Improviser A says "You forgot our anniversary!"

And Young Improviser B, surprised to learn this, will have a flash of small but genuine anger before saying "No I didn't! You MADE me forget!"

Even though the scene is stalling comedically, it's a real moment, emotionally.

I wish I could say "keep that honest emotional reaction, but be the unusual thing at the same time." But that's a tough, subtle point and I don't think it sticks.

What I usually say is some variation of "Make the criticism true" or "Say yes to what you're being accused of" or "You're being given the gift of being the unusual one, be it." Or "do more of what you're told not to." "Don't worry about winning the fight, win the scene."

I agree with those notes, but here's what I fear is accidentally communicated: "Do not trust your first instinct. Stop it and replace it with this rule." And then students are in their heads, because they've been told too often "your first reaction is wrong, don't trust it." By the time they've taken five improv classes, they are out of touch with their real feelings on stage. And we yell at them again "Trust your instincts! React faster! Don't think!"

Here's what I wish I could say concisely to Young Improviser B: "That small flash of anger you felt is real, and it's okay. Be a little angry. Be hurt. Fight back. Scowl, before you've even fully processed what has been said. That's acting truthfully. But then, also, be weird. Be the unusual thing you were just labeled. Do it in an angry tone so that you are honoring your own emotional reaction as well as the information that was given to you. Go ahead and win that fight, but win it as the person who is holding onto an irrational viewpoint. Trust your emotional instinct, but override the words with this big unusual thing. I know, you don't even agree that you were responding angrily, but trust me you were angry, a very little bit. I saw it, and that was you acting in a truthful way. Keep it up, just protect what's unusual. You are becoming a comedic actor."

Sometimes I do say that. And that ruins it for everyone because we're fifteen minutes late taking our break and all they remember is "The teacher talked a lot; we must have done it wrong." If I were Del Close I could say it in three words and people would remember it for the rest of their lives.

APRIL 11TH, 2010 at 11:17AM

FIGHTING, LYING, BEING STUPID

Some thoughts about teaching improv students to avoid fighting, lying and being stupid characters.

Communication is the payoff: First, you must appreciate that young improv students are not foolish for thinking fighting, lying and stupidity are funny ideas. Look at Shakespeare, or any comedy ever: these things get laughs. You must prove there's a payoff for giving them up, and that payoff is COMMUNICATION. It's easier to get on the same page at all times if we get rid of fighting, lying and being stupid. Way, way, way, way easier.

Fighting: Easy to teach people to avoid, because most fights won't get laughs. Side-coach someone to accept an unusual viewpoint, or to stop fighting until something unusual happens. (Although this creates a bad precedent for ignoring your natural reactions, a problem I fail to solve in another post—the "Young Improvisers Fighting" post right before this one).

Being Stupid: Being stupid gets laughs, albeit only short-term ones. To counter this, point out that being intelligent will help keep you out of your head—young improvisers are dying to feel like they are not in their heads.

"Try this scene again, and say what you'd really say—it will be easier." They'll feel the relief of saying what's obviously true and get greedy for it.

Lying: Lying gets huge, huge laughs. Fortunately, almost any game in improv that requires someone to lie becomes even funnier when the liar admits that he's/she's been lying and tells the truth—and the game won't significantly change. Make them hungry for that moment of owning up to their lie. "Try this scene again and this time admit the truth." The class will laugh and that will reinforce that decision more than a long explanation from you.

All three, wait for the game: Students see advanced improvisers fight, lie and be willfully stupid very often in their sets and get huge laughs. Point out that advanced improvisers wait until the game is set. So I used to say "no fighting." Now I say "no fighting before you know your game." That works better and is more true.

Sell the magic: It is amazing and awesome that improv is a subgenre of comedy that becomes funnier if you cooperate, tell the truth and are smart. Point that out to students, make them invested in how cool good improv is. I imagine one of the reasons Del Close blew people away was he was saying the exact opposite of what your comedy instincts tell you and he was right on the money. Say it in the form of a positive: "Cooperate, tell the truth, be smart." They work! They work like charms. Invite them to be part of that very cool, counter-intuitive genius.

I invite rebuttals, improvements, inspired digressions and slavish affirmations for/from any of this.

APRIL 16TH, 2010 at 7:38AM

KNOW EVERYTHING

When someone on your team is making a reference to someone or something you have never heard of—a movie, or tv show, some science-fiction b.s. that does not interest you or some reality show you've been avoiding because you still love yourself—what do you do? The audience reacted to what was said, so you know it means SOMETHING but you know you don't know what it is.

The textbook answer is that if you react honestly and yes-and, then the scene will be fine. It's okay that you don't know what the reference is. And that is true.

But I have an alternate back-up plan for people who are really investing themselves in improv: you should just KNOW EVERYTHING. I say you have a responsibility to be a smart, informed person if you want to be a good improviser. Okay, not EVERYTHING everything. But I've never known a good improviser who wasn't extremely smart and didn't know a LOT.

Good improvisers read books, watch movies, know what's happening in the news and know what the hit shows are. They are media-absorbers and remember everything. They talk to people and know what the general opinion is of the issues of the day. They know the Bible and the tenants of most major religions, they know classic television from past generations, books that your English teacher told you to read, they have a decent-to-great knowledge of history. They get lost in wikipedia, they like skimming through weird magazines. They know dozens of genres of fiction, movies, plays. They have a "Mad Magazine parody" level of knowledge of plots of all classic movies. They get out in the world and do weird things and talk to interesting people and remember it all. They have conversations with their weird relatives and they humor the annoying person in the bar and they learn and remember and learn and remember.

And then despite that, these improvisers will still run across scenes in which something is being discussed that they don't know. But rather than throwing up their arms and exclaiming with fear "But I didn't know! I had NO IDEA what that person was talking about!" they will react honestly and yes-and and make the scene work.

And then go home and look up what it was they didn't know and never forget it for the rest of their lives.

APRIL 19TH, 2010 at 9:23AM

DWELL ON GOOD SCENES, NOT BAD ONES

One of the biggest traps of teaching improv is to talk too long about bad scenes and let good ones go by. This quote from Mick Napier's Improvise really hit home for me:

> "...good scenes are a drag to talk about and many people wouldn't even know what to say. I've seen soooo many instructors watch a bad scene and chalk it up to 'too many questions' or 'talking in the future.' I've seen as many, after a good scene, say (with a half-laugh), 'Great, that's how it's done, two more."

That's how *what's* done?

I can't really blame them though. It makes sense to discuss The Rules in regard to a bad scene, but it doesn't feel right to break down a great scene. Students and teachers alike love to satisfy their left brain and analyze which failed, but nobody likes to mess with magic."

I have to remember: It's often better to edit a bad scene early, give a quick note and move on—let it fade away. And when a good scene happens bask in its magic. Compliment specifically what things the actors did well, ask the other students in class what happened that was so satisfying. Make it big and important in their memory of that class. Success begets success.

Related: I remember some UCB Theatre meeting years ago when Amy said she had walked by a class and heard a teacher letting a bad scene go on and on. "Cut them short," she said. "No one learns as much from a bad scene."

APRIL 28TH, 2010 at 12:22PM

Q: OLD DAYS

Anonymous asked: People are talking about the "old" days of the improv community constantly. Were things really, objectively better back then, or is this just run of the mill nostalgia and ancestor worship?

I'd say it's like 90% nostalgia and selective memory, and 10% truth about what was cooler when the scene was smaller. Which is to say that there are some things that are more fun when the scene is smaller, but there are also plenty of things that are better when there's more people involved. Example down side: My first Harold Night had like 30 people in the audience. Example up side: You could make a reservation to ASSSSCAT on Friday and go, and there'd be Tina Fey, Adam McKay and all 4 UCB there.

Example up side of present times: The average quality of improviser is way, way higher than it used to be. Example downside: you have to fight like crazy to find an open class (something we are working on, I promise).

APRIL 28TH, 2010 at 12:32PM

Q: IMPROV CHANGED SINCE YOU STARTED?

halphillips asked: How do you feel improv has changed since you started? I don't mean clear-cut changes like how many improvisers there are or what forms are popular; I mean subtler changes in style, approach, etc. Anything that would make a time traveler from when you started say "I don't know, that's not really how we do things".

Follow-up question: what is the best Gin Blossoms song that is not "Hey Jealousy"?

I'm going to speak mostly about Harold Night as I've seen it the most over the longest period of time.

Harolds are shorter and find games faster now. Initiations are more direct and idea-ful (not always good, but I like it better for the most part).

People used to do swinging doors a lot more. They always looked stupid to me.

There were longer and more monologues in the openings, which I don't miss.

Group games were overall not as experimental at 161. But third beats were longer and more experimental.

Openings were always a point of contention. There are slightly more options now but not much.

People are more comfortable on stage earlier in their development—probably because of the indie team scene. People are not as good at being simple straight men, also probably because of the indie scene (so supportive and experimental that people forgive crazy realities too much—a subject for another day).

The lack of a premier team like The Swarm, who could play slow and physical and still find game, has made it hard to get people to play interesting and slowly.

"Lost Horizons" is the second-best Gin Blossoms song. Followed by "Found Out About You" and "Pieces of The Night" and then "Mrs. Rita."

APRIL 28TH, 2010 at 12:34PM

BILLY MERRITT'S IMPROV PARTY

I asked for questions. Lauren Hunter asked this one:

People talk a lot about the idea that improvisers fall into three categories: "Pirates," "Ninjas" and "Robots." What do you think about this? Can you change your status? (For example, can a Robot become a Pirate?)

She's referring to a categorization first popularized and probably invented by Billy Merritt. Read about it here, courtesy of his fantastic 2002-2003 online improv journal Billy Merritt's Improv Party: Pirate, Robot or Ninja? The whole journal is a trippy, inspirational blast.

I don't think pirates / robots / ninjas fundamentally change into each other, but I do think they all learn how to temporarily emulate each other's strengths. I'm a robot for sure, but sometimes I catch whiff of a pirate energy and then I can be a pirate for a little bit. Sometimes I can even force that transformation in myself. So my answer is: kind of.

APRIL 28TH, 2010 at 1:02PM

Q: UNDERRATED IMPROVISER?

ryangdunkin asked: Who do you think the most under rated improviser is at UCB and why?

Lots. On Harold Night, I think Morgan Jarrett has transformed into someone who makes immediate reactions as well as follows game—a tough balance, and I don't think people are appreciating that. There are literally thirty people in the class system (and therefore in the UCBT world) who are fantastic improvisers and not on a team. Some, like Rob Stern, are correctly respected are seriously funny dudes. Do people know how good Lou Lasher is? Or how funny Dawn Luebbe is? Lotsa people. I should pick one and not cop out. I'll say Stephen Sajdak—yes-ands and adds to a scene in a small, real way every line. Don't let me down Stephen, make me a genius.

APRIL 28TH, 2010 at 1:05PM

Q: AVOIDING BREAK-UPS?

johnztownsend asked: More on the side of team psychology than improv talk, but what are the 'secrets' to keeping a team together and good for a long time? How do you try to avoid fighting and breakups?

I don't have a great answer. The truth is all teams fight and to some degree just tacitly agree to shut up and get over it. My only advice is when your team starts emailing each other like crazy about how they've been silent for so long about how much they hate the opening or your coach or even someone on the team to keep the emails short. A one line "I'm not happy with the opening, and don't think we're playing game." is less destructive and more effective than a seven page monologue. If you want to rant endlessly about improv, start a tumblr.

APRIL 28TH, 2010 at 1:08PM

Q: DISAGREE WITH UCB CURRICULUM?

Anonymous asked: What's the one dogma of the UCB curriculum you disagree with most?

I think I agree with all of the dogma. I'd like to improve the culture of teaching and coaching to be more exercises based and less note based. We've tried to become more consistent in what we teach when which means we talk about it more which means we talk more to students, which we have to correct. It's a process.

APRIL 28TH, 2010 at 1:16PM

Q: NERVOUS ABOUT CAGEMATCH?

katespencer asked: Are you nervous about getting your ass kicked in Cagematch tomorrow?

It worries me a bit, Kate.

But only a bit.

APRIL 28TH, 2010 at 1:18PM

Q: TOO FUNNY?

alexispereira asked: I feel like I've heard shades of this from some coaches and teachers, but do you sometimes find that some people are so naturally funny that it hurts their longform work?

Yeah. Though I don't like the idea of "funny" being thought of as bad. We're a comedy theater, being funny is good. I think of people who are so funny they change the game of the scene with everything they say. That's destructive. I count the unusual things in a scene, if I get to 2 then something's wrong.

APRIL 28TH, 2010 at 1:20PM

Q: FAVORITE STRUCTURE?

demuth asked: What's your favorite structure to perform other than the Harold? Why?

I like doing a Monoscene because audiences crap their pants as if you did something hard.

APRIL 28TH, 2010 at 1:22PM

Q: VENUES?

jokesfortalkshows asked: What are your thoughts on venues?

The venues all have their own energy. UCBT is big and cushiony—I feel quiet up there. Magnet felt more serious and theatrical—easier to be quiet but harder to get silly. Under St. Marks is my favorite place to just be funny. The small audience right on top of you while you're brightly-lit—that always feels comfortable and lo-fi in a nice way. The old UCBT was smaller and you were above the audience—it was easier to be funny. The Creek is nice but too warm and sleepy, if we're going to nitpick.

But non-crybaby improvisers never blame the venue... out loud.

APRIL 28TH, 2010 at 1:23PM

Q: NEGATIVE PARTNER?

emilyhoffman asked: How do you make scenes work in which your partner chooses a negative point of view to the one you established, initiates arguments, or denies things that you have said? In other words, how can make a scene successful scene with a partner who doesn't follow the rules?

Try to be on teams with people you like so that doesn't happen that often. And then when it does, treat it like a gift. Enjoy it. Worst case, just listen and react to each line with no regard for the direction of the scene and leave it to the Gods.

APRIL 28TH, 2010 at 1:42PM

Q: FANTASTIC SCENE?

Anonymous asked: what is one scene that you have improvised or witnessed being improvised that sticks in your brain as fantastic?

One SCENE? Geez Louise. It's easier to remember whole shows. The first one I thought of was the "JAG" scene from Team Roo Roo at Terry Jinn's Project. Brett Gelman was a roommate blocking Curtis Gwinn from watching his favorite show, JAG. But when he stepped out of the way it was revealed he was blocking John Gemberling, who was watching JAG on another television. Then he stepped aside and was blocking Will Nunziata. Joe Wengert and Neil Casey were on the side doing the voices of the episode which were "I need you to give me the codes for these missiles" and "I can't give you the codes for these missiles."

Then John said something in an Irish accent, and Brett said "you're not Irish." and John said "Aye, I am." "Well, you weren't a second ago." "Aye, I was." So Brett told them there was an Irish bar where everyone watched Jag, and then I think they went there and Joe and Neil were still doing the same dialogue, but in an Irish accent.

That one.

APRIL 28TH, 2010 at 1:43PM

Q: AVOID ONE-DIMENSIONAL STRAIGHT MAN?

Anonymous asked: How do you avoid playing a one dimensional straight man?

Be awesome at it like Will Hines.

APRIL 28TH, 2010 at 1:46PM

Q: REAL NAMES?

justcraig asked: What are your go to names for men and women in scenes? What are the best go to names?

How do you feel when people use real names in scenes (for instance, calling you Will or Mr. Hines in a scene)?

I like using real names, because I like when improvisers play the person in the scene as much as the idea in the scene. Like anything else if it's all you do you have to mix it up.

But I love fake names even more. On 1985, I had a pre-declared formula for all fake names which I told the team was more important to me than the quality of our shows. And that formula was COMMON FIRST NAME + HOUSEHOLD OBJECT FOR LAST NAME. Like "Danny Cabinet" or "Arnold Wastebasket." I once said "Leroy Handlebar" in a show and that's one of my proudest moments as an improviser. That team got better after I left.

APRIL 28TH, 2010 at 1:47PM

Q: FAVORITE BASTIAN MEMBER?

adamfrucci asked: Who is your favorite member of Bastian?

Molly Lloyd.

APRIL 28TH, 2010 at 1:48PM

Q: GET OVER SELF-DOUBT?

Anonymous asked: What is the best way to get over a self-doubt rut and/or allow yourself to make riskier moves in improv?

Do improv with people that you know like you.

APRIL 28TH, 2010 at 1:50PM

Q: AREA YOU WANTED TO IMPROVE?

adamconover asked: Earlier in your improv career, what was an area of your play you wanted to improve in, and how did you go about doing so? (For instance, you wanted to be more aggressive, so you ...) More generally, how do you recommend improvisers go about identifying and working on their weak spots once they've mastered the basics?

I might not have been great at this. Outside of just focusing on one thing at a time, playing with different combinations of people is a good idea. Each team has its own dynamic and each dynamic brings out a different side of you—playing with Erik Tanouye and Kevin Hines brings out a different side of me than playing with Chris Gethard and Silvija Ozols which is different than with Brian Finkelstein and Charlie Sanders.

APRIL 28TH, 2010 at 1:52PM

Q: YOUR SENSE OF HUMOR?

Anonymous asked: What do you find 'funny'? How would you define your sense of humor?

1. Deadpans stares of regard in the face of explosions of passion
2. Mimed top hats.
3. The logical fulfillment of a defined pattern in a surprising way.
4. Lists of synonyms.
5. Angry declarations of the obvious.
6. Rich kids being full of themselves.

That's it.

APRIL 28TH, 2010 at 3:19PM

Q: SECOND-FAVORITE MEMBER OF BASTIAN?

adamfrucci asked: Well Jesus Christ, who's your 2nd favorite member of Bastian then?

Brian Faas

APRIL 28TH, 2010 at 3:24PM

Q: BLASPHEMOUS

Anonymous asked: Is it ever okay to chose not to sell out your ideology in order to commit to a scene? Is it okay for say, a religious person, to refuse to partake in a scene in which something blasphemous is occurring?

Should be moot—it's not your ideology, it's your character's. You shouldn't sell out your view of reality, but if your view of reality is so narrow that you can't imagine someone being an atheist you're probably a boring improviser. Or if you can't imagine someone genuinely believing in Jesus Christ, for that matter. Be actors, you jerks!

APRIL 28TH, 2010 at 3:25PM

Q: BURNED OUT

nicolemarietherese asked: How do you handle those periods of time when you feel burned out or bored by improv?

Use my few remains ties to normal society to go hang out with non-comedians. Stay away from improv shows for a while. It usually only takes a week before I miss it, though. Or watch shows and take a break from performing. Skip a rehearsal and revel in being bad.

APRIL 28TH, 2010 at 3:25PM

Q: SCARED OF SKELETONS?

kellyqehudson asked: Why aren't people more afraid of skeletons? They are inside of us. That's insane.

It's an excellent point. I guess the same way we're not terrified by the huge hunks of metal hurtling down the avenues every day—we just don't think about it.

APRIL 28TH, 2010 at 3:29PM

Q: PRE-SHOW RITUAL?

Anonymous asked: Your pre-show mental ritual? or physical ritual? Or, interesting ones you've noticed of other people?

When I was in classes I would tell myself "listen and react" over and over like a mantra when I was backstage to stop worrying about all the notes I had been told. I used to visualize a steel column running down my spine to try and summon courage and commitment. I also went through a phase in which I pretended my Harold team were all strangers; it made me bolder. I used to not eat for an hour before a show, but at other times I had a beer as a matter of course. Sometimes I'll show up at the last possible second before we're supposed to warm up so I don't talk myself into a bad place. I like stretching my hamstrings. A very few times I've gone in the bathroom, dropped to one knee and prayed to God to not let me suck.

APRIL 28TH, 2010 at 3:33PM

Q: FAVORITE STEPFATHER?

blogalicious asked: Who is your favorite current member of Stepfathers to improv with? Is that an appropriate question to ask?

It is entirely inappropriate. Probably Shannon.

APRIL 28TH, 2010 at 3:45PM

Q: HAROLD TEAMS WITH MORE WOMEN THAN MEN?

Anonymous asked: do you think there will ever be a harold team with more women than men on it? is the proportion of men to women on harold night an accurate reflection of the proportion of good male improvisers and good female improvisers in the community? are there

always that many more men that audition then there are women? what is your general opinion about gender and improv?

(Edited to add: Craig Rowin reminds me that Bangs had more women than men. That team deserved a longer lifespan, I can see in hindsight.)

(Edited again: Kevin Mullaney reminds me that Ice-9 had versions that were half women also).

Yes, there will be a Harold team with more women than men. I don't know how the gender breakdown on Harold Night matches up with talent breakdown. There's more guys in class and auditions, yes. 101 classes seem to have a mostly 50/50 guy/girl breakdown and then it skews more towards dudes as you get more advanced. BUT it's not nearly as drastic as it used to be. I think when The Shoves were half women and then Bangs—that makes a difference to the students in the crowd who stay with it. Mick Napier said it best—good improvisers improvise the same, men or women. Bad male improvisers improvise their own way and bad female improvisers improvise their own way. In my family growing up, the women were funnier by FAR. Men in the audience forgive the men on stage and the women in the audience forgive the women on stage. I would like to think that we are not a dude-tastic testosterocracy. Any theater 25% owned by Amy Poehler shouldn't be, at any rate.

MAY 2ND, 2010 at 9:21PM

A SET OF 2-PERSON SCENES TO BOND OVER

An Advanced Study class I have which I like very much reached its seventh week. I walked in wanting to drill game, or maybe drill full Harolds. But after two rounds of pattern games and scenes, they looked a bit in their heads and tired. Or maybe I was tired. So I switched up the plan and ran a set of 2-person scenes. Everyone sits. 2 people up a time, give them a suggestion. Let them go 2 or 3 minutes. Laugh honestly but generously. Call the edit, don't give notes, and get two more people.

In a way, you're wasting time: no notes, no focus. The scenes meander and vary wildly in type. But by the end of it—and it only takes around 20 minutes to do 8 scenes—the class is refreshed. They've had a break, they've gotten to enjoy each other, and they've all gotten a chunk of time with no one tagging them out. They remember: oh yeah, improv is fun.

Then I had them do Harolds and put them all in their heads for the rest of their lives. But those twenty minutes!

MAY 7TH, 2010 at 7:16AM

ACT LIKE LIFE, EXCEPT...

We say to act like you do in real life, and to let reality be your guide. Not always true.

We want you to tell the truth far more often than you do in real life.

We want you to communicate out loud what you are thinking and feeling far more than you do in real life.

That's all.

MAY 8TH, 2010 at 7:45PM

Q: ARCHETYPAL CHARACTERS BORING

rileysoloner asked: Unless approached with some unpredictable, original take, I find some archetypal characters in improv scenes to be all but useless. Any scene where someone crouches down to play the monkey, or whenever someone's palms open up and their arms bend to a 90 degree angle to play a clunky, 50's style robot, I kind of sink into my chair. I'm all for being won over, but it turns into a real uphill battle when someone pulls those cards.

Are there characters that you're tired of seeing? Am I the only one sick of monkeys and robots? Do I need a chill pill?

You may need a chill pill, but I hear where you're coming from. It's very annoying when I see someone depict something not the way it IS but the way it is portrayed on already-too-dated tv shows and movies. That's not exactly what you're saying but it's coming from the same place.

One major exception: if someone is doing any of the above with tremendous joy, it's great. I remember someone coming out and doing a classic 50s style robot and all he/she said was "robot...bzz bzz.. robot!" and it was really hilarious and fun. You'd definitely need a chill pill if you didn't enjoy that.

You have the name robot in your handle, so of course you're sensitive to this topic.

MAY 8TH, 2010 at 7:47PM

Q: ETERNALISM?

totallymorgan asked: If you agree with eternalism or block time (I don't know if you do) how would/does it change your view of improvisation? Or do you completely disagree with that philosophy of time? Is improv something that is actually being created in the moment, or is it something that "has always existed" but that we as players/an audience are just tapping into as we move forward in time.

I'm not sure. This much I believe: that Einstein's theory of "spacetime" was right and time is just a property of things and can be different from object to object, depending on that object's energy. I also believe in suspended disbelief for everything from romantic comedies to pop songs that are not aimed at you to the inevitability of death. Whether I'm making my improv decisions or not, I just worry about my commitment and leave the mechanics of the universe to smarter people.

MAY 8TH, 2010 at 7:47PM

Q: HOW LONG TO NOT SUCK?

ryangdunkin asked: How long had you been improvising before you could go out onstage and know you wouldn't suck?

It took three and a half years.

MAY 8TH, 2010 at 7:48PM

Q: IMPROV HERO?

Anonymous asked: who is your improv hero? is there a performer, team or show that you remember watching and thinking "i want to to do THAT?"

The Swarm or Weirdass. I'm not close.

MAY 8TH, 2010 at 7:48PM

Q: OVERTHINKING

poupak asked: How do you keep your mind from overthinking it and getting in the way of improvising? I read somewhere that some improvisers think 5 steps ahead, while others just live in the moment... how do you keep this "5 steps away" from getting in the way of "living in the moment"?

If I get enough laughs I'm out of my head. Otherwise I'm back in. I have no other solutions that are true.

MAY 11TH, 2010 at 12:50PM

Q: PICKING SCENE PARTNERS MID-SHOW

charlietodd asked: Let's say I'm stepping out to set up a callback late in a show (in this case a montage.) I'm trying to set up Ben Rodgers to bring back a hilarious character, and I see an opportunity to make a connection by establishing a new scene with new characters that he will either walk or tag into. I know Ben will get what I'm setting up. The tricky thing is I don't want Ben to step out at the start of the scene. I don't care who steps out with me, it just can't be Ben.

When we want someone specifically to join us in a 3rd beat type scene we have an easy way to communicate it (pointing or strong eye contact.) Is there a way to communicate the opposite—that we specifically don't want someone to join us? Last night I handled this by pointing at Lennon, to ensure Ben didn't walk out. The danger in that though, is that by pointing at Lennon, I'm communicating to her, "I need one of your previous characters for this scene," which I don't. I run the risk of confusing her with my initiation when she doesn't get the connection to any of her characters.

It ended up working out and Lennon and Ben both nailed it, but I'm still left curious if there is a solution to this super specific improv dilemma.

Very cool question! There's no set convention that I know of for this, but I can guess what I'd do. You're right that explicitly pointing could create confusion since whoever you pointed at would be expecting the scene to be about something they had done earlier in the show.

So I'd step out, not pointing, but obviously looking for SOMEONE to step out—kind of already looking to my side as if someone were there on stage with me.

If Ben happened to step out, I would gently turn away from him and look for someone else, and wait. I think he'd know—"Oh, he didn't want me—what is he doing?"

When another person stepped out, I'd move a little closer to them—hoping to focus the attention of the audience on just me and this other person, making Ben kinda not there. Presumably it would soon be clear that I'm talking about Ben and he'd enter.

Right? That would work, I bet. If not I'd start prepping my standard "I am a fraud" apology for the team after the show.

MAY 13TH, 2010 at 1:59PM

Q: NOT BEN RODGERS

toyns asked: Let's say I'm on a team with Ben Rodgers and I don't ever want him to step out in a scene with me. Can I just tell him at our first meeting that he shouldn't do scenes with me? What if he forgets? I can remind him before each show. During a show, should I always point to other people on the back line at the start of a scene? If he steps out to do a scene with me, should I just ignore him, or should I tag him out immediately?

Just make a loud buzzing noise whenever he talks.

MAY 14TH, 2010 at 12:08AM

Q: BEST SHOVES SHOW WITHOUT ERIK?

benrodgers asked: Can you describe the best show by the old UCB Harold team the Shoves? I've heard so much about it and would like to know more. Did anyone from the team miss that show?

http://www.improvresourcecenter.com/mb/showthread.php?t=35957

I believe only one member of The Shoves was missing (Erik Tanouye).

(Though he was there for this one:http://www.improvresourcecenter.com/mb/showthread.php?t=34476)

MAY 14TH, 2010 at 12:09AM

Q: THEMED HAROLDS?

toastface asked: How does one go about attempting themed harolds? How have you worked on that sort of thing in the past?

Getting to this, I promise.

MAY 14TH, 2010 at 12:25AM

Q: PREMISE VS. ORGANIC

natedern asked: Hi Will Hines. What is your take on the difference between premise based improv versus organic improv. This was touched on at the last DCM, and to me it articulates a fairly profound difference between two different ways of approaching our scene work. On the one hand we're taught to generate ideas from an opening, ideally generating full game ideas, so that we can hit the ground running with our scene initiations (premise based). On the other hand, we're taught to be patient and listen, to Yes And and build a scene one line at a time (organic). Obviously they aren't necessarily mutually exclusive, and in fact are probably most effective when used in unison, but I feel

like sometimes it might be too easy to accidentally confound these different approaches.

Hello Nate Dern. Nice to see you. Semantics are fun, right? They are. I find the useful for discussing shows afterwards. Not much use when you're actually doing them.

Short answer: Some scenes start with games and some don't. You can be more assertive in the former and you need more patience in the latter.

Longer answer: For me, the scene feels differently once the game is found. Before the game, I'm an actor discovering things. After the game, I'm a writer, forcing crazy stuff to have fun with the game. So it's helpful to have a term for the scenes where there's a game very early, because then after the show I can talk about scenes like this "That was a premise scene, but I played it like it was organic—should've switched and just hit the thing." Or "I was playing like there was a premise, but it was organic—I should've been doing more discovery. Is anyone going out now?"

MAY 14TH, 2010 at 12:26AM

Q: ALWAYS GETTING BETTER?

halphillips asked: "You never stop learning and getting better" vs. "at some point, it is what it is and you play the hand you're dealt". Discuss.

Because on one hand, everyone theoretically COULD be a better improviser, right?

Whatever you're doing that's less than perfect, you could have done differently. Behavior can be changed.

But on the other hand, that is not realistic.

Is there a ceiling? Do you feel like you're still getting better or do you feel like you're the best Will Hines you can be?

You get set in your ways. I find it harder and harder to change my approach. Best way I know is to play with different people—forces different sides of you out. I'm not the best Will Hines I can be, Hal. That person would be seriously awesome.

MAY 14TH, 2010 at 12:35AM

Q: ALL-STAR TEAM?

halphillips asked: If you could make an all-star team of improvisers who have not performed in at least three years, who would be on it?

I know you remember more people than me, Hal. Is that what you're really asking?

Off the top of my head (forget "all-star" here's just people I liked seeing do improv):

- Maggie Kemper
- Dan Giberman
- Dave Blumenfeld
- Angeliki George
- Chris Schell (he's performed within three years but so what?)

A bunch of other people.

MAY 14TH, 2010 at 12:36AM

Q: DON'T WANT HOUSE TEAM

binu asked: It's probably just me, but is it odd to just want to be a terrific improviser as opposed to wanting to get onto a theater's house team?

Yes, Binu. You are messed up! Get with it!

MAY 19TH, 2010 at 8:54AM

THERE ARE DAYS WHEN I HATE THIS

And I'm sick to death of it and none of it's funny. And I'm ashamed of how long I've done it. And I'm sad that no one can remember the shows I can remember, nor will many people remember the ones we're doing now. And how the community turns over so quickly. And suddenly all the openings look stupid and so do the scenes. Everyone sounds ridiculous on stage. I'll think of the million other non-comedy things I could be doing and I think about the five or six nights in the last ten years that I genuinely explored New York City. I get like this now and then. It happens. It's part of it. So I go outside more and read books, and talk to friends about their kids. I listen to the Boston Red Sox over the Internet. I drink a pitcher of cold water and watch movies I've been meaning to for years. I buy the new Daniel Clowes comic, or go shopping for fresh produce and God forbid maybe try to cook something. Vacuum my rug and re-organize my books. And then I come back.

MAY 25TH, 2010 at 2:26PM

TANOUYE AND I DISCUSS THEMES

Will Hines: So students come up to me and ask how they can theme their harolds. 1) What are they talking about? 2) Your old Harold Team The Shoves used to theme Harolds really well, am I right about that?

Erik Tanouye: 1) I think "conceptual" might be a better term to use than "theming," despite (or because of) all its art rock baggage connotations.

There are different degrees of this sort of thing, such as:

- Harolds with unique structures (no sweep edits, no edits at all, in the dark, musical, etc). This would be the equivalent of Bruce Springsteen's *Nebraska* or *Young Americans* by David Bowie.
- Harolds with thematic unity (all scenes are about some sort of breakup, all scenes are about secrets). This is like Radiohead's *OK Computer* or Frank Sinatra's *In the Wee Small Hours*.
- Harolds with overarching narrative cohesion (all scenes involve related characters from the beginning as opposed to just making connections at the end). Like The Who's *Tommy* or Pink Floyd's *The Wall*.
- Harolds combining multiple elements from above. *Outside* by David Bowie and the classic Extreme III *Sides to Every Story*.

Sometimes these things happen as a result of the suggestion. Sometimes a group will decide to do them in advance. I think both ways are valid.

2) The Shoves did a lot of this sort of thing. It would be immodest for me to say we did them well. Instead, I'll just say that we were the most amazing Harold team of all time. And also, I'd give a lot of credit to Peter Gwinn who was coaching us at that time and pushing us to explore the limits of what a Harold could be.

Will: The Shoves were okay. I think students get excited about theming more than audiences do. Who cares if you have a consistent way of editing from scene to scene? Make the scenes good—that's hard enough as it is. I also only just now noticed you referenced Extreme in your last answer.

Erik: I think if a show's scenes aren't good, the audience doesn't care whether it's themed or not. But if it has good scenes and has a consistent theme or conceptual side, I think it's even cooler. Especially if the theme is related to the suggestion. I'd much rather look back and say "That apocalypse show was great" than "That show had a great apocalypse scene."

Will: True, true. How does a themed show get born? Does someone make a big obvious move up top that says "hey, i'm making a theme here?"

Erik: I think there's two obvious ways. One is a big move by someone at the top of the show. In a 1985 show where the suggestion was "Time Travel," Adam Pally stepped out at the top of the opening and said "Thank you, that's our show." The rest of the group jumped on it and played the show backwards from that point. In Bastian's recent "Tequila" Harold, Lydia Hensler made a choice at the top of the show to endow each member of the group with a degree of drunkenness.

Other times, it can develop from a series of moves in the opening or otherwise. In The Shoves' sports Harold, it started with Lennon Parham yelling enthusiastically at the end of the opening. Other players picked up on that and added to it until by the third two-person scene, it became clear the whole group was a sports team. In a different show, where the suggestion was "Hula Hoop," the organic opening started in the 1950s, then explored the 1960s and 1970s. When it was time to start the scenes, players filled in the blanks that the three two-person scenes should take place in those different decades in order. (Although it could have worked out that all the first beats were in the 50s, the second beats in the 60s, etc)

Either way, I think all the members of a group need to be on the lookout for show-wide moves. First, you have to be completely comfortable with the Harold form and structure to be able to devote enough of your collective brain towards considering the show as a whole. Then you have to agree with each other to be aware of what everyone is doing. If you're only thinking about your two-person scene, you might miss key information about the show as a whole.

Another strategy Peter Gwinn shared with us was to get the suggestion and immediately try to think of how the show should end, then work backward from there. Or, at least, think about the ending during the opening then try to play towards it. So, for example, if the suggestion is "Armageddon," the show might end with the destruction of the world. Not every suggestion lends itself to this sort of thing, which is why you'd sometimes wait until the end of the opening to figure out the ending of the show. If you're thinking of the opening as an overture, then that makes sense—the big closing number of the show should be the last song in the overture medley.

Will: Does it seem like a lot of themed shows have sound and movement transitions? Do they go hand in hand?

Erik: I don't think so, in terms of transitions, but in terms of sound-and-movement openings maybe. I think that groups willing to try organic/sound-and-movement openings are, statistically, more likely to be the kinds of groups that will take chances and trust each other enough to be able to find thematic arcs in their show. But I think sound-and-movement transitions probably make it harder to develop big-picture ideas, since you're so focused on each scene and its next transition.

Will: What exercises can a group do to start thinking "show-wide"?

Erik: Something helpful we did with Peter Gwinn was starting a lot of shows and then stopping either after the opening or after the first beats and talking about where a show could have gone or should have gone. (I think this sort of thing does take a lot of conversation and group mind—you have to be willing to talk about shows afterward and what other choices you could have made. I think if you're in a group that's too sensitive to have frank post-show discussions, it's going to be hard to do thematic stuff.) When Bastian was doing them recently with Chris Gethard, we just forced ourselves to do them over and over in rehearsals—sometimes you had to force themes into shows that didn't really need them, but doing so built up your muscles. I guess it's like practicing three-pointers. You don't always shoot them in games, but if the clock is running out and you're down two points, you're in a much better position if you've practiced a bunch of three point shots than if you've never tried one before.

I use sports metaphors because I am an incredible athlete.

Will: What's a great themed show you've seen that you weren't in?

Erik: There was a Swarm show at the 22nd Street theater where someone made a choice at the top to keep Sean Conroy out of scenes. He would get tagged out, or his characters would be kept out of scenes. He began fuming on the back line, and eventually pacing back and forth angrily, until he was able to barge into a third beat angrily as a character who had been kept outside for a long time. His character yelled at everyone for how rude they had been to him. It worked because the group made a pattern out of tagging him out initially, and because Sean was willing to play along with it too, he could have forced his way into scenes earlier in the show, but it was more fun to let himself be taken out so there could be a big payoff at the end.

Around the time of the writers' strike, there was a fwand show where the group went on strike and had their second beats performed by "scabs" (played by the members of fwand). That was a lot of fun.

And I think there was an Arsenal show where the group was sold to Disney halfway through the show and then had to perform sanitized, corporate-friendly second beats. (Or maybe that was Mailer Daemon?)

Other than those three shows, I have been in every great themed Harold ever performed in America.

Will: Final words, nerd?

Erik: The theme of this conversation has been themes! We decided that at the beginning of the conversation so we were able to stay focused. If we just had a conversation about improv, we might look back and say "Some of that was about themes, but not all of it." So you generally have to decide themey stuff at the beginning or near the beginning.

Will: I was just trying to wrap up.

Erik: Sorry, I missed the blackout.

MAY 27TH, 2010 at 2:58PM

TWO FOLLOW-UP QUESTIONS TO THEME DISCUSSION

I liked my interview with Erik Tanouye about themes so much that I asked two follow-up questions:

Will: What if the suggestion sucks? Or at least doesn't immediately lend itself to an obvious theme?

Erik: I took a workshop with Matt Walsh once and he said there was no such thing as a bad suggestion. Or at least that we should pretend there wasn't. If the audience says "dildo factory," you say "Thank you" and then prove to them why "dildo factory" is a good suggestion and do a show that really tells them something about society and the modern world.

In terms of themed Harolds, some suggestions wouldn't seem to lend themselves to conceptual Harolds as easily. But that's why you have the opening–you can take the suggestion and spin it into a bunch of larger ideas, once of which can help provide a show-wide theme. To stick with the "dildo factory" example, you might discover that the show is all about feigned masculinity and the scenes relate to each other that way.

Will: Is there ever a time when the theme starts fun but gets oppressive to the show, and you have to bail on it? Can you think of an example of this happening?

Erik: I'm sure there have been shows where the theme is oppressive, but I have blocked them out of my memory.

Most likely if the theme is oppressing the show, then the theme is a little meta and you've lost the ability to start new scenes and begin again because you've broken the fourth wall too may times. Otherwise, I think the third beats can feel oppressive sometimes in a closed-world conceptual show, but I don't know if that's any worse than being stuck in connection island in a non-themed Harold. In any case, I think it's hard to throw something away and start again in a Harold. Because even if you throw away the conceptual side, you've still got its first beats. And even if you try really hard to get away from them, then your scenes are just reactionary.

One show I remember that relates a little to this discussion is an Optimist International show from Cage Match. I don't think they were intentionally trying to create a theme for the show (it was Cage Match after all), but a lot of their scenes had a misogynist tint to them. It started to get kind of uncomfortable as the show went on and the ratio of funny to creepy tilted towards the creepy. Then with about three minutes left, Jack McBrayer made a _retroactive_ thematic move by stepping out and saying directly to the audience: "Ladies and gentlemen, we've seen a lot of scenes tonight where women were abused and mistreated by men. But what if we lived in a world where women did the mistreating..." And then they redid the whole show quickly, switching the roles in all the scenes so female characters had the upper hand and men were mistreated. It was amazing and completely won back the crowd. So they kind of rebooted, but in a way that was informed by the earlier part of the show.

EDITED TO ADD a correction from Charlie Todd: *McBrayer said "...let's find out what would happen if the shoe were on the other foot." So not only did he make an incredible retroactively thematic move, he also did so in the folksy rural Georgia way that was uniquely Jack.*

MAY 30TH, 2010 at 8:26AM

MY VISION QUEST

The Stepfathers took me on a vision quest Friday night during the second half of our show, off of the suggestion "sweat lodge."

Delaney had read my post about how there are days that I hate improv. Backstage before the first half he proposed that I go on a vision quest. I agreed but asked what that entailed. He said something like that that depended on me, and then we got introduced and did our first half.

Then for the second half we got the suggestion sweat lodge and I saw Delaney move out to initiate, walking in a regal fashion. I stepped out with Delaney, who said to me something like "Congratulations on starting your vision quest." I was going to answer exactly as I had backstage, but I worried going in 100% as myself was going to make me too unreactive so I adopted a sort of happy douchebag energy and said "I'm on board, man! What are you talking about?" Chris was already sitting cross-legged behind Delaney and Shannon was standing there mimicking Delaney's regal posture.

"Well, that depends on you," Delaney answered. And for the rest of the show all the Stepfathers were endowing and pimping me through a Wizard of Oz style vision quest which included me riding Zach's wise mountain puma character, consulting with Silvija who was sometimes a talking bird and sometimes Neil Young, answering the riddles of Chris's "balancing egg" creature, meeting with the decapitated head of my dead friend "Hoagie" (Delaney again), and Shannon putting me through literal physical challenges including catching all the chairs on stage as she threw them at me, and also carrying Silvija on my back while using the chairs as stilts. All to reconcile with my wife Marjorie (Silvija again) on whom I had "freaked out" on the night before and was now being seduced by Chris' 12-year-old character from the first half at a screening of Sex in the City 2.

I don't think anyone else on the team heard Delaney refer to a vision quest before the show, and certainly whoever gave the suggestion hadn't heard that. It also wasn't the goal of the team to "heal Will Hines" or do anything other than play as things developed. But it does happen like that—the shows you do feel like direct reactions to your emotional state. Or maybe they're like Rorschach ink blot tests—you see in them what you choose. Like when you're dumped and every song on the radio is torture.

But it was the silliest and most fun I've had in awhile. And reminded me how lucky I am to be on that team, and at the theatre. And how you'd be hard-pressed to construct a more blessed improv path than I've gotten to walk. An appropriate vision quest for a discouraged improviser, I'd say.

I'm embarrassed gushing over it—it feels uncool and inappropriate to discuss. But I offer this as a balance to my expression of the discouragement which I posted, which we all feel at times. There's this other half that happens too.

JUNE 1ST, 2010 at 6:16AM

THE HARD PART IS CONNECTING TO SOMEONE ELSE'S IDEA

This one might be overthinking and overanalyzing. But here we go anyway....

So the pattern games in my classes were too stilted, so I told students to preface everything they did in a pattern game with "That makes me think of..." So instead of people looking at each other's shoes and saying

> "icicle
>
> snow day
>
> chicken soup
>
> chicken soup day
>
> holidays for specific meals..."

it'd be

> "that makes me think of an icicle
>
> that makes me think of a snow day
>
> that makes me think of how awesome I thought morning television shows, just because I couldn't see them normally
>
> that makes me think of how I had terrible taste as a kid
>
> that makes me think of liking terrible things because they're new
>
> that makes me think of blogging"

And it's more chatty and conversational, and truer and more personal. At least everyone is smiling and out of their heads and the funny ideas aren't so crazy or abstract. "That makes me think of..." was a powerful tool to making the pattern game more accessible.

That's interesting, but not as much as what happened next.

Because THEN I thought there were too many ideas, so I split the group in half. I asked one half to always start with "that makes me think of" and the

OTHER half to focus on support. The "support" half had to label what was already said, to think of other examples of what was said, to flesh out the ideas of the "that makes me think of half." That would help cement ideas with repetition rather than constantly have new ideas.

So now the pattern games would go something like this (contributions from support people in italics):

"that makes me think of an icicle

that makes me think of a snow day

local news broadcasts

that makes think of terrible toupees

that makes me think of my uncle's terrible toupee

insecurities of getting older

plastic surgery

that makes me think of heidi montag

terrible people on television

local news broadcasts"

I liked these pattern games better—fewer ideas, and more labelling of games and nailing things down. HOWEVER I noticed that the people who had been assigned "support" were in their heads. They were looking at the shoes of the people across the circle. The "that makes me think of" people were smiling brightly and totally engaged.

Maybe it's the support that makes pattern games so hard. It is easier to connect to yourself than it is to other people's ideas. But in a pattern game you're told "connect to the last idea" or "label the patterns" or to "A to C" or whatever and you go in your head, because it's hard. You have to process it, internalize it and come up with another example or another way to say it, or an aspect to isolate. Necessary, but harder.

In other set openings—documentary, scene painting, invocation—you spend more time on your own contribution and less time processing what other people are saying. Maybe?

We know that support is a muscle, but how strong you are at it may be very directly related to how in your head you feel. By "support" I mean to hear someone else's idea and focus on it—create another example of it, highlight part of it, label it.

So if you're feeling in your head a lot—maybe practice being an echo machine—spend some practices / shows / classes amplifying everything that everyone else is saying and doing. In the long run, you need to be connecting to yourself as much as anyone else—but it might be connecting to other people's ideas that slows you.

JUNE 7TH, 2010 at 7:12PM

TRY IT WITHOUT ANY RULES

The more improv you do, the fewer rules there are. You start to go more and more by your actual reactions.

This is only true after you are comfortable being watched. Being uncomfortable on stage creates false and weird reactions. Just like how most people, when they see a camera pointed at them, suddenly stand unnaturally straight and put a weird smile on, and no longer look like themselves. In that same way, young actors will take the stage and suddenly forget how to ask for gas for their car, or how to be upset that you have to fire someone, or how to hold a fork.

I believe that's one reason we give young improvisers all these rules—they help prevent the natural bad habits that come from the self-consciousness of being watched.

>NO QUESTIONS
>
>DON'T ARGUE
>
>AGREE AND DO EVERYTHING
>
>AVOID THE MEAN GAME
>
>PHYSICALLY MATCH
>
>HAVE A BIG EMOTION
>
>HAMMER THE FIRST UNUSUAL THING
>
>CONFESS

(I'm trying to state them the way I think they feel, not necessarily the way they're said or taught.)

But then you do enough scenes (100? 500?) and you chill out and can maintain a mostly-normal reality and react to things with appropriate importance. At that point the above "rules" hinder you. They block your intelligent, informed reaction. You need to throw all of those rules away and just do this:

    LISTEN. REACT. And TELL THE TRUTH.

If you're a student at this I recommend now and then going into a practice session or a show or even a class with only one rule: "listen, react and tell the truth." Don't worry about game, or avoiding fights, or starting in the middle or anything. It's a way of seeing how you're doing with all the crutches of rules stripped away. You'll definitely fall back on some bad habits—let it happen. Because you'll also start playing like an independently thinking and acting person—far more interesting than a student trying to "do it right."

Then next practice go back to trying the rules, then later try it without, repeat.

What I've found is I'll need to bring those old restrictions back now and then one at a time. I'll realize after a show that I'm being hostile for no reason, and so I'll temporarily tell myself "no fighting, Will Hines—don't be angry." I'll carry that one rule only around with me the whole next show for my own good. But just the one.

JUNE 8TH, 2010 at 6:56AM

Q: TJ AND DAVE

Anonymous asked: When I watch improv duos like TJ and Dave or Adsit & Gausas I feel like I'm seeing a different kind of improv being practiced than what is taught at UCB. Is the difference their immense amount of experience or is there something else to it?

Lots to address here! It is true that our core improv courses teach the Harold and thus focus on a group doing a series of short funny scenes inspired by an opening—a very different feel than two people doing long scenes with no opening. (Our advanced courses teach a wider variety which do address things like smaller sets and longer scenes—but I won't cop out and say 'we teach everything.')

That said, I think the success of TJ & Dave and Adsit & Gausas is the quality of the players more than the form. Gausas was on a UCBT Harold Team when she moved to NYC, then she was on Stepfathers, and she does Gravid Water—and she makes them all look easy and great.

The magic of a small set of improvisers building one long scene is mesmerizing. But to me, it's not inherently more noble or better than a group of 8 doing a series of shorter, more quickly-developing funny scenes. They are both magic to me.

JUNE 8TH, 2010 at 6:57AM

Q: COMEDY OR THEATER?

Anonymous asked: Improv for you is mostly: comedy or theater?

Comedy, definitely! Great question. I will be writing about this in an overly-opinionated way soon!

JUNE 8TH, 2010 at 7:00AM

Q: BIG A-HA MOMENT?

coreybrown asked: What was your biggest ah-hah moment?

I'd love to hear everyone's answer to this. I've had many. One was when I took a series of acting workshops, and the teacher pointed out how much I was sounding fake breathy when I was trying to sound serious. Another was when James Eason side-coached me to "participate" in a group game. Another was when Ian Roberts said to try pulling from your real life in every line. Another was when John Gemberling suggested I try "matching energy" rather than thinking about whether the first line made sense. Another was when Brett Gelman suggested doing a whole Harold without initiating. Another was about week seven of Kevin Mullaney's Meisner-y "Improvising From Your Gut" level 4 class.

JUNE 8TH, 2010 at 7:00AM

Q: CHARACTER VS. GAME

Anonymous asked: What's more important to do in a scene: establishing a strong character or a strong game?

Both equally important and usually overlap tremendously. Whichever set of words works for you.

JUNE 8TH, 2010 at 7:02AM

Q: DEMISE OF STRAIGHT MAN

realbenrameaka asked: Good Morning Will Hines,

I've heard several senior improvisers lament the passing of the "Straight Man" at the UCB theatre. As an improviser continually looking to improve how can I better my straight man ability (apart from the standard answer of "Watch Kevin Hines")?

Follow-up question: Why doesn't the Training Center teach a straight man workshop?

Hello Ben Rameaka. Yeah, I've felt that. Maybe a better way to put it is that I feel like I recently went through a phase at Harold Night in which I saw multiple unusual things per scene—an unusual thing is born and is met with another unusual thing. Theoretically, someone being a straight man would fix that but it's probably better to just support the first unusual thing however you'd like.

Interesting idea for a workshop. It sounds like it'd be a bit too narrow. Maybe? Let's talk about it.

JUNE 8TH, 2010 at 7:03AM

Q: BLACKOUT ON YOUR MOVE?

coreybrown asked: Do you get a slight chub when a show is blacked out on your line or move?

I really do. But I'm not proud of that.

JUNE 8TH, 2010 at 7:03AM

Q: WHAT DOES IMPROV MEAN TO YOU?

Anonymous asked: What does improv mean to you? Why do you do it?

I love this question. Everyone answer this.

JUNE 9TH, 2010 at 8:59AM

YOU SHOULD WANT TO BE FUNNY

The best compliment you can give my improv show is to tell me it was funny. That's why I'm doing it—I want to help make a funny show. I like being funny and always want to be more funny more often. I love when my shows get laughs and I super-love it when I in particular get laughs.

I'm saying this to counteract something that drives me nuts which is lionization of slow improv shows over other kinds of improv. "Slow" does not mean "better"—"slow" is just one kind of show, which can be great or can be terrible.

I love that UCBT improv classes almost always have graduation shows. It sends the message: we are studying this in order to perform shows that are funny. I like that message.

Not that I dislike slow shows. I like them a lot—if they're good. And "good" means "funny." TJ and Dave are smart, invested, patient—they are also hilarious. Without that last part, the first three parts would NOT MATTER!

Fwand was impatient, abstract, disorganized—and also hilarious. I loved fwand shows.

Gravid Water is measured, thoughtful, often solemn. It is also hilarious.

ASSSSCAT is crazed, frantic, very fast-paced. It is hilarious.

Creep's Harolds were slow, character-filled, patient. And hilarious.

Adsit & Gausas? Of course: amazing, hilarious shows that are slow and patient. So is Neil and Anthony's two-man movie, which is frantic, shapeless and full of zombies.

All good shows. But they were/are all shamelessly hoping and trying to be funny.

Being funny is not bad! It should be the whole fucking point!

When we tell people to slow it down, it's not because we want them to be slow. It's because they are not paying proper attention and commitment to funny ideas that are passing them by. WE TELL THEM TO BE SLOW, BUT WHAT WE WANT IS FUNNY. FUNNY. FUNNY. FUNNY!

Okay, sure: sometimes the desire to be funny creates destructive behavior in our shows. Being funny off the game is bad. Being funny at the expense of the reality of the scene is destructive and problematic for the show. Being funny at the expense of your teammates' performances is unlikable and therefore bad for the show.

But you shouldn't be ashamed of wanting to be funny. If you don't, you're in the wrong field.

JUNE 27TH, 2010 at 10:32PM

IMPROVISING BETTER

Improvising Better, by Jimmy Carrane and Liz Allen.

Jesum Crow, what a great book! Slim, smart, knowing—and every point is backed up with simple exercises. They directly address almost every problem area I struggle with as a teacher and performer in less than a hundred pages. I had never heard of this book until Mullaney mentioned it on his blog last week. And then today Ben Rameaka dropped off a copy on my desk as a donation to the UCBT library. "The universe wants me to read this," I thought and so I have. It'll be on the shelves at the offices tomorrow. Check it out.

"This whole nicey-nice syndrome results in boring scenes. Stop being so damn nice and play life! We want to see two selfish characters fighting for what they want. Give yourself permission to emotionally hurt your partner's character onstage, and they should do the same to you. So, take the plastic wrap off your improv and let your characters get down and dirty."—Chapter 3, "Nice People + Nice Choices = Boring Scenes."

What other improv books should I read? What am I missing out on? This book has been out for 2 years and I just heard of it a week ago.

Edited to add: I've read Truth in Comedy, Art by Committee, Group Improvisation, Improvise, Something Wonderful Right Away, Guru, Funniest One in the Room.

JUNE 29TH, 2010 at 7:32AM

CONVERSATION: WHY DO IMPROV?

An email conversation with Anthony King.

Will: My question for you: From one person who's done improv for a long time to someone else who's done it for a long time—Why do improv? I'm asking you to speak as improviser, not as Artistic Director of UCBT. Don't you ever think that we've put just like way too much time into this?

Anthony: This is a good question. And one I ask myself a lot—especially when I'm feeling lost, bewildered, or depressed about my career or the current state of my teaching and performing. And almost every single time I start to feel like I'm doing really good work, I think "Congratulations! You're great at something that no one else cares about."

But one of the great things about improv is that it's 100% about this moment, right now. And in less angsty, clearer-headed moments of my life, I'm able to look around and think—"You know what? Some of my happiest memories have happened before, during, and after improv shows with the people I met because of improv." That's not so bad. And I really do love it. That feeling of anticipation as you step out for a scene? That rush when an audience erupts at a moment you helped create? The satisfaction of pitching your teammate a home run? There's nothing better. Reveling in a great show? Beating myself up for weeks about a bad show? Cringing in shame about a terrible move YEARS later? I love all of that too. The artform just speaks to me. I'll never be the funniest person or the best actor or the best writer—or even the best improviser. But the philosophy of longform improv gives me strength. The ability to learn from success and failure, and immediately put those lessons to work in the next show? I'm not perfecting a product, I'm perfecting myself. Which is impossible. And never ending. And frustrating. And wonderful. And so so so rewarding.

But here's a question I wrestle with a lot: What if there is nothing else? Could you be happy if you spent the rest of your life teaching and trying to master this simple but impossible artform? Is it truly rewarding enough? Or is improv really just a frivolity, a learning exercise, a workshop of skills that's a lot of fun—especially when you're young—but ultimately a first step you have to leave behind and use in other more lucrative artforms that will, we assume, be more satisfying because they can get you money/fame/something else? Would devoting your life to the study of improv mean you're a failure?

Will: Hmmm. I suppose if you have the sense of moving forward, then you COULD be happy being a career improviser. I see teachers from Chicago writing books, or designing their own classes and shows—there's ways of finding new challenges. But I've always unconsciously assumed I would move onto something else at some point and that improv would just have been an education. The main problem is that in improv the work vanishes as soon as you finish. I find myself hungering for something permanent. Even something like this blog gives me a certain satisfaction because it exists after I stop typing on it. I will always consider myself an improviser, but I'd like to find a non-improv area where I could apply the philosophy and things I've learned.

Then again, I bet I would have said that in 2003. What I think about, ironically, is how little I think about the future. If you're an improv performer with a regular gig, you can let time FLY by. You're performing, right—so that means you're doing something? Except that outside of your own evolution of a person—what are you building? Improv does not punish laziness. How many brilliant improvisers can't write a second draft of a script? I'm certainly including myself in this assessment. The same awesome ability to be in the moment on stage comes with a dangerous tendency to ignore the future! I think that last sentence is from a Spider-man comic.

Anthony: Maybe improv is a drug. You do it while you're young, you have fun, you open your mind. But eventually you have to get off of it and do something real with your life. Or you start selling it (teaching, writing books about it, etc.).

Maybe my question was really, "Would you be happy being a drug dealer hooked on drugs for the rest of your life?"

But let's embrace this dark, sad idea for a second. Is this drug doing anything for us? Are we all just wasting our time getting high when we could have just been writing from the start? That's really what we're talking about here, right? Writing? Actors don't really have anything permanent to hold—only recordings of moments they created, the same as improvisers.

But many, many creative types—comedians, writers, artists, etc.—have used drugs to facilitate their art (for better or worse). Maybe the most empowering thing we could do is to embrace the idea that improv is our drug. And to say—If you're not using this drug to facilitate the creation of something more permanent, then you're not an artist or a comedian at all. You're just a junkie.

Too harsh?

Will: No, not too harsh. That describes perfectly the worry I sometimes have. We should be writing, and if all we do is improv shows than we are putting off making a more permanent creation out of laziness.

Keeping the drug metaphor, what about people who are lifelong pot smokers? Not in a way that ruins their productivity—but it's something they enjoy, that's part of their lifestyle, that at one point opened their mind and that just become something that provided happiness? Could that be an analogy for a career improviser, if they have some other way of making money, some other field that they are working on. Like a dentist or something who enjoys improv and finds ways to do it for years and years? That doesn't SOUND unhealthy. Is there a way to keep drugs in your life in moderation? Does everyone who enjoys an evening glass of wine become a debilitated alcoholic? Legalize improv!

I'm not ending on a question here. Do you have a comment on this, if not I've got more to say about why I do improv separate from career goals.

Anthony: So I guess to answer your original question—Yes, we have put way too much time into this. We're the guys with the vaporizer saying, "You think you're really smoking pot? Nah man, you could totally smoke it better."

Will: That is a good closer to this, BUT I HAVE MORE TO SAY! Because actually this whole pot metaphor makes me feel better about how much time that I've spent on improv. I mean, in moderation, the use of some sort of mind-altering substance isn't a bad thing. It changes how you think about things, gives you something in common with others who partake, has its own culture and aesthetic and vocabulary. It doesn't HAVE to lead to something, although you do have to guard it from becoming so central that it takes away from other activities. I mean, moderation is possible, even desired. There is a middle ground between lifelong drug addict and abstainer.

Or I am just an addict finding the rationale necessary for me to continue?

Anthony: I don't think drug rehab programs would agree with you, but since neither of us is going to stop using, let's agree to that rationale and try not to end up in the improv gutter.

JUNE 30TH, 2010 at 6:39AM

Q: SLUMP

Anonymous asked: Will—maybe I am in a slump. Maybe I need to take a break. Here's my question.

That unusual thing we're looking for in the scene. What if it comes up and it just doesn't excite you. YOU (the improviser) just don't find it funny. Maybe your scene partner doesn't either (he/she doesn't seem excited)—but it got a laugh. You know why it got a laugh but it's just fucking BORING/NOT FUNNY to you. Do you owe it the audience to play it? Or your scene partner? Or your team? Or yourself? If you don't think it's funny, should you play it just because of the rules of improv? Or can you hit it and move on?

Has this ever happened to you? Am I doing this improv thing wrong?????

It sounds like you're asking permission to do the scenes you want to do. I grant you permission.

JUNE 30TH, 2010 at 6:47AM

Q: TOO CRAZY TOO SOON

halphillips asked: Say you're in a show that's getting too crazy too soon, and you think it needs to be pulled back. If you can't think of a way to ground the show while also supporting the craziness that's been established, which do you think matters more?

I keep thinking about a move I made in your class yesterday (the lonely hearts Harold). We had talky meta-edits that bled into the first group game, and I was worried we were gonna get unfocused and go off the rails, so I did a sweep edit and started the second beats. I hoped that would ground the structure a little, so we could keep the meta stuff going without losing the Harold. But I keep debating whether that was a flat-out denial of the structure we'd established.

I don't know if that's the best example—but I think in general, "this show is too X and needs a little more Y" is tricky, because Y can feel like a denial of X. Giving the show what it needs vs. honoring what it's become; which wins?

I wrote so many drafts of this question.

Oh yeah, I remember that. As an audience member watching that I didn't mind. And I understand that urge to rein something in. But I would bet it's better practice to "yes" the big decision and do it in a way that addressed what you're concerned about—do the meta-transition but then initiate in a way that clearly moves away from it—keep it alive but improve it. Easy to say.

Meta stuff is tough, but I would guess that most times supporting the big idea on the table is a more important muscle to work than being worried about what will happen. Let it go off the rails, since I think that shows go off the rails way way less than students fear.

JUNE 30TH, 2010 at 6:56AM

Q: MENTAL RUT

coreybrown asked: When a group is going through a period of bad show after bad show, do you have any tips to help them get out of their mental rut?

It's tough. In practice, run a bunch of two person scenes. Everyone watches as the team goes up two at a time. Don't work on the opening or group games. Two person scenes in practice are fun and nice and remind you that improv is fun and you are good.

Ask the coach to focus exclusively on support. Listen, commit and connect. Set aside game or pushing the envelope or doing some new form. Shows don't feel as bad if you believe that everyone is on your side. Don't just tell each other "Guys, we need to have fun." That's vague and everyone does it differently and you'll be separate on stage. say "Guys, we need to support and listen and connect."

But really the only sure-fire cure is to have a good show.

I'm honestly kind of guessing here. Hello Corey!

JUNE 30TH, 2010 at 7:10AM

Q: IO VS UCB?

legospaceship asked: What do you see as the main difference in the Chicago vs NYC schools of improv thought? More specifically what's different about iO vs UCB?

I've gone to iO in Chicago maybe 10 or 15 times since 1998—not that often—and always loved it. I'm not qualified to answer. I will now answer anyway:

First, it feels like going to an alternate universe where I don't know anyone and yet everyone looks familiar. I constantly map the performers I'm watching to ones I know. "Ah, that person is like Jon Gabrus." or "Look! That person is playing like Shannon."

The piano players who accompany a lot of improv shows is the first and most noticeable difference. Changes the atmosphere a lot though after watching one or two sets I notice it much less. I prefer no piano player but that is likely just how I was "raised."

The hosts at iO only host, they don't seem to plug shows.

Having a bar in the same room and nice tables and chairs to sit at feels more professional somehow. Feels more theatrical and less rock club. I don't have a preference.

I was there LAST March and saw two nights of shows. What I noticed then was there seemed to be less commenting and directly calling out weirdness. Sometimes that made shows feel too soft and indecisive—I was hungry for someone to call shit out. Other times it made the shows feel braver and more committed. I ended up thinking that it was probably good there was less calling out—if that even IS an actual difference.

A major part of my experience was watching shows where I literally did not know ANYONE on stage. With no pre-conceived notions I was far more aware of people on stage smiling and grinning at each other in support of each other. It stood out a LOT. I don't think they do that more at iO; they may do it less. But I became aware of it. I wanted them to stop. That put me in my head for my next ten shows "The new people in the audience see you smiling and don't like it," I thought to myself.

iO is where the UCBT was born—I always feel lucky to be there and to be watching shows. It's Mecca to me—so I like to be respectful and dig it. Even the shows that don't work, I like getting to see them.

Groups I have seen at iO over the years: People of Earth, Prefontaine, Baby Wants Candy, Georgia-Pacific, Five Chinese Brothers, Zumpf, Lindberg Babies 2.0, Gold Rush, Bullet Lounge. Others too, I just can't remember the names. I kind of like going randomly and just seeing whatever is there.

JUNE 30TH, 2010 at 7:13AM

Q: NO WAY YOU'LL BE A SMART IMPROVISER

ryansimmons asked: I just started 201. When you first started out, did you also ever feel like there was just NO WAY you were ever going to

be a smart improviser? How did you get over that?

Yes, I felt like that for a long time. For me, my thing was I felt like I would never be comfortable on stage and I would always be a boring presence that killed the energy.

I got over it because I knew if I quit that I'd wander back and watch a show two years later and some fellow student of mine that I knew was worse than me would be on a team and I'd want to kill myself for not sticking it out. Persistence beats talent. So I just waited like FUNGUS THAT WOULD NOT DIE! BE A FUNGUS! THAT'S WHAT I'M TELLING YOU!

JUNE 30TH, 2010 at 7:13AM

Q: EMOTIONAL FIGHTS WITH YOUR BROTHER OVER IMPROV?

coreybrown asked: Have you and your brother ever gotten into a for real emotional fight over theories in improv?

My brother and I do not have emotional discussions with each other or anyone.

JUNE 30TH, 2010 at 7:18AM

Q: INVOCATION "ELEMENTARY?"

Anonymous asked: Will Hines,

The invocation is my favorite opening to do. But, I've recently heard both it and the pattern game called "elementary" by improv students more experienced than I. And I do notice that the more senior groups on Harold Night tend toward more advanced openings like the organic. Does a simpler, more basically, structured harold opening strike you as being for younger groups or students? Is there something that can be done to elevate them or make them more advanced? Is there a group out there that still does these basic openings in a

more interesting way?

Don't listen to snobs who say what's hip or not hip. The only rules are "yes and" and "if this then what else." Any opening is fine and no opening is fine. Structure is good, and so is less structure. Starting from a suggestion or an opening. Time dash or analogous. Starting a scene with a digging motion is okay, so are surgery scenes and job interview scenes. Just say yes, commit, listen and support.

We all have too many opinions on everything that the audience isn't even paying attention to. It's like rock bands arguing that they have the wrong color guitar picks. Just play a good song—no one will notice.

JUNE 30TH, 2010 at 7:19AM

Q: SAN FRAN IMPROV?

Anonymous asked: Any tips on where to do improv in San Francisco?

I don't know! Got to be some, though.

JUNE 30TH, 2010 at 7:20AM

Q: TERRIBLE SHOW

Anonymous asked: I just had a TERRIBLE show. What do you do to regroup after shows like that?

Try not to think about it until you can have a show that's good. Go see a movie. Be nicer to everyone to wash away the guilt you feel. Drink more water.

JUNE 30TH, 2010 at 7:20AM

Q: HATE SKETCH?

reasonsilovemymother asked: Do you and your tumblr hate sketch comedy?

Yes.

JUNE 30TH, 2010 at 7:24AM

Q: DOUBTS

Anonymous asked: Dear Will,

I am a 301 student and I am on a long form group back at my college, Uconn, and I am having some trouble. When watching a scene or Harold I can almost always identify the game and then think of steps to heighten. This changes when I perform in class, where I find myself focusing too much on responding truthfully to everything my scene partner says and I end up missing potential game and afterwards end up feeling like I have no idea what game is. Is this something most improvisers go through or does it mean that maybe I would just be a better fit doing sketch instead of performing?

Are you mentioning UConn because you know I went to UConn? Did you like it there? When I was there I hated it—I was a real snob about myself and felt I was a genius and deserved to be at a better school, not that I was willing to accumulate the massive debt that would have entailed. But I did make terrific friends there that I still love. And Storrs was truly beautiful in the fall. I used to like walking around the older buildings at the center of campus and wonder what it would have been like to go there in like 1920 or something. I signed up for a stand-up competition when I was 19 and went to it, and then when they called my name didn't move and pretended to not be there. What was I thinking? I was also in the marching band which baffles me to this day. Mirror Lake was disgusting, wasn't it? I liked going to Ted's Grinders and ordering the hamburger sub with ketchup and mayonnaise—I still have dreams where I'm eating one!

I don't have a good answer to your question.

JUNE 30TH, 2010 at 7:24AM

poupak asked: Answer to the question: Why do you do improv:

I started improv a little by chance. I have classical theater training from college but have been working in the corporate world ever since. I was also a TV producer and a journalist for many years, working on live shows, and have always had the "live entertainment" bug in me. 2009 was a difficult year for me, like for many other people, so I decided that I needed something fun to do. I signed up for Improv 101 with Silvija. I guess I was just lucky—I had amazing people in my class with an absolutely AWESOME teacher. It's hard for me to improvise: English is my third language, I am older than everybody at the UCB, including the teachers, and I didn't grow up in this country... my cultural references are sometimes different from everybody else. But now, I can't live without it. That live entertainment bug I was talking about has become a consuming passion for improvising on stage and making people laugh. First, it allows me to physically relax. You need to be on your toes when you're on stage to support the team, and this tension and the warm up exercises before the show are just the type of physical exercise that I like and that my body responds to. It takes my mind off my own little world. Improv is all about supporting the team and making everybody look good while they are doing stupid things, so it doesn't leave room for me to torment about my personal little problems. It helps me perform without being the center of attention. I was never a "front of the camera" person. When I did theater, I was a director and a producer. When I was a TV producer, I wrote the show for other people, and I directed and edited recorded segments. When I was a journalist, I was an off camera journalist and a writer. Performing without being the center of attention, yet bringing comedy to people, is the absolute definition of fun for me. Because at the end of the day, I love improv because it's the most fun I've ever had.

I love it! Thank you for answering.

JUNE 30TH, 2010 at 7:27AM

bubblebathosbands asked: when meeting people in non-improv contexts, do you wonder, or can you tell, what they would be like as improvisers?

I do form that opinion all the time. I was riding Metro North back from CT once and in the seats behind me were two guys talking about what sounding like engineering—I presumed their jobs. Blueprints, proposals and such. When the train got into Grand Central the conductor said over the loudspeaker "Everyone please leave the train. This train will be departing for the yard." And one of the engineers said to his friend "The yard. They are going to the yard." and the other guy responded in a very dry voice "I hope to go there someday." And I thought "Those guys would be good improvisers."

JUNE 30TH, 2010 at 7:29AM

Q: POOP OBJECT WORK

spotastic asked: Any advice on how to my my 'poop' object work more realistic?

Two schools of thought on this: one is to really pay attention the next time you're working with poop in real life. Watch how you handle it, how your actual physical work is. Maybe do some of it in front of a mirror.

I think Owen Burke would suggest not thinking about it though—just DO IT on stage with the same casualness and familiarity you do in real life. "You've worked with poop a million times in your life, just do it."

For what it's worth, I've always admired your poop object work, though I'm glad to see you're not resting on your laurels.

JULY 1ST, 2010 at 9:01PM

WHY I DO IMPROV

Someone asked "What does improv mean to you? Why do you do it?"

The **short answer** is that I like being around funny media-absorbing sarcastic jerks who also put a premium on being truthful.

A **true but cop-out** answer is: I liked doing it day 1, and then again on day 2 and so on and so forth for 10 years.

A **more cynical** answer: I need so badly to be thought of as smart and/or funny that I paid an institution thousands of dollars for that illusion.

A **selfish** answer: Prettier girls started talking to me after I started getting good at it.

An **idealistic** answer: Because I believe it makes the people who do it more interesting people.

My **long pop psychology** answer is: My mother was a genuinely hilarious woman, as are her sisters. She and they were from Ohio, and in the midwest everyone regards everything with folded arms and a raised eyebrow. My family was raised in her presence, learning from her to regard everything in the world with smirking suspicion and to assume that everything was bullshit to be mocked. Then she died of cancer and we were all devastated. Ironically, the way she taught us to behave—doubting, sarcastic, regarding everything as bullshit—left us unequipped emotionally to deal with her being gone. I'd meet people in college and not know if I should make fun of them or break down crying for how sad they seemed. I was an engineering student, then a journalist, then a computer programmer—mostly resigned to being a wandering watered-down creative type in a room full of people talking about last night's television shows.

And then when I was 29 I found improv. And in this world, people were simultaneously pressured to be hilarious and suspicious but also honest and forthcoming—seeing the unusual but being emotional. It meant everything to me that my teachers would tell me to react, to say what I was truly thinking and that they called me on it when I was lying—but still appreciated funnyness. Scene Work healed me from being a complete jerk but also complimented me for sometimes being a complete jerk. Improv shows were emotional lie detector tests and also places where being funny was valuable currency. It felt like my home, with the bonus difference that you had to talk about what you were thinking at all times and you couldn't lie. I couldn't have prescribed a better place for me if I had a fucking genie's lamp.

A **practical** answer: I've done it too long to really stop now! What am I going to do, go back to school and research how to purify water? Come on! Two more up, please!

JULY 4TH, 2010 at 9:35PM

Q: LEAVING A TEAM?

2ndguesscorrect asked: Hey Will, I just graduated college and am getting ready to move across the country to pursue comedy and film. I am super close with my college improv group and I'm so scared that

I just won't fall in love with my new teammates and be totally unmotivated. I know who I am in my improv group and I know my teammates and I know how to play with them-they keep me going. What if I get out there and nobody thinks I'm funny and I can't improv good no mores?

I think leaving a team you're comfortable with is a justifiably nerve-wracking thing. But you will undoubtedly become a much more powerful improviser when you learn how to find your own voice again with new people. Every good improviser I know has had at least two long tenures with different groups of people. It is disorienting, but I think it's common and essential. You'll be okay.

JULY 4TH, 2010 at 9:39PM

Q: SUPPORTIVE STRAIGHT MAN?

frankgarciahejl asked: What makes a good supportive straight man in a scene? It's something I've been really trying to focus on personally in rehearsals and performances. It's tricky because you want to react honestly, but you don't want to just be pointing out over and over, "You're crazy! What?! That's insane!"

People like Ian and Matt W. or You, Kevin, Curtis and Anthony K. always seem to make the straight man work perfectly while still playing the reality of "wait a minute…" but still seem to make the scene move forward and make it fun.

What are some things to look for in your behavior as a straight man and reactions to go for to make it an effective in a scene?

Aaaaand also… Favorite albums or songs that you might listen to on the way to a show that get you excited about performing?

My instinct is that the pitfalls are 1) neglecting to add info and 2) being unaffected. If you are saying "you're crazy" it's only bad if that's all you say and you say it in an "i don't care" tone. Give the crazy person some more fuel. Be agitated, disturbed and point out that not only are spiders NOT currency but there is a tarantula in the cash register drawer.

I don't have a fixed routine of songs but some stuff I've listened to lately Don't Stop Me Now by Queen, Accidents Will Happen by Elvis Costello, Alex Chilton by The Replacements, Stratford-On-Guy by Liz Phair, Another Nail for My Heart by Squeeze, Revolver by the Frigging Beatles and Everything Right is Wrong Again by TMBG.

JULY 4TH, 2010 at 9:40PM

Q: HOW FAR LOVE?

jokesfortalkshows asked: Disregarding talent, how far can a team go by simply loving each other?

I think far, though it matters more that that "loving" is happening on stage. And by loving I mean listening and supporting and committing. Off-stage stuff—book clubs, dinners, movie nights—it helps but I think 1% more respect on stage is better than 10 karaoke nights off-stage.

JULY 4TH, 2010 at 9:42PM

Q: SUPPORT VS. UPSTAGING

emilyhoffman asked: Where is the line between support and upstaging your teammates in a scene? In theory if your intent is to be supportive then that should come across, but how do you know that you're not undermining what they are trying to do?

Interesting! Maybe.... honor system? I think? If you mean to support, then you are supporting. Though a good guideline might be—does your support move completely confuse and surprise everyone in the scene? If so, you might be rewriting the scene to something they are not looking for—which is okay once in while, it's your scene too. But most support should be there to confirm and help them push the scene the way they are already expecting. In other words: support what they are interested in, not what you think they SHOULD be interested in.

JULY 20TH, 2010 at 3:51PM

Q: VONAGE POINT?

Anonymous asked: I'm working on an improvised show about the intramural football team at an internet-based phone company. It's called Vonage Punt. Would you be interested in directing it?

Erik Tanouye, disregarding your terrible puns, the show I am directing is called Vantage Point and it's happening tonight.

JULY 28TH, 2010 at 3:25PM

Q: IMPROV TEAMS = CLASSIC BANDS

iamachilles asked: Not a question, but an assignment:

Equate all of UCB's great Harold teams to the great bands of modern popular music. (Modern popular music = From Elvis, on.) For example, if The Swarm are The Beatles and Respecto Montalban are The Rolling Stones (not even sure if those are,even correct analogies) what are Mother, Dillinger, fwand, et al?

This is an irresistible game to play. I first heard of this proposed by Charlie Sanders, and I've been part of long email chains devoted to this. Swarm = Beatles and Respecto = Stones works. Talking about it here in the office, I'll add that the best suggestions I've heard in addition are Mother = Beach Boys. Optimist = The Who. Roo Roo = Zeppelin.

Dillinger and fwand are tough. Dillinger might be Elvis Costello? Fwand = Guns and Roses? Or either one could be Nirvana. Or The Clash? Dillinger might the Clash, though weirdly The Shoves feel more like the Clash to me.

Fun game! DOES NOT END ONCE YOU START PLAYING.

Edited to Add: Dillinger is The Talking Heads. Creep is Duran Duran. As you were.

AUGUST 5TH, 2010 at 8:36AM

Q: UCB GENERATIONS?

silvija asked: How many improv "generations" has the UCB been through? How, in general, do you define a generation? By year? By a series of seminal shows? When one group literally "topples" another (like Dillinger beating the Swarm in Cagematch)?

Dillinger stacked the house.

Hmmm. I don't know. When the classes were synced up, it felt like every new Level 3 graduating class was a new generation. Lately it feels like every YEAR is a new generation, starting with each Harold Night shakeup. If I had to break it down, it feels roughly like this in my brain:

"Solo Arts / original" people

"Cowbot / Feature Feature / Real Real World"

"161 – Swarm / Respecto / Mother"

"Neutrino / Optimist / Monkeydick"

"PCR / Dillinger"

"Reuben Williams / Shoves / Arsenal / Creep"

"fwand / 1985"

"the year with a million teams"

"now"

I typed this without thinking.

Edited to add: I realize I obviously define generations by Harold Night. You could make a different list without mentioning Harold Night—something like Solo Arts, 161, Amy on SNL, early 26th street, derrick comedy, mono scene, college humor—but it'd be more difficult and not how I actually think of things.

Edited again: Anthony King points out "Dillinger came long after Optimist, Neutrino, and Monkeydick. Those teams all existed before PCR. And PCR was formed almost a year before Dillinger. Methinks you've crammed two generations together."

It's true! Dillinger and PCR now separated from Optimist / Neutrino / Monkeydick.

AUGUST 5TH, 2010 at 8:50AM

Q: BESSER CONTRADICTS YOU?

Anonymous asked: I noticed that during Matt Besser's lecture at DCM that you appeared to agree wholeheartedly with everything was saying while it seems to contradict your expressed teaching/thoughts. Can you expand your thoughts what was discussed at the lecture?

How does it contradict? If you could be specific at all I'd be happy to answer. Well, crap, I'll answer anyway.

Besser's workshops are among my favorite classes ever. They're smart, focused, informed and reflect the way he plays, which is to say the way one of the best improvisers around plays! I find them fascinating and like going to them.

If there's a contradiction, it's because Besser focuses mostly on the opening and initiations in his talks. Not exclusively but mostly. And there are strategies and things to do in your opening that do not apply to other areas of the long-form set.

Like he talks about the opening, and using that opening to build premises, and then unapologetically using those premises to start scenes. I do agree with that. For years people did openings just as weird verbal/physical gymnastics then disregarded it and essentially started their scenes from the suggestion. I think Besser got us using the opening more directly and more practically.

What I have noticed over the years is that students will go to Besser's workshops, love it and then spend a few months obsessed with the opening and getting ideas from it. It's not bad, per se, but during this time they will be in their heads and be more connected to the opening than to their scene partners. They act more wooden. They boss around more. It's okay. They're just... learning. So at some point they need a coach or teacher to remind them that the scene continues after then the first two lines, and that they need to support and listen and react regardless of how good your opening is. I don't think Besser would disagree with that.

There's initiating with premise and there's initiating with half-ideas or less. And they are different muscles. The first is a bit more writely, the second a bit more actorly. But you're an improviser so you can do both.

I also went to a Kevin Mullaney workshop that was focused on improvising from your gut. Reacting honestly. Using the natural energies of you and your scene partner. It was the exact opposite approach to starting a scene from using a verbal opening.

But I loved them both! I don't think they're exclusive. They just work different muscles.

AUGUST 5TH, 2010 at 8:51AM

Q: IMPROV IN EXISTENTIAL CRISIS

Anonymous asked: Why is it that improv seems to be constantly suffering an existential crisis, certainly more than any other art form? Improvisers are always asking questions like, "What is the point of improv, to what end am I doing it?," "Improv performances are so ephemeral, shouldn't I be devoting myself to something more tangible and permanent?," "Is improv just a way to hone comedy skills that are better applied elsewhere, is it merely a stepping stone to a greater endeavor?," etc. There is so much introspection about the point/purpose/meaning of improv, all emanating from a place of doubt and skepticism about improv's inherent worth or validity. Why, Will? Sure, this goes on in other fields, but not to this extent. I can't imagine ballerinas aren't up all night pondering whether they're wasting their time dancing because the recitals are transient experiences that don't leave an indelible cultural mark. And I'll bet professional puppeteers aren't incessantly tortured by the suspicion that what they do is an indulgent hobby, a fun distraction lacking nobility. So why not with

improv? Why do we hate ourselves? Why are we often so sheepish about this passion (and how oxymoronic does that sound!)? Why is it so hard for us to be confident in the notion that what we do matters, that it's worthwhile, that it is good and valuable in and of itself???

P.S. Happy DCM!

Great question! My initial reaction is that we're a bunch of self-centered boobs, myself included. Fun, smart, media-absorbing boobs but self-centered ones nonetheless. Thankfully we're noted so hard to build group mind or we wouldn't pay attention to anyone else ever.

AUGUST 5TH, 2010 at 8:52AM

Q: BAD MOOD = BETTER SHOW

chrisreblogs asked: I've started to notice a pattern about myself. If I am in a bad mood going into a show (outside stuff... or actually feeling negative about the project itself), the shows go better. I play better. I listen more attentively and I respond quicker, stronger and clearer. I don't inflict my teammates with my bad moods pre-show. I bury it down and put on a smile and to the whole cheerleader thing. My question: Is this messed up? And what the hell does it say about me?

You're messed up!

I have noticed this about myself! Maybe we're better listeners when we're in a bad mood because we're not so full of our own joy? Maybe sad songs are better than happy ones? Maybe we're both broken human beings?

AUGUST 5TH, 2010 at 8:57AM

Q: MOST EPICALLY RIDICULOUS SHOW?

halphillips asked: What was the most memorably, epically ridiculous show you've ever been a part of?

December 19, 2003. The UCBT was between theaters and doing shows at Access Theater—the fourth floor walkup on Broadway below canal, Monkeydick faced Mother in Cagematch. Curtis and Gemberling were at the premiere of The Two Towers. Brian B. was somewhere else I think? It might just have been Rocco, DeCoster, Lathan, Mitch and myself. Our show went bad early and we just kept throwing more ridiculous stuff. I know we blacked out on John F. Kennedy getting assassinated by The Bee Girl from the Blind Melon video while one of us was a buddhist monk or something. Actual silence after the blackout. We got three votes.

AUGUST 5TH, 2010 at 8:58AM

Q: IMPROV INNOVATIONS

benjaminapple asked: I'm always impressed and fascinated when people mention the fact that Jazz Freddy (right?) invented the tag-out. Sometimes I amuse myself by trying to imagine what kind of improv innovations might happen in the next few years. Do you ever try to come up with "things" we could do in shows but don't? Do you have any pet forms or devices you kind of want to become popular?

I am fascinated by how conventions get developed and become accepted. I prefer a group choosing or excluding conventions (tag-outs, "we see" or whatever) instead of forms. The Macroscene wasn't a form, it was agreeing to a set of conventions to use.

I have tried to come up with others, but failed. The closest I know is trying to copy 4 Square's "liquid transitions" and cross-fading from scene to scene.

Edited: I'm hearing The Family invented the tag-out. Regardless, your question about imagining when certain conventions were consciously created is interesting.

AUGUST 5TH, 2010 at 9:00AM

Q: IMPROV PEOPLE COMMON ENERGY

benjaminapple asked: One of the things I like about improv is that sometimes I feel very at-home in the community of improv people, i.e. I feel like there's some kind of common thread running through the type of people who devote so much time and energy to this thing. Is that true, or do I just imagine it, and if you imagine it too what do you think it is?

I don't know but it's one of the best things to ever happen to me.

AUGUST 5TH, 2010 at 1:11PM

Q: CLARIFY TERMINOLOGY

benwarheit asked: One of the big things i took from the Besser seminar was that it may be important to clarify the definitions of our artform's terminology. Words mean different things to different people, and that might not be the best thing when we're all struggling to learn and get on the same page. Besser defined 'heightening' as 'taking what's funny and making it funnier'—a simple concept that a non-improviser could understand and work with.

How would you define the following terms, simply and concisely, to a johnny-everyman?

heightening, exploration, commitment, yes-and, group mind, straight-man, the first interesting thing, a-to-c, analogous, game, and premise.

Also, in a recent post you said you prefer sets of conventions to the notion of a form. How, then, would you define form?

It is very important to be picky about terms. Simple terms convey a lot of information if you pick the right ones and disregard others. One of Del's talents, I am guessing, was fostering simple mantras that created good improv behavior (things like "yes, and" though it can be bent to defend any situation does tend to make people improvise better, for example.)

Like we're trying to say "base reality" instead of "who, what, where." It's more accurate for sure, which I like. Will it stick? Remains to be seen.

Sometimes the mantra is more clear than its actual importance. "A-to-C" is a nice clear idea but in my opinion way overused probably BECAUSE it's so clear. People use the term "A to C" to defend making huge leaps from opening to scene, from first beat to second—where it's a far more valuable skill to repeat what was already funny without changing it too much. For example. Just use A-to-C to get away from the suggestion, then try hard to connect and repeat. But already it's getting confusing.

In general, you want fewer and fewer rules and terms in your head. The UCB—and really anyone who teaches/coaches a lot—fight to reduce the terms. You want the fewest number possible. A lot of what Besser talks about is throwing out terms and strategies that seem not helpful enough to remember ("relationship" is maybe only as important as it defines our base reality so don't waste conscious thought on it while you're performing beyond that, maybe).

I'm ducking your actual question of defining terms because I'm lazy.

Forms? I think of them as structures and orders for shows. Conventions are tools to use at the actors' discretion. Harold is a form. Tag-out is a convention. Monoscene is a form. Cross-fade edit is a convention.

AUGUST 6TH, 2010 at 6:29AM

MORE UCBTNY GENERATIONS THOUGHTS

From purns: "That G3 group covers all the groups from, say MKV up to Reuben/Mailer Daemon. PCR/Syndicate/Dillinger/Shoves are obviously central to that era, but MKV and Reuben/Daemon sort of bookend the era. This was so much easier when we all started at the same time. If we wanted to really nitpick, I'd say the G3 group started basically with the November/December '01 set of classes post-9/11, with Dicktrino/Menuky and Pound's Black Harold as big markers of the G2 experience, and the Nomad period generally/Dillinger debut as a big marker of the G3 experience. Whuh boy."

From lifeisaslowharold: "Ok, this is very specific to just me. I'm trying to figure out which generation I'm in. I started taking classes in early 2005, which would be G4, but the Harold teams I watched were Reuben, Mailer Daemon, The Shoves, and Creep, which would suggest end of G3. Which am I? Who am I?"

From halphillips: "I think I'd split it up into more, smaller generations than you and Purnell did. Maybe about a year? I've always thought of a "generation" as people coming up through classes around the same time, which translates into who's in practice groups and indie teams around the same time. I think of my generation as Big Tobacco, Kid Dervin, Chantico Warfare, etc., followed by Thank You Robot, Baby Grenade, Orphan Tycoon, etc., followed by Fat Penguin, Bad Data, Stamp & Coin Club, etc. Each of those feels to me like a wave of new people. I wouldn't go by Harold teams, unless it's for purposes of who the new students are watching, i.e. the Shoves or Fwand influencing respective generations of students. Two years seems WAY too long to me; the people at the beginning would be coaching the people at the end."

For me, I prefer fewer generations rather than more. I like making all the time that's gone by feel accessible and simple. Might just be a fear of death or at least a fear of information clutter.

More thoughts. This from katespencer: "Charlie Todd speaks very specifically about the Class of 2001, people who started taking class that summer right before 9/11. To me this generation starts with PCR (how can anyone overlook PCR from the Harold Team generation list? My all-time fave) and ends with Dillinger, kinda resulting in the birth of a bunch of other groups along the way (M.D., Reuben, etc). I started classes in 1/2002 but latched onto the tail-end of this generation."

AUGUST 30TH, 2010 at 6:25AM

QUICK THOUGHT ON OPENINGS

It isn't what opening you do, it is that you are doing one at all, that changes your form.

Does that seem obvious? It is not. I used to obsess, as a teacher, over the difficulties of teaching pattern game, or scene painting, or sound and movement, or organics or whatever. But really—the hardest thing to teach is INITIATING WITH PREMISE. Getting the actors to be on the same page at the top of a scene after an opening.

Going off just a suggestion—the actors may be struggling to get ideas, but they have much less trouble staying on the same page with each other. You introduce an opening and they have ideas but aren't really listening and reacting to each other as much. I'm talking about students more than veterans.

Yet we just obsess over the opening itself. Did we A to C too much? Too little? Was it grounded? Were we repeating? But really you should watch the tops of your scenes AFTER that opening. Are you still listening and reacting as honestly as you would if you are coming off just a suggestion?

WELL?

I've been away from this blog. But look! Here I am! I hope you are all doing well.

SEPTEMBER 10TH, 2010 at 8:05AM

DOPPELGANGER; MULLANEY; TWO-PERSON IMPROV

A round-up:

A belated thank you to Doppelganger, the improv trio that lasted eight weeks in UCBT-NY'S Cagematch. Their shows were a clinic on trust, agreement and commitment. And it was exciting to see a new team announce itself to the UCBT world with convincing authority. They had to lose sometime, and I'm glad it was to a team as cool as Rogue Elephant—the granddaddy of indie teams, whose shows are a clinic of a truly funny team whose members love each other in a genuine, unaffected way.

Kevin Mullaney's latest post on practice and how it means more than talent and how it applies to improv is a great read, as all his improv thoughts are great reads.

Did a two-person set with Kevin Hines on Monday, and a two-person Harold with Dyna Moe last night at the Creek. Two-person shows are so unfairly fun to perform in. So much stage time! No possibility of getting in your head!

Basketball and jazz are the two best metaphors for improv, that's clear. One addendum: being at bat in baseball is like improv. You have to be relaxed and instinctual but also totally focused and analytical. Note: I am a terrible baseball player.

Other stuff.

SEPTEMBER 15TH, 2010 at 8:35AM

MAYBE WHEN GIVING NOTES

Maybe when giving notes we should check the following things and note them in this order:

1. Are they listening and reacting and understanding each other?
2. If yes, are they committing to their own choices?
3. If yes, are they creating a world that seems truthful rather than just silly?
4. If yes, did they find a game and hit it?

And you don't address later questions until they're doing the previous ones. Like that. Instead, I think coaches/teachers note the thing they are interested in regardless of what the actual problem is. That's not fair or true what I just said. It's a worry I have.

This topic deserves way more thought than the time I just spent typing this.

NOVEMBER 25TH, 2010 at 11:09PM

STOP FOCUSING ON INDIVIDUAL NOTES

Students love individual notes. But I'm not so sure they help, certainly not as much as students want them. In fact, I think too many of them can make players more self-centered, less confident and worse listeners.

But students ask for them. As the person in charge of teachers and curriculum at an improv school, it is the number one request I hear from students (outside of being told a room is too hot/cold, which is still far and away the number one concern of New Yorkers Pursuing Improv). Could I get some notes? Students wait after class in a line, wanting more notes. They write in their evaluation of class that they had questions about their notes, or they liked a teacher because "he/she wasn't afraid to call me out on my bullshit."

Why are improvisers so masochistic? Why do they love, in class at least, being told specifically what is wrong with them?

Well, individual notes = individual attention, first of all. People love, understandably so, individual attention from their teachers and coaches.

But also, people believe that there are magic words waiting that will transform them into the improvisers they want to be. One brave teacher who will just tell me like it is, they think, and I'll be able to do it all.

Unfortunately, I think the more a student is noted individually the less he/she is paying attention to his/her scene partner and the less he/she is paying attention to the work. Also, the focus on FAILURE over STRENGTH just reinforces the self-doubt that we all have. A culture of noting individually is hobbling students. How about an individual note that praises you and tells you what you're good at and what you should do more?

A well-placed concise individual note is helpful. But not every class, not every show, not even every teacher. Individual notes should be like a big hammer you apply once in a great while.

Most of the time the best notes you can receive are not the ones you want to hear, but the same fundamental rules: Say Yes. Listen. Commit. Support. Play to the Height of Your Intelligence. Find the First Unusual Thing. Do More Scenes.

Note to all of my students: it is okay that you ask for more notes. I would do it too. I just mean that you and me and we all put too much weight on them.

NOVEMBER 25TH, 2010 at 11:26PM

Q: IMPROV HAT TRICK

silvija asked: In hockey, a Gordie Howe hat trick is when a player (1) scores a goal, (2) records an assist, and (3) gets in a fight all in one game. The Detroit Red Wings' Pavel Datsyuk (possibly my favorite player) had a Howe hat trick in October.

Define your own improv hat trick and name it after somebody who embodies its spirit.

My suggestion: The Brian Huskey Hat Trick—When an improviser plays (1) a straight man, (2) a crazy character, and (3) an inanimate object, all in one show.

The Erik Tanouye Hat Trick:

1. Initiate a scene with a clear simple game from the opening
2. Initiate the second group game as a parody of a smart movie/book
3. Use mimed binoculars at any point

NOVEMBER 26TH, 2010 at 7:23AM

Q: WORDS OF WISDOM THAT STUCK

justcraig asked: I feel like I usually remember one or two specific notes or words of wisdom that really stick with me from a teacher or coach. Are there any ideas that you remember from specific teachers or coaches that really stick with you? What are they?

Also, what did you eat at Thanksgiving that made you fart most? Can you pinpoint it?

Someone, I think Delaney, told me "the second beat starts where the first beat started, not where the first beat ended."

Armando described second beats using sound effects: "If the first beat is you going 'grrr!' and the other person going 'aaaah!' then that's what the second beat should be."

James Eason once side coached me "Will, participate!" during a group game where I was miming photographing taking photos of everyone else eating a bear and it had a big effect.

Besser's "if Lorne Michaels gave you three minutes to come up with ideas for an SNL submission, would you spend it doing a sound-and-movement exercise with your team?" or whatever—that make a lot of hilarious sense.

Also, I remember coaches/teachers laughing at things and that would make me do more of them. Billy Merritt laughed at big stage pictures. Delaney laughed at long pauses followed by simple confessions ("um... that hurt my feelings.")

Second question: I presume the two cups of strong coffee.

NOVEMBER 27TH, 2010 at 10:06AM

LET THE EXERCISE DO THE WORK

We teachers often note too much instead of letting the exercise do the work. This is especially true in exercises that have a lot of rules. Like a mono-scene, or Scene Painting, or even Big Booty. We explain these rules, the students do the exercise and then we start noting them on all the subtleties of things we know about those exercises and the philosophies behind them. Just let them play. Let them do it in an amateurish way. They'll get it—you don't need to talk once they start doing it.

2011

JANUARY 5TH, 2011 at 6:18PM

HAROLD NIGHT SHAKEUPS AND BASTIAN

New Harold Teams at UCBT, both in NYC and LA!

There should be more shakeups, more often. Everyone on Harold Night is a great player, but chemistry is elusive and unpredictable. Best way to get the most chemistry MIGHT be to just roll the dice more often. Take Sandino—there were one of three new teams last April and in my mind seemed the LEAST cohesive. But one show and you could see—holy shit, this team works.

So more shakeups! That sounds right, except that improvisers—myself DEFINITELY included—have a tendency to instantly sentimentalize the teams they're on—take pictures, having bonding trips, etc. All great things! But that allegiance makes it more emotionally tough to break apart and try other combos.

Is it true that at the LA UCB theatre they don't even take pictures? Maybe that's smart. Or maybe it shouldn't happen until a team is around for a year. At iO, there's so many teams that people maybe don't get attached to a team until it survives and ascends to the front of the pack, I am totally guessing?

We've had times at the NY theatre where there were frequent shakeups and cuts and people freaked the fuck out. Maybe we need a thicker skin for the sake of letting the unpredictable effects of different combinations play out?

—

NOW I will go against the idea of being detached from a particular combination of people to say my best wishes to the long-running giants of Harold Night (comedy and height wise)—BASTIAN. I saw their first and last show and even though the lineup changed a lot they always remained the smart, funny, confident tentpole of the night. (I keep resorting to tall, thin imagery because their original lineup with Frucci, Gardner, Barrett and Maggie Carey was hilariously tall and thin.) How many Harold Nights would feel off before Bastian came out and killed it? They gave a clinic on doing a Harold right. Then when every coach started moaning that they were too smart and careful they were brave enough to try really hard forms, and then loose ones, and everyone opening you could think of, and they traded second beats with Badman and were all to a member, the nicest people on the night! They rehearsed twice a week for their first year! They were the anchor for like ten years! They've been around so long that almost no one taking classes knows a Harold Night without Bastian! A great team. They are all superheros: brandon, brian, adam, maggie, john, lydia, molly, oscar, abra, erik and faas! Too good, jerks! Too good! Thank you Bastian for caring a lot and being so good and being a bright spot for so many nights.

Okay, now stop mythologizing teams!

Yours,

Uncle Contradiction

JUNE 1ST, 2011 at 9:28PM

ACCEPTING OFFERS, RICH SPECIFICS, PHYSICALITY AND COMMITMENT

This post is about things you can do in your improv sets that provide instant gratification in terms of laughter from the audience and are also usually (though not always) healthy for your scene overall.

I'm thinking about when you're about to do an indie show and you just want to HAVE FUN, but so often that urge results in terrible aimless chaotic shows.

Here are things you can do that are easy, that get you INSTANT LAUGHS, you validation-hungry whores, and will USUALLY help your scene even though they are not technically things that address directly the fundamentals of a good scene.

QUALIFICATION AND APOLOGY: This post is also a ridiculous

over-simplification of things but I will accept no criticism. Express any dissatisfaction through means which I cannot detect. It is also too long to be considered diligently written. I forgive myself as I'm shaking off dust. Thank you, improv 301 students, who will hopefully read this whole thing.

I. IMMEDIATELY ACCEPT OFFERS

So I was in a Stepfathers show and was kinda lost—I had initiated that I had come to town hall to look up a birth certificate of my grandfather and then immediately forgot why I thought that was a good idea. My scene partner, Silvija Ozols, made a suggestion in the form of a tentative question in the way that improvisers sometimes do when they feel things have gotten foggy: "Wait, are you they guy who's trying to fake that your grandfather is a citizen?" And I considered it for one second and then without really understanding what I would have to do just said "Yes."

And the audience laughed.

I think we're all familiar with that situation—someone half-offers an explanation or an idea of what another character is up to. "Are you saying you're going to quit your job?" "There's something else going on. Are you trying to tell me something?" Saying yes to these questions will almost always please the audience. I'd go so far as to say you will always get a laugh in saying "yes" to those questions which are really tentative offers.

I'm NOT saying it's always good for the scene. If there's a game established, blindly saying yes could muddle things. And now you have to prove it—to make true whatever you just agreed to.

But it's always always good for the MOMENT to say yes to those offers. It's a guaranteed happy moment and often the right move since you are agreeing with your partner.

Why is this so reliable? I guess because the audience can see that Person B thought of the idea, and Person A is now going to enact it. It's like a pimp or in a small way like a short-form game where one person is controlling the other. Or it's just good cooperative improv. Person A pauses, Person B makes an offer and Person A accepts. Or it's the magic of saying "yes."

Another way of looking at this: when I watch indie shows that are going poorly, it's the number one thing that stands out to me, that people are constantly saying "no" or finding reasons to dismiss or ignore the half-hearted tentative offers from everyone else. Next show at the Creek or Under St. Marks: you count how many times someone softly brushes aside comments like "you're angry, aren't you?" or "is that MY briefcase?"—it is surprisingly constant.

II. RICH SPECIFICS

Making any generic item specific, or making any would-be generic setting specific—is always immediately fun. When Jack McBrayer moved to NYC and was doing an improv show, and the world here had yet to discover how awesome he was, he stepped out in a Harold and someone said "Pick up that basketball" and Jack said "I'd love to. It's a SPALDING."

And the audience exploded with laughter.

That's partly because the audience loves anything Jack McBrayer says but they also loved the specificity.

Magazine titles, types of food, saying particular names all are fun and easy things to do—as long as they fit within the reality you establish and are not jokes in an of themselves are always a delight. No more *Johnson File* for *Jenkins At the office*. It's a *list of fire alarms that need repairing* for your boss *Bert Purdy at the rock quarry headquarters*.

I admit these will not always serve the scene, and if a game has been established you will risk distracting from it—but it will absolutely be fun in the moment and very often inspire future choices. And if you're in a show that you're thinking of as a fuck-around show, it's a good way to practice keeping the writer side of your brain active.

Related but just slightly harder: starting with a rich world—the future, the past, a fantastical land—each with its own laws, codes, cultures, jargon—that's fun to play with and is instantly fun. A dystopian future where you say "Greetings citizen" is not that much harder than asking your modern-era roommate about the rent, and it's way more fun. A small midwestern neighbor who comments that the Kiwanis Hall needs fixing—that person sounds more interesting than a doctor asking for a scalpel.

III. COMMITMENT

Commitment is obviously a big part of good improv and something that does help your scene fundamentally and is something all improv teachers should constantly talk about. But what you might not appreciate is that, ironically, *even half-assed commitment works*.

What I mean is: you don't have to work yourself up to a Robert Duvall level of immersion for your commitment to help your improv. I think just saying to yourself as the scene is starting "be there" or "be this person"—just that short mental check in, and your whole posture will change. Your face will slightly drop its smirk, your eyes will focus. The audience will detect that you are much more in the scene and they absolutely will love it more at that very moment.

Better example: The suggestion is "plaster" and you decide you're going to be a guy in a hospital bed, and as you walk out you also decide that maybe you're going to be asking the doctor if you can bribe him for a better room because why the fuck not? You need an idea and that's one.

As you sit in that chair and lift your leg, just tell yourself "be in the hospital"—and without thinking any more than that, I bet your acting will get 20% better. The audience will notice. How many indie shows are two people facing each other on stage with a big grin, giggling through their lines? Just being a notch more into it would set them above most of the rest of the pack *in one instant*. Yes, you too can be a GREATER IMPROVISER WITH JUST THIS ONE STEP OF HALF-ASSED COMMITMENT! NO FORETHOUGHT OR GREAT GAME MOVES REQUIRED!

IV. SUMMING UP

So I don't know: none of these things address the fundamentals of a good show. They don't guarantee you a grounded reality, or supportive environment, or smart games. They don't lay down seeds for third beats—they don't really do the work.

But they increase the quality of play, they increase the percentages of good things happening. They provide instant gratification and are easy. I suggest you try them at your next low stakes show and feel how much fun you will have.

BONUS: None of these things really require that anyone on your team be on the same page with you. You can do these in a show all by yourself.

JUNE 14TH, 2011 at 7:44AM

HAVE AN OPINION AT ALL TIMES, TO EVERYTHING

Here's something that improv made me do: ALWAYS HAVE AN OPINION on EVERYTHING in the show. Not as a comedy snob thinking about what it's like to watch the show, but as a character in the show. Everything that is said, that happens—your character should notice it and be able to turn that into a strong point of view and attach it to the scene.

- Someone's ironing? You have an opinion about domesticity.
- Someone's buying a sandwich? You think about the ridiculousness of over-branding and that this person is making it worse.
- Someone says hi casually, and you think that saying hello is a brave act, and that the person saying hello is coming out of their shell.

When you do this, you are connecting with yourself.

I dabble just a tiny bit in stand-up but in the days before a set I'll really be watching everything, trying to get ideas. And that will really work that muscle of me checking in with what I really think and feel about things.

JUNE 15TH, 2011 at 10:14PM

TWO TYPES OF CONNECTING

Lately as I write these posts and teach classes, I find two general categories of what i want the advanced students to do more of:

1. Connect to themselves—their real opinions and thoughts and reactions filtered through characters and specifics. Okay, you're an upset parent—what kind of upset parent would YOU be? What are things that would make you that person?

2. Using other people's ideas: specifically ECHOING other ideas, giving other instances of others' thoughts and inferences. mirroring

characters, repeating, confirming. Can you observe someone else and do what they're doing, adopt their philosophy—like, immediately? It's not what could happen, it's what HAS ALREADY HAPPENED. Can you make it happen again?

Here's what's more: number 1 is pretty easy to get students to do, number 2 seems to confuse everyone.

JUNE 18TH, 2011 at 10:03AM

#

Something to teach: Male improvisers should be chivalrous to female improvisers on stage. I use that word "chivalry" because it communicates "respect" but also acknowledges that there is a double standard. Chivalry dictates men's behavior more than the women's. This isn't because female improvisers demand it but because the audience demands it. For example: In general a woman can be verbally abusive to a man on stage and the audience could enjoy it. But if a man were verbally abusive to a woman—the audience would likely get uncomfortable. The sooner the male improvisers understand that, the sooner they'll be more successful on stage.

You know what chivalry is in life. It means a man holds the door open, pulls out the chair, offers to pay for the check. On stage it means the men don't say anything sexually crude to the women, don't physically challenge them, don't scream in their faces, don't put them in weird sexual conversations or scenarios. Not because the women are such delicate flowers that they would wilt, but because it's goddamn polite and we are going to be polite and sensitive to the rules of chivalry until we've earned the right and the confidence of our teammates to break them.

This is a separate issue than general improv respect. General improv respect and support applies to everyone. Everyone has to listen and react and cooperate with each other regardless of gender. Saying we need chivalry also is simply acknowledging that the audience sees you as men and women and they do not forget it.

In lower improv levels, there is always a generous peppering of guys who treat girls like weird robots. There are also girls who are unsure how much they can stand up for themselves without violating "yes and." Chivalry or maybe politeness are useful terms there. "We're going to be chivalrous in this class," I'll say after the first scene with sexual subject matter in it. "Guys should never put girls in a situation that isn't cool on stage. No one ever puts anyone in uncomfortable situations, and in addition guys will be chivalrous to the girls."

It's tiring and difficult to parse what's right and wrong for men to do to women on stage (and vice versa). And people love to argue the specifics. "What if the female actor ASKS the male actor to be sexual?" "What if the opening was all about dildos?" "What if the monologue was about a creepy uncle who gives weird neck massages?" Internet threads about this topic are always hugely long. Articles about men vs. women in comedy get disproportionate attention.

In class, I cut that discussion short and say "We could argue forever about hypotheticals, but guys: you know what's rude; don't do it."

That's because there are no hard rules. It depends on how well the actors know each other, on what topics the opening developed, on the level of self-awareness of the actors, on what has happened in the show already, on the confidence and talent of the actors, etc. And everyone has different levels of personal tolerance.

But you KNOW when you're being rude. And the words "chivalrous" or "politeness" let me discuss the easily-argued standards of men treating women well in a quick, not provocative way. "Not chivalrous," I'll say to the nervous 201 student who is doing only his 20th full improv scene ever. "There's no obvious reason for your character to give a neck massage there, seems not polite." (actual quote) End of discussion, no foul, start the scene over with a new suggestion.

I've seen a lot of weird starts to scenes between men and women with all degrees of malice and naivete. I've seen guys grab girls whom they do not know well and pretend to mime fuck them from behind as a INITIATION. I've seen guys call girls cunts in line one. I've seen 12 guys all gang up on the only girl in class in a group game when she was 100% mirroring what everyone else was doing. Those are the bad examples. Teachers should stop those scenes immediately, quickly note that it's rude for a guy to do that to a girl and not allowed, and either restart the scene or move on to two more people.

I don't think a lecture is necessary there, it puts the male student on the defensive and asks him to be resentful. And students are allowed to screw up in class. Abruptly stopping, saying it's not cool and restarting quickly saves time and send a simpler stronger message: just don't do it.

I've also seen far more cases of things that probably aren't meant as that bad: guys initiate scenes by endowing the girl as being a nymphomaniac, or guys screaming in girls' faces a little too closely and loudly to be justified. Or guys labeling the female actors as guys and then challenging them to a fistfight. Those types of things will happen from guys who maybe are just too socially awkward to know that they are being rude. I'll sometimes let those scenes go on a bit so they can feel the awkwardness, then stop it. I'll quickly and directly note it feels rude.

"I didn't mean to!" he'll protest, embarrassed. I'll briefly discuss those scenes, acknowledging that there could be cases where such things are the right move. I'll also point out it's not bad, especially in class, to try embodying offensive points of view and testing those boundaries. But the truth is the male actors cannot be seen as mistreating the female actors. "Maybe it's earned," I'll say. "I could see it being a game. But we have to err on the side of being polite, it's not worth it."

I like putting it in terms of the audience rather than the feelings of the female actor. The female actor, if she's the type who likes improv, probably isn't as easily offended as an audience would be, and probably doesn't want anyone to fight her battles. It's not fair for me as the teacher to presume what she feels and frankly, it doesn't matter. It's not about any one student as it is creating a standard of politeness for everyone for the audience to see.

Being at the UCBT gives me a great trump card if anyone argues me: "This is Amy Poehler's house. Girls are not mistreated here." Everyone loves Amy and invoking her makes everyone behave.

Girls are sometimes rude and inappropriate to guys, also, which needs to be noted. But it doesn't happen as often and the audience has a much higher tolerance for it.

Most people get chivalry without discussion, and are happy to live by it. More importantly, once everyone knows they are entitled to expect that type of good behavior they will stand up for it on their own.

JUNE 19TH, 2011 at 2:09PM

STOP NAMING PEOPLE "JENKINS"

It stands out.

JUNE 29TH, 2011 at 10:35AM

Q: LABELING A WOMAN AS A MAN

tragichamster asked: I thought I'd ask a question related to your blog on chivalry (since this is an interesting topic that actually comes up a lot). I was recently in a scene with a male improviser (I initiated) and my first line was (likely) more consistent with a man's behavior on a date than a woman's. Consequently, my scene partner labeled me as a guy, and the scene went on. Afterwards, the note we got was that my scene partner shouldn't have labeled me as a man right off the bat. What are your thoughts on this? I know we can all play anything or anyone in a scene, but is it unchivalrous to label a woman as a man in the first few lines?

I don't think this is a chivalry question, simply because it sounds like no one was being rude or weird in their intentions. I meant my chivalry post to apply to blatant weirdness between men and women that makes the audience uncomfortable.

The case you're describing addresses a more subtle point which is that playing opposite gender should be no big deal—not a weird thing in and of itself. So if it served the scene for you to be a guy, then your partner was right.

The problem your coach might have been worried about is when people get really hung up on making someone a particular gender when it doesn't matter. "Oh, only a girl would be freaking out about X, I better make this character a girl" when it didn't matter.

But I think that's most often a problem when people WON'T switch genders. Among beginning students, I'll see two guys sort of back into playing a gay couple because neither one thought to play a woman. Being the gay couple is fine, but being hesitant to switch genders will hold you up in other scenes. So I'll explicitly say "be ready to play opposite genders and not have that be the joke." They need permission or something. The book "Improvising Better" has a chapter on this which says it better.

I think your coach was well-intentioned but noting a problem that didn't exist there. Tell him/her I said those notes were totally wrong.

JUNE 29TH, 2011 at 10:36AM

Anonymous asked: How do improv actors make a living, especially in NY, where the cost of living is so high? Is their income mostly from teaching classes? Or is a "day job" required?

You either get money for coaching/teaching other improvisers and/or you have a job. Basically no one makes money at this unless you open your own theater and even then maybe not.

JUNE 29TH, 2011 at 10:39AM

zhubinparang asked: Do you think the NY improv community is over-indulging in the "fuck-around" shows? I recognize their value in blowing off steam, but in the past couple of years it seems to me that the number of these shows has exploded, and that there's been a corresponding rise in lazy, uncommitted improv, even at ostensibly "serious" shows.

Probably yes. I've heard a lot of veteran improvisers say the same thing. If there's no coach or director then usually stuff gets sloppy. Another thing that will cure that is a real audience of non-friends, who will have zero tolerance for nervous grins, talking heads and people quibbling on stage.

JUNE 29TH, 2011 at 10:48AM

Q: THINKING ABOUT THE BUTTON

Anonymous asked: How early on in a show do you start thinking about the end of it? Are you like "oh, yeah, that's the button," and you hold onto that, or is it just something that comes up all of a sudden?

I try to notice things throughout the show that feel like would be fun to revisit at the end. If a couple is talking about a party, maybe we'll see that party. If they mention a weird uncle they have a home, maybe we'll see that uncle. My group had a show recently talking about werewolves where people turned into terriers rather than wolves, and I thought "werewolf transformation would be fun for the ending segment." Shannon O'Neill and Silvija Ozols do this better than me anyway.

I never worry about the last line—I never know the button until I hear it.

JUNE 29TH, 2011 at 12:32PM

Q: JUSTCRAIG: EVER FARTED ON THE BACK LINE?

justcraig asked: Have you ever farted on the back line and been like, "oh boy."

I have done this. I have.

JULY 24TH, 2011 at 10:57PM

THINGS I KNOW ABOUT ONLY FROM WATCHING IMPROV

- The plot of the movie "Goonies."
- That there is a thing called The Thundercats and among them is one called Liono.
- MMA competitions

AUGUST 25TH, 2011 at 9:45AM

PLACEHOLDER THOUGHT: EMPATHY

The ability to sense what the other person intends, expects, thinks—that might be the most difficult skill to acquire in improv. It might be what separates people who can do this from people who can't. More than wit or ability to emote.

Separate: This is also a reflection of weakness in my teaching technique, but no request seems to befuddle more students or put them in their heads more than to say "do more of what the other person is already doing." That shit slows them down so much you'd think I'd asked them to build clocks.

I'll flesh this out later maybe. Or maybe someone else can figure out what I mean?

AUGUST 29TH, 2011 at 10:23AM

BETTER CONVERSATIONS

Improv can make you funnier, will likely make you a better actor, and could maybe even get you work. But one thing it will definitely do is make you better at having conversations.

You listen better, you speak to the heart of the matter more, you lie less, you speak more concisely.

But also, you will be better because most of the human race is so unbelievably bad at conversations. After years in improv, I can barely stand speaking to anyone who either isn't an improviser or is someone who would just naturally be good at it.

Most people, in conversation, speak solely about themselves, and in a way that matters only to themselves, with no ability to sympathize for the other conversational party may think or feel. They listen to other people only for opportunities to speak about things they want to and once they get going cannot be dissuaded. They speak inefficiently and amazingly redundantly. They rarely laugh at what's funny and instead only at what makes them nervous or at recognizable references to famous things.

Improvisers do all these things too but less often and they know enough to feel badly about it.

PEOPLE TALK ABOUT WHAT THEY WANT AND DO NOT LISTEN

A few months ago I was on a shoot and we broke for lunch. I sat with a group of people including one of the producers, meaning he's in charge and is not answerable to anyone and that's probably a position he's usually in. Someone remarked that the plastic utensils we'd been given were a bit shoddy. He breaks in:

"You know, my wife was yelling at me the other day for stirring my soup with a knife."

We look at him. Someone says "oh?"

"Yeah! She's like! 'Hey, what are you doing? You can't do that?'" I'm like 'Why not? It stirs, doesn't it?'"

And it's clearly some story he's told before, and he's locked into it. And maybe he's nervous and he's trying to be nice so he's forcing in one of his anecdotes and if I think of that way it's endearing. But I am an asshole and all I can think of is: *That has nothing to do with the shoddiness of utensils, or of our lunch, or about us! It's not that good a story and leaves everybody currently sitting with you out.*

"You could scratch the bowl," someone says. "That's why it's bad."

He looked at them. "Right. But I said 'Come on! What's so bad about using a knife?'"

Which did not answer the point. All I could think was how locked in he was—he could not recognize that someone had asked a question that essentially deflated his story and he didn't seem in touch with how no one was really encouraging him to continue. In his own bubble, broadcasting like a radio station.

PEOPLE DO NOT ANSWER QUESTIONS

He also remarked that until he was 20 he had no idea that Piglet in the Pooh stories was a pig. I found that interesting and wondered how he could not know that.

"Wait, yes he does—he looks like a pig," I said.

"No he doesn't. He barely looks like a pig!" he said.

"Okay. But he's named Piglet—the type of animal he is is in his name. That didn't tell you?" I asked.

He responded "Well, like how do you know what Goofy is?"

Except that Goofy isn't named "doggy," that's just a reference to a conversation in *Stand By Me*, and that doesn't answer my pretty reasonable question, and... I mean, the guy wasn't thinking about what he was saying, he wasn't listening to what was being said. He just had a story and wanted to tell it and didn't really want anyone thinking about it. What is the point of talking with people like this?

But he's far more typical of people's conversation—and it's what I run up against when teaching 101 and 201 improv courses. MOST PEOPLE ARE NOT PAYING ATTENTION TO WHAT THEY OR ANYONE ELSE IS ACTUALLY SAYING.

FOR MOST PEOPLE, BEING FUNNY IS JUST POINTING AT WEIRD STUFF

Once you throw in trying to be funny, it's almost impossible for most people to make sense. My youngest brother Brian told me a story about being in an elevator in Las Vegas with a group of strangers:

One of them was a woman holding a large stack of souvenir cups, and another was a woman holding an ice cream cone. A third person said out loud to the first person "Hey, got enough cups?" and everyone kind of laughed. Okay, fine, fine.

But then a fourth, presumably idiotic, man, blurted out "Yeah, but SHE'S GOT THE ICE CREAM!" and pointed at the ice cream and laughed. The whole car burst out laughing. Except for my brother, who remained stone faced because being raised in our family had schooled him to be an alienated snob.

I know that by pointing this out I am a cold unfeeling jerk, but *it makes no sense to point out that someone was holding ice cream*. It did not follow; it was not a joke. But it was a noticeable and strange thing in the elevator, and for a hugely high number of human beings—pointing at weird things (or celebrity references) counts as humor.

When I heard that story, I shuddered with the idea that that guy will take an improv class and I'll have to explain to him that most of what he is saying does not follow what his scene partner is saying, and he'll walk away complaining that UCB focuses too much on game.

VAGUENESS

How many conversations do you have, out there in the real world, in which people finish an anecdote just by making a face and shrugging? Or ones in which someone makes their point using a non-committal phrase like "and you can imagine what THAT felt like!" or "so, needless to say I wasn't too happy with THAT." or "let's just say things ended there."

How about we just say... what actually happened? Or what you felt about it?

There are even worse problems when two strangers try to complain about the government together. Or try to speculate on what their local sports team is doing incorrectly. Or when they have to make an official quote on behalf of an organization. "Ideas were utilized in a way that let's just say are going to leave things in a not bad way" or whatever.

I AM AN ASSHOLE

Guys, it is difficult for me to maintain friendships.

AUGUST 30TH, 2011 at 9:35AM

HEY, ANTHONY KING

Thanks for putting me on 1985 in March of whenever that was.

Thanks for coming and telling me directly when Monkeydick's run ended. And letting us have a big last show.

Thanks for coming to watch Porter's, Flynn's and my improv show in the Red Room on that Sunday during a week when you'd already watched a million shows. There were like six people there I think and you were one of them. Kate went too. Hello, Kate!

Thanks for coming over to my desk to tell about something that happened in your class that you liked, or realized, or that worked, or didn't so I could think about it and tell other people about it.

Thanks for creating Maude night. And Beta Teams, and who knows what else.

Thank you for emails of encouragement when things sucked in my life, whether by my own hand or just by bad luck.

Thanks for running those theater meetings smartly, back when we had them. First theater meetings to run on time.

Thanks for answering ten million emails, including some that questioned Harold team placements, and hosting protocol, and worries about the direction of the theater community as a whole, and dumb bits. For always being willing to articulate why you were doing something.

Thanks for worrying about your improv, which you were good at right away, the whole time you worked here— even when I bet your brain told you to not worry about it so much. You were on two of the best teams ever to be here: Dillinger and Reuben Williams. That is pretty awesome.

Thanks for being happy when hundreds of people advanced their careers because of exposure you helped them get, and people you helped them meet, and advice you gave them, while you sat at your desk and answered ten million emails about god knows what.

Thanks for somehow being organized and creative at the same time. For being invested but not taking too much personally. For loving theater first as well as comedy. For seeing this place as a theater and not just a clubhouse of comedians.

Thanks for sometimes coming storming in like a southern lawyer with a notepad full of suggestions for shows. For paying attention, for wanting things to be better.

Thank you for caring about Harold Night! For wanting it to be great, for making it better.

Thanks for watching all those Spanks. I honestly don't know how you did that. I think I've watched one Spank in which I didn't know anyone. For five minutes.

Thanks to Charlie Todd for telling you about this place.

Thanks for being the kind of person that even if I disagreed with you, I knew you were being fair and making the decision that you thought was best for the theater. That is impressive. What is the word for that? Integrity? Whatever it is you have it.

I know you're not dying or anything, and that this type of open letter of thanks and compliments can be weird and awkward—but I have to say something: it is just going to be really really really weird to not have you around. Send me a meticulously organized email now and then outlining something complicated so I don't feel disoriented.

AUGUST 31ST, 2011 at 10:36AM

BETTER CONVERSATIONS FOLLOW-UP

Friends have made some great points in response to my "better conversations" post.

1. First and foremost, that improvisers are not always better conversationalists because they tend to be self-centered and self-absorbed and prefer doing bits to talking about real things. That's true, especially

in groups. Like try telling the rest of your improv team you had a bad day in the green room before a show—no one is going to hear you, they will be busy talking about how you're wearing the same shirt as somebody once did on Dawson's Creek.

I still feel that good improvisers will be aware of their shortcomings in that regard, and will still find a way to answer any questions asked of them directly while ALSO forcing the topic back to themselves, Maybe it's that they DO hear you and simply CHOOSE to talk about themselves so it doesn't bother me? Regardless, I don't have a good rebuttal to this point.

2. Second, that my post was arrogant and obnoxious. I agree. I wanted it to be. It's how I feel while I am striding around the world.

3. Third, and this is my own feeling: I ranted too long about the one producer guy and I wish instead I had come up with concrete examples of:

- People making jokes that are funny only from their point of view, and not the people they are making the joke for. The musician who jokes with the audience about how long it took roadies to tune his guitar, the boss who jokes about how funny it would be if he fired everyone, etc.

- People making the same point three times in a row. Witness: Someone who is upset that their favorite reality show did not favor the proper contestant. The classic "Not to beat a dead horse, but (beats a dead horse)"

- People saying the word "yes" but then saying something that disagrees with what they ostensibly are agreeing with. "Boy, CNN really sensationalized their coverage of the hurricane in New York City" "yes, i agree, it was terrible. And did you know that was one of the biggest storms of the last 40 years?" Witness: all discussions that happen at bars.

Obviously, I touched on a topic that people are interested in—but I don't feel I really nailed it. That happens a lot. I should take more improv classes!

SEPTEMBER 4TH, 2011 at 9:51AM

YES (PAUSE) AND

I see two common but contradictory problems with new groups:

1. They don't react at all to anything, they're just looking at each other or maybe not even looking at each other.

    Improviser 1: When we hold up the bank, grab the gun with your feet.

    Improviser 2: (nothing for a long time) Okay.

2. They are blindly and over-enthusiastically reacting to everything so much that they sound kinda dumb.

    Improviser 1: When we hold up the bank, grab the gun with your feet.

    Improviser 2: Awesome! I have fingers for toes!

Or whatever. And by trying to fix one of those problems, they create the other.

Maybe this? Maybe we need to hear an explicit yes right away always, but then you can wait and consider and feel things before you and.

Improviser 1: When we hold up the bank, grab the gun with your feet.

Improviser 2: Yes, got it. (pause, feels it out) You know, we're trying too hard to be a really cool gang of thieves.

Does that matter? I don't know. That quick yes buys you time, I'm sure of that.

I have an insanely long post coming so I'm writing this just to prove to myself that I can write a short one.

SEPTEMBER 4TH, 2011 at 12:06PM

Q: REPEAT (PAUSE) AND

ericscott asked: You could also Repeat (Pause) And. "You want me to grab the gun with my feet? (Pause) You know, we're trying really hard...." Doesn't have to be a repeat question, could just be a statement.

I agree, that's a good, common way to buy time also.

SEPTEMBER 4TH, 2011 at 1:15PM

ACCEPT OFFERS: SPEAK TO THE TOPIC OFFERED

Full disclosure: when you teach or coach, you go through phases in which you fall in love with certain mantras, or certain priorities. I've obsessed about justification, about reacting, about reality, about game. I'm in one again, and this time it's all about "**making and accepting offers**." And as suspicious as I try to be about how I have in the past over-reacted and overly-relied on a particular strategy—I cannot escape from the belief that this phrase may indeed hit on the very central tenant of what is missing from teams that are not working. They do not, by default, look to accept each other's offers.

They will not, comedically and theatrically speaking, dance with each other.

I wrote something about accepting offers before—but before I meant specifically to accept any suggestion or question half-heartedly stated by your scene partner. I stand by that as a fun thing to do which almost always helps your scene.

But now I think even more fundamentally that telling teams to accept each others offers—and to look at every line as an offer, to hear every line you make as an offer—solves a great deal of agreement and teamwork problems.

I think Delaney was the first guy I heard use the phrase "make and accept offers"—he says it's a Del thing. I don't know.

What I do know is when I watch a team and I choose to observe the scenes with the mindset "how well are they accepting each other's offers" that I can see many many moments of dismissal, of ignoring, of misunderstanding that would likely not happen if these people kept as a point of pride to recognize and accept the offers being presented to them.

Really, it's just a re-stating of "yes, and" (like so many improv mantras are) but I like it because a) it's new to me and b) it's more active.

SPEAK TO THE TOPIC OFFERED

Initiation: "Honey, come on, the car's running, we gotta go."

What should the response be? This is pretty wide-open initiation. There's no game or unusual thing in it (unless it was some comment on the suggestion). Speaking conservatively, all you really "have" to do is accept that you are in a couple with the initiator, and that you guys had plans to go somewhere, or at least your partner thought so.

A possible response which seems fine but I will argue is not good:

Response: "Hey, I can't go! I'm still making all the salads!"

That response agrees that there is urgency, and it adds a specific activity and agenda for the responder. It "yes, ands"—at least enough that we can get going.

However, if I think of the initiation as an "offer"—I suddenly see it as an offer that *let's talk about this thing we're going to*. Suddenly, anything that refuses to address this thing that we're going to feels like a denial, a distraction, a refusal.

To accept the offer fully and simply, the responder should speak to what the initiator is speaking about. I would accept either of these responses:

"Just had to get my coat. Oh I hope your Dad isn't upset that we're late for his party," or

"You know what, sweetheart? I think I don't want to go. I think I'm just not the church-going type."

Meaning, I don't care if the character accepts the offer of wanting to go—but the actor should accept the offer that "the focus right now is that we have to go somewhere." Don't bring up salads, or something else in your life. Your partner has offered a topic, you should speak to it. To do otherwise is to dismiss your partner and focus instead on carving out your own separate piece of land to live on.

I see lots of people in the first 3 lines worry exclusively about giving themselves something to do, preferably something funny and wacky—and what their partner is talking about becomes second priority.

I have SEVEN OTHER PARTS TO THIS. Dear lord. I've tried to set up Tumblr to publish one a day, so we'll see. Some of these are really good.

SEPTEMBER 5TH, 2011 at 9:00AM

ACCEPT OFFERS: ACCUSATIONS/ COMPLAINTS

How about the very common case of a complaint or accusation? What if we see that as an offer?

> Initiation: Bill, why are you so insistent to spend your whole paycheck on this meal? You need that money!

We discourage our beginning students from fighting, since it often stops the scene from moving forward. But it's okay to fight, as long as the actors are smart enough to see the accusations as an offer. A gift.

The worst response to the above line would be:

> Response: Hey, YOU told me to spend all that money! I was just doing what you said!

That's what a 101 or 201 student would do. But we can see that that's essentially a denial, right? The next higher level student would accept the truth but spin the context:

> Response: Yeah, but this the only time I'm allowed to eat all week! I need to get all my food in for the whole week right now!

It's better—it's accepting the idea that you truly are going to spend all your money. But it still feels off to me, it's justifying the complaint so much that the complaint isn't interesting anymore—you denied the gift of yourself being ridiculous.

What if we look at that accusation as an offer: *you are the kind of person, very central to your nature, that spends all his/her paycheck on a meal.*

What if it went like this:

> Initiation: Bill, why are you so insistent to spend your whole paycheck on this meal? You need that money!
>
> Response: This is how much I love food. [or] What can I say? I'm horrible with money.

I bet they would get a huge laugh of satisfaction. And not because there's any brilliant game in there, or brilliant comedic idea. They are unoriginal, obvious statements. But I believe they would work because they accept in full the offer of the previous line.

I believe the audience rewards us for being smart and realistic. But it also rewards us for playing together. For recognizing what we are implying about each other, for being cooperative.

There is one game that exists in every improv scene, and that is the game of following each other's cues.

SEPTEMBER 6TH, 2011 at 9:02AM

ACCEPT OFFERS: HERE'S WHAT'S FUNNY

How about when someone offers something funny? An offer of a game/unusual thing/premise/joke?

> Initiation: Thanks for helping me move. To pay you back, here's a bag of fish.

I say the offer is *paying with fish is what's gonna be funny about this scene*. That at his/her heart, the actor wants that big of fish to be a ridiculous thing. Your character can accept that bag of fish as appropriate or inappropriate but to be supportive, the actor must help keep that idea of paying with fish as a funny thing. We call it a "game move" at UCBT.

> Response: Fish? A bag of fish is not the right kind of payment for me helping you move. (framing it as a weird thing)

Or,

> Response: Wow, a whole bag! So generous! (you're character is going along with it, but we can tell that the actor knows this is a silly/funny thing we're playing with).

I think either one shows that you understand that *the fish payment is funny* and will be central to at least the start of this scene.

That's what you have to realize: once someone makes a game move, what you have to confirm is that it's the funny thing. Who/what/where and everything are not as important until we've agreed on that offer.

DON'T JUSTIFY AWAY THE SILLINESS

Like if you want to justify it, and you should at some point want to—just make sure you don't make the fish so normal that it's no longer a funny idea. Like this would be bad:

> Initiation: Thanks for helping me move. To pay you back, here's a bag of fish.
>
> Response: Thank God. You know I love fishing, I can use this as bait.

You took away the silliness. That was what your scene partner was offering and you took it away.

A good justification gives us a philosophy that we can use to expand this moment into a bigger story, without making the moment un-silly:

> Initiation: Thanks for helping me move. To pay you back, here's a bag of fish.
>
> Response: Stop paying me with fish. I'm not a seal trainer anymore, this doesn't mean anything to me now!

IGNORING / REPLACING

Worst possible answer ignores it completely:

> Initiation: Thanks for helping me move. To pay you back, here's a bag of fish.
>
> Response: Thanks. You want a beer?

That's a blatant example of the character agreeing but the actor dismissing. Actually, there's one way to make it even worse:

> Initiation: Thanks for helping me move. To pay you back, here's a bag of fish.
>
> Response: Thanks. Man, you had a lot of weird furniture.

Because now you're ignoring your partner's offer and replacing it with one of your own.

Maybe that mistake seems obvious in the context of this essay, but I see this happen ALL THE TIME. I think it happens when someone is not listening, or someone has gotten too accepting of crazy things. They have forgotten to hold their scenes to a high standard of reality, and so silly things are no longer noticeable.

All I'm really saying is that if someone wants to make something The Funny Thing (the game, the premise, the unusual thing—call it what you want), that you agree to make that thing The Funny Thing.

EASY IN CONVERSATIONS

We do this in conversations with our friends all the time.

> Friend 1: So did I miss anything at the party after I left?
>
> Friend 2: Yeah! You did! These totally beautiful girls came by and we all slept together.
>
> Friend 1: Wow, I knew it. I could tell it was going to be that kinda night.

Or maybe this:

> Friend 1: Really? Because it didn't seem like that was going to happen. When I left you guys were arguing over whether Tom Baker or David Tennant was a better Doctor Who.

And you don't bother thinking about "unusual thing" or "framing" or "justifying." You could tell there was a joke, and you kept it alive. It's like that, do that when someone is making the offer of "X is a funny idea."

Although, ever trying to make a joke in a conversation with someone who just isn't on the lookout for jokes in conversations?

> Friend 1: So did I miss anything at the party after I left?
>
> Friend 2: Yeah! You did! These totally beautiful girls came by and we all slept together.
>
> Friend 1: Really? Wow, that's... kind of gross, actually.
>
> Friend 2: I was kidding. We didn't meet anyone.

I guess improv requires that you have a sense of humor and presumes that you are on the lookout for funny things to happen. Or else the joke is just that someone never gets a joke?

UNFUNNY PRESENTED AS FUNNY

Speaking of that, how about when someone offers an unfunny thing as if it were funny? What are you supposed to do?

> Improviser 1: My son did bad at science again, so I had to hit him in the face.

This is not that uncommon a thing that happens in lower levels, and contrary to what you might assume—very nice and balanced people will make such a choice. They're mistaking "outrageous" for "funny." They don't have stage experience, they don't know what's gonna land with a clunk because it's so mean.

In the interest of accepting offers—and I am saying the offer is *the funny thing is that I hit my son in the face*—then you should accept that offer and improve the idea without denying any part of it.

> Improviser 1: My son did bad at science again, so I had to hit him in the face.
>
> Improviser 2: Right, yeah. I'm telling you, social services is going to be upset with you. (framing it as an unusual thing)

OR

> Improviser 2: Great move. I mean, "spare the rod, spoil the child" right? Might as well go for it and just pop him right in the face. (giving it a philosophy, also restarting the touchy thing in a way that makes it clear it is ridiculous).

I'm not saying you made an unfunny thing funny. But you accepted the offer, and you are edging it closer to a comfortable comedic premise. I'm proposing that's the order you should do it: accept the offer, then improve as you can.

And then hopefully the coach/teacher notes that a parent hitting a child is not in and of itself a funny thing.

SPOILER 1: It is easier to do improv with people who are funny and know what's funny.

SPOILER 2: Tom Baker was a better Doctor Who, because he was awesome first.

SEPTEMBER 7TH, 2011 at 9:00AM

ACCEPT OFFERS: AFTER AN OPENING

A team does an opening and now has a handful of ideas, evolved to various degrees. Some obvious, some not. The problem is people will assume they understand what the other person has decided about the idea, and charge ahead without listening. Let's say in the opening there's an idea about a kid trick or treating at a famous person's house and not knowing who the famous person is and also that famous person was really chincy. (this example is from a very good team, to show that all levels of improvisers do this)

Initiator: "Trick or treat."

Response: "Hey, great costume, kid!"

Initiator: "what does this sign say? Sammy... Hagar? Who's that?"

Response: "That's me. Here's half a kit kat, kid. Have a blast."

Initiator: "Thanks. I've never heard of you."

Response: "That's all right. Here's a single candy corn."

If you didn't speak English, you would assume these two actors were getting along. But they are each playing a different game, and each refusing to react to the other one. The actor playing the kid is not noticing how cheap the candy offered is. The actor playing Sammy Hagar is not reacting to how the kid doesn't recognize him. It doesn't matter that the characters are getting along—they actors are refusing offers in each line after line 2.

SEPTEMBER 8TH, 2011 at 9:00AM

ACCEPT OFFERS: AGREEMENT BEFORE REALITY

The trickiest case I think is when someone is making an offer for you that requires you to ignore reality. Then you have to make a really tough choice:

do you support playing at the height of your intelligence, or do you support your partner's offer? Like this:

> Initiation (in a broad, hammy, wide-eyed musical theater but bad delivery): "These pens! These pens are so expensive! My wife is going to leave me!"

And let's assume this big energy is not like a fun genre choice. You can't just blindly match energy. It's just aimless and silly noise. So you've got a problem: your scene partner is over-acting, and is being guided by unrealistic logic. And it's confusing. What do you do?

I would advise: accept the offer first, and then as the scene goes on do work to make it more realistic, without ever refusing anything. The scene won't be great, but you will keep your improv muscles proper. And actually, if your partner is a just someone having a bad moment, your cooperative acceptance will snap them out of it, and things will get better quickly.

> Response: $500 a pen? Are they crazy? They're going to ruin our lives! We gotta get some nice pens!

I haven't solved any of the problems of the scene ignoring reality, but I showed my scene partner that I accept what he/she is putting down. The actors are connected, there's a chance to save this scene.

If you can think of a justification to make things make sense, do it. But it's gotta be something still accepts what is being offered. In other words, it can be this:

> Response: $500 a pen! It's our own fault for not bringing pens on the plane! Now we gotta buy them here in the airport!

I know, it's not great. But it's way better than this:

> Response: Calm down, you are so crazy. Pens are not that expensive. You can buy a really great pen for $10, here's $10.

Because the initiator is not offering that he's crazy. I mean, he IS being crazy. But that's not the dance he's starting. He is starting a dance about pens. If you're a top tier Olympic improviser, you will dance with your partner in the way he/she is expecting to be danced with. Metaphors mixed, I know.

My point: A better approach is to accept first, and deal with reality second:

Improviser 1: These pens! These pens are so expensive! My wife is going to leave me!

Improviser 2: $500 a pen? Are they crazy? They're going to ruin our lives! We gotta get some nice pens!

Improviser 1: I know! We're so screwed!

Improviser 2: We're so touchy about how good we look in our offices! (justification offered)

Improviser 1: That's what we get for working at a law firm (scene maybe starting to make sense?)

It's not great. But it shows what I think is a more productive process: agree first, accept first—then work from there to improve the reality, the justification.

SEPTEMBER 9TH, 2011 at 9:00AM

ACCEPT OFFERS: DO IT CASUALLY, EASILY

Even though I'm making a big deal about it, accepting offers should be no big deal most of the time. You should be poised to say yes to anything implied about you in an effortless way. A lot of the time, the offers won't be a big deal—but it's good form to accept them anyway.

Let's say you're a character taking a girl on a date, and you and the other character get into a little groove where you're each trying to apologize for things going badly.

Guy: I'm so sorry, this night has been such a mess.

Girl: Don't feel bad! I know you've been trying.

Guy: Who cares if I've been trying? The waiter brought us this horrible meal, everyone's been rude. We should go.

Girl: No, you paid so much for this meal! We should stay!

Guy: It wasn't that much. Let's get out of here.

Right there in the last line, the guy is rejecting an offer. I mean, not really.

He's just saying his character didn't consider it that much money. It fits his character and the momentum of the conversation, and he has not hurt the scene. But I bet if he were really disciplined about listening to his partner's lines for offers, he wouldn't have said that.

Without adding any new information, I will tweak this to show offers accepted explicitly and simply:

>Guy: I'm so sorry, this night has been such a mess.
>
>Girl: **It has, it has.** But don't feel bad! I know you've been trying!
>
>Guy: **I have! So much!** But who cares? The waiter brought us this horrible meal, everyone's been rude. We should go.
>
>Girl: **We should just leave immediately.** But you paid so much for this meal! We should stay!
>
>Guy: **It really was very expensive. Still,** let's get out of here.

I don't think I've really changed the scene, but this conversation sounds like two improvisers who accept everything hinted as a matter of course. It shows better form.

This is all semantics. You could correctly argue that I'm just talking about "Yes, and"—and that the previous example is simply making a bigger, more explicit "yes." But as I said at the start of this (monstrously long?) piece, the phrase "accept offers" demands more explicit action from improvisers.

SEPTEMBER 10TH, 2011 at 9:00AM

ACCEPT OFFERS: WHEN YOU'RE NOT EXPECTING IT

You've got an idea in mind, but your partner implies something else. Your first instinct should be to go with it.

>Improviser 1: Thanks for stepping into my office. I just wanted to tell you that you are a terrible employee and I think you're a jerk.
>
>Improviser 2: Okay, you know what? I've had it with this place. I quit.

Improviser 1: What, are you going back to your band?

Improviser 2: It has nothing to do with that! You just insulted me, that's why!

The final line rejects an offer, even though it's being faithful to reality and the momentum of the conversation. Better would be this:

Improviser 1: Thanks for stepping into my office. I just wanted to tell you that you are a terrible employee and I think you're a jerk.

Improviser 2: Okay, you know what? I've had it with this place. I quit.

Improviser 1: What, are you going back to your band?

Improviser 2: You're damn right I'm going back to my band! The reggae world never disrespected me like this.

It's obvious when I'm presenting these examples but in the heat of a conversation, when you're committing to your emotion, it takes training to remember to say yes to what's offered to you.

SEPTEMBER 11TH, 2011 at 9:01AM

ACCEPT OFFERS: DON'T BREAK GAME

Don't accept an offer in a way that makes you break a game.

Improviser 1: I know that I'm 50 years old, but I'm here to take the SATs.

Improviser 2: You're too old to take the SATs sir.

Improviser 1: I'm going through a hard time in my life and I need to do something I know I'm good at.

Improviser 2: Fine, you're allowed to take the test but I think you'd be better off dealing with whatever is bothering you in your life.

That last line kind of sounds like an offer, but if Improviser 1 accepts the advice of dealing with his life directly he ends the game he started. The scene is no longer funny. I think it'd be okay for Improviser 1 to say:

Improviser 2: Fine, you're allowed to take the test but I think you'd be better off dealing with whatever is bothering you in your life.

> Improviser 1: No! I'm not dealing with my life! I'm dealing with the SAT! GIVE ME THE TEST!

Although, being super conditioned to just say yes to offers shouldn't really hurt the scene. You can come back to it. Like this:

> Improviser 2: Fine, you're allowed to take the test but I think you'd be better off dealing with whatever is bothering you in your life.
>
> Improviser 1: You're right, I should do that. I'm sorry to waste your time.
>
> Improviser 2: Wait! I can't see you give up. Come back here and kick the shit out of this reading comprehension.

Or even:

> Improviser 2: Fine, you're allowed to take the test but I think you'd be better off dealing with whatever is bothering you in your life.
>
> Improviser 1: You're right, I should do. I'm sorry to waste your time.
>
> Improviser 2: Good, you'll be happier.
>
> Improviser 1 leaves the scene, re-enters): I thought about what you said, and I'd like to express my thoughts in the essay section.

That sort of thing happens a lot. You inadvertently walk away from the game early, realize it, and come back. Saying yes, accepting offers—in this case it delays the game, but I would say in the long run you will do better having that instinctual reaction.

SEPTEMBER 12TH, 2011 at 9:00AM

ACCEPT OFFERS: WHEN IT'S REFUSED

Here's a weird one: You make an offer. The other person quibbles with it. Don't back down: re-make the same offer and address whatever the person quibbled about.

> Improviser 1: If we drill for oil here, we'll hurt the environment. We should march right into the CEO's office and just quit.
>
> Improviser 2: This is ExxonMobil. We can't just march into someone's office.

> Improviser 1: You're right. We'll send an email right now, and then we're going home.

Choose to see it like this: Improviser 2 is basically saying "I see you're making an offer, but I'd like you to make it a little bit better, please."

I know this contradicts a lot of what I've been saying, but every great improv team has an unspoken level of acceptable quibbling. It's a way to make our scenes smarter:

> Improviser 1: If we drill for oil here, we'll hurt the environment. We should march right into the CEO's office and just quit.
>
> Improviser 2: This is ExxonMobil. We can't just march into someone's office.
>
> Improviser 1: You're right. We'll send an email right now, and then we're going home.
>
> Improviser 2: It just doesn't feel right. Us quitting won't have any effect on the environment.
>
> Improviser 1: Maybe not, but for our conscience's sake.
>
> Improviser 2: Okay, for our consciences, yes let's quit.

Offer improved and accepted, scene can progress.

A few things:

- Quibbling/rejecting an offer can be a bad habit, even if you're doing it for noble reasons. Be sparing.
- Quibbling is bullshit if you're doing it just to get laughs out of making fun of your partner's offer. I do it a lot. I suck when I do that.
- I think when you quibble, that you're obligated to try and accept the offer once it it's offered a second time. Certainly a third.
- If someone quibbles/rejects three times, just give up and move on. It's bullshit that someone would do that but it happens and it's better to move on.
- Quibbling happens, regardless of whether you approve of it or not, so you should learn how to handle it (stick to your guns a bit, then move on)
- I like bullet points, I'm just realizing that now.

Here's something I realize now is true, even though it contradicts everything I've been ranting about. I'm okay with people refusing offers! Sometimes it has to happen. As long as they realize it's a big deal and they should only do it if they really really think the scene needs it. And they should expect to defend themselves to the coach after the show. What I see too often is people doing it with no regard to how much they're hurting their scene work.

SEPTEMBER 13TH, 2011 at 9:00AM

ACCEPT OFFERS: CONCLUSION

Leftover thoughts:

- The other phrase I've heard Delaney use is "culture of agreement." That's a great sounding phrase, I like what it inspires in me.
- An initiation can be thought of as accepting the offer inherent in the suggestion, or the opening.
- Accepting an offer is very often having the character say "no."
- I wrote a lot (too much) about "Accepting Offers" not because I think I have it figured out but because I'm working it out. When/if I revise all this I will condense these a great deal.
- I admit that a lot of this is restating stuff. "Accepting offers" is just "yes and." But a new mantra, that's part of the fun: you get a lot of old stuff re-awakened.
- People have disputed my examples. I can see why. I don't like a lot of my examples either. Coming up with examples is hard. But to leave them out would have been cowardly. Criticize away, it's fair—and the criticism helps me improve. But give me credit for being willing to state examples. CREDIT I WANT CREDIT.

Okay, I'm done.

SEPTEMBER 14TH, 2011 at 3:02PM

Q: MORE ON ACCEPTING OFFERS

Anonymous asked: I just want to say that I loved this accepting/agreement stuff. I just did an ASH with Delaney where he said, "Anytime someone asks a question, if you can answer it 'yes' without hurting the scene, do it." I'd never heard that note before, in two years! That's insane! Once it was drilled into me a few weeks later, scenes became hilarious. If someone says, "What, are you retarded?" And you say "Mildly, yes" it's so much funnier than no, and you get to explore it! So ... thank you for these posts.

I agree with that note! Also thank you for reading this blog.

SEPTEMBER 14TH, 2011 at 3:23PM

Q: "SMART" PLAY

brynna asked: Hi Will, we recently had a pretty in-depth discussion in class on the definition of "smart play," and it seems like everyone has a different definition. Some people thought it was reference-based, some thought that the performers were intelligent as people, and others thought it was how much people honored each other's' ideas. What we did agree upon was that there were really good performers on both "smart" teams and non "smart" teams. I was curious to hear your opinion on the phrase.

I'd never thought of this distinction. I guess it depends on what someone's expression is when they say a show is smart. If they look impressed and happy, they mean good improv that has a strong sense of a smart reality, and if they're mad and disgusted, then they're talking about some bunch of show offs who are making references for no reason, which would be a show I was in.

SEPTEMBER 15TH, 2011 at 7:53AM

Q: OUR MUTUAL FRIEND ROBBIE

ericscott asked: Hey Will, the other night me, Joe Wengert, and our mutual friend Robbie went dancing and we were talking about Ben Rodgers and how we think he does "cool improv." Do you think Ben does, in fact, do "cool improv?" Or who else do you think does "cool improv?" Also, what is "cool improv?"

Ben does a form of cool improv for sure, which is to say his characters mention a lot of birds. Mentioning birds is to me the main barometer of how cool improv is. There are other kinds of cool improv but I don't understand them. Glad to hear you and Joe and Robbie are all hanging out.

SEPTEMBER 15TH, 2011 at 2:56PM

YES OVER AND

When people are new to improv, all they notice are the ANDs. "Did you hear that line?" "What a great move!" "How did they think to say X?"

But once you've done it a while, you appreciate much more people who can just say YES: "He re-states the most important part," "She keeps the idea alive," "He understands everything that everyone is saying," "She listens."

Your little indie group of people who are all new—the ones who will be doing this in 3 years will not be the flashy ones, but the ones who take care of the ground under your feet.

UNNECESSARY BASEBALL ANALOGY

There's two components of hitting—On Base Percentage and Slugging Percentage. On-Base Percentage is how often you reach base, whether it's through a hit or a walk. Slugging is how many bases you make once you do get a hit.

To me, that's the YES and AND of hitting—YES (getting on base) and AND (slugging). In baseball, amateur fans talk about the home runs, but people who make trades look for the guys with on-base percentage.

In fact, a common measure of a hitter's worth is to multiply the on-base percentage by a factor of 115% and then add it to the existing slugging percentage. They both matter but ON BASE matters more.

Say yes, say yes, say yes.

SEPTEMBER 16TH, 2011 at 9:00AM

PRACTICE VS. CHEMISTRY

Good chemistry is worth 100 practices.

SEPTEMBER 16TH, 2011 at 12:18PM

Q: WHERE CAN I PUT THIS LINE?

alexispereira asked: Sometimes when somebody initiates without an opening and without anything really unusual, I think in my head, "where can I put this line that would make it unusual yet still sorta make sense?" Bad? (Asking for a friend...)

I am against initiations that are so small they are boring and in fact will be rambling about that tomorrow. But if someone dumps a small boring initiation on you, worry about just agreeing the first time, and then make a big jump in the next line. Because maybe he/she has something in mind? Even if not, it's a bad habit to try and AND before you've YESSed which is what it sounds like you're describing, or so I think! Standard qualification of this being just my opinion here.

SEPTEMBER 16TH, 2011 at 3:00PM

Q: JUSTCRAIG: WHAT PERCENTAGE WEARING A HAT?

justcraig asked: What percentage of the time is your character wearing a hat in an improv scene, but people wouldn't be aware of it because you never make reference to it?

100% of the time.

SEPTEMBER 17TH, 2011 at 9:01AM

SOMETHING TO UNPACK

A good initiation has "something to unpack." That's a phrase that Curtis Retherford came up with in a class I was teaching last weekend, as I tried to find a way to describe what made an initiation good, even if it didn't have a premise in it.

First of all, I do like initiations that have premises (or funny ideas, or games, or unusual things—say what you want—ones that have a sketch idea in it, in some form):

- "Excuse me, miss? We've been in this McDonald's for ten minutes and no one has waited on us."
- "Here at this gym we fuck the weight off you."

Still, I don't like depending on having an idea. You need to be able to start with nothing. But I don't mean starting with NOTHING, like these:

- "May I borrow a pen?"
- "Nice day, isn't it?"
- "I see you're wearing a tie."

Yes, they can work but YAWN.

When you don't have a premise or any kind of idea, you want to start with what Curtis identified as "something to unpack." Something intriguing, something to figure out, to propel us through the first few lines.

- "I guess I have a lot of guitars here."
- "So you built this dock yourself?"
- "These obituaries practically write themselves."

These are small initiations, but there's something interesting in each one. When I hear them I'm curious to know more. If the other person is a good improviser and will speak to the main points being offered we're going to have at least an interesting scene.

SEPTEMBER 19TH, 2011 at 9:00AM

MY FAVORITE WOODY ALLEN JOKES

Typed from memory and therefore slightly wrong:

- My wife is so immature. Well, you tell me if this sounds immature to you. When I was taking a bath, she would just burst in without any warning and sink my boats.
- This is my pocketwatch. It means a great deal to me because it's been in the family for ages. On his deathbed, my grandfather sold me this watch.
- I recently encountered a very effective case of oral contraception I want to tell you about. I asked a girl to go to bed with me, and she said no.
- I was thrown out of NYU for cheating on my metaphysics final. I looked within the soul of the boy sitting next to me.
- It's fun to play sports with neurotics. When we played softball, I'd steal second base, feel guilty and go back.

No reason. I just like these.

SEPTEMBER 20TH, 2011 at 9:00AM

MAYBE EVERY GAME IS JUST "OPPOSITES"

What makes a good game of the scene? I think a decent rule of thumb is to make sure your scene has **two components that are kind of opposite** or at least funny in contrast to each other.

1. James Eason described an interview his father once conducted with Mel Brooks. James' dad asked Mel something like "what makes things funny" and I think it was supposed to be worded, for fun, so that it was basically impossible to answer. Like "I know this is a ridiculous question but 'what makes things funny?'" But Mel said "Actually, I have an answer. 'Juxtaposition.' All comedy is juxtaposition."

   I thought of Young Frankenstein singing "Puttin' On The Ritz," of Broadway producers desperately WANTING a failing play, of a man walking up to another man and then punching out, not the man, but the man's horse.

2. Earlier this year, Kevin Hines was teaching SIX classes concurrently. He was also coaching a bit. At the end of one of these exhausting weeks, after something like 40 hours of watching people do improv, he stumbled into my office at UCB looking wiped out, sat down and sighed "You know, sometimes I think every game is just 'opposites.'"

I thought of my favorite sketches: super smart Ronald Reagan, Mother Theresa trashing a hotel room, a man politely insisting a dead parrot was alive.

Juxtaposition. Opposites. Two things, in contrast to each other.

WHEN GAMES GET THIN

Okay, so let's say games are thin in two cases:

1. A scene has one fun thing, but it doesn't feel like a full game.

   So I look to add in a contrasting element.

   Like maybe you've got three people on stage and because they matched each other they are all singing a Christmas Carol together, and that feels fun in the way that improv scenes are just fun—but there's no joke other than it just feels a bit silly. What could we add to juxtapose with people singing Christmas Carols? Are they in prison? Are they a judge, bailiff and stenographer all in a courtroom? Are they Jewish?

2. A scene WAS great, but now there's been a tag run or a second beat and it feels thinner.

I'll think back "what were the TWO components juxtaposed that made this thing work when it started?"

So maybe a character is yelling at another character for not being peaceful enough, let's say. And that's working. Then someone tags in and yells at the character for not being patient enough, and then someone tags in and is just yelling at them for being a jerk. So now it's just yelling, whereas first it was yelling on behalf of things that were not at all like yelling. So you tag in and yell at him to whisper—to bring back the other component of the scene that was missing, comedically.

I won't do this in the first 1/3 of a scene—that's when I'm prioritizing getting on the same page and playing to the top of my intelligence. But once things are underway I'll do a mental check—do we have two things here?

We say "only ONE unusual thing" but that's because TWO unusual things do not juxtapose, they collide. ONE unusual but also ONE usual to contrast.

Rule of thumb, not a rule.

SEPTEMBER 21ST, 2011 at 2:02PM

AMY POEHLER QUOTE

"I think the hardest thing, frankly, as an improviser, is to get to that point where you can live life onstage. Where you can just have a funny, interesting conversation with someone and be able to get up onstage and have that same conversation without it being this weird, hyper comic version of it."

SEPTEMBER 28TH, 2011 at 1:23PM

WALK-ONS VS. TAG-OUTS

Walk-Ons and Tag-Outs are two ways to support a scene from the backline. As coaches, we often group them together when making adjustments "let's not have any walk-ons or tag-outs for the first beats." Or "Hey our second beats need more group support—let's practice doing more tag-outs and walk-ons." But they have very different effects. In general, I think you should do walk-ons more and be sparing in your tag-outs, especially if your team is having communication problems on stage.

Tag-outs more easily feel dismissive. They increase the pace of a show so much that it's very hard to slow down once they've started. They are often snarky comments on what was just happening before. They do not exist outside of improv—non-improv audience members will likely not know what's going on at first. To be tagged out stings.

Walk-ons feels more warm—you're joining someone's scene without removing anyone. They require you to at least agree with the current location of the scene. They are generally logical in terms of the who/what/where. They exist in the standard convention of theater. They make a scene feel more rich. Someone walking on your scene feels like a compliment.

If a team seems like they're quibbling and bickering and also not committing, I'll run a montage with "no tag-outs, no sweep edits." It makes the whole piece feel more rich because you've taken out two conventions that do not happen in plays. And you're allowing walk-ons which lets the ensemble still practice playing together.

My brother Kevin says "A scene needs to breathe and find it's depth. Walk ons and support might help find that. Tag outs rarely do." Scenes might need a walk-on but they almost never NEED a tag.

GOOD TAG OUTS

Still, I do like tag-outs! They let scenes have an explosive run of jokes. They are great, especially to end a scene. Last night I saw (UCB NY Harold team) Very Good Kiss do a textbook tag run.

First beat has Jeremy Bent as a guy who felt uncomfortable saying it hurt when he ejaculated so he tells his doctor "Doc, listen, I'm having a lot of pain in my PANTS, if you know what I mean." And the doctor, Matt Mayer, doesn't understand. They have a lot of fun awkward pauses, and nice organic moments of Matt trying to guess what Jeremy might mean. Second beat is Jeremy trying to explain sex to his son using the word pants instead of penis. At the end of that scene we see this tag run:

Laura Wilcox, as a pharmacist: "What do you want to buy? A rubber balloon for your pants? All we have are these condoms." (Jeremy winces)

Arthur Meyer tags, says: "We don't have any 'you know what I means.' I honestly don't know what you're talking about." (Jeremy is flustered, stammers)

Johnny McNulty tags: "You haven't said a word since you walked in this sex shop." Laura edits.

They waited until well into the second beat. By then they had a good feel for Jeremy's character. He's prudish, he's vague, he says "you know what I mean" a lot. And each move was a new twist from the previous one—they weren't simply replacing someone and doing what they were already doing. They let Jeremy react to each one. They were each funny and worded well.

But if they had tried to do that in the middle of the first beat, they would have lost what was a really funny and measured conversation between Matt and Jeremy. They would have thrown off the pace of their show. They waited until they had a strong handle on it, then nailed it!

OCTOBER 18TH, 2011 at 7:03AM

Q: AD-LIB VS. IMPROV

benjoseph asked: In a lot of interviews, I've noticed older comedians and dramatic actors use the term "ad lib" instead of "improv." Thoughts on the terminology? Implications of the two different words?

This is a great question I had never thought about, but I believe is very true.

My reaction: "ad lib" is an old school's comedian's term for someone who can come up with a well crafted joke on the fly: something you'd say about Groucho Marx, Jack Benny maybe even Johnny Carson. It's a compliment for a great stunt.

"Improv" probably sounds like the same thing, but has come to mean something else. It means the art of collaborating on a scene together in front of an audience. It has more to do with reacting specifically and honestly while being suggestible than being witty. Improv is long-form—a great conversation, not a great line.

BUT people who don't know still expect improv to just be a series of jokes. That's what audiences expect. "Ooh, based on that suggestion I wonder what jokes they will say? Will they 'win' with that suggestion?" And then they get disappointed when the first two lines are about something only related to the suggestion, but then (hopefully) are won over by a funny and dazzling scene that they then realize was made up in front of them.

We don't ad-lib. We improv.

NOVEMBER 2ND, 2011 at 10:03AM

KITCHEN RULES

This past summer, Michael Delaney sent me an email decrying the state of improv. That in itself was not unusual (Hello, Delaney!). But in this particular email he outlined what I think is a brilliant way to measure whether someone has become an advanced improviser:

1. A good improviser habitually accepts the offers made to him.
2. A good improviser habitually makes active choices rather than passive ones.
3. A good improviser justifies.

He said these were based directly on "Del Close's Kitchen Rules." I had never heard of this, though according to "The Funniest One In The Room," it's actually Elaine May and Ted Flicker who made them during a run of improv shows in St. Louis in 1957. Del became the rules' most ardent preacher. Elaine and Ted seemed to have called them the Westminster Place Kitchen Rules which sounds funny.

Regardless of where he got them, Delaney's email rang very true to me. It's an elegant summary of what goes into compelling scene work.

Accept Offers.

Take the active choice.

Justify.

You can solve a lot of problems in bad scene work by using those mantras, and I think we should all start using them. We already use "Justify" but the other two.

Like any other set of mantras, this is a restatement of things we know. "Accept Offers" is just "say yes." And "take the active choice" is a neat summary of things like "have this be the day where the person speaks their mind" or "talk about people who are here in the scene." And "Justify" is under the "play it real" umbrella.

But I like these three better. Short, direct, imperative. Good mantras are important in a medium taught mostly through oral tradition.

These rules leave out game, but we're good at game. Or at least, we're good at analyzing it and parsing it.

BAROMETERS

Some quick ways to analyze whether a scene is following these rules:

For "accept offers"—how do the players respond to *accusations and criticism* in a scene? Do they take it as a gift? How do they respond to *half-hearted offers their* partners state in the form of a question? Like when someone goes "wait, are you saying you want to fire me?" Does the other person shrug it off without even considering that?

For "take the active choice"—how often do the players put themselves in the center of the action vs. assignment responsibility to characters not on stage? How often do they try and say that this is their first day, they didn't know any better, it was a mistake and won't happen again?

For "Justify" how often do they explain how the action of the scene could actually happen in the real world?

NOVEMBER 4TH, 2011 at 11:34AM

AN IMPORTANT PHASE IN IMPROV STUDENTS' DEVELOPMENT

is when they stop high fiving in scenes.

NOVEMBER 5TH, 2011 at 2:31PM

STAGES

Taught a 101 class recently. Saw them go through this:

First, with every yes-and they did, they were **surprised**. "Wait, *I'm* your boss?" Literally almost every line was said in a questioning tone.

That went away and then with every yes-and, they were **not responsible**. "Well, I just got promoted so I don't know this department. It's my first day."

Then that went away and then with every yes-and, they were **defensive**. "So you're MAD at me that I'm your boss? You wanted to be the boss!"

For a while everyone was **crazy**. "I'm your boss! I love being the boss so much! I'm going to give you a raise of *four hundred thousand dollars*!"

Then THAT went away and every yes-and was just... **boring**. "Yes. I am your boss. Shall we review the reports, Jenkins?"

Then, after that, sometimes, it was **good**. "Yeah, I love this job. Remember the blood oath we took about increasing sales?" I mean, is that even good? You know what I'm saying: they got comfortable just accepting new information and adding to it as if they had been in that world all along.

I forgot how hard it is for "normal" people to just yes-and each other. There are a lot of defenses in place that you have to wear away just to get started.

EDITED TO ADD: Upon re-reading I realize this all sounds like a criticism. I mean it as sympathy. Yes-anding is tough, takes practice and patience before it's casual and easy.

NOVEMBER 9TH, 2011 at 2:07PM

Q: PIMPS VS. WEAK OFFERS

mopula asked: Would you please clarify the difference between a question that "pimps" your partner, a question that is a weak offering, and a question that is ok to ask within the context of the scene? I'm especially confused about the latter two. Thanks.

I don't know a hard rule. A pimp feels more like asking someone to perform a stunt, like talk in spanish or juggle or dance or do an impersonation. A question is often just a statement that is said with some hesitation ("is this because of your anger management classes") and should be accepted by the other person as if it were said with full confidence.

NOVEMBER 22ND, 2011 at 9:38AM

THE DANGER OF CLARITY

Another pretentious theory post. I talked about this in the talk I gave this past Saturday at UCB, and by saying that I'm mentioning that I gave a talk at UCB on improv theory which was fun but is also ridiculous but below is some of what I talked about and hello! hello.

—

The semantics of the game of the scene have become wonderfully clear in the last four or five years.

- If this is true, what else is true
- React to the first unusual thing
- Justify
- Peas in a pod
- Straight man/crazy man
- Framing

So clear that, tragically, they get overused! We talk game to death and ignore if we're actually simply saying yes and building! We need our agreement and scene work vocabulary to be just as clear as our game-analyzing one is.

HUMANS LIKE CLEAR IDEAS

People overuse concepts that are neat and clear. For example: the Kubler-Ross "Five Stages of Grief."

Most people are at least partly familiar with this: Denial, Anger, Bargaining, Depression, Acceptance. It's a nice clear idea that feels right.

Unfortunately, most therapists and psychologists say that this model is not accurate. It's an interesting clear model of different emotional strategies that people use in the face of grief—but people don't go through them in that order, not everyone goes through all of them, and there are others.

Still, when people talk about depression, someone will bring up the five stages. It's got such great clarity that it's easy to mentally apply to different situations.

A TO C: CLEAR, BUT OVERUSED

Some concepts in improv get more importance than they deserve because they are so clear. "A to C" is my favorite example of this. "A to C" (or "third thought") is a great simple concept for getting a unique idea from a commonplace suggestion, or for changing the subject during an opening.

But for a while, students would apply "A to C" everywhere they could—going from first beat to second beat, within otherwise simple conversations, with walk-ons into scenes. You ask them why they're making moves that shake everything up so much and they say "I'm just A-to-C-ing."

How could they resist? It's such a clear concept. Except that it destroys a scene if you're trying to do it every line.

GAME MANTRAS

I read the student's evaluations of classes at UCB-NY. In describing exercises they liked or didn't like, many students refer to their ability/inability to see the "game", to use "the unusual thing," to "if this then what."

But they don't ever directly refer to "yes-anding" or "agreeing" or "understanding."

Almost all game/comedy mantras, very few scene work mantras. (They DO mention "listening" and sometimes "justifying"—that's not enough.)

NEW AGREEMENT MANTRAS

Okay, so now we're comfortable discussing game—the comedy of a scene and what powers it. But we're paying so much attention to it that we're playing like hostile, commenting, uncooperative jerks (my observation of many students at the intermediate level).

I don't blame the game mantras. I blame the lack of agreement mantras. "Yes and" is genius but we're numb to it.

We need to improve how we analyze basic agreement so that it is as clear and precise as how we discuss game. I propose Delaney's restatement of the Kitchen Rules:

- Accept offers.
- Take the active choice.
- Justify.

Which I ramble about in a separate post.

NOVEMBER 23RD, 2011 at 1:01PM

Q: GOOD AND BAD JUSTIFYING?

Anonymous asked: You have been saying "Justify" a lot lately. Not long ago, I got a note in practice not to "justify away the unusual thing". Can you explain the differences between good and bad justifying?

Nope!

NOVEMBER 23RD, 2011 at 1:02PM

Q: CUT DOWN ON TERMINOLOGY, IMPROV NERDS

dangurewitch asked: Your latest post reminds me of a post I wrote last year. Tumblr won't let me link it; it was titled "Improv Nerds Only." The central idea: in discussing improv, we might be well-served to cut down on terminology & increase use of the word/concept "fun." I still stand by it—my problem with all of the interchangeable terms/concepts is that it creates a tendency toward mathematical improv; people trying to fill in blanks, but forgetting to follow their gut humor instincts. Am I full of shit?

I don't think you're full of shit but it makes me laugh that you ended this question with that. I remember your improv nerd post. I sympathize but disagree or at least have a different reaction. Meaning, I agree there's too many rules and semantics and we should ultimately be guided by our inner sense of fun more often. BUT: I still think a small pouch of the correct mantras and be good. And I'm going to spend THE REST OF MY LIFE figuring out what those mantras are. Happy Thanksgiving Dan Gurewitch!

NOVEMBER 23RD, 2011 at 1:05PM

Q: MICK'S BOOK

alexispereira asked: Will, would you kinda touch upon this quote on Mick Napier's Wikipedia page? "He founded The Annoyance with the philosophy that training improvisers to be individually powerful is the best way to support those with whom one improvises, an answer to the Yes, And philosophy, which he found led to weak, polite improvisation more often than powerful, good improvisation, a subject that he elaborates on in his book, Improvise: Scene from the Inside Out." Sorry I don't have a more specific question.

I really like Mick's book. I think it's perfect to read after you've been doing improv for about a year or so. The idea of being individually powerful rather than meekly responsive is a great one! But I think built into Mick's book is the assumption that you will listen to and be able to generally understand what the other people in the scene are saying. And when I watch lower level improvisers and in fact when I watch people in regular real life—NO ONE LISTENS, NO ONE UNDERSTANDS. So I think people gotta spend time being "meek and polite" until they can reliably understand what the fuck people are saying. Hello Alex.

NOVEMBER 23RD, 2011 at 1:06PM

"BABY GOT BACK" APPEARS IN 100% OF HOT SPOT WARM-UPS.

Fact.

NOVEMBER 27TH, 2011 at 10:26AM

HOW ARE YOU SUPPOSED TO REMEMBER STUFF FROM THE OPENING? I CAN NEVER REMEMBER STUFF FROM THE OPENING! DO YOU HAVE ANY ADVICE ON REMEMBERING STUFF

FROM THE OPENING?

Be smarter?

Remember everything?

Enjoy it so you remember it like you remember your favorite movie/tv show?

I don't know. Just do it. Remember stuff or don't do improv.

DECEMBER 2ND, 2011 at 7:26AM

BEST RECURRING CHARACTER IN ANY IMPROV TEAM'S HISTORY

"Sideways Dracula"—Bobby Moynihan, Police Chief Rumble.

Note: Improv teams should not have recurring characters.

DECEMBER 14TH, 2011 at 10:31AM

AMY POEHLER QUOTE

"The stage is my church and long form improvisational comedy is my religion and I want to practice it at every moment in my life. When I have felt most myself and most alive is when I have been living this way. Now, rock out with your cocks out."

DECEMBER 18TH, 2011 at 12:44PM

HOW TO SAY NO

A theory: teaching someone to say "yes" and be on board is important but straightforward.

Teaching someone how to say "no" to things that are bullshit in a way that does not stop the scene is much trickier, and therefore a more valuable skill.

AGREE WITH ME OR YOU ARE A BAD IMPROVISER

EDITED MUCH LATER TO ADD: I didn't mean to imply that someone's MOVE—someone's improv decision—would be bullshit. I meant more that characters will offer to other characters circumstances that few people would ever accept, and that knowing how to say "no"—in character—to things because they are bullshit situations you would not put up with in real life is an important skill. Bullshit circumstances offered to a character, not bullshit moves. Though I can see how in re-reading my post it looks like I said "bullshit moves."

DECEMBER 30TH, 2011 at 2:31PM

Maybe this: "yes" requires one move but "no" requires two.

Characters say yes and get excited about things, or they say no and fold their arms.

Yes needs one move. You say yes and you're done with that.

No needs two moves. The no and then some move to repair whatever no did to slow things down. A justification, a reason to stay.

Doesn't mean no is bad. It just takes more work to do it right.

Students learn that it's easier to just say yes and start being characters who say only yes—literally, the word 'yes.' But that is the wrong lesson. You very often have to say no in order to keep the scene truthful. Just do it right—make the second move: Add a justification, be sympathetic to what you are saying no to, find a reason to stay.

EDITED LATER: Folding yours arms is not bad. It's just bad if you stop with that.

2012

JANUARY 2ND, 2012 at 10:18AM

FUNNY, SMART AND NO

Here's things that I bet upper level improv teachers/coaches would be uncomfortable to say:

- "Being funny is good in improv!"
- "Characters should feel comfortable saying no!"
- "You should know a lot of things if you want to be a good improviser!"

But all of these things are true.

(NOT for beginning improvisers. These sentences would be destructive in a level one improv class).

I believe that people will read that list and interpret them like this:

- "Make jokes that are off topic and that decrease your emotional commitment!"
- "Stop forward action and reject your partner's offers in order to be funny!"
- "Make references for their own sake!"

That is not what I was saying.

Go ahead, define "funny" "smart" and "no" in a context that paints them as dangerous improv advice—it's easy to do.

OR: realize that we get scared of those words and that it limits our improv. Yet those words are an essential part of compelling comedy and theater.

I'm interested in a discussion on this, although I don't need you to tell me how people can use the words "funny" "smart" and "no" dangerously.

I need ways to use those terms well. At the advanced level, it is often what is missing.

This is one in a series of me trying to figure out the proper way to teach "no."

JANUARY 3RD, 2012 at 10:09AM

KNOW EVERYTHING!

I get in trouble for saying that because I deliberately say it in a jerk manner. KNOW EVERYTHING. When someone says "I didn't know the movie my partner was mentioning" I'll sometimes say "Well, you don't HAVE to know it but it would be easier if you knew it."

And then people are like "Why do I have to like Star Wars?"

And I say "Who said anything about Star Wars?"

"All these improv nerd boys love Star Wars and can't stop mentioning it. I hate that HAVE to know it."

I know. It's annoying.

Here's movies I've never seen but have watched be referenced a million times in improv shows: The Goonies, Dead Poets Society, Home Alone, Robocop. I finally saw Terminator 2 last year.

TV shows I've never seen: Full House, Family Matters, Quantum Leap, Star Trek the Next Generation, Top Chef, The Bachelor, Project Runway, Survivor, Duck Tales, Fresh Prince of Bel Air

Books I've never read: any Jane Austen book, barely any Harry Potter, Are You There God It's Me Margaret?, not to mention Hunger Games and Dragon Tattoo.

Musicals I've never seen: West Side Story, Company, Rent

Sports I know nothing about and never watch: Football, Soccer, Hockey, Tennis

I mean, it's a drag when everyone in the group is all excited to do their movie parody and you don't know it. You have a right to be weary of nerds pushing their thing. You never have to do anything on an improv stage that you really don't want to.

BUT it WOULD BE EASIER if you knew it.

And then here's the part that people get mad at me for: forget the principle of the thing—if you really wanted to be prepared and to know everything that is going to be brought up in an improv scene I think there's a finite list of things that would cover like 90% of it. A lot of it is male nerd stuff, which is annoying, and you should not be restricted by that—but with maybe one hour of wikipedia reading you could know enough about ALL OF IT.

As a purely practical solution it would be easier if you just knew the basic plot of Star Wars.

And then I start to make this list and people get mad. But I don't think people should get mad because I'm not saying you HAVE to. However it's a fact that things come up multiple times and you can put yourself in a position of confidence by knowing about them.

The Stepfathers (my group) has gotten Jersey Shore (a show I've never seen) as a suggestion on three different occasions. Back when my improv group took a line from a movie as a suggestion we got "We're gonna need a bigger boat" (from Jaws, a movie I did not watch until that team broke up) at least five times. I never really knew a Radiohead song until my level 3 class ended a class show with everyone signing Paranoid Android at the end, a song I had never heard and which sounded like the most aimless humming I'd ever known, except that the audience was laughing.

So: I made sure I knew the basic plot of Jaws.

I found out about Jersey Shore.

I listened to OK Computer.

I know a thumbnail sketch of every thing mentioned in this post, enough to fake an improv scene.

I don't walk out of any improv scene mad at the culture. I look shit up and learn things.

I guess it's distasteful but there are like probably 50 movies you should know, maybe 50 tv shows, 50 books and plays, 50 bands. That sounds like a lot, but it isn't since you probably already know a lot of them.

I would be interested to construct a list. If it just offends you to no end then you could ignore it. But they WILL come up, and it WOULD be easier —FOR YOU—if you knew.

I had a student who didn't know the basic story of Cain and Abel. Another who didn't recognize what The Godfather was. Another who had zero idea of what Occupy Wall Street was about (thought it was a movie, not an actual protest). I mean—it's just harder to improvise with people who disavow any responsibility to know shit.

And, it might be a correlation and not a cause: but every single person I know who is really good at improv knows a shit ton of things. Be offended if you wish. It is the truth.

EDITED LATER TO ADD: People who have disagreed with me in the past tend to disagree with:

1. my confrontational defensive tone, which is the tone I use when making this point. Understandable to not like that.
2. the narrow nature of most common things brought up in an improv scene—so much white male nerdiness. Understandable. Although I'm saying that as an improviser it's just smart practice to spend a tiny amount of time learning it for your own comfort and then don't feel restricted by it or even beholden to it. So, it is gross how often improvisers bring up the comic book The Watchmen. But you could spend a few minute reading about how The Watchmen is a story of how superheroes, only one of which has real powers, try to solve the real world problem of the US and Russian approaching nuclear war.
3. because reference-prov is gross and some people are wary of any advice which seems to condone it. So my attitude seems to condone it. It seems that way because I DO reference-prov a lot and it's gross and I shouldn't
4. the list itself, which I have not included above. I will make the list and post it. Then lots of you will not like this either. I'm ready for that.

MEANING: I get why people argue with me when I say "KNOW EVERYTHING," especially when I make it quickly and off-handedly and in a hostile manner. In this case, I've deliberately stated things above in a way that's hard to disagree with. Or maybe I've just learned how to say it better over time.

JANUARY 13TH, 2012 at 9:21AM

PLAY IT REAL?
A POLICE STATE

Watching the Improv Jam two weeks ago, sitting with Neil Casey while a scene started where someone did a tag out that transported characters from a fast food restaurant to a police interrogation room. Neil leaned over and said this to me:

"I've noticed that for students under 25 a lot of them walk on or tag out as the police coming to shut things down for being out of line. These kids either live in a world or they think they live in a world where if you step out of line the system comes crashing down on you like a ton of fucking bricks."

After he said that, it started to stand out. Someone in an improv scene starts cheating on their company, security comes crashing in to ask them questions. Some tag-outs were just people being police. Other were smarmy investigators who came in with a sort of "good cop" attitude: "Hey, we're just here to ask a few questions."

Once you start thinking about this, a lot of improv gets really creepy.

"They might be right!" Neil said to me today when we were talking about this. "We live in a system where you're allowed to fuck whoever you want and eat whatever you want but you can't' really do anything that gets in the way of the moneyed or powerful," he said. "In fact if you do try to run off to the woods they'll send out helicopters to make sure you're not smoking weed."

Maybe it's because those who grew up after 9/11 only know a subway where there's cops waiting to check your bags?

Chris Gethard talks about the overly oppressive straight man: someone who, in an effort to make a game right away, jumps on something that's not that unusual with too much force.

Scene starts: "Look I found a gold nugget in my desk!" Answer: "Well, what are you doing with it! Hide it! You're spending too much time looking for gold! Get it away!"

What Gethard talks about has always been, but maybe that oppressive straight man is now more often a military agent of the government.

Playing devil's advocate: I can remember a lot of interrogation scenes for as long as I've done improv. And police coming in with guns in a cliche so frequent that The Office made fun of it when they showed Michael Scott's improv class.

Am I just more sensitive to such things now that Neil has made his observation?

OR IS THE WORLD TURNING INTO A TERRIBLE PLACE?

JANUARY 16TH, 2012 at 9:00AM

TEACHING INTERVIEWS: CHRIS GETHARD, PART 1 OF 2

This is a series in which I ask great improv teachers to write down their thoughts on teaching improv. We start with **Chris Gethard**, who was the second person to ever run the UCBT-NY school after Kevin Mullaney.

Gethard wrote the first full curriculum for the school, taught dozens and dozens of very popular classes at all levels and also coached some of the best teams to ever develop at the theater. For a majority of the people who have considered themselves UCB performers in the last 10 years, Chris has been one of their prominent coaches/teachers.

He also has a new book out, "A Bad Idea I'm About To Do," which you could check out.

Q: What are common notes you give to students?

Gethard: Here are pretty much all the notes and speeches I give, all the lines I draw in the sand. Honestly, I think if anyone reads all these they don't even need to take a class with me:

1. Chill the fuck out.
2. You had the potential for a good scene. Trust that potential. Shouting and scrambling to the joke made you stop listening and stopped it from actually being a scene.

3. Stop talking about things and people that aren't in this scene. Why these characters? Why right now?

4. Companion to that—stop initiating scenes about the vase you inherited from grandma. The vase is invisible. Grandma's not here. Stop putting roadblocks like that between you and your scene partner. You will never convince an audience that that invisible vase has higher stakes than the living, breathing human being you are up there with.

5. Take the content you are generating and make an honest effort to be an actor while delivering it.

6. Start with the honest part. If we believe that a character has some recognizability, some traits we identify with, some relationships to the world and other people we can respect as true, you can always make that funny. If you head right to the funny and miss with a joke, you can't all of a sudden try to convince an audience that it's real. They won't buy it. Real can turn into funny, it's harder to turn funny into real (especially because you generally only have to when the funny goes away.)

7. Try something you haven't tried before. It's great that you are good at what you are good at, but don't be the person who does that one thing.

8. Just because you can get laughs with bullshit moves doesn't mean you're doing good improv.

9. Not every scene needs a straight man. If there's nothing crazy going on, let's not make the scene about why someone shouldn't be doing something.

10. The straight man wants things to stop; the actor playing the straight man wants them to continue. Let the actor's impulses guide the scene, not the characters.

11. Once a straight man is on the record, they can often just go away.

12. Characters get laughs, but I'm more impressed to see you play close to you. (This is a point of personal preference, but a note I do give a lot.) Characters often strike me as dumb and cheap. Keep them light.

13. The second line of your scene almost never needs to be telling someone else to stop. We all rush way too much to stop things. Way too many scenes are framed around the person who initiates an idea

trying to convince the person responding to it to just try the idea. Slow down the straight men.

14. If you could be matching your partner's energy and helping to forward the scene, and it would still be a good scene, do that instead of arbitrarily playing the straight man because you think every scene is supposed to have one.

15. All of the rules and structures are actually guidelines. A structure is only there to help you. If you do a hilarious show where the Harold structure gets fucked up, no one will care. If you do a textbook Harold that isn't interesting or funny, it is no accomplishment. All of the rules are like traffic lights—you probably should stop at a red light. But if you really want to, you can hit the gas and drive through it—you might crash and die. But you also might get away with breaking that particular law.

16. 90% of your problems can be solved by looking at your scene partner. The floor holds no answers. The thing that is about to happen isn't happening, stop rambling about it. Talk to that person standing up there with you and listen when they talk back. It will solve a lot of your problems.

17. When done well, improv should feel easy. Remember that we are a lazy people. We don't write things down. We don't do second drafts. We show up in old jeans and charge people money. Let's embrace that we want it to be easy. So many scenes run into trouble when we pass on fun, simple, clear, easy ideas and over-complicate things through too much talking and not enough listening. Easy, simple games can still be handled in a smart fashion.

18. A lot of the best improv falls under this general umbrella—smart people doing dumb things in a smart way.

19. 90% of the performers you see on the UCB stage break the rules all the time. Just because someone is on a house team doesn't mean they're doing good improv, myself included. Strive to master the rules before you strive to be one of the people allowed to break them.

20. Longform Improv is a young art form. You might be the one to discover the next cool device. You might be the one to have that legendary show. Any show can by definition be your best one. Believe in that, bring that excitement to the stage. Look down the line, really try

to know the people you're up there with, and understand that you and every other person standing on the stage with you has the potential to do the best work they've ever done in the next half hour. Facilitate that by any means necessary.

21. Walk ons and tag outs aren't the only forms of support. In fact, they're not always supportive. Sometimes a tag out feels like the cold hand of judgement.
22. Sometimes the best way to support is to stay out of the scene, even when you have a good move.
23. Too many moves early can be like throwing a big log on a small fire—technically it's fuel, but it can smother the fire itself. Build to it.
24. You have a right to feel like you can try anything; you have a responsibility to make everyone else on stage feel like they can try anything too.

Q: How about for someone who's had 3 or 4 classes—more than a beginner but not a vet—what notes do you give?

A lot of what I alter with people right on this cusp is to make sure they don't get off the hook for bullshit while also encouraging them to think about WHY the things working for them are working. Getting a confident person to shed fear is a long but rewarding process. I find myself constantly asking people to think about why one thing works and one doesn't. It is on this cusp that part of your job as a teacher isn't just to give notes, it's to encourage good students to get better by defining their own philosophy and approach to improv, and to make them confident in their beliefs. I often find myself pointing out how often good moves don't hit at this stage entirely due to a lack of confidence the audience can sense.

Q: Advice for running warm ups?

I hate running warm ups. Luckily I work with advanced students and can ask them to run their own. When working with more junior groups, I like to keep them quick. Something to wake their brains up. Something to wake their bodies up. Some scene work with an exercise attached to it that reminds them it's ok to fuck around.

Q: Stuff for top of class?

Quick light scene work exercises. Then I usually isolate habits or tendencies presenting themselves via those scene work habits and do a few exercises to deal with those specific problem areas. Then we move into the core of what the class or group has been going for.

Q: End of class?

I never plan for the end of class. I talk too much and usually go over.

Q: How do you note loud angry dudes?

I like to give some version of this speech—"We live in New York City. People are angry and in a rush all the time. We spend enough time being in a bad mood—be in a good mood while doing this. It's not fun to be angry. This should be fun."

Q: How do you note people who play in a broad clownish style?

I eviscerate these people and make them feel bad. Broad, clownish play is my personal pet peeve. I do not respect it, and I do not hide my feelings on that. Students of mine quickly learn this and even those very good at playing cartoonishly tend to avoid it, knowing I will probably come down on them harder than necessary.

Q: When is it right to note game?

A lot of the time, but primarily:

- When a game was possible but missed entirely.
- When a game didn't get played in a way that allowed the most forward momentum.

Q: What should a 101 class feel like?

It should feel like the adrenaline rush of realizing there are likeminded people participating in an artform truly devoted to collaboration and open-mindedness. It should be fun and exhilarating, not because we're faking it, but because this stuff is the most fun thing in the world.

Q: What mantras/ sayings do you use?

I put a lot of them in the notes I listed. Instead of answering this directly, I'll tell you about my favorite Del quotes:

"The Family was amazing not because they were flawless, but because they played like six guys who were falling down the stairs—but managed to land on their feet."

"Good improv should look like people putting the plane together while they're already in the sky."

"Aim to be a poet. If you can't do that, aim to be an actor. If you can't do that, do your best to be an improviser. And if you can't even pull that off, you'll have to settle for being a comedian."

I also tell that one Fwand story everyone is tired of hearing a lot, as an example of how groups committing to each other's' ideas can trump every expectation we have of an audience. And of how little work greatness can entail if we can present things in their purest forms.

Q: Any breakthrough moments in learning how to teach?

Teaching improv is the only thing I ever felt naturally good at. Luckily I'm not the funniest dude, so I have to think about how it works and know how to articulate. That helps. One of the biggest steps that made me a good teacher was when I got to a point where I could admit that I didn't have all the answers. It's ok to be a teacher and be wrong about stuff. It makes the stuff you're right about seem that much more valid.

Q: What were you favorite classes / things about classes you took?

I was lucky to take classes from Delaney when Delaney was in a truly weird, experimental phase. Even outside of specific things I learned in those classes, I look back and realize how much Delaney was instilling in me a real desire to bend things, see what could be done differently, see how existing conventions could be left behind or adapted to find newer, weirder, things. Really clicked with me.

Ian's scene work classes were flawless. They were clinics on comedic acting and how to generate comedic ideas.

Also, I was lucky to take Mullaney for levels 1 and a level 3. Watching him taught me how to teach. He had an amazing ability to work with the best people at their level while not short changing the people who were catching up to them more. He knew how to give hard notes while being kind.

Q: Do you have any general advice for teachers?

Speak in universals—if you tell two people why their scene is off, two people can get something from it. If you tell those two people how what they're doing is emblematic of common problems and tendencies, everyone in the room can learn from it. It is on you to make sure the whole room knows that all the notes are for everyone. The people in the scene are at all times the guinea pigs that the rest of us can learn from—so make sure you're making that easy with how you approach notes.

Sidecoach, and make it clear why. Stopping a scene and giving a note in the middle allows the person getting the note to put it into action on their feet, as opposed to having to wait 30 minutes until the end of a Harold so they can think back and remember that scene they did where they knew something was off. Be concise when sidecoaching. Be direct. And be as gentle as one can be while stopping someone who is already clearly scrambling to get this right.

Point out every time you have to give the same note twice. This serves a dual purpose; it makes sure everyone in the room focuses on what's happening at all times. It also reiterates to students that there are very few actual rules to break in improv—most notes relate back to listening, commitment, justifying, rushing, etc. Your ability to articulate specific notes into examples of the big overarching notes will be appreciated by your students.

Don't give your notes in question form. Tell the student what went wrong from your perspective. If they knew the answer to your question, the scene wouldn't have gotten messed up in the first place.

Failure is a skill everyone has to learn. Get good at it. Encourage your students to get good at it by making your classroom a place where they know failure is ok. That being said, make sure they understand that integrity comes with failing for the right reasons. Don't fail because you're being lazy or unfocused. Don't fail because you're bailing on your scene to go for the cheap joke. Fail because you are pushing yourself to take chances you haven't taken before. Take a chance you haven't taken every time you step foot into a classroom. It's why classes exist.

Remind your students: Sometimes teachers are wrong. It is ok to ignore them when you know in your heart that is the case. Know that sometimes you will be wrong and your students should be ignoring you.

Be compassionate, kind, and professional. Your students have taken your class or asked you to coach them because they respect you. Don't abuse or betray that respect.

Sometimes giving mean notes is the only option. Usually, that is not the case. Look for every other option available before you are a dick. Really, the only reason to give a mean note is when someone's individual behavior is so egregious that the class will not respect you if you don't bring the hammer down on it. Nine times out of ten, this behavior is rooted in off stage issues, not on. There are very few times where you *need* to be mean to someone who is actually trying their hardest.

You will burn out. Do yourself and your students a favor when this happens, and stop teaching. Do not give them a sub-par product, especially when you are in many ways the product itself. Put your students before yourself.

Don't exploit the community by charging too much for coaching. Just because you can get a lot of money doesn't mean you have to, or should. Teach this because you are someone with the authority to pass on an oral tradition, a set of skills, an artform that largely lives through us. Don't teach because you want to feel like a big man on campus or because you know level two students will give you $90 for three hours. Improv is about giving, and it's sad that coaches have become exploitative.

Stop talking about relationship. It's a moot point. Of course if there are two characters in a scene there's a relationship. It's like saying "Humans breathe air". Characters have relationships. But that's not the funny part. The fact that you're my dad isn't funny. It's the unusual aspects of this particular version of that traditional pairing that we focus on. Our students need to stop thinking about relationship. It puts you in your head as much as thinking about it every time you needed to take a breath would. And our teachers need to stop preaching it. It's a non-issue and a waste of time.

PS—Anyone who says they like improv but don't like game sounds as dumb to me as someone who says "I like cars but I don't like engines."

JANUARY 28TH, 2012 at 10:35PM

Q: IMPROV ORDER OF OPERATIONS?

natedern asked: Have you ever heard anyone discuss an "improv order of operations"? In high school math we have the acronym PEMDAS to help us remember that the rules must be followed in a certain order. I think it might be useful if we came up with one for improv students. I've found that when I'm teaching or coaching and I note someone on disagreement, they'll say, "Well, I was playing top of my intelligence." I think agreement should be first. I'm not sure what the rest would be or what order. Thoughts?

I love stuff like this! It's also kinda like Asimov's Laws of Robotics, in which each rule is only followed if you don't break the previous one. Ok, here's my pitch:

(presented like I'm describing a pyramid)

>BOTTOM LEVEL: **agreement** (yes anding, accepting responsibility for accusations, making/accepting offers)

>NEXT: **truthfulness** (top of your intelligence, reality, what would one really say)

>NEXT: **active choices** (making this about the people in the scene, deciding you are invested, making things matter)

>NEXT: **justifying** (philosophy, POV)

>TOP: **game** (irony, juxtaposition)

I think seasoned improvisers do four out of those five every time they make a move.

Hello Nate Dern!

FEBRUARY 10TH, 2012 at 1:09PM

Q: PEOPLE WILL ONLY IMPROVISER WITH EACH OTHER?

Anonymous asked: I teach improv, and I have two members, who are friends, that constantly go out in scenes together. They don't completely refuse to improvise with other team members, but if they have the option, they will always race to the other one and take them out. How should I deal with this situation?

Tell them to stop doing that.

FEBRUARY 11TH, 2012 at 11:04PM

Q: IMPROV SPECIFIC TO ITS HOME CITY?

Anonymous asked: There's an interview clip with Noah Gregoropoulos where he describes improv being culturally specific to its locations; New York being brash and fast, Los Angeles being a character showcase, etc. Do you agree, and is there an inherent difficulty in being a patient but slow player?

Ooh, I'd love to hear that interview! Generalizations like that are fun but ultimately pointless. I mean, I do them too. There's a germ of truth there but there's room in every city mentioned to do whatever kind of improv you want to do. I saw Bullet Lounge at iO do a brash, fast (great) set, and I saw Sentimental Lady from LA do a monoscene that would make TJ and Dave fans applaud. And one hour ago in good old NYC I did a set in which a ship at sea used sound-and-movement to turn into an amoeba that contained in it a house and, oh, I don't know. Who knows? Can't you often trade "Annoyance" and "NY" pretty easily when someone uses either one to describe a type of improv? No? Okay.

Re: being a patient player. There's difficulty in doing anything well. I can't believe it ever works. Good night!

APRIL 11TH, 2012 at 10:52PM

Q: SHOULD EVERYTHING BE JUSTIFIED?

coreybrown asked: Do you think every unusual thing should be justified? Do you think that sometimes a justification undoes what makes the thing unusual and decreases the potential comedic value?

I don't think any improviser should give herself/himself a reason to not justify.

Though the way I've been thinking about it is that a justification is bad if it deflects responsibility away from the people on stage. If the justification is because of something your character or another character did on purpose, I think that usually works? So "I ate the couch because I believe wood is good for you" is better than "I was prevented from getting normal food so I had to eat the coach."

I'm beat. What should I watch on Netflix?

APRIL 12TH, 2012 at 10:21AM

Q: JUSTCRAIG: SILLY OR GOOFY?

justcraig asked: In an improv scene, is it better to be silly or goofy?

Ideally both but speaking pragmatically you generally have to settle for one or the other.

APRIL 19TH, 2012 at 9:32AM

IMPROVY MOVES IN MOVIES

I'm going to write an article about "improvy" moments in movies. Not moments that seem to be improvised, but story decisions that seem like the kind of decisions that an improv education would encourage.

I have two main examples:

- How in Teen Wolf, the movies treats the emergence of a werewolf as a normal part of high school life
- How in most Wes Anderson movies, people mostly respond to direct questions with the truth, done for comic effect.

Yep, I'm giving away the goods here. But I'm doing it to ask you all to help me think of other examples in movies where it really feels like an improviser made the story decision.

And yes, my references are all old.

MAY 13TH, 2012 at 4:01PM

Q: EXAMPLES OF GOOD FIGHTS?

shrave asked: On April 9, 2010 you posted about "Young Improvisers Fighting." I think this sentence summarizes the point of that post: "I wish I could say 'keep that honest emotional reaction, but be the unusual thing at the same time.'" You provided an example of the wedding anniversary. Could you provide other examples of when a player is confronted with a line that basically initiates a conflict, they respond honestly but add something unusual? I find myself getting stuck in argumentative scenes.

I think about this so much it's hard for me to be simple in response. Almost all young improvisers fight too much and they fight early, and they get offended by things that were just meant as endowments, and they accuse rather than gift. A lot of it has to do with tone. Teachers and people who watch a lot of improv grow immensely weary of all hostility in scenes—it generally goes along with bad insecure improv.

It's hard to get people to stop. If you FORBID all fighting, then all the scenes seem to become toothless hug-fests in which everyone just says "I LOVE [the suggestion] so much!" and the other person goes "Me too! It's SOOOOO great." And that's annoying and dumb.

I've tried to teach how to "fight well" which I think means to see all accusations as gifts which you should own. Someone says something about your character that implies something negative or maybe is straight-up presented as an accusation—say yes to it by owning it.

Someone says you're late for dinner—admit it, then justify why you are late with a philosophy. Don't blame it on traffic or your boss—that's deflecting. Even if it's a reasonable excuse, you are deflecting the gift. Don't be surprised to learn you are late. Own it—it's a gift.

Related: "Sympathetically disagree" is something I've been saying lately to people so that they can have differing points of view without getting mired in an angry, stalled scene.

I tried to write something here:
    http://improvnonsense.tumblr.com/post/9836442948/accept-offers-accusations-complaints

Former UCB Artistic Director Anthony King talks about this in his essay about Harold Auditions:
    http://theanthonyking.com/post/18958200344/harold-auditions

Chris Gethard talks about avoiding being an obstructionist protesting straight man for no reason in his essay on improv advice (numbers 9, 10, 11 and 13):
    http://improvnonsense.tumblr.com/post/15952067691/teaching-interviews-chris-gethard-part-1-of-2

I don't know. Don't fight. Say yes to accusations. Be sparing in how often you accuse? Watch how good teams do it. Let me know how you beat it.

MAY 25TH, 2012 at 2:23PM

IN CAGEMATCH

It's not the teachers, or any gimmicks, or who goes last. The best show wins. Everything else is just stuff for us to talk about at McManus.

MAY 25TH, 2012 at 3:33PM

NOTES: DECEMBER 22, 2000

I think I've posted these before; I can't remember. Here's notes I took the night after I did my first Harold night ever with the amazingly ungood team Fire, Hot, Burn!

12-22-00

—

Two shows last night.

First one, I fucked up a scene—I was supposed to be getting married and I didn't realize it. Frank Shea made it work, but it effectively left me out of all three beats. That sucked. Well, it sucked for me—the team covered so it did less damage to the show than it might have. I felt out of it—like the Shitty Guy on the team that I fear becoming.

Word: Hello. I—Curtis Gwinn owns comic shop owner; John O'Donnell is customer, II—Josh Comers the psychiatrist and Michael Bosniak the timid patient, III—Frank the groom and Will the Guy Who Fucks Up Scenes and Just Stands There. Game I—Watching guys in front row. Game II—sheep call.

The second show at Cagematch wasn't good either for me, but it was better. It was looser and sillier overall. My scene was poor, but we struggled through without too much stopping. I had two silly walk-ons that were fun, though they didn't add to a 'game' per se.

Word: pancake. I—John O'Donnell and Frank are hunting ants. II—Josh is funeral home director passing it on to Curtis. III—Mike and I are brothers. Hilary is a mom. Mike is dumb but extremely powerful. (?) Game I—Episode of BBC Mystery. Game II—hmm. we might have skipped it. We did a Laser Tag time-out.

Fuck! The team doesn't know what to do with me! I just fucking sit there! I've become my nightmare? How to beat it? How to get better? I don't know. It's frustrating. I feel it's time to put up or shut up and I don't have anything.

I need to act and to add information. And to react. And to play tone. Shit, I don't know.

I definitely felt over my head. Everyone on the team is nice. I guess I am over my head but I hope I can improve quickly, which I think I can do. Having an audience is a totally different feel from being in practice. It's like I'm learning everything over again. I'm acting just like I did in my early classes—scared, without characters, with fear. One mind game I tried last night was pretending that the team was my Level 3 class, where I felt confident. When I did that, I noticed I paid less attention to my team backstage and just focused on getting ready. I smiled less. I think I smile at people when I'm nervous. I also tried remembering what it felt like to be around Monkeydick folks.

My brother goes to all my shows, which is great. He had to go to 3 this week! He always supports me, but I could use an honest voice. Well, no I guess I need my friends to cheer me on. I need to be my own honest voice.

After Pat McCartney's coaching session ("you're[sic] characters are all the same, it gets boring"), I felt bad, but I think I had a grip on what I'm missing as a player which made me feel I could get what I'm missing. But now, and even last night, I couldn't remember the feeling of knowing what it is I'm missing.

My team backs each other up. That's cool. It's fun, even when I suck.

Maybe it's just that I'm tentative. But I don't want to be a spazz and not add anything specific. No, my problem is being timid. I started to come out of it at the second show last night. I didn't feel nervous at either of them. I just need to make bigger moves—especially as a character.

Addendum: I remember what I hated about my cagematch scene. Mike was a brother laughing at the TV. Hilary Kimblin was a mom laughing at the TV. But because I was nervous I didn't laugh. I didn't become a character like Mike did. And so I had to call out being the normal brother. Maybe that was what made it seem lame. Or maybe it would have been alright if I just named things a little better. I don't know—somehow I feel like I screwed that scene up and can't figure out why.

—

Honestly, I could have written this six months ago.

JULY 7TH, 2012 at 5:23PM

DON'T ASK QUESTIONS = DON'T BE SURPRISED

We say "don't ask questions" but what we mean is "try to not be surprised."

I point this out because "don't ask questions" is one of those pieces of improv advice that I've always thought does a bit of damage down the road as it helps at first. You need to ask questions because questions are such common things in everyday conversation—it's very hard to sound like a natural human being without asking each other questions.

But you DO have to be able to avoid acting surprised, unless your scene partner specifically needs you to be surprised and a lot of times even then it's not needed.

In students' first improv class, they say almost every single line like a question. "Wait, *I'M* the boss?" or "You're behind on the rent?" They are so new that they can't process any new information without having a moment of barely understanding what it is.

The teacher will say "don't ask questions!" and the students restate their sentences as statements: "I see. *I'M* the boss" or "You've got to stop being behind on the rent!"

Better, though I wonder if the note should be "don't be surprised—act like you already knew these things."

At Cagematch I saw a terrific set from the three man group Outlook of the Poet. They played a monoscene featuring three cousins who were police officers getting ready to take on Chinese gangsters called the J-Dragons. Lots of the scene involved endowing each other with information, or confessing information about themselves. But almost 100% of the time, they made the decision that they already knew the information, even when it was being presented explicitly as new information.

For example, about one third of the way through their set, Jon Gabrus' character says "Guys, I have to confess something. I'm adopted."

Ben Rodgers responds with "We know, man."

Jon: "I knew it, you guys already knew."

Ben: "Yeah, because you're Chinese. Your parents aren't." A big move since Jon's character has spent a lot of time talking about how much he hates the Chinese gangs and maybe Chinese people in general.

Jon takes it in and says. "I know. God it was so hard growing up. I kept hoping I was just Hawaiian but pale."

Setting aside their ability to play somewhat racist characters intelligently, they also demonstrated how much more powerful it is if the characters decide to already know the information being discovered by the actors.

Am I the biggest asshole who ever walked the Earth?

JULY 10TH, 2012 at 1:15PM

Q: IMPROV TEAM OF HISTORICAL FIGURES

brennanleemulligan asked: Hi Will! Today I heard a story about something Albert Einstein said. When a philosophically-minded student asked him "Why does time exist?", Einstein responded "So that everything doesn't happen all at once." This struck me as being great. It also made me think that Albert Einstein would have made a great improvisor. If you could put together a team of All-Star improvisors, using only non-show-business historical figures, who would be on it?

- Sherlock Holmes*
- Mata Hari
- Sigmund Freud
- Amelia Earhart
- Harry Houdini

*If I can't pick him since he's fictional, I'll go with Joseph Bell, the doctor who inspired the Holmes character.

My all-authors team (no Shakespeare, since he was also an actor)

- Jonathan Swift
- Virginia Woolf
- Gabriel Garcia Marquez
- Nikolai Gogol
- Sylvia Plath (for the edits)

JULY 10TH, 2012 at 3:43PM

Q: JUSTCRAIG: FUNNIEST VOLUME OF YELLING?

justcraig asked: When you're in a scene playing a disapproving dad meeting your daughter's new boyfriend, what's the funniest way to disapprove? Also, what's the funniest volume of yelling (as the dad).

Furrowed brow followed by resigned sigh. On a scale of one to ten, funniest volume is always the reliably-surprising EIGHT.

JULY 24TH, 2012 at 5:14PM

Q: IMPROV EXERCISES FOR WHEN YOU'RE ALONE?

westcoastcharlie asked: Let's say it's 2am. Monday morning. There are no classes or shows going on, your teammates are asleep and even if they were, there's no coach available to rehearse in front of. Can you recommend any improv exercises that can be done alone? I've heard people say to do object work.

Put in your headphones and play your favorite song while thinking with extreme focus of your favorite friends and loved ones. After like half an hour, if you're not tired, read a good book until you fall asleep.

JULY 24TH, 2012 at 5:17PM

Q: FUNNIEST THING ERIK TANOUYE HAS DONE?

Anonymous asked: Hi, Will. This is Aaron Jackson from UCBNY. What is the funniest thing you've ever seen Erik Tanouye do on stage? And what is the funniest thing you've ever done on stage?

My personal favorite Erik Tanouye move was after Charlie Sanders initiated a scene about tourists going to Williamsburg, Brooklyn looking for colonial Williamsburg Erik did a tag out to show that (then) seminal Williamsburg Brooklyn club Galapagos was filled with giant turtles.

The most inadvertently funny thing I ever did on stage was during a Stepfathers show, when I was still new to that team. I ended the show by curling up in the fetal position alone on stage until the show ended in bewildered silence. That is true and the context would not help this description.

The actual funniest thing I ever did was probably some quip that was all wry and shit.

I highly doubt this is really Aaron Jackson because Aaron turns into light when he tries to use the internet.

JULY 26TH, 2012 at 4:40PM

TRIANGLE

In computer programming (and probably in lots of fields) there's the expression "Fast. Cheap. Good. Pick two."

I feel like there's three aspects of good scene work: **cooperation, reality, activeness**. Maybe the challenge is doing all three at once, and maybe students can only ever do two of them at once. And we teachers are always noting them on whichever one they leave out?

So **cooperation** means listening and going with each other and being sensitive to what the other person is expecting and playing together. Saying yes, accepting offers. Someone brings up pickles, you speak to the importance of pickles.

Reality is being sensitive to how you'd be in real life, what the audience's expectations are, being truthful and savvy. So if you obey "cooperation," but that makes you have this five minute conversation about how important pickles are, you've ignored the reality that no one would talk about pickles. So you must speak to the topic of pickles, but in order to respect reality, you can only talk about pickles in a way you really would, and let it naturally lead to something else that you really would talk about.

Activeness is being interesting, having it be about the people who are currently in the scene, about things that matter to them, dramatic events. So you speak to the importance of pickles, then somehow be sensitive to how that's a bullshit conversation and so you make some big choice that could maybe really happen, and it lets you speak about pickles except now it's important and you have to and it's funny and it all just... works.

Is this something?

EDITED 10 HOURS LATER TO ADD: I don't know what my point is in "pick two." I mostly just wanted to express what i see as the conflicting aspects of good scene work and express sympathy for people trying to do all at once. I like models and metaphors and such. I didn't think it through.

JULY 27TH, 2012 at 10:15AM

EMPATHY

"Improv taught me to really say YES" is something I read whenever a non-improv media source writes about improv. "SAY YES TO EVERYTHING" seems to be the big eye-opening moment that journalists take away from improv classes. Even accomplished comedians look back at their time in improv and speak to the revolutionary concept of being cooperative and then when pressed for specific examples will talk about the joy of saying yes to things one would say normally say no to.

I think that is over-simplistic and wrong. Yes-And is not about SAYING YES TO EVERYTHING and in fact, an important part of becoming a good improviser is learning how and when to say NO on stage, so things stay truthful. It makes for a good story, but saying that "improv taught me to say yes" is like saying that comic books aren't for kids anymore.

The revolutionary game-changing skill of long-form improv is: EMPATHY.

Seeing things from another's point of view. Furthering agendas that you do not personally agree with. Adding to a story from the viewpoint of a different character in the scene. THAT is the skill that separates the rookies from the veterans in improv. It has nothing to do with whether they say YES or NO. It has to do with if they can see things from more than one perspective with credibility.

Tests to see if you have empathy in your improv, from easiest to hardest:

1. **Being an intelligent version of a character who believes something you do not.** Like if you're a passionate liberal, can you play a right-wing politician with strident religious beliefs—but not sound like a jerk? Can you set aside your distaste for that person and indeed advocate for them?

2. **Yes-anding another character who your character disagrees with, WITHOUT CHANGING YOUR CHARACTER'S MIND.** Like if you're a right-wing religious zealot and the other character is someone trying to legalize heroin, can you do something like "I remember how you took that economics class, and it convinced you legalizing drugs was a smart idea—but it's not worth it, it's morally wrong." Holding onto one viewpoint, while being able to further another one. It's tricky, but the sign of someone who's getting good.

3. **Yes-anding an accusation lobbed at your character which genuinely surprises you, the actor.** You're a right-wing religious zealot and someone says to you "That never stopped you from shoplifting from my store." Even if that's an ill-conceived move, the person playing the zealot should be able to accept it and justify it with ease. "I steal to protect the free market, which is a way of honoring God." A non-empathetic move would be to fight back and re-accuse the other character as a way of trying to "win" the scene. "I only stole because you had slept with my wife!"

4. **Yes-anding the other character while justifying an accusation that surprised you.** "That never stopped you from shoplifting from

my store." And you say "You're good at noticing people's hypocrisy. I admire that in you." Wait, is that funny? I bet it would get a laugh, just for being a surprisingly generous response.

Other handy tricks that empathy will give you:

- being able to respond to what someone MEANT to say, rather than quibble over their wording of what they actually said
- speaking to the suggestion in a way the audience intended you to. If someone suggests "snowstorm" during a week of an actual snow storm, they are thinking of different aspects of snowstorm than what someone might be thinking of if he gives that suggestion in July
- Giving endowments to the other actor that they are happy to have been given. Giving gifts people want.

Anyway, SAYING YES TO EVERYTHING is not only an obvious lesson from improv, it's an over-simplistic one that you do not do when you're making a comedy show.

EMPATHY, though, is a good barometer of someone's ability to make up stuff in front of an audience and have it all fit together in a funny way.

AUGUST 1ST, 2012 at 9:21AM

CONDITION

Some people's problem with doing improv is they can only think of what MIGHT HAPPEN next rather than thinking about what must have ALREADY HAPPENED.

AUGUST 14TH, 2012 at 2:50PM

LIKE MINDED PEOPLE

I guess the most important thing UCB improv gave me was: all of my friends. This is a sentimental recollection of what it felt like to take an improv class and realize that I liked everybody in an entire community.

I moved to NYC in 1996 when I was 26 and found I could not accumulate friends. I worked at PaineWebber as an "electronic reports editor" (which meant I manually converted Microsoft Word docs into text documents with proper codes so that they could be submitted to electronic news services like FirstCall and Bloomberg). Most people there were either humorless robots, straight-up sad, or passionately devoted to leaving the city as soon as possible every day to go hide in a New Jersey suburb.

There were cooler people among the temps, but I couldn't upshift pleasant small talk during lunch into social invitations. There was a really cool girl who was getting her PhD in sociology and whose boyfriend wrote for the goddamn Nation, and I desperately wanted to be adopted into her circle of snobby intellectual friends, as I desperately wanted to be snobby and intellectual. She invited me to a party somewhere near Columbia and I remember meeting the guy who wrote Lemony Snickett and otherwise standing by myself and feeling boring.

I did stand-up at open mikes (Rebar, Detour, Gladys) but never talked to anyone. It's tough to feel creepy in a room full of asocial creeps, but I somehow did it.

I taught myself computer programming and started working for software developers. I got along with them, but I had to kind of adjust myself to do it. Like watching old movies where you mentally allow for the slower pace and ham-fisted delivery—at work I found myself forced to relate to people's opinion of what was on tv the night before. People talked about Howard Stern a lot, and whatever scandal was afoot, and whatever was on Saturday Night Live the week before. I didn't mind, but it was sort of like eating without breathing through your nose.

People did not do anything at night. They went home. Or maybe they went to a bar and left by 8pm. There were no parties on the weekend. My college friends (UConn) all lived in Boston or worse, Hartford! I imagined all these cool things going on in the city that I felt I had no access to.

And in general, New Yorkers are just always BUSY. Everyone's agenda is full.

For years, I sat in my room and thought: *how does anyone in this city make friends?*

Then, in November of 1999, I took an improv class. I did that not to make friends, but just because I liked the shows at UCBT and despite having almost no experience on stage, somehow considered myself funny. Something to do.

Class was Monday night, taught by Kevin Mullaney, on the stage of the UCB Theatre on 22nd street. DAY ONE, at the end Jake Fogelnest said to the room "Anyone want to go to McManus?" And we did, and stayed out until five in the morning. It was a terrifically fun night of everyone in class exchanging their stories of how they came to take improv, what UCB shows we liked and (already? yes) theories of what good improv was.

And right away, what I noticed was: *I was talking like myself.* I do not think I had felt that way since HIGH SCHOOL. These people had seen the same movies as me (*Annie Hall, His Girl Friday*, all Marx Brothers films), heard the same music (Elvis Costello, Smiths, Ray Charles), had the same general disposition to what was funny (some of SNL, all of Conan O'Brien). They were speaking from the same context as me. I didn't have to explain why I watched a Woody Allen movie, which i something I would have had to do at my computer programming job. I didn't have to explain how I came to have heard old episodes of the Jack Benny radio show. Or why I would be excited to take an improv class.

Some of my favorite memories from that first batch of nights at McManus:

- Mitch Magee and Jake Fogelnest, arm in arm, singing the ENTIRETY of Pet Sounds at double speed.
- Brian Berrebbi getting Jessica from our class, who worked as a dominatrix, to tell us sex stories about weird Wall Street jerks
- Frankie Tartaglia sermonizing on how great sandwiches were, for maybe 45 minutes Capped off by his promise to "smoke me up" since I had never tried marijuana and was about to turn 30.
- Michael B.'s description of losing his virginity when he was 24. I guess a lot of these nights were getting people to confess personal things.
- Jake Fogelnest deciding that two guys sitting on stage and listening to Paul Simon's "America" in its entirety would be a bulletproof comedy bit.
- Brian Berrebbi's fake wedding. He had a party at his apartment, proposed to his then-girlfriend and brought in a (supposed) preacher and they got married. We all bought it. I was best man. Then found out the next day that he and his girlfriend and the preacher were all in on it. I think I was mad? Jake's take was "Good bit."
- Many passionate discussions of movies. *Magnolia* was just out and

polarized the group. *Rushmore* was sacrosanct.

- Making Josh Perillo do object work for an hour or more. "Grate cheese!" "shuffle cards!" "piano!" "MATRIX! DO SOMETHING MATRIXY!"
- Mitch Magee's one man Harold by the big long table in the back of McManus. (Sample group game: "You guys are assholes!" "No we're not" Sweep.)
- A night where I had to be convinced over a long period of time (no smart phones) that yes there was a movie filmed in Esperanto and it did in fact star William Shatner, and no, that is not something that people are making up.
- Mitch's toasts. He always had very serious, considered toasts. He's raise a glass, wait until everyone else had raised them and was silent, and then say very earnestly: "To a new way of living."
- Also Mitch's emails. My first email to him was something like "Is this email right? Let me know that you got this, I'm planning a practice session for Wednesday. Or is the phone better?" And his response in its entirety was "I fuck fat chicks for money."
- Carrying Jokers. We heard from someone that in Chicago people would carry Jokers in their wallet and you could show yours to anyone, and if they didn't have a Joker they were required to drop their pants. So we all started carrying Jokers. That was dumb, right? I just threw mine out a week ago when I got a new wallet. CORRECTION: Brian Berrebbi introduced this to us. He worked or interned at Blue Man Group and there were people there for whom it was a tradition.

I'm not doing this justice. There is something supremely comforting when you are talking with a group of people and you have full confidence that you will be understood by all of them. Not DEEPLY understood, but that they get the context in which you are telling your story. They know where you're coming from when you hope that you're not "disappointed" by a movie. You could say things like "We need to downshift into small talk; I'm emotionally exhausted" and they got it. It was intoxicating. The rest of my life sharply paled when compared with these evenings.

When the teachers hung out, we were unbelievably psyched. We made Mullaney and Armando tell us about Chicago shows, and old UCB stunts.

We'd see people from new level ones peep in and sometimes regard them suspiciously, and other times aggressively adopt them to our tables.

We started practicing improv together on Wednesday nights in my office (after everyone else left at 6pm) first without a coach, then with Seth Morris. We would go to Harold Nights on Thursday and go out after that too. Generally we'd see either the Friday (Marooned, Naked Babies, Immortal Combat) or Saturday (Real Real World, Feature Feature) UCB shows and then go out. ASSSSCAT we'd go to but not as much as it was more of a pain to get into. The smartest thing the UCB ever did was keep its shows to five bucks, because it meant you could go ALL THE TIME. Cheaper than a movie, by half.

Rarely just two of us—it was a group thing. Rob Lathan, John Gemberling, Brett Gelman, Frankie, Josh, Brian, Mitch and myself just started doing everything together. There were others who hung out but dropped out: Mike Fine, Mike Bosniak, John Marshall, Jessica S., Amy Halpin. We started getting picky about who we'd let practice with us, we kicked people out, we got mean. People left. The core of us got made into a Harold team eventually (Monkeydick).

Unlike the drones at work, these people were interesting. Brian's stories of growing up in Canarsie. Mitch's painter friends from Cornell. Jake and Frankie's stories of a Quaker school in Philly (is that right? am I remembering that right?). After our level one grad show is when I discovered (how had I not known) that Jake had hosted an MTV show and knew, like, famous people.

Improv people were forthcoming with details, not shy about answering questions unlike the vast majority of adults who seem to go to great lengths to not be bothered by words.

Mitch started inviting me to parties of his friends, which including a group of girls who literally all had the exact same glasses and I got crushes on all of them simultaneously. He gave me a tour of the then-not-yet-overrun bars of Williamsburg. Jake had a birthday party in the basement of the Chelsea Hotel where, weirdly, Claire Danes was in attendance. He also hosted a weekly karaoke night at some place on Bleeker Street and we'd go to that (I remember we did "Welcome to the Jungle" which is a terrible karaoke choice but I had only done karaoke once before in my life). Brian and I would talk on the phone once or twice a week, analyzing the shows we'd seen: who was good? who was bad?

Recommendations given to me in McManus Pub: I got introduced to Neutral Milk Hotel, Love's "Forever Changes", Beach Boys' "Pet Sounds," A Tribe Called Quest's "The Low-End Theory," Minor Threat and Fugazi. I tried sushi, Indian food on 6th street, Polish stuff at Veselka. I discovered the Russian and Turkish baths on East 10th Street. I borrowed Preacher comics, rented Kubrick's *The Killing* and Kurosawa's *The Seven Samurai*. I went to see Proof before it went to Broadway.

I was doing things.

We were all sitting in the green room at UCB after New Team Harold (which at that time was Monday nights 8pm) when Matt Walsh came in and asked everyone in the theater to go with him to Marc Maron's show at Luna Lounge where we performed as a 50-member improv troupe. "How about a Harold?" Maron said. "We prefer party quirks," said Walsh. We all did a sound-and-movement for two minutes, and then freeze tag. At some point I was frozen with David Wain.

I went from having no one to talk to, to having a full calendar with a league of ready conversation partners.

The city was suddenly available to me. I had allies and agents to give me access.

I felt like myself, all the time, for maybe the first time. What was it that made us all get along? Some combination of showmanship, media savvy, timing and an attraction for maybe trying to be funny on stage? I don't know. Whatever it was, it was immediate and durable.

And it remains true! There's been, what, one million generations of people since then? I have always been able to feel comfortable and to enjoy a conversation with the people who float through this world.

Having people to hang out with: It was so crazily tough before, and then suddenly it was just so easy. Oh my God, thank God I took that class.

I've having a down week, and I wanted to remind myself of how lucky I am that I found this world. I am lucky, I do still love it.

AUGUST 15TH, 2012 at 3:38PM

Q: PEOPLE LAUGH WHEN NAMES ARE GIVEN

halphillips asked: You know how sometimes people laugh when a character gets named? Doesn't even have to be a funny name. Just a normal name, and everybody laughs. Right? Why is that? I still don't know why that happens. It's weird.

I agree! That is weird. I think, and someone suggested this to me but I can't remember who, that all names have connotations and so you are automatically assigning a whole history to someone when you give them a name and the audience laughs at however that instant history contrasts with what we know. So if a character is a pharmacist filling a prescription and someone calls that character "Bernard" someone will laugh because his association with Bernard somehow funnily contrasts with being a pharmacist?

AUGUST 16TH, 2012 at 2:31PM

Q: JUSTCRAIG: FUNNIEST FOOD?

justcraig asked: What's the funniest food to prepare using object work? Also, is it funnier to be a guy who sits in a subway scene, or is it better to hold onto one of the poles? Thanks.

Questions we should all be thinking about.

AUGUST 16TH, 2012 at 3:48PM

gabrus asked: You want to gift your scene partner with the fact that they just sneezed which of the following is the funniest -god bless you, -salud, or -gesundheit

Thank you for your help, Gabrus.

AUGUST 20TH, 2012 at 8:02AM

HOW DO I GET MORE INVOLVED?

People ask me that consistently. They're talking about the UCB Theatre though I would imagine it could apply to any improv/comedy community.

For UCB, I don't know what to tell them. I started watching shows at UCB in August 1998, took a class in November 1999 and then never left. It's not an easily portable model.

What is it people are looking for? What does it take to feel "involved?" To see people on stage and then be friends with them? To perform on stage? How much? To be on a TEAM? Regardless of how actually helpful that is, is being on a TEAM the only way to feel part of an improv theatre? Or do they want an agent/manager/paying comedy job? (good luck asking your improv teacher—if he/she knew they wouldn't be there)

Because to some degree, everyone in this community feels left out. I get emails from people who are definitely friends with lots of people here and who perform a lot asking "why am I not in X show? what do i have to do?" It's demoralizing to think how far up the ladder people are still saying "why am I not farther up the ladder?" Because a lot of that depends on what ladder you're envisioning.

THERE IS NO LADDER, FOOLS! Except the one in your mind.

Okay, there's ladders, but there's a lot of them: friends, stage time, career ammunition, comedic voice.

Still, it's a question a lot of people ask. So I put it to you, insiders:

1. what is it people want when they say they want to be more "involved?"
2. what is it that ultimately makes someone feel "involved?"

EDITED TO ADD: This topic deserves more thought, I shall return to it in a typically ambling essay IN THE FUTURE.

AUGUST 20TH, 2012 at 11:50AM

WAYS I FELT INVOLVED AT UCB THEATRE

My last post about "feeling involved" and now I'm trying to remember what things happened that made me feel involved. I tried to include the ways in which I met people who later helped me get performance/job opportunities.

NOVEMBER 1999–SUMMER 2000

Met friends in a Kevin Mullaney 101 (as detailed in this post) and we started practicing together. We hired Seth Morris and then Billy Merritt as coaches. Billy started saying hi to us at Harold Night and at McManus.

Kevin Mullaney would be at McManus and we'd get what felt like insidery stories about Chicago.

Saw enough shows that I knew who the main players of the UCB stage were. I knew who the stars were, and who was struggling (in my opinion, from an audience member's perspective). At McManus after classes, I would be the one telling people about what shows were good.

Saw other non-UCB comedy shows, like the Luna Lounge crowd, around town. All free or cheap East Village type shows. Seeing shows like that— ones that had minimal advertising, maybe just listed in a paper or something—made me feel connected.

Brett Gelman, who was in my practice group, asked me to tech his sketch show The Grizz. Met Jon Daly, Vadim Newquist and their director John Bowie. Started saying hello to those people, chit-chatting about improv shows here and there.

We all just talk about improv. That's the way in. What shows are good, what moves are good, what was good and bad in whatever show just happened.

I take improv 2 with Michael Delaney. I take improv 3 with Armando Diaz. I re-take improv 3 with Armando Diaz. I take improv 4 with Ali F, then improv 4 Ian Roberts, then improv 4 with Kevin Mullaney. Practicing once a week with Monkeydick outside of class the whole time. Doing sets at Freaks Local with whoever is around. Watching The Swarm, Respecto, Mother.

My brother started taking classes. Went to his grad shows, hung out after. Met Chris Gethard, MC Chris, Kevin Cragg, Sean Taylor, Dave Lombard, Ed Helms.

Run into Jon Daly at a party being thrown by Mitch Magee, also in my practice group. He tells me he hears that I'm funny, that I'm getting really good.

Billy asks me, Brian Berrebbi and John Gemberling to do a hosting bit with him at Harold Night.

NOVEMBER 2000–DECEMBER 2001
Armando Diaz puts me on a Harold team. Jake Foglenest is the one who tells me, on the phone from the UCB box office. ("You're in the program! You're on a team! You gotta step up, show everyone how awesome you are.")

My practice group Monkeydick gets in Cagematch. We win for 4 weeks and get made a Harold team.

Brian Berrebbi starts coaching and introduces me to his favorite team, The Dark Champions. I meet: Eric Scott, Chris Kula, John Reynolds, Risa Sangurai, Sarah Burns, Alan Corey.

I take sketch classes from: Ali F, Ian Roberts, Armando Diaz. I meet Shannon O'Neill. She gets on a team.

Mitch and I write a sketch show, get a spank, get a short run.

I take another Ian Roberts sketch class. Meet Erik Tanouye, Dan Powell, Julie Klausner.

Theatre gets closed because of fire code violations! I go to tall the "sub" shows at Raffifi and Access Theatre.

SPRING 2002–SPRING 2003
I take an improv class outside of UCB. I meet Joe Wengert, Neil Casey, Ryan Karels, Amey Goerlich. Joe and Neil, who liked Mitch's and my show, ask me to direct their show. They split their Spank slot with a guy named Anthony King. It's one of the best Spank hours I've seen!

Kevin Hines tells me Charlie Todd is the best new improviser coming up. I watch him on My Kickass Van and agree. Not sure if I told him. I try to tell people.

Rob Lathan rents Under St. Marks for a series of variety shows called "Osgood Schlatter." He and I write a sketch for each one. Lotsa Repsecto guys do bits: Rob Huebel, Paul Scheer, Jackie Clarke. Lathan also does a "one man" show that features Gemberling and me. Owen Burke directs.

New theatre opens. Monkeydick is in the first Cagematch there, vs. the Swarm. We get pummeled, like always.

Kevin Mullaney wants a team of Wiliamsburg improvisers to get the UCB brand into Williamsburg. Charlie Sanders, Brian Finkelstein, Will Becton, Mark-Sam Rosenthal, Jeffrey Campbell and I start doing shows there every week. Harold teams are ordered to perform out there. I watch all the shows, hang out after. Get to be really good friends with Neutrino folks, Police Chief Rumble. I see Dillinger's first bunch of shows—Joe, Erik, Risa, Sarah introduce me to the rest of the team: Lennon Parham, Brett Christensen, Anthony King and Zach Woods.

The PIT opens. Armando puts me in a show there, which closes two months later!

Spring 2003-*Things start to get hazy now.*

John Reynolds, formerly of Dark Champions, now of Harold Team Van Buren asks me to coach them. Julie Brister gets added to Van Buren. She recommends me to be a sub. Kevin Mullaney calls me and asks me to be a sub.

Brian Finkelstein hosts a stand-up night at R Bar in Williamsburg. I start going and writing jokes. Meet Ritch Duncan, Mike Dobbins, Carter Edwards, Michael Martin, Eugene Cordero.

2004

I coach Police Chief Rumble, other teams.

Owen Burke books a commercial and a few other things has to miss most of a 101 class he was supposed to teach. He asks me to take it over. I meet Lydia Hensler.

Lathan and I write a parody of A Christmas Carol for a show. Huebel stars. Owen directs. Jon and Jackie are in it. Joe, Neil, Ryan, Amey are in.

Mitch, Rob, Joe, Neil and I form a sketch group called Game Face. We write five shows. Nick Kroll directs us. We rent Under St. Marks for 5 weeks. One of those weeks we take off and I host an indie improv night with Rogue Elephant, who start doing shows there all the time.

I also write a separate show, Seven Fights, with Matt Decoster which we premiere at the Red Room on East 4th street to an audience of four people: Kevin Hines, Brett Gelman, Jackie Clarke and our director Dyna Moe.

My brother Kevin forms Primal Bias, with Tanouye, Lombard, Cragg, Gavin. Silvija joins later. Gethard has a group called Five Dudes and at some point the two teams do a run of shows on Saturday nights, with different indie groups opening: Big Tobacco, Kid Dervin, Sherpa.

2005

Tony Carnevale brings Channel 101 comes to NYC in the form of Channel 102. I had met Tony when he co-hosted a weekly variety show called Variety Underground with Sean Taylor. I make a show for the first screening and win. Make videos there for a year or two. I meet (over email) Dan Harmon, other LA Channel 101 people. Sara Schaefer submits a video, I meet her.

Armando at some point leaves The PIT and forms the Magnet. Terry Jinn puts Primal Bias in a show there. I do Ash Wednesday on Wednesday nights, get to be friends with Ashley Ward, Matt Oberg, Chris Schneider, Stan Laikowski and Rachel Korowitz.

Monkeydick gets a weekend slot, we lose it. We get it again. We get broken up.

I do stand-up at School Night, at shows in Williamsburg. I ask for slots from people I remember from R Bar; from people that I saw at shows when I would see shows outside of UCBT.

Nick Kroll lets me do a set of stand-up on Oh, Hello! at Raffifi. I meet John Mulaney and Joe Mande.

2006

I get put on Arsenal, then Anthony King put together 1985.

I leave my computer programming job and start a video production job at AOL and learn a lot more about cameras, editing. I get that job because Sara Schaefer was working there and suggested me because she saw my Channel 102 videos and knew from the improv world.

Charlie Todd puts me in an Improv Everywhere stunt as a guy threatening to jump off a three-foot ledge.

I meet a million people.

Anthony King suggests me to submit monologue packets. Someone calls me into audition for commercials. Andy Rocco (from Monkeydick) and I book one. I get a commercial agent. I do a featured extra part in a web series that Seth Myers directs. I almost get cast in a terrible MTV show.

2007

Chris Gethard calls me and asks if I want to be on Stepfathers. Chris and I had started here at practically the same time. Delaney was my level 2 teacher. Silvija was on my indie team Primal Bias. I would be replacing my second ever coach Billy Merritt. Also joining at the same time is Shannon O'Neill who I'd known since a sketch class seven years prior. I'd known Zach since watching his old Dillinger shows. I'd coached Bobby in PCR. So that's one way to get on a weekend team: be friends with and be good in front of the entire existing cast for years.

The Derrick guys make a movie. I audition, get cast as the principal.

Sean Clements asks me to direct his Maude Team. He writes scripts for videos and I direct those. Justin Purnell suggests I work with Todd Bieber.

Christine Nangle asks me to coach her Harold Team. I meet Dan Gurewitch. He writes me into a College Humor thing. I meet Sam Reich, head of College Humor videos. Christine gets hired for SNL.

2008

Rob Lathan and I write a book. We hire Damian Chadwick (who I met coaching Sean Clements Maude team, and then other teams) to do the graphic design.

Joe Wengert calls me and asks if I want his job running the school.

Todd Bieber suggests I work with Nate Dern, and so we get him to be a video intern to work on ucbcomedy videos. We make Indie Cup, Checkmates, Snapple Facts, others.

I coach Gramps, meet Elaine Carroll. She puts me in Very-Mary Kate videos.

I teach a class that has Spencer Griffin who is a producer at Collegehumor. He gets me some directing gigs there. I meet a ton of CH people.

2010

I get all into Twitter at some point and in a gross way try to write things that will "be successful" on twitter: better jokes, shorter, poppier things.

Neil approaches me and says it's been too long since we've done a show. We write Small Men.

Gethard does his stage show, I do that.

Start this improv blog.

2011
Connor Ratliff starts doing shows. We message about comic books on Facebook. Gethard proposes him for Stepfathers, he joins. He puts me in his Presidential campaign bits.

I start recording my stand-up bits. I do 30 minutes (invited by Aaron Glaser, who I'd met at Maude Night).

2012
Finally launch Small Men. Direct Spo videos (I'm behind, I know). Improvise with the PKD group. Teach a lot, think about it a lot.

THIS WEEK
Today I'm doing a stand-up showcase at the Beast for Comedy Central. Wednesday I'm acting in a web series that stand-up/CH guy/good dude Adam Newman wrote. Thursday night I'm performing Small Men and then my youngest brothers comes to town and we are going to do Cagematch together.

—

I don't know how it happens! Be around, talk to people, put yourself in situations in which you are genuinely enthusiastic. Talk to your peers about the things that excite you. Wait 10 years.

AUGUST 30TH, 2012 at 11:29AM

Q: I WASN'T INVITED TO AUDITION.

Anonymous asked: I wasn't on the invite list for Harold auditions and I know that my last audition was rough to say the least, but I feel like I've made great impressions on my teachers and I'm a strong improviser—though I'll admit I'm at my best when there's no added pressure of a Harold audition. Class and an indie group are all I have time for

without feeling overwhelmed sometimes. How much of "getting in" is about networking and show-going and how much is it about being a strong improviser?

First, you tell me why other people haven't hired me to write TV shows and I'll tell you why other people haven't picked you for improv auditions.

Second, I don't know!

Third: Networking doesn't matter for things that are picked via auditions. Though meeting like-minded people is more fruitful in the long run than being put on a team with people you didn't pick to play with. Also I hate the word "networking"—just do things you love and talk to people who also love them about those things and that's all the networking you need to do.

Fourth: Auditions are a weird process: they pick shiny people more than workhorses, by design. I don't believe that anyone picking a team is doing anything other than trying to make the best team possible. I do not believe there is nearly the bias and corruption and attention to "politics" that I hear some people suspect. It's more that the nature of picking 8 people from 800 applicants means only the shiniest, brightest torches get snatched up, leaving plenty of dependable workhorses behind.

Think of all of your classes. Who would YOU pick from those people to be on a team. Now think of who you are NOT picking. Why not them? Could you defend yourself to all those people? Are you playing politics by not picking them? Why do you think of some and not others?

Think of the current teams on Harold Nights: which ones would you say deserve a spot on the weekend. Now think of the teams you did NOT pick. Are they bad? Aren't they comprised of strong improvisers? What is it that makes us pick one thing over another? It's not favoritism that plays a part but an intangible sometimes hard to articulate opinion in your gut that some people/teams are just inarguably BETTER than others.

What could the other teams/players/classmates do to win your favor? Do all those things in yourself.

Fifth: You're a strong improviser, but do you leave an impression on teachers and fellow classmates? Do you have a comedic voice beyond just competent rule-following? Or are you just a utility infielder? Utility infielders don't get picked during auditions. That is a flaw of the audition process, or at least the nature of the audition process. It is not a result (probably) of favoritism or social politics from the people at the front of the room.

Sixth: What is it you want from being on a team? Can you get that another way? Teams are valuable but also overrated. There are many people whose careers would have been better served by never having been placed on a time-demanding improv team.

To sum up: I really don't know. It's a really hard thing to do fairly and the vast majority of people get told "no."

Wrote this in 60 seconds. My apologies to everyone.

AUGUST 31ST, 2012 at 8:24AM

YOUTUBE COMMENTING IN REAL LIFE

A group of people. Someone tries to tell a story. "Oh that reminds me of this thing that happened at work..." or "I've been meaning to tell you guys..." But the person can't tell the story because everyone snipes and quibbles at the way the person is telling the story, the phrases used—unimportant details. They don't care about the story, they just want to use the exposition as ammunition for their jokes! It's like people who comment on YouTube videos and only talk about how the soundtrack is lifted from a movie that isn't that good, or how someone's shirt betrays that the video was made 10 years ago. Those are people that won't be able to play a group game. There's something about people's inability to just... listen to the point that someone is trying to really make.

SEPTEMBER 3RD, 2012 at 9:03AM

GETTING SWEPT UP IN IT

For the people who get hooked, improv is a religion. You punish yourself when you do bad scenes as if you have sinned, and you feel noble when you do a scene the "right" way. When Ian Roberts told me "that was a well-acted scene" in a class I felt like I had been decreed inherently good.

It's supposed to be comedy, but very soon into learning about it, you forget about funny and you start chasing some elusive noble idea of artistic purity. My level 1 classmates and I nodded reverently when we'd watch Rob Riggle mime throwing aside his newspaper while sitting on a supposed toilet. "Very real," we'd all approve.

By the end of their first class, improv students are discussing amongst themselves the "right" way of doing things vs. the wrong way. Everyone is very sure of themselves. They watch shows and are very confident they know who's good and who's bad, which teams are good and bad. At my level 3 grad show, my brother's level 1 show was in the audience, picking among us who seemed good or bad—we had had SIX MONTHS of improv—but were being judged with an air of solemn finality.

And these are people who are reverent about nothing else! Atheists, scoffers, skeptics who are skeptical of others' skepticism. But they square up and toe the fucking line with expressions of absolute commitment when their improv teacher tells them they have to do a sound-and-movement PROPERLY or else NOT BE GOOD AT IMPROV.

I can't imagine this happening in a cooking class, or at least not as frequently. Or a dance class.

Stand-ups get reverent about their craft (witness the million podcasts in which stand-ups almost break into tears discussing their respective climbs to the middle) but there seems to be a higher priority in maintaining your own point of view.

But in improv, you give yourself over. You do sound and movements and pattern games, and do practices at noon on a Saturday after staying out until 5am, you help senior improvisers with their shows, you plan elaborate stunts that demonstrate that you understand improv—you're going to do yes-anding FOR REAL IN THE REAL WORLD BECAUSE YOU'RE SUCH A BADASS.

Is it the built-in hierarchy of most improv communities? The class system is built into levels. Then the top students get put on teams. The teams have a hierarchy—Harold Night, weekend shows. You can feel a definite amount of validation from where you are in that system and it drives you FORWARD.

When I got put on a Harold team I went to Cap 21 and rented a one-person room meant for people to practice singing. I stood in there for an hour pretending to get suggestions so I could practice initiating. Meanwhile I had a lucrative computer programming job which I was skipping out on to do this.

The money from my job: *valueless*. My place on Harold Night: (at that time a Thursday night show which about 40 people a week watched?) *worth devoting extra time and money to.*

We value the hard notes, the ones that hurt because we think those are going to make us better. "I like teachers who call me out on my bullshit," says everyone. We do warm-ups that we hate because we think it's important to be humble and suffer. We see bad shows but justify in our heads how they are good because we think it's noble to appreciate the good side of an improv show, to yes-and it from the audience. "It was so brave the way they made no decisions for the first 20 minutes," I once said.

You go to shows and you laugh, but you're not even laughing you're trying to demonstrate that you GET IT.

You get off stage and instantly beat yourself up. Has anyone ever walked off stage from an improv show and said "I was awesome?" No, it's always "Oh god, what did I do? Why did I say X? Why couldn't I fix Y? I'M SORRY, I WAS SO BAD." Backstage after a show I remember what it felt like to attend a Catholic Church.

Being good in improv feels like a capital G good. After my practice team's' second Cagematch (Feb. 8 2001), Michael Delaney came backstage and said "Hey, guys, that was a good Harold" and it made me so happy that I just smiled NOW. I don't remember any jokes from the show, just that I felt capital G good after.

It's a long time before you look up from your studies and remember your own opinions. Remember the things you think are funny. It's a necessary phase to learn to say NO again after so desperately trying to say YES to everything.

It's weird. Also, it annoys all our friends and all of the show vanish.

SEPTEMBER 3RD, 2012 at 11:27PM

Q: IS UCB/IMPROV A CULT?

Anonymous asked: I sometimes wonder if (UCB) Improv is a cult. What do you think? I think there are cultish aspects, but one aspect where it doesn't apply is providing skills that can ONLY be used in a cult. Like, improv training is also Good Adult training: listening, responding truthfully but kindly, supporting ideas...

It is a cult except that you can leave at any time and no one will try to stop you.

SEPTEMBER 4TH, 2012 at 10:32PM

Q: IS UCB TRYING TO BE MORE DIVERSE?

Anonymous asked: It is my understanding that UCB has been active trying to diversify its community & stage but the question keeps poking me—is that merely a formality? Diversity is about variety but the only thing I notice are more people of color or more gay guys making the same jokes & writing the same kinda of solo shows—lots of jokes about scratching nuts and Star Wars. Isn't that sort of like straight-white-male-washing it all? Wouldn't it be more diverse if UCB celebrated difference comedic voices?

I don't agree with your tacit assumption that all the shows are the same. Nor that all the jokes are the same. I just got back from Harold Night, and The Pox' ambitious second beats full of physicality and space bending felt very different from Johnny Romances' slow patient human first beats. Liked 'em both. My sketch show with Neil Casey is super different than the very cool This is Not A Sketch Show by Messers. Moskovciack and Stadler. Doppelganger's improv is way different than The Stepfathers and The Law Firm is different than both of those! YOU HAVE A PRECONCEIVED NOTION AND YOU ARE GATHERING EVIDENCE TO SUPPORT IT IN YOUR BRAIN, ANONYMOUS!

To answer a different question about the same topic: is it worth it to consciously try and change demographics in a community? And to that I honestly say: I'm not sure. It FEELS just and right to do, and we're trying to do it so we can just see what the community produces when it's not all white dudes and then we'll just say "well, that feels like it worked" or we won't. It already feels somewhat different to me and I am INTERESTED.

I haven't seen a Star Wars joke in some time. Ninja Turtles and Duck Tales are still all over the place though.

Scratching nuts is funny.

SEPTEMBER 5TH, 2012 at 11:27AM

INITIATION ETIQUETTE

...is extremely important to teach in the first three levels of improv. I think the simple and pragmatic step of letting students know they have a lot of time when they step out would improve the happiness and confidence of early classes an enormous amount, and prevent the "sameness" of initiations you often get in third and fourth-level classes.

Main point: **Teachers should make it clear that when someone steps out, her/his scene partner should grant a generous amount of time for the initiation to finish.**

As I watch improv levels 1 and 2—the a large portion of questions from students are in the category of "what is fair?"

- "can i just say what the place is if I didn't do the first line?"
- "am i allowed to edit a scene i'm in?"
- "if this person doesn't understand my idea and they get it 'wrong' what do i do?"

They are understandably asking about the general sense of boundary and decorum in playing together.

Teachers know these rules are very grey and that you ultimately have to be able to roll with anything. Long initiations that go as planned; early reactions that change everything; a place being named much later in the scene which changes the context dramatically. Everything can work. Treat it as a gift.

So the teachers often say that anything is right, and you have to accept everything.

BUT I think in the early levels it's fair to expect a generous amount of patience from each other as players, and the teacher should enforce a sense of etiquette towards each other especially at the top of scenes. Let people take a moment to gather their thoughts, let it be more verbose than it will be once people have more practice.

It's one of the main things students comment on when asked if they enjoyed a particular class—if they feel they were heard and understood by their scene partners.

SEPTEMBER 5TH, 2012 at 2:17PM

Q: CODDLING TIMID PLAYERS?

boshtunes asked: I can understand how encouraging initiation etiquette harbors a nurturing early class setting, but I worry that it would teach more timid players that it's okay to step into a scene cautiously instead of being confident with their initiations. As a student, something that always made me feel more free in class was seeing my classmates do something ballsy and awesome—it changed the feel of the room. At what point would you start wanting students to step off the back line with an initiation?

I am sympathetic to this worry and I considered that as I was teaching but from my observations it doesn't happen. The opposite happens. Once someone knows they have time, they get more decisive and bold. Note that I said this is for early levels: one and two the most and a bit for level three. Watch an early class: there are always three or four bulldogs who interrupt and make big choices and who do not wait. If the teacher lets them get away with that, even in the name of "you have to be decisive!" then you are breeding a bunch of loud obnoxious HURRY UP AND GET IT ALL OUT IN ONE LINE improvisers who are the people that are ruining the reputation of my art form.

SEPTEMBER 9TH, 2012 at 1:07AM

Q: WHY NOT RHYME?

Anonymous asked: I'm confused by musical improv at UCB. I recently heard that UCB's musical improv classes don't focus on rhyming at all. Why? Part of the cleverness of musical improv to me has always been using a song format and rhyming on the spot. I wouldn't like watching improvised rap if it was just sentences that were said fast. And when I watch musical improv without the rhymes and, a lot of times, without the vocal musicality I sit there wondering why make the scene a musical scene at all.

Be smarter?

SEPTEMBER 9TH, 2012 at 9:15AM

REMEMBER, DON'T INVENT

Improv works better when we talk about the past.

When an improviser says to another in a scene "Hey are you going to the game tomorrow?" the response is invariably uncertain and often disagreeable. "I'm not sure, I don't know, maybe."

But when an improviser says to another "Hey, did you go to the game yesterday?" the other person almost always just says "Yes."

EDITED AFTER A TEXT EXCHANGE WITH CHRIS GETHARD:
It's wrong to say "speak about the past" because that can lead to inactive scenes where we're talking about stuff that isn't on the stage now. What I'm talking about in this post is just something I've noticed during recent classes. When students make choices about their characters' pasts, everyone agrees. And when students make choices about their characters' futures, people tend to quibble and refuse to sign off.

I don't actually think it's better to talk about the past vs. the future. It doesn't matter. BUT I DO think it's true that students for some reason have an easier time agreeing on the fictional pasts of their characters.

Ok, the examples I gave ("Hey, are you going to the game tomorrow?" and "Hey, did you go to the game yesterday?")—I deliberately put them as questions, because a lot of questions are really just half-hearted offers. They are things that the asker wishes to be true, but they're having a moment of indecisiveness or uncertainty, or maybe there's another cause, and so they put it as a question. I believe that usually it's good to say "yes" to these types of questions.

But if the student poses a question about the future, they are often met with quibbling, adjusting, qualifications. And if the student poses it about the past, they are met with a quick, unqualified "yes."

I think that's interesting! Gethard speculated that "People instinctively want to control their destinies, even as characters."

So I saying, upon further reflection, is NOTICE that improvisers have an easier time agreeing on their fictional pasts, and try to have that same attitude of agreement about everything your partner says.

Hello. Yeah. Yep. Hi.

SEPTEMBER 10TH, 2012 at 10:24AM

Q: IMPROV A ROAD TO NOWHERE?

Anonymous asked: Is improv a road to nowhere? Neil Casey is arguably the best improviser in New York City, and he's genius performer with an incredible character range. But what ended up getting him his break? I'm guessing the packet of excellent written material he submitted, not his latest Roo Roo or 2-man movie show. So should one admit to themselves that as fun and enticing as improv is, if your ultimate goal is to achieve something like Neil, that improv should not be your main commitment?

(Neil Casey texted me this response to this thread: "I heard you got a job as a choreographer. Do you regret having spent so much time dancing?")

As a man with almost no commercial success, it is hard for me to answer this but I find myself with an multipart opinion anyway so here it is:

I think a career in improv has seriously diminishing returns for stuff that translates into a paying job. At first, it can connect you to a network of like-minded people, and help you develop your voice and your confidence. And then after some amount of time, you've met the people you're going to meet and your voice is as developed as it's going to and you should get rid of all that time you're spending in rehearsal and write your own stuff.

But I find that life isn't so clean as all that. You don't know which of your day's activities is going to flower forth into a huge part of your life later. When Neil started improv, he was a 20 year old University of Delaware commuting up to NYC to take classes with his friend Joe Wengert and he loved it for its own sake. It clicked with him and he followed the joy and love he felt for it. He met friends he liked (including me) and was happy spending his days doing it. I highly doubt he was directly motivated by the idea of a possible writing job, except in an abstract "maybe someday" sense. He was motivated by the idea of doing a better Harold, a better sketch show THAT DAY.

I think Neil DID—I mean, I'm really kind of guessing—it sounds like you should ask him. Maybe I will ask him. But anyway at some point Neil did decide he was not spending enough time on his own career. He walked over to my desk in October of 2010 and proposed we write a sketch show, which we did. This spring, he talked to friends about getting representation, which he got. He started submitting to shows via his friends.

But road to nowhere? Neil wouldn't have been able to get representation without years of being awesome in front of hundreds of people. Directing sketch shows for years, impressing dozens and dozens of the best writers and actors with his acumen.

What got him his break? He didn't have a Harvard Lampoon background, or a starring role in a Groundlings show or a part on the Second City main-stage. He had a decade's worth of friends at the UCB Theatre in NY, at a time when that theatre coincidentally was becoming more and more nationally prominent, who unanimously pointed at him and said "he's good."

It was partly improv, but it was more an adult life spent following his nature and not worrying about how far up the mountain he was.

When he was 20, riding up from Delaware, SNL was not on his mind. He was thinking "I hope I have fun in this 11pm Owen Burke improv class show in which I dress up like a superhero for an hour."

When he was 27 and he agreed to direct Stone Cold Fox (a house sketch team at UCBT) he wasn't thinking "I bet a number of these people will work for SNL someday," he was thinking "I love sketch, this seems fun, we're going to make a fun show." And then they were the fucking best team at the theatre.

Two-Man Movie started because Anthony Atamanuik and Neil—one of them was co-teaching a class on improvising movies and they demonstrated for their class the form by doing a set by themselves. And that felt good enough that they did a one-time fill-in show at UCB Chelsea. And THAT was good enough that it became a frequent fill-in show. And then UCB East opened up and they got a regular show. At no point was there any real look to the future. Just: what is fun today based on what happened before. Yes, and.

If something is fun and enticing, you are victorious. You should keep doing that. If you're a zombie and going through the motions it's time to move on.

If he never got a job, and now I can speak from experience, then he'd only have a life spent being happy behind him.

Road to nowhere! Good heavens. I mean, ALL ROADS LEAD NOWHERE. Try not to think about that. Spend your days in love with what you're doing as much as fucking possible and thank the stars for your chances to do that. Be nice and honest and brave and hopeful and then let it go. The improv stages of Chicago and NYC and LA and elsewhere are filled with super talented people on roads to nowhere! I am one of those people! But I'm not in a cubicle giving my precious breath to a dumb company which I could give a shit about and so that's what I've got.

MORE YES MORE I'm going to be redundant: the packet is what got him attention at SNL. But also doing ASSSSCAT with Seth Meyers, directing an improv group which contained his future manager, his time on Roo Roo talking to Curtis Gwinn and John Gemberling and everyone else about what opportunities exist—visualizing and picturing how it might go down, and of course 10 years of making up funny things so that when he sat down in July to write his packet in three frenzied days it was good. He included a sketch he wrote for the show with me, and that happened because he took an improv class with me in Two Thousand and Fucking One! He's sharing an office today with Bobby Moynihan whom he probably met in the back of

McManus in 2002 deciding which Harold Teams would be which member of Star Trek The Next Generation or something like that.

Hi. It's a fair question, I don't really know how to answer it. I turned 42 last Monday and have had the craziest year of my entire life.

SEPTEMBER 10TH, 2012 at 10:56AM

Q: SHOULD I HAVE SKIPPED CLASS?

Anonymous asked: I missed an improv class. But it was for pursuit of true love. Did I make the right choice in skipping class?

Yep.

SEPTEMBER 10TH, 2012 at 3:09PM

Q: EXERCISES FOR EMPATHY?

Anonymous asked: In an earlier post you mentioned that a good skill for an improviser to have is empathy. Can you think of or have you done any exercises that work this empathy muscle?

Two people up. Someone initiates an accusation against the other person. Other person agrees to it and justifies it, by which I mean has a reason for doing what he/she is accused of.

Another one, that I think Amy Poehler used to have people do (and I imagine she got from Chicago). Everyone walk around the room taking turns saying true facts about themselves. "I am six feet tall" "I am from Ohio." Then on the teacher's cue you switch to saying true opinions that you have. "I think the Republicans are dumber than ever." "I think television is a terrific medium." Then for the third round, on the teacher's cue, you say opinions that you do NOT have but that you could imagine someone having—and it should sound just like round two. You don't telegraph that you don't agree. "I think gay people should not be allowed to marry." "I think that war is a necessary evil and is ultimately a good thing."

SEPTEMBER 10TH, 2012 at 3:15PM

FOLLOW-UP TO "ROAD TO NOWHERE"

It's not a dumb question to ask if improv is financially viable. I'm sorry I was so dramatic in my response. A more concise version:

1. In Neil's case, improv was not a road to nowhere. It was part of his life, which consisted of improv and a lot more, done one step at a time for happiness first and then eventually led to opportunities, almost all born out of things that were at one time NOT done for opportunities' sake. In my opinion. I am not Neil Casey, who is a human being who is still alive and has his own view of this. Still.

2. Improv does have diminishing returns in terms of what leads to a paying job and it can be a rut if you are no longer enjoying it, etc. No shame if that's true.

3. Things aren't so black and white. It's not like a ONE or ZERO: IMPROV or NO IMPROV. You can quit a practice group, but come back in a year and take a workshop. Your friends or WEIRD ANALOGOUS VERSIONS OF THEM will be around. I've advised people to quit their indie groups and write stuff, sometimes. But then those people get asked to audition for a house team and I say "do it" because why not?

You know if you're stuck or bored. If you are, change it up.

SEPTEMBER 11TH, 2012 at 6:47AM

Q: LA IMPROV SCENE?

Anonymous asked: What are your thoughts on the improv scene out in LA? I think Quartet, Dr. God and Delicious Moments could match up with any show in Chi or NY.

Don't know them but I would imagine every city with an improv scene of decent size has amazing improv going on within it. It's fun to generalize cities down to little personalities ("Chicago is ARTFUL; New York is FAST" etc) but I think that always falls apart when you get down to specific groups. It's not a competition, not least because almost no one is paying attention to this.

SEPTEMBER 14TH, 2012 at 1:39PM

Q: TMBG LYRIC?

hellyesbrandon asked: If you had to summarize your approach to improv with a They Might Be Giants lyric or song title, what would be it? (I will allow for one Flansburgh and one Linnell lyric/song if necessary)

Thank you for asking this question.

Linnell: Every jumbled pile of person has a thinking part that watches what the part that isn't thinking isn't thinking of.

Flansburgh: I've got my house surrounded. I know I'm in there. Come out with both my hands up and don't make me come in and get me.

SEPTEMBER 17TH, 2012 at 10:35PM

Q: PET PEEVES?

Anonymous asked: Any pet peeves that young improvisers do that bother the hell out of you? (so we can avoid)

1. High fiving.
2. Jenkins, Timmy, Janice and the Johnson report.
3. Things going wrong in the second line.
4. Being scared (like as an actor, being scared to do things, though I understand it and still am scared myself)
5. "That's the last time I get something/one off of Craigslist!"
6. "Wow, that's not what it said on your dating profile!"
7. "It's my first day!"
8. "You don't look like you mean it."
9. Parodies of: American Idol, the Real World, an audition room, anything.
10. "Guys, we need a new idea for [whatever]."
11. "You're a terrible roommate!"
12. Improv vets making lists of pet peeves like they've got it figured out, which I don't. But I mean, oh, well, you asked.

SEPTEMBER 17TH, 2012 at 10:38PM

Q: ONE LEADING, ANOTHER FOLLOWING?

Anonymous asked: I think a lot about two-person scenes, partly because they're usually the main metric by which we judge ability, and also because I think they're usually more elegant and intimate than group games. One thing I've noticed in these scenes is that there is usually an asymmetric relationship between the improvisers akin to the one between the Lead and the Follow in partner dancing, where the lead is whoever is wilder/worse at yes-ing/better at and-ing. Is this a valid way to think about improv?

Mixed message (on my part, in the following answer) alert: I think you're parsing things too finely, and that all scenes are group games even when only two members of the group are off the back line. But I like the dancing metaphor and agree that a lead-follow thing is constantly going on in all improv scenes. And even though I think you're doing an unproductive categorization of scenes as "two person" vs. "group" I do love this sort of theorizing and making formulas out of things. It's fun. I think something more fun to think about is counting the points of view in a scene. Regardless of how many characters are in the scene, how many opinions total? I've actually never thought about it this way before, but at the moment I feel like you can't have more than THREE points of view in any one scene, and even that many is assuming one of them is a just a brief recurring sub game (like Eric Idle saying "a pointed stick?" in that Monty Python sketch about self-defence which was not improvised but I mean, whatever). Regardless of how many actors, it's the differing points of view that are the axes of the jokes, I think.

SEPTEMBER 18TH, 2012 at 1:04PM

Q: POPULAR IMPROV NAMES?

sussybuckets asked: I don't think I've ever heard a single person name someone Janice in a scene, at least in class/coaching. Do you think

there are regional differences when it comes to popular improv scene-names? Like, once a name is out there in the air everyone in that city overuses it? Or do you think you just create a Janice-y vibe in class? Are you the architect of your own misery? In case you're wondering, my biggest improv pet peeves are shitty gifts and shitty vacations.

Hi Sussy. I miss you around here.

That's genuinely interesting to me that you don't hear "Janice" that much. You know my old Harold team named itself Janice for a while after we used that name like 6 times in a show. So maybe I just give more weight to the times I hear it. But no, I'm sure of it: the improv classes/practices I see have people giving the name "Janice" more often than almost any other female name. Maybe that is a regional difference. Do you notice a preponderance of any specifics—not counting pop culture. Like types of jobs or cars or even cities. I don't know.

I am likely the architect of my own misery, but that seems beyond the scope of this document.

Shitty gifts and shitty vacations: I'm not specifically sure what you mean, but any possible example I can think of I agree with you.

SEPTEMBER 18TH, 2012 at 1:31PM

Q: WHY DON'T YOU CALL OUT NOAH FORMAN?

mymotherwasright asked: 100% serious: Noah Forman names characters Janice ALL THE TIME. WHY DO YOU REFUSE TO CALL NOAH OUT FOR THIS, WILL HINES?

When he was in 301, Noah Forman sacrificed a goat to the ancient albeit minor demon Azazel, asking the dark (minor) lord to grace Noah with a magic protection against any coach criticizing his name choices. Many a coach and teacher in the UCB-NY community has privately lamented on their inability to note Noah on his terrible choice of names. I report that the experience is strange. You sit there, and hear him say "Janice" and want very badly to say something, but you find your mouth simply refusing to move, as if for that moment that you are trapped in paralyzed body able only to observe. Then your mind moves on to a new thought and lo and behold you are able to speak. Our hope is one day that his contract with Azazel ends, and we coaches/teachers will all descend on Noah at once and chide him for his choices with tremendous venom and a thick air of condescension.

SEPTEMBER 18TH, 2012 at 8:27PM

THANK YOU

To two entities:

1. All the nice people who have said nice things about my "All Roads Lead Nowhere" post, which is a surprisingly cynical viewpoint to get so many nice things. Nonetheless, thanks.

2. Also someone sent me an anonymous message to this tumblr which was terribly nice and I appreciate it.

SEPTEMBER 22ND, 2012 at 7:10AM

QUOTE

Any community that gets its laughs by pretending to be idiots will eventually be flooded by actual idiots who mistakenly believe that they're in good company.— Anonymous

SEPTEMBER 24TH, 2012 at 12:58PM

Q: FAVORITE PART OF PLAYING WITH CONVOY?

coreybrown asked: What was your favorite part about performing with Convoy?

That they asked? And that they were so friendly and trusting? Fernie sent me an email. Fasen did bits about it on Twitter. We hung out backstage for a bit before the show and then had a great time.

SEPTEMBER 24TH, 2012 at 2:22PM

Q: LEAST FAVORITE PART OF PLAYING WITH CONVOY?

ferniecommaalex asked: What was your least favorite part about performing with Convoy?

Having to tacitly admit by taking the stage that I at least somewhat approved of the improv of Alex Fernie. Who is this, by the way?

SEPTEMBER 30TH, 2012 at 10:25AM

Q: WHEN TO SUPPORT?

Anonymous asked: It's hard for me to feel like I know how to support a piece. Whether it's a montage or a Harold, when I'm on the sidelines, I'm never sure when to edit or when a scene might need a walk on, help from the sides, etc. I worry that if I make a move it'll change rather than build on what the scene is already doing, and I worry it'll be stealing focus from other players. Do you have any tips on how I can work on that?

Trouble is, there's no hard and fast rules. It sounds like you're in your head, though, so you need to get out of that. I'd be quick to walk-on, but hesitant to tag-out. Edit when you feel your body naturally move forward—follow your foot. When you've done it "right" your partners will smile and get more energized because you've helped push the scene how they were hoping it would go. Allow yourself to screw up, you'll get a feel for it.

SEPTEMBER 30TH, 2012 at 8:00PM

THE MUSIC, NOT THE LYRICS

How you say it matters more than what you say, in terms of your partner understanding you more quickly.

OCTOBER 4TH, 2012 at 3:00PM

Q: ONE PERSON I DISLIKE?

Anonymous asked: What do you do when you are on a team you love to perform with, but there's one member you dislike? He mows over games and offers with spite. He critiques other team members and he does passive aggressive, catty things towards everyone except the team leader, whom he kisses up to. I've tried to bond with him but he's unresponsive. Everyone else supports one another and eventually he'll likely get the boot. In the meantime, how do I make the best of being onstage with a mean-spirited improviser?

A tough question which I appreciate you asking very candidly. I don't know for sure but here are some contradictory reactions.

FIRST: everyone deserves to play with people they like and the best teams tend to like each other. As you advance in your "career" you will have more and more say and you should try to play with people who are good to you and you are good to, both on and off stage.

Now, some major caveats:

1. EVERY TEAM, CERTAINLY EVERY GOOD TEAM, HAS A DIFFICULT PERSON. Someone who breaks improv rules, who shows up late, who loses his/her temper after shows too much, who wants the team to do something even though he/she is the main culprit of NOT doing that thing. To some degree, if the shows are decent, you have to live with this. If you kick off your difficult person, you will then notice someone new being difficult. So make sure this isn't the case you're noticing here.

2. TALK TO HIM, ONE ON ONE. People deserve a chance to change their behavior. Behind the back bitching festers. I think the high road is to have a one on one talk with this person where you gently bring up a specific thing that bothered you. I think on-stage stuff is easier than off-stage stuff. Giving notes is wrong, but a particular incident that is bothering you—you can bring that up in private. Tell him it's been bothering you and that you need to talk about it. Don't make a showdown out of it. This can establish trust. Improvisers are like drunks: they respond

in the same tone of voice they are spoken to. So speak concisely and respectfully and he'll likely answer that way. You will feel better. "I need to talk to you. This thing you did in a show really bothered me and I've been stewing about and I wanted to tell you rather than let it grow in my head. I really don't like it when your characters literally scoff in the second line. I can't let it go." Notice that you're not telling him to stop, you're telling him it bothers you. See what he does with that.

If he's still a dick, then you'll have a chance at some point to get away from him—he'll get cut or you'll get moved. It'll happen.

I don't know. It's tricky. This is a sub-culture of weirdos. The more you can live with, you more improv you will be able to do.

I'd be curious for other opinions. This is one I've gotten bitten on both ways.

OCTOBER 8TH, 2012 at 7:52AM

Q: GUM CHEWING?

Anonymous asked: What's the general consensus on gum chewing during an improv set? Bad manners, or no big deal?

It's no more disrespectful than a violinist playing paddle-ball during a concert. By which I mean it's dumb, though I've done it (chewing gum, not paddle-ball or violin).

OCTOBER 8TH, 2012 at 7:56AM

Q: NOTHING IS FUN.

Anonymous asked: you're in a scene and you're in your head. nothing is fun and nothing is easy. you feel stuck. what do you do?

Walk off stage and take a deep breath. Try to feel supportive healthy dynamics around you, like maybe dinner with good friends. Pick a place with some style but not too pricey—like that Chinese restaurant on 9th Avenue. While there, be vulnerable and earnest in conversation. Be responsible and own up to things you've done wrong. Be generous in your praise. Establish an emotional connection with these people whom you may take for granted. Go on an internal mental journey that re-awakens dormant parts of your personality, like the athletic confidence you had for just six month in high school when you thought about joining the swim team, or the ten months in college you got really into Graham Greene. Plan a four-day trip to somewhere extravagant: Vancouver? Iceland? New Orleans? Write letters to your oldest relative, then your youngest friend. Find a job in another city. Move there. Walk to public transportation each morning holding a hot cup of coffee. Read old books. Fall in love. Make a family. Create a dynasty. Don't look back.

OCTOBER 8TH, 2012 at 8:15AM

Q: JUSTCRAIG: IS SUE GALLOWAY UPSET?

justcraig asked: You failed to respond last time I posed the question, but when I fart on the back line is Sue Galloway pretending to be upset, or is it genuine.

If she's miming that she's wearing enormous high heels, then yes, she's upset.

OCTOBER 9TH, 2012 at 11:03AM

Q: NOT EMOTIONAL PERSON

Anonymous asked: We're often advised to respond to initiations with a "big emotional choice." I'm not a very emotional person. I once copied down a list of human emotions from wikipedia in an attempt to learn them. For some reason, the only emotions that come easily are mad, flirty, jealous and proud. Are these emotions enough? I generally try to respond to initiations by just being pleasant and adding some more grounding information. Is that a waste of everybody's time? Is emotion the core of good improv?

Not every scene needs a big emotional choice, but an improviser should be able to easily make emotional choices and be affected in emotional ways.

Mad, flirty, jealous and proud are not enough. That's really only two: mad, jealous and proud are from the same family of defensive angry "yang" emotions and "flirty" is a sweet "yin" one. Though maybe you're doing it in an aggressive demanding "yang" way which means you're basically only doing ONE emotion. Whatever, not enough.

Speaking as someone for whom acting does not feel natural, a trick to making an emotional choice is just to make it internally. Like just really BE there and don't worry what it looks like—the audience will pick up that you changed internally. You can tell that a soft-spoken person is filled with rage just from the curl of a lip. Also, the audience knows what you are feeling before you do so be honest with yourself about what you feel like in a moment and try to use that if you can.

Take a Meisner-inspired acting course.

Emotion is not the core of good improv. Listening, reacting, commitment, and truth are the core of good improv. Emotion is just a frequent tool. If improv were basketball, comedy is scoring baskets, listening/reacting is dribbling and passing. Emotional choices are... I don't know, emotional choice is the ability to pass more than five feet? Like you don't technically need it but anyone who plays a lot does it without thinking and it happens all the time so just be comfortable and good at it.

Metaphors fall apart a lot, I find. There's something to be said for just answering these questions rapidly and then again, maybe I should think twice, just once, before I answer these.

OCTOBER 12TH, 2012 at 6:36AM

Q: CAN YOU TELL IF SOMEONE WILL NEVER BE GOOD?

Anonymous asked: Hey Will, I'm wondering if there's ever a point in early improv training where you can tell that a student could be really good at improv or will never be really good at improv, and if yes, what kind of early-on improv behaviors you associate with each.

You can't tell early. I mean, you can tell if someone is already good. But

I've seen a lot of people fundamentally transform from where they were at in their first year of studying to some time later. I count myself in that group, and Kevin Hines, and Alan Starzinski, and .... I mean even really great people like Neil Casey took quantum leaps UP after a certain amount of time. Jocelyn DeBoer was always good but at some point leapt up in quality to become the scary improv ninja she is now. Never lock your impression of anyone or write anyone off. Perspiration beats inspiration and all that. It's who loves it more, who works at it more—that is a greater indication of future success.

OCTOBER 15TH, 2012 at 7:28AM

Q: FINISHING MOVE?

dwmurray asked: If you were a character in an improv fighting game, what would your finishing move be?

I think mine would unfortunately be a dry remark wrapped in a withering glance! Anyone else like to guess what theirs would be?

OCTOBER 15TH, 2012 at 7:30AM

Q: NOTES AFTER SHOWS

Anonymous asked: My team coach has a very busy schedule and cannot attend our regular shows. Any thoughts on getting notes from a coach who has seen your set only on video? And getting notes via email 1 to 2 days after the show? I'm uncomfortable with it. HOWEVER, since the majority of my team is into it, I have to go with the flow, right?

I'd go with the flow if only because going with the flow is a good skill to have as a Good Improv Citizen. I mean, you should (and it sounds like, did) express yourself, but go with the group. A coach who sees your practices a lot can still see a lot. If you find someone who can be even MORE devoted later you can switch. See how it goes. Find it on its feet.

OCTOBER 15TH, 2012 at 7:36AM

Q: I'M NOT STANDING OUT

Anonymous asked: I just know I'm not standing out. I think I do pretty well in my classes (UCB or otherwise) and I am out doing or seeing shows pretty frequently, but I can just feel like I am not making much of an impression on people. What else could I be doing? Am I focusing on the wrong things to begin with? Does any of this crap even really matter? I should probably just go read a book or something.

I felt like this a lot for my first few years. Scattered advice follows:

1. Except for the very talented, almost everyone is ignored by default. Realize that on the nights you are feeling unnoticed, that almost everyone is also feeling that way. It's not as urgent as you think.

2. Economy of words and movement. Newer performers spread their energy out over three long sentences instead of one punchy sentence. Or they move aimlessly instead of of decisively.

3. Switch tactics often. On some nights, focus on being yourself. On another, try playing a character filled a very not-you energy. On others, initiate with a premise. On another, start with just the tip of an iceberg. On one night, have a big meal before the show. On another, go in hungry. Pretend that someone you are desperately hoping to impress is in the audience, or maybe that your best friends who you know love you are there. When you do shows, try pretending that your team are all strangers—see if that makes you sharper. Or try pretending that it is an improv class in which you felt particularly strong. Maybe tell yourself right before the show that your number one priority is to "be playful." Find a friend's three year old and see if you can hold his/her attention with a story—notice how broad and simple your manner is in that moment. Mind games are a big part of this thing.

4. Getting out of your head will help. Ask around for a coach who is good at this. It's a particular skill to create a practice like that and not everyone can do it.

5. Maybe try a different improv school, teacher, style. Musical improv? Storytelling?
6. Take an acting class, something that makes you bring in a monologue and deliver it. Just trying it will boost your confidence.
7. When in doubt, throw it all away and just tell yourself "listen and react" and see what happens.

Repeat for three years.

OCTOBER 15TH, 2012 at 7:38AM

Q: DO IMPROVISERS MAKE TERRIFIC LIARS?

brennanleemulligan asked: Hi Will! I hope all is well with you! I was having a conversation with an old pal from college, and he suggested that improvisers make terrific liars, what with all the quick invention we do in scene work. I tried to explain that we use our powers for good, not evil, and our training emphasizes honesty. I then theorized that improvisers might be great at spotting liars, due to active listening/first unusual thing noticing. Do you think improvisers make good liars, or good lie-detectors?

I think this is such an interesting question that any valid attempt to answer will make it less interesting. I'll say that good improv contains within it mind reading and minor telekinesis.

OCTOBER 15TH, 2012 at 10:16AM

Q: MISSING THE SENSE OF "HOW DID THEY DO THAT?"

probablysean asked: The first time I saw improv, I was overwhelmed with the sense of "HOW DID THEY DO THAT???" and pretty much felt that way for at least the first few months of seeing good shows.

Nowadays, it's pretty rare, but it happens. I'm only in my second year of doing this and it's already so rare. Do you still get that "HOW DID THEY DO THAT???" feeling? Or does that just go away completely?

Yep, though it's rare. Last two times was watching a show called Improv Nerds (not sure if you're a NYC person or not) do a set with transitions and callbacks so simultaneous that it felt scripted. 4Square style fluid transitions: very awesomely done.

Joe Wengert doing BatmanProv in the DCM this past June made me laugh like I have not laughed in some time.

Most improv I watch is in classes and I've seen a few scenes that have been impressively awesome: an old west shootout where they thank each other for skin products; three women stranded on an island in which 2 of them keep making cool crafts; there was some X-Men parody (sorry) that I really liked but I can't remember the hook. I've been into overt premise stuff lately, but that's just where I'm at.

OCTOBER 15TH, 2012 at 10:17AM

Q: WHY 3 YEARS TO GET GOOD?

Anonymous asked: I think you said it takes ~3 years (of hard work) to get not bad at improv, correct? I have to agree completely, but I am wondering how you arrived at that number? Is it just your experience, or have you watched others move at that pace?

I heard Michael Delaney tell it to someone at a party in 2000 and just held on to it as a plausible sounding answer. The real answer is "a doable but not easy amount of time."

OCTOBER 17TH, 2012 at 6:10AM

Q: HAVE WE SEEN IT ALL?

andrewyg asked: Hey Will, there's a term in chess called "going off the book" I heard from a Radiolab episode called "games". It's the moment in a chess game when a move is made that hasn't been made in the history of recorded chess games. I know thinking about improv scenes the same way isn't ground breaking. But, I thought the parallel was fun to consider. I know we've all done a million roommate, cop, firing/hiring, etc. scenes, but going "off the book" seems like the fun part to me. Thoughts?

I loved that episode and that concept—going off book. I think it does apply to improv in exactly the way you're describing. You see a setup/framework/context/base reality you've seen a million times, but then something happens that you've never seen before. I guess the trick is it still has to somehow fit what's happened. It can't feel forced or invented solely from one player's head.

First example I think of is from ten million years ago in 2000 during one of Mother's Harolds.

Jon Daly stepped up to Stephan Bekiranov (references in this post are now officially so old that they are themselves 'off-book') and said "Dad, I'm changing my name."

Stephan said "Well, Bill, what are you changing it to?"

And Jon paused a very little bit then said "Dave."

Stephan was surprised and waited.

Then Jon said "You thought I was going to say something crazy."

And that was incredibly hilarious to me. I don't think that's what Jon planned. He felt something in the moment and went that way. It felt right. It also surprised me. Haven't seen that since.

OCTOBER 18TH, 2012 at 12:43PM

Q: WHAT TEAMS WOULD YOU BRING BACK?

Anonymous asked: If you could bring one former Harold team back for one night only, which would you pick and why?

Dillinger, fwand, Swarm (i'd rank it higher but I saw a ton when they existed), Bangs.

OCTOBER 18TH, 2012 at 12:44PM

Q: WORST ADVICE?

Anonymous asked: What's the biggest piece of improv nonsense you've ever heard, IE, the worst advice?

"Let's just have fun out there tonight."

OCTOBER 23RD, 2012 at 1:46PM

Q: HONESTY THE BEST POLICY?

Anonymous asked: As a beginning improviser (almost one year), I often hear "Just be honest and real." But, sometimes, when I'm really honest in a scene, I feel like I'm a huge bummer, or that I upset/freak people out. I'm not trying to be a creep. Is honesty always the best policy in improv?

More often than not, yes. "Live life onstage" is a way to put it. Talk about things how you would in real life, react how you would react.

But you also need to make "active choices" to move the scene forward. That's the trick. You must be honest but also move things forward.

So: a character says something to you which in real life would make you be silent and look for the first opportunity to end the conversation. Or would make you call the police. You need to find the part of yourself that would engage with this person so that you are still being yourself but also moving it forward.

You either have or will do many crazy and irrational things in your life. Choosing to be invested in the situation will help you make active choices. What if the person talking to you was someone you had a crush on? Someone you looked up to? Someone you felt responsible for? There is more than one honest choice—make the fun one.

ADDENDUM: You worry about being a bummer. Being a bummer isn't bad, as long as you're not making the scene passive. Can you be a bummer in a way that provokes a reaction from your scene partner? Or in a way that makes you able to participate in whatever is going on? Or in a way that makes it so your character gives more a shit? You can bring up cynical philosophies as long as you are being someone who acts on them.

OCTOBER 23RD, 2012 at 3:39PM

Q: WHY NOT "HAVE FUN OUT THERE?"

Anonymous asked: You said that "Let's just go out there and have fun" was a the most nonsensical piece of advice you received. Isn't that a part of improv? Having fun, enjoying yourself, enjoying the moment on stage? Are you casting aside that aspect of improv?

No. But in my experience, when you're backstage and about to go on, and someone on your team says "let's just have fun out there," what follows is a bunch of people not listening or reacting and kinda just making a lot of noise. The urge to take the pressure off of your show is understandable and good, but saying "let's just have fun" doesn't work. Maybe "let's not worry about game—let's just react and make big choices." That could work. But you can't ignore stuff. You have to react to everything. Even if you fight and act dumb, if you're reacting (and therefore cooperating, in some sense) it can work. "Let's just have fun" a lot of times means everyone in his/her own bubble jerking off. And yes, everyone in a bubble jerking off COULD be a good improv scene.

OCTOBER 27TH, 2012 at 5:56PM

Q: IAN'S "WORST YES-AND I'VE EVER SEEN"

Anonymous asked: On the Nerdist Writer's Panel episode with the Key and Peele staff, Charlie Sanders says that he first met Ian Roberts when he took a class with Ian and Ian said that Charlie did "the worst 'yes, and' I've ever seen." do you know this story? Do you what specifically Charlie did? I can't stop wondering. Thanks.

From Charlie:

I had actually met Ian before because I interned at Assscat. But, this class was the first time I had been in a class of his. We were doing a yes and exercise... And the person said something like "I got the car for the party tonight." And I said something like "Oh I'm not going." And Ian stopped the scene and said something like "Stop. Okay, that was probably the worst yes and I've ever seen." This was level 4-ish by the way. It was funny.

OCTOBER 29TH, 2012 at 1:38PM

SOMETHING FOR ME

Teaching group games, I see at first everyone making choices that are too big. They're accustomed to doing two-person scenes, so they are used to adding big big choices and now that there's six or seven or eight people in, they don't need to do nearly as much. Okay, so that's to be expected.

But I noticed a particular type of choice that is prevalent during group games that is not as prevalent during two-person scenes. And that is the "what my deal is" choice. Someone declaring what their character's deal is. They're the mother of the main character, or they are a religious person, or they're a stoner, or something.

Like they're all in a football huddle and about one minute into the scene it's settling into being something about how they're all feeling sorry for the other team. But then someone pipes in, probably right in the middle of someone else's sentence and says "Guys, I'm the ref—you almost finished here?"

And whoever said that—his eyes had been glassy and unfocused until that moment, and only after he declares himself the "ref" does he seem to be listening to the scene. But if everyone declares something for himself the scene is too crowded with ideas and it seizes like a car engine flooded with too much gas.

I might be making too big a deal of this.

But once I noticed it, I started to visualize the students with imaginary fences around themselves, marking their territory. They are so mindful of having these fences, of labeling them. They feel they don't belong in the scene until they've paid the entrance fee of giving themselves a specific thing, generally very strange and exaggerated.

Even if a scene begins smoothly, the students will start to quibble and jostle and try to separate.

A scene: everyone is miming that they are in an assembly line. Someone says "Santa sure is working us hard this year," and then someone else says "Yeah! It's only August" and the teacher thinks *hey, this might be good* but then someone says "Hey, did you get the shoes?" and the other person says "No, I was waiting for you to finish with the toy trains" and then the first person says "Hey! I need you to get the shoes!"

You can see the fences going up, everyone separating themselves, via accusations, into different camps. *We can't move on*, they think, *until each of us has a job.*

This is MINE. That is YOURS.

We had something—something about a slave-driving Santa, but then we needed to assign jobs and so now we're fighting.

You might say "Well, it's the fighting that's the problem" and that's true, but the root cause is this internal itch that the students feel "Oh my God, I need to say why I'm here."

On the first day of level 1 there's an exercise where you get 4 people up and you endow them with something they all have in common—"You all wrote a cookbook together" and then you the teacher interview them so they can practice agreeing on shared history. And the first move is almost always someone assigning individual jobs. "Well, I did the desserts, and he did the entrees, and he just did the salads."

Everyone wants to be part of a bank heist team, with specialties. No one's allowed to just be there for the same reason as someone else.

But group scenes work better if the characters are a **family of acrobats** with **matching costumes** and lots of things in common, not a **team of superheroes** with **separate back stories** and powers.

Fences, bubbles. Everyone drives down a highway alone in a big car when we should all be together in a bus.

Improv is continually teaching people to give up their ego, their individual definition. Find ways that you have things in common with what's already there. Let yourself be connected to the whole. Bend and change to fit. You are defined very much in terms of something else. We are all in one bubble. We are all the same.

NOVEMBER 2ND, 2012 at 6:21AM

Q: IMPROV ON VIDEO VS. JUST AUDIO?

stophittingyourself asked: The essence of improv is notoriously difficult to capture with video and film, though of course there have been notable successes, many of the videos on ucbcomedydotcom for example. But having just listened to your episode of Make Yourself Comfy with Abra Tabak about a dozen times during editing **I still find it re-listenable. Listening to Make Yourself Comfy doesn't leave me with that hollow, late-to-the-party feeling from which even good improv may suffer when experienced after the fact. Why?**

I don't know but that's reassuring to hear. Maybe radio improv is a way to record this magic for the masses.

NOVEMBER 2ND, 2012 at 6:30AM

Q: WHAT SHOULD I DO TO GET BETTER FOR ADVANCED STUDY?

Anonymous asked: So, I finished 401 a couple of months ago and I got rejected from Advanced Study but I want to get better. The notes my teacher gave me read: " I think you have great instincts and a solid understanding of the basics. Keep making more moves, since your ideas are usually correct and over time you'll get more adept and making every scene work." Is there a 410 class I should be on the lookout for or should I just retake 401? I love improv and your blog so any advice would be greatly appreciated.

For non-UCB readers, this person is asking about the individual notes that get mailed after someone takes improv 401. And how you have to apply at that point to get into advanced (post-401) classes and how if you get rejected you can take these 4-week courses we have that each have a focus: 410 (game), 411 (performance/range), 412 (listening/reacting).

Um, okay to your question. I mean, what do YOU think you need to work on? As a teacher and a guy who runs an improv school I'm torn on the issue of individual notes. They are important but flawed. Students cast aside all else, it seems, when given the chance to hear an INDIVIDUAL NOTE. But, like, those are notoriously unreliable. Even the most devoted and intuitive teacher has seen you go, what, 15 scenes? While dividing his/her attention among 15 others times whatever other classes he/she is teaching?

The notes we are most sure of are the ones we say over and over to everyone: "yes and" "commit" "start grounded" "if this then what" "top of your intelligence" "don't be coy" "take an idea from your opening" which of those do you need to work on? You have paid attention to yourself more than any teacher ever will.

Just to avoid copping out, it sounds to me from those notes that you are doing it basically right, but that it looks too rigid and tentative. That it needs to be more fluid and effortless. The quarter beat it takes you to process what is being said needs to be an eighth of a beat, your reactions need to come more instinctually and less from a place of "what SHOULD i do"—you need practice, reps. Don't think so much. Play, play, play. Get in touch with your honest and real reactions. Say what you really think. YOU. No class is gonna give that to you as much as doing this once a week on your own. But if you want to pick a class I'd go with 412 "listening and reacting" though the other two would be fine. Just try to play with a fluid swagger, fearless, a bit sloppy, let yourself be seen, warts and all.

I have no idea who you are or what your improv looks like.

NOVEMBER 2ND, 2012 at 2:58PM

Q: MINIMIZING "COMPARING MYSELF TO OTHERS?"

Anonymous asked: I feel like in 101 and 201 I was really good about not judging myself and not comparing myself to others, but since finishing 401 I've been doing it constantly (especially the "comparing myself to others" thing). I'll get anxious if players I love and respect seem to talk to other people in my classes/groups but not me, which I know is all total mental bullshit that's just psyching me out, but was wondering if you had any tips for minimizing it?

I don't except to say everyone goes through it, on and off, as long as you do anything at all related to performing or writing. So be strong and look for ways to focus on what is within your control. I'm not always able to do that (focus on what is within one's control) but it's a habit that gets easier.

NOVEMBER 3RD, 2012 at 12:18PM

Q: FAMILY TREE OF HOUSE TEAMS?

Anonymous asked: First of all, thank you for bringing the Podcast back. Secondly, in the inaugural episode with Tim Martin, UCB NY

house team pedigree was briefly discussed. Is there a "family tree" of house teams in existence? If so, do you know where to find it? I know there are pictures of the teams at the training center, but it would be neat to see it mapped out!

Not a family tree exactly but there's a pretty full list of Harold Teams at the UCB Theatre in NYC on the internet.

NOVEMBER 3RD, 2012 at 3:13PM

Q: BEST WAY TO LEAVE A GROUP?

Anonymous asked: Hey Will. I've been with my current group for a year and feel like it's not working out. What's the best way to gracefully leave a group? There are one or two people who I'd like to perform with outside of the group in a format different from what the group does. Would asking them put them in an awkward position? Could it potentially strain friendships?

I've never done it. My instinct is to be direct and concise. You're stepping out to make time for other things, and just to switch it up. When you do things with a subset of the group—don't make that a group right away, just do one-off things now and then and see how it feels before you make THAT a group. Maybe? DON'T send a ten page long email explaining how much the group has meant to you. See the scene in "Moneyball" when Brad Pitt explains how to tell someone he's been traded. You just tell them, no song and dance. CAVEAT: There are people who no longer speak to me.

NOVEMBER 15TH, 2012 at 2:18PM

Q: WHAT SHOULD COACH'S CHARGE?

Anonymous asked: There are coaches now in the indie scene that are charging 20-25/hour (even 30!). It seems like many of them don't care and are just phoning it in. They don't seem like they enjoy it, as though

they are just doing it for the rent money. Do you have any advice on this and did you ever have issues with this as a performer?

It's a free market, and they're allowed to offer what they want and you are free to say "no" based on their price or their ability. There's no hard rule.

But in general, if a coach is doing it ONLY for money they're probably bad and you shouldn't use them.

In the interest of not copping out, I will assign numbers to what I'm saying. But I do not coach often now, nor do I hire them. So I'm out of touch. But maybe these real numbers will shed some light on my perspective.

When I was coaching a lot (circa 2003? sheesh) I'd charge $50 for the whole 3-hour thing and that was standard. My Harold team paid $50 for three hours. Some coaches who had kids would charge $80 or $90 and we'd sometimes use them but not often.

Then around 2008 I started charging $60. Nowadays I'll charge $30 an hour but I don't coach very often. I try to earn it and bring some helpful perspective that someone might expect from me since I've been around. I try to keep them on their feet and have them enjoy it and also articulate something that maybe they've had trouble articulating, or suggest some way of doing it that will let them be great. Doesn't always happen but I'm looking for that.

If it's a Harold team from my theatre and it's a one-time thing I'll charge $50 or nothing because I feel like I'm lending a hand for one evening to something which is part of the machine that creates my world around me.

Some people make their living coaching and will charge $30 an hour or even more. Hmmm, what do I think of that? Well, I can see charging $30 an hour if you're good, and you're attentive and you've got experience. But that feels like the top limit of what should be a standard rate. More than that I don't think is worth it.

$20 an hour I'd accept a wide variety of coaching experience. It'd be okay with me if you were still figuring things out as a coach at that rate, providing you give a shit and you're trying.

If someone is not great and doesn't seem to care are charging a lot, say no. Go more junior. Enthusiasm can often trump status.

The very best coaches are not the most expensive money wise, but they only do things that interest them. They're being paid in the experience of the chance to work with a great group or to teach something new.

Someone email me if I'm spreading bad info in regards to the numbers I'm saying.

NOVEMBER 15TH, 2012 at 2:19PM

Q: IMPROVISE WITH ANYONE YOU'VE NEVER MET?

Anonymous asked: If you could improvise with anyone who you've never met, who would you choose?

Susan Messing. Christopher Guest. Ringo Starr. For some reason I think Ringo would be terrific, and I am not kidding.

NOVEMBER 15TH, 2012 at 2:20PM

Q: SHOULD COACHES TAKE NOTES ON THEIR PHONES?

Anonymous asked: How do you feel about coaches using their phones to take notes during practice?

I think it's okay, but they should say in advance "I'm taking notes on my phone not being an asshole."

NOVEMBER 15TH, 2012 at 2:21PM

Q: IS WRITING SKETCH PART OF THE TRANSFORMATION?

weirdlessbeardo asked: Do you consider writing sketch to be something that plays a big part in the transformation of someone from good improviser to great improviser?

Yep. At some point you have to shamelessly embrace that writing is part of being a great improviser and you should work the muscle of being a sharp phrase maker and having a strong sense of heightening and being into the math of it.

NOVEMBER 15TH, 2012 at 2:23PM

matthewsstarr asked: Hey Will, how do you believe improv changes based on venue, meaning how do you believe improv is different in a small room versus a very large room? Further, how do you think improv today would be different had it originated and been developed being performed in symphony halls rather than black box theatres? Thanks!

Improv feels very different from venue to venue to me. Under St. Marks in NYC is the easiest room to make work, somehow. UCB-Chelsea is fun but demanding—so big I have to really project. The Producer's Club makes me feel literate and theatrically important and shit. Parkside Lounge is really hard to make work (for improv).

Symphony halls! Hah. Um, it wouldn't have worked? But we would all have tuxedos.

NOVEMBER 15TH, 2012 at 2:40PM

Q: INDIE TEAMS DON'T CARE?

toyns asked: There are teams now in the indie scene that are paying

20-25/hour (even 30!). It seems like many of them don't care and are just phoning it in. They don't seem like they enjoy it, as though they are just doing it to use up rent money. Do you have any advice on this and did you ever have issues with this as a performer?

Erik Tanouye is good at second beats.

NOVEMBER 15TH, 2012 at 4:08PM

Q: I WON'T BE AT STEPFATHERS.

spotastic asked: I won't be at The Stepfathers show tomorrow. But I want to make sure a mentally challenged character still gets in the show. Can you do that for me?

Will do.

NOVEMBER 15TH, 2012 at 4:09PM

Q: JUSTCRAIG: FUNNIEST THING TO ORDER?

justcraig asked: What is the funniest thing a person can order at a restaurant in an improv scene? Thanks in advance.

I don't have a complete answer but I know that I try to throw in "teriyaki sauce" and "french dip sandwich" as much as possible and am only now realizing that a french dip sandwich might not be a real thing.

NOVEMBER 15TH, 2012 at 10:23PM

Q: I'LL BE AT STEPFATHERS.

connorratliff asked: Hi Will. I'll be at The Stepfathers show tomorrow night. I saw that Shannon used this forum to tell you that she WON'T be there tomorrow, and I assumed that this is how we're all communicating now. Are you excited about the show tomorrow?

I am excited about it! See you there. Probably going to watch Riley's show before.

NOVEMBER 18TH, 2012 at 7:42PM

Q: HAROLDS NOT MAKING IT 20 MINUTES?

Anonymous asked: What are your thoughts on more and more Harolds at UCB getting blacked out at barely past 20 minutes? Harolds in Chicago take 30 minutes minimum. What's the point of doing a Harold if you black out on the first big laugh after the 2nd group game before any connections? The last 5 minutes of a Harold done right are the most important, but at this point it's actually rare to see a Harold team get that far.

My reactions to your thoughts:

In my experience whenever someone says "in Chicago, it's like this..." or "in NYC it's like this..." they're usually oversimplifying and being pretty selective in their observations. Hi.

I haven't seen Harold Night at UCB-NY for some time. But when I've gone over the last 14 years, I've usually liked at least one of the sets a lot.

If the Harold's done, it's done. 20 minutes could be right, 30 minutes could be also.

It's okay for things to change and adopt new shapes for a while or maybe even forever. I understand that Harolds in the mid-1980s USED to be 45 minutes minimum. Why is the Chicago of your story in such a rush? Maybe the next 15 minutes is where the Real Art happens?

Maybe let's just talk about the show that happened, and not worry about the one you were imagining, which didn't happen, meaning it's something no one else can really speak to. Did you like the show as it occurred? If not, can you say why without referring to hypothetical SHOULDS you brought into your experience of it?

Today I tweeted about Vin Diesel.

NOVEMBER 18TH, 2012 at 7:43PM

Q: PERPLEXED BY SOMETHING NEW?

Anonymous asked: I love the idea that no matter how much we achieve or how many obstacles we overcome, that there is still infinitely more to learn during one's life. Is there a moment in your life, as someone who has done so much, when you were perplexed by how difficult something new in your life was, considering how much you had already been through and accomplished?

This question is hilarious.

NOVEMBER 19TH, 2012 at 11:34PM

Q: WHERE'S THE LINE AT HOW SHORT HAROLDS SHOULD BE?

Anonymous asked: Based on your response, why not black out Harolds at 15 minutes? Why not 10? You can't bake bread in 30 seconds. I concede that things used to be different even in Chicago, but the point is really solid callbacks/connections/3rd beat runs are a very rare thing to see Harold teams do on a UCB stage. It is much more common just to kill the lights at the first big laugh after 20 minutes. If longform is about the payoff, why are we in such a hurry? Where's the line?

I don't know. Is it really fair to say that every harold at UCB is blacking out at 20 minutes? I think you're making an unfair generalization to support a notion you had before you started collecting evidence. Or else maybe you are blowing up the significance of one or two particular shows in your mind to be representative so that you can make an argument? You're using the generalizing provocative language of a polemic, not the rational observant language of something who's truly trying something out. Instead of pointing to selective evidence as your justification, why not just say "I prefer longer Harolds" and not worry about casting a particular theater or city in a single light so that you feel okay sending an anonymous post to a blog?

If I go to Harold Night tomorrow night and time the shows—how many will be 20? And if I count connections / callbacks, even just "really solid" ones— am I gonna come up with "zero?"

Go to where you are happy, instead of insisting that where you are should be different so that you can be happy? There's something infuriating about your assumptions and your rhetoric. I think you had your answer before you asked your question.

I haven't seen a ton of Harolds lately. I saw one in the first week of September and The Pox did a Harold that was about 28 minutes and had extremely cool connections including angels watching Law and Order, which had been the object of obsession of a housewife who was ignoring her child in order to catch up on TV and a trial of murderers where the jurors were looking up at the clouds. It felt like a great Harold to me with "really solid" connections. But what do I know? I'm just citing an actual example.

NOVEMBER 19TH, 2012 at 11:47PM

Q: WHY ARE COUPLES ALWAYS A MAN AND WOMAN?

Anonymous asked: How come if you find yourself in a scene with another male where you play a couple one of you will inevitably find yourself as a woman? I always find it would be less awkward to just play it as a gay couple assuming it doesn't contradict anything that went on earlier in the show. Playing a woman might get a cheap laugh, but not a very big one so what's the point?

Young improvisers seem hesitant to play opposite gender, so as a teacher you look for a chance to encourage it. They're not as hesitant to play homosexual couples, which is cool, except that I think this willingness comes not from a progressive sensibility but because to be gay in an improv scene you just have to say the word "gay" once and then keep acting exactly as you are, whereas to play opposite gender requires you to act differently than you are a little bit.

NOVEMBER 19TH, 2012 at 11:47PM

Q: HOW HARD TO DO AN IMPRESSION?

Anonymous asked: If you're in a scene and your scene partner declares that you're a certain celebrity or the President or even a person of the opposite sex, how hard should you try to do an impression? Is it better to do a half assed and awful impression of President Obama or to just say in your own voice "Yeah, sure. I'm President Obama."?

Commit.

NOVEMBER 19TH, 2012 at 11:49PM

Q: I HAVE HUMPED PEOPLE IN THE LAST TWO SHOWS.

connorratliff asked: Over the course of the past two Stepfathers shows, I have "humped" almost every other member of the team on stage. (You, Delaney and Gethard on 11/9; Silvija on 9/16) Is this more likely a sign of A) poor improv or B) a personal problem on my part? Should I be concerned?

I'm not sure. Riddle me this: I was thinking of how your character humped Silvija's character after she had died (granted it started before she died but then continued after) and considering that in a way that might be more chivalrous than the genuine leg-humping to did you Delaney and I. I thought about this for several minutes. Should *I* be concerned?

NOVEMBER 21ST, 2012 at 6:21AM

I'M NOT GOING TO YES-AND YOU SHITTING ON ME

So the person who asked this:

"The point is really solid callbacks/connections/3rd beat runs are a very rare thing to see Harold teams do on a UCB stage. It is much more common just to kill the lights at the first big laugh after 20 minutes. If longform is about the payoff, why are we in such a hurry?"

Asked why I'm attacking someone just for asking a question. It's a sincere question, he/she says. Why am I so defensive about UCB?

Well, it's because... I learned improv there, was on a Harold team for like 7 years and then a weekend team for 5 more. I've taught there for 7 years and currently run the school in NYC. I am defensive about it.

To me, your question sounds like this: "Don't you think the way your family has terrible manners is bad? In this other metropolitan city, all families always have good manners. Why not be that way? Let's talk about manners. Yours, anonymous."

And my response: I don't really want to talk about manners, I want to talk about how you just shit on my family. It is true I'm being a bad "yes-ander" by dodging your proposed topic of early blackouts. I feel the emotional truth of being attacked in a passive aggressive way is more important than your proposed topic, so I'm speaking to that.

What the fuck? Why would you think I'd be excited to talk about your conversation that opens with you taking a big old shit on my house? This is my fucking blog! I'm not going to allow an opener of "Ok, we all know your theater is shit. That's a given. Now let's be polite and talk about my sincere topic."

Especially when I genuinely do not agree with your initial assumptions! And I don't think you have the data to back it up! I also don't always need to see big long third beats since some times and for some teams, a quick third beat suits them!

I guess I'd be more into a topic where I agree with the assumptions. "UCB focuses on game of the scene in their teaching. But I think this hurts improv training for X reason." That would not offend me. It starts with something which is true and that we admit, followed by your opinion. Ok, let's talk.

Nor would this: "I hate when Harolds black out in the first big laugh after the second group game. My favorite part is rich connections in the third beat. I want a generous amount of time there to discover them. Why do some teams / directors black out so early?" I'd be into that discussion too.

But the whole "UCB blacks out harolds at 20 minutes. That's a given. In Chicago all Harolds are 30 minimum. And everyone agrees the best part is the third beat connections. So why is this?" It sounds like this to me: "It's rare to see a good show at the place where you have spent your adult life. A good show being shows where third beats are really long. Why is that? Why not do good shows like they always do in this place where you have never spent a lot of time? Let's talk."

NOVEMBER 21ST, 2012 at 8:07AM

Q: YOU ATTACKED ME. ENJOY YOUR HOODIE.

Anonymous asked: I'd like to ask a question about longform improv, but I'm worried I won't structure it right for you to deal with the substance of it without attacking me as some haughty asshole for deigning to suggest I didn't like something I saw on the UCB stage. This blog started as a wonderfully transparent discussion. I'd never expect a "company man" response to a question as benign as asking, "How short is too short for a Harold?" supported by my observations as a student. Enjoy your Don't Think hoodie.

You didn't ask "how short is too short for a harold?" You asked why UCB always blacks out harolds at 20 minutes.

I do enjoy my hoodie! Enjoy your self-corrected/improved copy of Viola Spolia's "Improvisation for the Theater!"

NOVEMBER 21ST, 2012 at 5:45PM

Q: EVER PLAY MO'NIQUE?

Anonymous asked: Hi, big fan of yours. I was wondering if you thought of expanding your characters? Like playing Mo'Nique in a scene? I think it will be enjoyable for everyone involved. It would probably be something people would talk about for years. Just something to think about.

Hello, Nicole Byer.

NOVEMBER 21ST, 2012 at 5:47PM

Q: CHICAGO HAROLDS ARE OFTEN 22-25 MINUTES.

shoemakerdr asked: Actually, the Chicago Harolds are usually anywhere from 22-25 minutes on average. I've seen them longer for more established teams, but on the whole, they are not much longer than 20. And I've never seen a UCB Harold, but I expect the truly great UCB Harolds to be the same as the truly great iO Harolds.

I would think so too. I've only been to iO Chicago maybe six or seven nights but even in that short time I saw some amazing stuff. A People of Earth Harold from long ago. Also one from Prefontaine. Five Chinese Brothers. Georgia Pacific. Saw Bullet Lounge three years ago and was blown away.

NOVEMBER 21ST, 2012 at 5:49PM

Q: YOU WERE A SMUG ARROGANT JERK.

Anonymous asked: I did ask that question. You ignored it. Since you said a Harold can be done in 20 minutes I asked if the same could be said for 15 or 10? I asked "Where is the line?" But no my stupid **OBSERVATION** meant I was "attacking your family." And your smug dig about a self-annotated copy of Spolin's book? No wonder UCB has such a reputation for arrogance. Maybe you should say "Sometimes it's okay to ask questions so long as you agree UCB is infallible." Who knew it takes 12 years to have a valid opinion?

Not sure what to say to that.

What I AM thinking about is that I did let myself get involved in a flame war in which I had to choose to publish your questions, and I should have just ignored them all if I knew I couldn't answer them without resentment. Improv is about walls going down, defenses going down and I let mine go up. Not good for anyone. Fittingly (or is it ironically) this tendency hurts my improv too. The ego, the sense of territory, it is hard to let go of.

NOVEMBER 21ST, 2012 at 5:49PM

Q: JUSTCRAIG: BEST NAME FOR A MALE BUTLER?

justcraig asked: Best name for a male butler in a UCB improv scene? Also best name for a male butler in a Chicago-based improv scene?

...

NOVEMBER 23RD, 2012 at 6:50AM

HOSTILE CHARACTERS

Taught some early levels this summer. It was fascinating to watch when characters got angry at each other. Most of the time it was because the actor had become surprised/confused by a move the other actor did. Like they were expecting the other actor to say "yes" and he/she said "no" or vice versa. Saw this scene in a class show:

> Person A: "Hi, I'd like some lotion from your store. I saw a sign outside that says this is 'Everything Lotions.'"

Person B: "Um, sure, do you need anything specific?"

A: "Something for my headache? I have a terrible headache."

(And she's referring to something in the monologue—the monologist made some reference to using lotions for 'everything')

B: "Oh, that doesn't sound like a lotion. You mean aspirin? I think you have the wrong store."

(and that response is because that person does not remember that part of the monologue, and also she has been noted hard to play things truthfully, to not do things on stage that she would not do in real life, so she's sticking to what a real lotion store would have)

A: "But your store says 'Everything Lotions!'"

B: "We have lotions, not headache medicine. I think you want a different store."

A: (suddenly angry) "You are giving me terrible service! I'd like to speak to your manager!"

B: "I'm the manager. I own the store. You're talking to the manager."

A: "Well, I do not like this store!"

And then someone walks on with headache medicine, which the store owner is confused by, and the scene goes south.

Person A wasn't expecting to be refused the lotion. She had a game in mind, or least a scenario, and when that didn't happen her character lashed out. We teachers say to be suspicious of fights in improv, and this is why: a lot of fights are not justified by reality of the scene—they are actors frustrated with the vagaries of doing improv.

I'm not sure how to teach people to avoid that, because they don't really know it's happening. I think they don't really feel that mad. They don't notice the shift: that their characters are suddenly mad when they weren't mad, when they likely would not get mad in real life.

It's weird to watch people learn improv. They are scared and hostile at any new information or surprises. Is that something evolutionary? To fear the surprising?

I get hostile a lot, still. Tough to quell.

The strongest and the fittest of a species would be bad at yes-anding, I think. They'd swat and bat away things that made them start.

NOVEMBER 23RD, 2012 at 2:32PM

Q: AGREEMENT TOO PASSIVE?

halphillips asked: Do you think part of why people tend toward arguments when they get frustrated in scenes is that agreement seems too passive? Like they fear that just being cool with everything doesn't add information, so they have to find something to pick at just to feel like they're contributing? Is there a good way to make simple agreement feel like an active, aggressive choice, instead of a lack of doing anything?

I think this is a great question! And I agree that an argument FEELS like an active choice often more than a non-argument. I do not know offhand how to make the non-argument feel more SOLID. I say "accept offers" a million times but I concur this is ineffective.

NOVEMBER 25TH, 2012 at 8:49AM

Q: HOSTILE CHARACTER EXAMPLE SEEMED GOOD.

improv4thought asked: I don't see what's wrong with the example in the Hostile Characters post. Obviously I didn't see the scene, but based on the example, it seems like it was set up to be a straight man/crazy man scene, where the game was Person A thinks "everything lotion" means lotion for everything, like headaches or back pain, when in fact it just means they have a variety of different lotions. Person B could very well have argued so as long as he acknowledged the unusual behavior of Person A.

Hmm. You're right! It doesn't read as that bad a scene. My opinion was formed by the tone. My hunch was the actor was getting angry not because of being committed to the scene but because of being flustered. I may have been wrong in this instance. But I did see in early levels lots more incidents of characters being angry than I see in advanced levels.

NOVEMBER 25TH, 2012 at 9:22AM

Q: WHY IS THERE BITTERNESS TOWARDS UCB?

fromthemindofjon asked: Some of my improviser friends who have gone through other schools generally knock UCB as being elitist in deciding who gets to perform and too focused on game when teaching. I try to defend UCB's methods as best I can because I believe in the theatre and my training. Do you think there's any legitimacy to these criticisms? Why do you think some people are so bitterly against UCB, the fact that it takes a long time to get to perform on stage, or the idea that game is so important to the scene?

I think about this a lot and don't have an easy answer. Also, it's hard for me to speak to your friends' viewpoints when I'm not hearing them specifically. But I have some guesses as to why people who don't like UCB feel that way. Several things going on at once.

1. **SUPPLY AND DEMAND.** The school and community and theatre is huge and there isn't enough classes and stage time to go around. There's generally 800-1,000 people taking classes at any one time. Over the course of a year, about 4,500 different people will take a UCB course / workshop on each coast (9,000 total). The classes sell out right away, the shows sell out right away, there's barely any chances to perform on a regular basis. Even long-time talented veterans have to scrape and fight for the chance to get their shows on stage. This scarcity of resources vs. demand is the NUMBER ONE REASON, I think, for the feeling of harshness that happens at UCB. There's not enough to go around. And no matter how polite you say it, "NO" is a tough thing to say and to hear. We ARE looking to expand the physical size of the

school, but even when we do there will be limited number of class shows, limited number of performing opportunities for alumni.

I don't see an easy solution for this one.

2. **COMPETITIVENESS.** The UCB very consciously promotes competitiveness in its culture. Auditions for performing, notes for teams at most levels, people being cut and replaced. Teachers ask "is this funny?" earlier and more often (I think) than other improv schools. We ask that you write an essay to get into advanced classes. It's tough! That can be a drag for people who are more drawn only to the "say yes to everything" and "treat everyone likes poets and geniuses" of improv fundamentals.

There is an aspect of swagger that gets favored in this kind of culture. Alphas push ahead further than others when you make people compete.

But I don't mind the competitiveness. I think this is the factor that let the UCB theatre flourish where other improv communities do not. The audacity to ask its members "Could you be funnier?" is a bummer but also fair. We're a comedy theater and most non-improv comedy cultures accept very early in their development that you have to be good or go home.

For this one, the UCBT (which includes me) is responsible for creating this aspect, for good and ill!

3. **GAME OF THE SCENE.** The school very consciously puts a priority on seeing improv comedy as GAMES. We ask students to articulate the games all the time and more jarringly, to defend themselves in terms of game. It's heady and abstract and cerebral and often, no fun.

Classes where I teach to commit and be specific leave everyone with glowing smiles. Classes where I teach being aware of games leaves everyone staring at their shoes in heady regard. That's probably partly a comment on my teaching! But it's also that game is thinky.

But learning to see scenes as games is at least helpful and for some, revolutionary. Like, it's a technique—it doesn't seem right to get, like, mad at it, just because it's not fun or even isn't effective for you? I do get that game of the scene can be a drag, but some students end up making the same faces about improv that they made about math. If you don't like math, do you BLAME math? Or just accept "Well, that's not my approach."

HOWEVER, I do see teachers and coaches unfairly hiding behind the phrase "X can't play game" when what they really mean is "I don't like that person's taste." That's bullshit when that happens. If you say someone can't play game you might be right, but you should be more specific or else in my opinion you haven't yet said anything.

Do you mean: a) doesn't sense the irony of a situation b) can't consistently repeat a comedic pattern c) can play it but can't verbally articulate it? d) plays his/her own weird viewpoints well, but can't further a weird world?

Similarly, when a former student says "UCB was too hard on game" I wonder if he/she is not being specific enough. Was it really that? Or was it that you didn't get on a team, or a class, or that a teacher was harsh, or that you felt lonely in a big community?

Somewhere in that discussion some people's talents get ignored and the community's strengths gets ignored and it's annoying.

4. **HAVE NOT MENTALITY.** Not unique to UCB, but people in communities tend to focus on what they don't have rather than what they have. I used to help run Channel 101 in NYC. In that system, people submit abbreviated TV pilots. Ten would get shown, the audience would vote back five. Everyone, to my ears, EXCEPT FOR THE FIRST PLACE SHOW, complained. By the time I left, it seemed like no one was happy. I think that maybe wasn't as true as my defensive nature was seeing, but it was true enough that I had to get away from it.

   Similarly, in UCB there is no more demoralized time than after auditions for Harold Teams. 16 people out of 900 are happy, the rest have to square up with their disappointment as they will. I guess see option 1.

CHANGES AFOOT

I do believe the opening of UCB East has made a sea change in the foundations of the school towards a happier more inclusive culture. The Wednesday night jam, the Sunday night Improv nerds show, Indie Cagematch, BYOT and the multiple open mics for stand-ups and storytellers—I think it's helping people feel a part of the community without the brass ring of being on a team. We'll see in a year if there's a palpable difference. I bet there are fewer people who complain about the elitism when they feel they had a chance to perform and meet like-minded people. We'll see!

NOVEMBER 26TH, 2012 at 9:36PM

HOW DO YOU ALL DEAL WITH IMPROV RUTS?

A very common question I get is "what do I do when I'm feeling like I'm not getting it / in a rut / not doing well?"

It's so common that I think everyone probably has advice. What is yours?

Mine is: best way to get over a bad show/class/practice is to have a good show/class/practice so shrug off the bad and get back on the horse.

NOVEMBER 27TH, 2012 at 7:42AM

Q: CHOOSING CHARACTERS WHO ARE COOL

halphillips asked: If an improviser's attitudes can bleed over into their character (like when an improviser gets frustrated with how a scene is going and their character gets frustrated too), do you think it works in reverse too? Does choosing for your character to be cool with everything help the improviser be cool with how the scene is going?

Yes, it bleeds both ways.

NOVEMBER 27TH, 2012 at 7:45AM

Q: RACIST CARICATURE?

Anonymous asked: I was listening to your podcast with Achilles. Near the end, to demonstrate initiating with a big character off of a single suggestion, you initiated off of "purple hoodie" with a brash character yelling at John to get off his porch. You skillfully avoided turning the character into a racist caricature, but a less-experienced improviser might not know how to toe that line. Question, then: how do you keep a character that might have some features that touch on racial stereotypes from devolving?

I think I probably WAS being a caricature. I don't think that was a textbook example of good improv. It was an example of stepping up and letting myself be displayed for good or ill to a sort of improv challenge. I guess to whatever degree that was a non-caricature—what I try to do is be inspired by real things—I was half thinking of people from my dorm floor at college and myself when i'm mad at people. And I try to let the person be smart and learn and be affected and change his mind as stuff happens—so it's a real person. Talking about the speed of light always makes a character seem like he has depth. Start with a voice or tone and as it goes make him smarter and more specific, if i can which i can't always. when in doubt pray someone sweeps and deny you ever did the scene for the rest of your life and only tell people about the good stuff you do and that's it.

NOVEMBER 27TH, 2012 at 11:57AM

Q: CAN SOMEONE ASK WHY THEY DIDN'T GET INTO A CLASS?

Anonymous asked: Is it ever appropriate to talk with a teacher about why you didn't get into an ASP class or what you could work on to end up in one next time? What about asking someone who judged a

Harold/Lloyd audition a similar question? I assume the answer is "no" so I wouldn't do this, but I'd love your comments here... Will, you're a peach. I said it because everyone's thinking it.

Don't bother but maybe we can put something on the message board that says how many people applied vs how many got in? Students do seem to be affected by this.

At UCB, ASP is "Advanced Study Performance" which used to be called 600s and they are classes that work on particular forms or other performances—the movie, monoscene, or something the teacher dreamed up. not every students gets to do them because there aren't enough. i did a "philip k dick" improv one last fall and there were 90 applicants for 16 spots. i included harold team people and those who i knew that loved PKD and even that only got me down to 30 people, then i cut it to 16 i don't even know how.

don't ask the teacher. you can email the school (will or erik at ucbcomedy) though it's mostly just a supply/demand thing.

harold/lloyd auditions: even less reason to ask. auditions are notoriously hard to do and hard to articulate why someone is advanced or not. i guess that's a cop-out but i honestly don't know how to articulate who goes on or not. yes-anding under pressure in a decisive funny way is goddamn hard and almost no one can do it, really. Anthony King wrote a good piece on the mentality of people watching improv auditions and how they are rooting for the people to do well—google that shit. but don't ask. there's too many, the reasons won't satisfy you.

you've taken improv classes, right? were you told any notes during the class? if not, what notes did the teacher say to everyone over and over again? maybe see if you're following that?

think of your improv classes—in your head pick the top 8 people. now think of what you'd tell the next 8 runners up. whatever notes you're mentally giving them, you take those notes?

sentences ending with question marks because i don't totally know why people make the choices they do. i've applied for a bunch of television writing jobs. Amount of information I have received back: zero. Not even a "no"—just no response. I presume there were better submissions that excited and got the attention of the reviewers, and I'm back in the mines trying to be funny and precise and shit.

I'm no peach, but thank you. i'm sometimes shabby sometimes great just like you, human!

NOVEMBER 28TH, 2012 at 9:30AM

Q: INITIATION ETIQUETTE EXAMPLE

Anonymous asked: Student-level scenario re: Initiation Etiquette— Your partner initiates with a premise that isn't unusual, but their energy hints that they're saying "Hey, this is the thing." Playing the reality might be blocking their shot, but a big reaction seems like taking the ball and running toward the other basket when the other person was looking for an assist. At least we're moving now? (Related: Who is the John Stockton of UCB right now?)

Commit. And make your partner look good. Make his/her choice the right one. Don't think like "premise that isn't unusual" because that's a thinly veiled version of "whoops, he/she is doing it wrong." Nope, it's the right move, the only move. Whatever they think is important, it's important and you know why, and your reason why makes it work and that move looks good and your partner is glad you stepped out.

"Oh man, the lightswitch is right by the door." (said in a tone that implies it's a weird and interesting thing)

"Oh, no. We're doomed. Why THERE?"

Re: John Stockton. Thank you for using circa-1990 references. Though I have no idea.

DECEMBER 3RD, 2012 at 7:36AM

Q: LETTING SOMEONE KNOW I FELT DEMEANED

Anonymous asked: I was recently in a jam where a male improviser made a move that felt demeaning to me as a female improviser. Do I Facebook him and let him know (in the nicest possible way) or do I let it go and accept it as one of many terrible jam scenes?

You don't have to tolerate jerks, ever, but I don't think a message will do anything. Assume he will stay a jerk. Going forward, you adjust by a) pushing back on stage b) choosing to spend most of your time with better people. Jams contain multitudes including jerks: learn to deal with them rather than trying to change them. I'd advise differently if this were someone in your practice group or maybe even in your class.

Trying to think when I've been demeaned. I did a scene once there were two people talking in an apartment. I entered as someone on their fire escape who leaned in their window and said something. One of the two came over and shut the window in my face and turned back to the other and said "don't know what THAT was about." Big laugh from the crowd. I felt dumb. Had I ruined a scene? Was it that dumb? Maybe I'd walked on too early and irritated them. Or maybe they were jerks? I stood there, and waited and every time one of them would glance over I'd wave. Eventually one opened the window and I picked up my sentence right where it left off. Big laugh. Edit. I never sent a message. This was on Harold Night so maybe I felt I had validation enough from being on an Official House Team that I didn't feel I had to fight. I don't know. I've never sent a note to anyone asking them to change their improv mostly because I don't believe people easily change?

DECEMBER 3RD, 2012 at 7:37AM

Q: 10,000 HOURS?

Anonymous asked: What's your take on the 10,000 hours theory?

It's good! Someone should turn that into a book that everyone buys!

DECEMBER 3RD, 2012 at 7:39AM

Q: AM I A NINJA, PIRATE OR ROBOT?

Anonymous asked: So there's this idea that any given improviser is naturally a Ninja, Pirate, or Robot (an idea invented by Michael Delaney, correct me if I'm wrong). I don't know which one I am. Do you think that knowing which one you "are"—or I suppose knowing how you improvise and what your strengths are—is something to focus on?

It was Billy Merritt. Delaney believes everyone is either Led Zeppelin, Rick Moranis or one of the seven pillars of fine art. That's not true. Anyway, if that metaphor isn't illuminating your view of yourself just move onto to another metaphor? Yes, knowing yourself is important. Then again, no one fits completely into any one box so prepare to be seeing yourself differently over time as circumstances change etc.

DECEMBER 3RD, 2012 at 1:42PM

Q: DEALING WITH HARASSERS OUTSIDE THE THEATER.

Anonymous asked: As a lady improviser, I am sometimes at the end of comments that are somewhat offensive to me because they are sexist. Those don't bother me as much, because hey! You gotta live with a lot of people who just don't get it. But when an improviser you know starts harassing you and being inappropriate outside the theater, should the theater be informed, or should you deal with this on your own?

Inform the theatre. At UCBT we have student advocates you could contact, or any teacher you felt comfortable taking with about it.

DECEMBER 3RD, 2012 at 5:34PM

Q: SHOULD I JOIN A TEAM RUN BY SOMEONE I DON'T RESPECT?

Anonymous asked: Kinda stupid question. I'm a beginning improviser at university, and my uni has an improv team that has some problems. The guy who runs it resists any suggestions from anyone, isn't good about encouraging improvement on any level, has been doing this for years, etc. The team also has a lot of cheap, gimmicky habits (imo, I guess). But the team performs. A lot. Is it better to play with them and get performance experience or stay away because I just wish it was a better environment? Thanks.

I feel I'm handling anonymous questions of hypothetical situations badly here, so I'm not sure exact what to say without having seen the examples of this group or what's being done or what's a cheap, gimmicky habit.

But I'm going to answer anyway.

This is not a final answer, and it may not be right for your situation, but your description reminds me of what a lot of people go through when they want to do improv, but they don't yet have a show or group which feels exactly right. Unless you're being personally disrespected, there's probably a lot to learn in terms of saying yes to the vibe and strengths of the situation, rather than find reasons to stay back. I'd say do it, enjoy it, embrace the things that feel like gimmicks and find a way to have fun and down the road there will be opportunities that are more what you envision. An inner judge and censor can grow so strong that it could become hard to defeat later.

If it really just feels demoralizing and distasteful to do, then no, it isn't worth it. But if it COULD be fun, and you don't have an immediate better path—it feels like something you should try in order to practice doing stuff.

I'm really not learning my lesson because without knowing the specifics of your situation, I'll bring up a situation from my life it makes me think of. It may not really be similar. But my freshman year of college I met a group of friends who loved, without reservation, top 40 pop music. In high school

I had been a discerning music snob of the highest order. But now that I had friends who seemed to truly love whatever the radio was playing all the time—I kinda learned to love pop music. And I learned to dance (Or at least to enjoy dancing) and to let go of the idea that the music I was playing was my identity. When I graduated from college, I worked as a journalist with a bunch of music snobs and found that my snobby taste had not left me and I went right back to digging for old Replacements CDs and whatever. And I don't regret learning to love something I had been put off from.

I really liked my friends, and felt happy around them. So that might be the difference.

DM me for a zipped file of Bobby Brown's "Don't Be Cruel" album.

DECEMBER 11TH, 2012 at 8:55AM

SHOWS AND SCENES I LIKE REMEMBERING

Remembering old scenes and shows I loved, all from circa 2000-2002. All memories subject to nostalgic revision and fogginess of time:

—

CORNDOG, ALLRIGHT! (CIRCA 2000)

Harold Night, first scene. Owen Burke walks out as some kind of scientist with a test tube and says something to Victor Varnado like "Ok, this potion should..." but as he approaches Victor, Victor weirdly leans towards him and kinda bumps into him, and then after they contact Victor slumps into Owen. Owen adjusts his sentence and says "okay, well, hold on..." and tries to prop Victor back up, who is now fully learning into Owen. Owen keeps stammering "yes, well, okay, wait, let's see... hold on... this potion, yes, wait" while Victor increasingly flops around. Owen grabs Victor's shoulders and they are full-on wrestling, with Victor in a kinda dead-armed Harpo Marx slump and Owen's voice remaining totally calm as he tries to right Victor's body. Finally gets Victor in a chair. Owen exhales. "There." Edit.

—

THE SWARM, CIRCA 2000

First group game. Andy Daly initiates "Okay, thank you for coming, everyone. As you all know, I've murdered a member of each of your families, in sometimes brutal ways. So please think of this as an 'I'm sorry' wine and cheese." The rest of the Swarm angrily noshes on the food. "You've got a lot to apologize for, mister! Hey, this is terrific hummus."

—

RESPECTO MONTALBON, 2003

Cagematch, when they were doing the Evente. Rob Huebel endows himself as a cashier at a fast food restaurant who "has a very private rape fantasy." Audience groans. Other things happen. Then the restaurant is robbed. Huebel mimes grabbing a gun from under the register and points it at Jackie Clarke's character, who is a male cashier. "Now you rape me! Now you rape me!" Huebel screams. Jackie shakes her head "No! I'm not going to!" "YOU HAVE TO! WE'RE GOING TO DIE! YOU RAPE ME NOW!" Jackie looks at the audience and shakes her head and says "fine." And mounts Rob "I DON'T AGREE WITH THIS!" she shouts. "YOU RAPE ME NOW!" says Huebel. "I AM! JESUS, STOP WHINING!"

—

DILLINGER, 2003

First beat is Zach Woods and Risa Sang-Urai as a couple in a bar trying to pick each other up. Zach admits to having sold his soul to the devil, but it was only so that there would be no more keyboards in pop songs. Risa wants to know why he didn't get more out of the deal, like maybe they could be together or Zach could be wealthy? Second beat: Zach and Risa have a prolonged and real discussion about the promise of love and how sad it is and they get frustrated and the scene seems to stall and then Erik Tanouye enters as the Devil and says "And now you know what it's like to live in a world without keyboards."

—

Joe Wengert, in class, 2002. Suggestion "pendulum." His initiation, directed to Matt Pack. "Captain Lightning, I've escaped! I was trapped on a platform, and the knife was swinging back and forth over me, and it got closer and closer, but then at the last minute I broke free and I ran to the headquarters of Dr. Darkness and when I got in there he was fucking your mom."

Matt Pack (breaks, recovers): "Again?"

Joe: "Yeah! I don't know, I think you have to get out of the superhero business. All these villains keep having sex with your mom. Oh, you know who gets out of prison tomorrow? Rhino man."

—

ASSSSCAT, 2000

Matt Walsh (maybe, or was it Adam McKay? Ian?): "Okay, class, today is dissection day. But because of budget cuts you are going to have to kill the frogs yourself before you dissect them."

Andy Richter: "Mine's a kitten!"

Walsh: "Yes, some of you have kittens. We couldn't afford to get everyone frogs."

—

MONKEYDICK, 2002
(AS I WITNESSED FROM THE BACK LINE)

First beat: Rob Lathan gets caught in a series of bear traps.

Second beat: Rob Lathan gets caught in another series of bear traps.

Third beat: Rob: "Hope there's no bear traps." There's not. Blackout.

—

WEIRDASS, DEL CLOSE MARATHON, 2002?

Bob Dassie and Stephanie Weir play two dudes and also two girls in a club and then they all dance with each other, with Bob and Stephanie quickly shifting characters mid dance to each play both their parts.

—

FILTH, (YES, FILTH), 2003

Neil Casey, initiation: "Railroad's cancelled."

Sean Taylor: "The whole thing?"

Neil: "Yep! They decided it wasn't working."

—

ANOTHER FILTH ONE! ALSO 2003

After a whole Harold in which Adam Koppel is a guy who comes in and reveals that the current scene was just a test and not for real, he enters in the third beats and says that the entire Harold has been fake. Amey Goerlich "So when do we do the real Harold?" Kevin Hines: "Right now! Can we get a suggestion?" Then Filth does a new Harold in 5 minutes and beats Respecto in Cagematch.

—

CAGEMATCH, OPTIMIST INTERNATIONAL VS. STOMPING GROUND, 2003

Third Beat, Jack McBrayer steps out and says "The female characters in this Harold have really had it rough. Let's see what it's like if the shoe was on the other foot." Then Shannon O'Neill, Chris Gethard, Terry Jinn, Seth Morris, Jack, Rhea Dates and maybe Dave McKeel re-do their Harold in 5 minutes, switching the gender of every main character.

—

JOE ROSS TRIBE, 2001

Debut Harold for Gethard and O'Neill.

First beat: O'Neill is giving Gethard a blow job, implying that his dick is as long as the stage.

Second beat: Gethard is eating out O'Neill, also from across the stage. Their kid enters and leaps over the clitoris like it's a jump rope.

(I left out this one the first time I typed this out because it was so crude but it was so insane and ridiculous, done to a screaming audience, that I have to include it. God, It was funny.)

DECEMBER 16TH, 2012 at 10:25PM

SCENES I SAW IN CLASS OR PRACTICES THAT MADE ME CRY LAUGHING

These might not translate. Adjust your mirrors as needed. These all left me crying laughing in class. A lot of these are sex jokes and fart noises. I am a fraud.

1. D'arcy Erokan as a photographer trying to get corporate executive Matt Chesmore to pose.

    D'arcy: "I wish we could get you to look… just a hair less, JUST A HAIR less—I don't want to say it…"

    Matt: "Creepy?"

    D'arcy: "Yes! Yes, just a bit."

    Then Matt silently posing for about 60 seconds, subtly adjusting his expression while D'arcy kept softly shaking her head.

2. Tom McKenna as a Home Depot salesman who before telling people where to shop accused them of stealing nails, frisking them, then rustling their hair and insisting that it was all just in good fun. For Frankie Zemel, McKenna tickled him and spun him completely around in the air.

3. Mark Dowling as a real estate salesman who knew nothing about the houses he was selling. "How many bathrooms?" someone would ask. "You know, I have no idea."

    That was all just a normal class scene. But then the client would say they were leaving and Mark, a relatively deadpan guy would for some reason brighten up and say in the cheeriest voice "All right! See you later!" I'm laughing now remembering it. I made him do that scene for like 15 minutes.

4. Don Fanelli and Tim Dunn entering the first scene of a first beat doing a million high kicks.

5. After a pattern game which proposed unfortunate names for superheroes:

    Patrick Kovich-Long: "Hello everyone! It's me: Tuberculosis Man!"

    Boris Khaykin: "Kids, get inside."

6. Jill Donnelly in the second minute of the first session of Improv 201 when for her entry in the name game she made the world's quietest fart noise.

7. Benjamin Apple in the apocalypse class as a guy who wanted to steal someone's Chipwich, and his strategy was to crunch halfway down, repeat in a whisper "Ok now, everything's fine, everything's fine now, don't worry, everything's great" until he got close enough to steal the Chipwich. People—Chris Scott? Adam Bozarth?—frozen in place in what seemed like genuine confusion.

8. Same class. In a frozen post-apocalyptic hellscape, Frank Hejl played happy go lucky, could not be depressed uncle Pepe.

9. Brian Faas as a zombie losing all his limbs one by one.

10. Sebastian Conelli walking on a physically abstract scene to label it with "Wow, you weren't kidding when you said you were raised by wolves!"

11. Martha Hearn as a redneck husband sexually molesting his crying wife Ryan Ramirez. That should not have made me laugh as hard as it did but the object work was too creepily specific.

12. Seth Reiss to Maggie Carey in their improv 101 grad show. I can't remember the scene except that Seth broke and then said "Could you give me a break? I'm incredibly short." As I recall, no relevance to the scene.

13. Tracey Wigfield as a mother who in order to teach her daughter a cautionary tale in emotional dependence, executed a teddy bear.

14. Murf Meyer as a principal who, while being mercilessly criticized by parents Karin Hammerberg and Katey Healy-Wurzburg, kept mispronouncing every brand name he said.

15. Still Mike practice: Michael Kayne and Don Fanelli as two cyclops talking to Terry Withers' Professor X. Michael Kayne: "Mind you, were are TWO Cyclops." Terry: "Yes, I understand that."

16. $12,000: Chris Schell describing to Michael Paoli his dream of walking through Candyland.

17. Captcha: Moujan as a bike shop owner who kicked out Ellena as someone whose body was "too weird" to deserve a bike. Then Matt Mayer walks in miming a weirdly big belly and said in a British accent "Hello! Just thought I'd check! No? Okay! Okay!" And then Dan Black entered walking like a crab so that he was a creature with no head, saying "I know we've had our differences in the past, but I was wondering if you had a bike?" And Moujan sold him one and then Dan's weird body rode a bike.

18. same practice: Eddie Brawley spent an entire group game getting initials wrong. "OJ? You mean Orange...... Julius?" "Oh, you're looking for the WC, you mean the... Walter Cronkite?"

19. Same practice! Connor Ratliff as a jazz musician named "Sambo Johnson."—"Terrible name! Uh, let me explain.." and then Dan Black enters with a name which I cannot reprint in this political climate.

20. Whorenado: Paul Downs spends 3 minutes starting a car.

21. Police Chief Rumble: David Martin tags everyone out so he could cut to General Noriega in Nicaragua doing something. This might have been a show.

22. Lou Gonzales as a wrestler named "Whole Lotta Salad."

23. Manny Hernandez as the man who inspired the red blow-up guy that used car lots use to attract attention.

24. Alex Charak and Ethan Silverman who are locked out of their apartment talking about how they should get more copies of their keys made.

25. Later in the same class Ethan and Tim Dunn were two guys wearing capes who were mad that other people had more diamonds than them.

Okay, I'm tired. Good night!

DECEMBER 18TH, 2012 at 6:16AM

THE MESSINESS MAKES IT REAL

The movie Argo features the CIA posing as a film crew to rescue diplomats from Iran in 1980. The people in charge use the phrase "Argo fuck yourself" to cheer each other up. It has a nice ring to it, but it also doesn't quite make sense when used to cheer on a colleague. But it feels right. I believe, based on that, that it was a real phrase used in the actual CIA mission this film was based on it. A writer would have made something neater. I like it. It feels real.

One big advantage improv has over sketch is that the sloppiness that comes with making stuff up gives it an air of truth. Things are sloppy in real life, they are not written. Neil Armstrong said "That's a small step for man, a giant step for mankind" which is obviously a slight mistake. There is a popular saying "it is what it is" which adds zero information still FEELS right. Actors who get caught shouting racist tirades at police hold press conferences and give non-apologies and everyone forgives them. Everyone collects money when you land on Free Parking even though that is not in the rules. Everyone misquotes Casablanca. Everyone says "time to flush this out" or "for all intensive purposes." It doesn't quite add up, it just FEELS right so we accept it and move on.

And improv captures that feel along with the corresponding illogic. Improv produces jeans that are pre-washed and distressed. It makes books that have already inherited the mistakes of their editors. Films with missing scenes. And that makes it feel real.

DECEMBER 22ND, 2012 at 6:28AM

PLAY LIKE A GREAT TEAM

Sometimes, I see house teams do shows in which they technically get everything right: clear premises, getting on the same page, careful listening, speaking truthfully and logical heightening.

But the show was boring.

What is needed is: swagger. A posture of confidence. Without that, a house team looks like a bunch of students.

Through timing and cadence, they ask the audience if what they were doing was funny. But that's not how it works. Teams SHOW the audience what's funny, they don't ask. The first time you hit the game, you're not asking—you're teaching the audience what the joke is. When you hit it a second time, you're confirming for their sake what the joke is that you already like. If they don't laugh, it's not that you did it wrong but that they missed it.

This isn't condescending, it's what it means to be deserving of being on stage. You play like you're right. When the show starts, you are in charge.

DECEMBER 26TH, 2012 at 1:40PM

TRYING TO WIN THE SCENE

Saw this in a class:

> A: So you hated the dog I bought for you.
>
> B: Yeah, well I already had 4 cats. The dog is going to murder those things. You buy me the worst gifts. You always buy me gifts that just don't fit.
>
> A: (*side coached to say why he bought a dog as a gift*) I got you it because I think you're more like a dog than a cat. It represents you more. You're not agile like a cat.
>
> B: Son, I'm 75 years old!

It's a decent scene since they're agreeing with the facts and justifying. And they were both good players. But still, there's something weirdly angry here. Initiated with an accusation, responded with another one. The lines feel like gotchas. They're trying to win the scene, not write a story together. they want their character to come out on top, when that doesn't matter.

The instinct to protect your character is a strong one—people who can't think of ideas in scenes very quickly think of ideas to protect themselves or to strike down someone they perceive as attacking them. It's very natural and pervasive in lower levels of improv. It's a sign of maturity (in improv and probably elsewhere) when someone is able to yes-and evidence against themselves in order to further a funny pattern, or play a game, or make the scene more interesting.

—

I wrote this a few months ago and now that I'm coming back to read it I can see that that scene is fine. They're yes-anding each other and it's funny. But there something in the tone. They were inspired first and foremost to win the… if not the scene, the line. They weren't in concert, at least in feeling.

I think maybe I just wanted to see some explicit yessing. Like this, maybe?

> A: So you hated the dog I bought for you.
>
> B: **I did. I hated it tremendously.** Of course, I already had 4 cats. The dog is going to murder those things. You buy the worst gifts.
>
> A: (*side coached to say why he bought a dog as a gift*) **I do buy terrible gifts, it's bizarre.** What I was thinking was that you're more like a dog than a cat. You're not agile like a cat.
>
> B: **I'm clumsy as all get out.** Although, I'm 75 years old!

I like that better. I'm trying to change what they did as little as possible.

Though if you read this you can see that if they explicitly confirm what was said about them, that their follow up statements feel a bit more like they are undoing what was said. Am I onto something? Or should I just go eat dinner?

DECEMBER 27TH, 2012 at 1:44PM

YOU GO TO THEM

One of the most common categories of questions I get to this improv blog is the "I'm playing with someone bad. What do I do?" Variations include that so and so is sticking out amongst the group, or maybe is behind everyone else, or playing really broadly, or mugging at the audience, or is somehow hurting otherwise good scenes. Many varieties of "when am I allowed to tell this person they're bad" or "what do i do if I'm stuck with someone who's bad?"

(A qualification: I'm not talking about off-stage terribleness, like people who mistreat you or are jerks or are mean. I'm talking about people that you think are bad improvisers and for whatever reason you're about to do a scene or show or class with them.)

Without knowing the specific situation, here is my first instinct every time that question is asked: YOU GO TO THEM. You stop questioning what's wrong with the other person and you focus on what you are doing. You say "yes and" and get on that page and play. If they won't budge, you go to them and you don't even hesitate. Don't even think about what might be wrong them, you just play.

You are thinking: "No, you haven't seen this person." Not that person, no. But I have played with every kind of player, often for YEARS. And if you're asking me how to play with that person the answer is: YOU GO TO THEM. If they are literally denying their own reality each and every line, then yes-and the last thing said and change with them if need be. No excuses. This is the answer, and the sooner you learn it the sooner this will be fun.

Would you rather be right or be in a great scene?

The performers MUST connect and meet else the scene does not exist. Agreement before all else. In fairness they should meet halfway, but if you find yourself in a scene with people who won't budge, then for the sake of the scene you go all the way to them.

In the second improv workshop I ever took in a black box theater on Ludlow St. in Manhattan in 1998, I did a scene with a guy who was, I can say in fairness, a terrible improviser. He contradicted facts I said, he mugged for the audience. He interrupted me and talked about sex nonstop. Problem: the audience (rest of the class) loved him. They cracked up at everything he did, laughing at his outrageousness. I sat stewing, knowing that I was doing it "right" and was getting no attention for it. I was brand new and could not get my thoughts together while playing with this jerk.

At the break I said to a friend of mine "That guy is so annoying" and my friend, who was grinning from ear to ear, shrugged his shoulders—"it's hilarious."

And he didn't mean that my frustrating predicament was hilarious. He meant this guy's outrageousness was enjoyable, and that my friend had not been paying attention to my artistic pain because who gives a shit?

And I realized I had to choose: did I want to be right, or would I prefer to be part of a fun scene?

I wish I had just said yes and made it work. That I had agreed that I was here to see the doctor for "dick pills." That my name was "Roger Roger Roger." That I was bribing him to tell my ex-wife that I was no longer on heroin. That I was "super gay." That even though I got flustered, that I amped up the fluster, so the audience could enjoy that more since they already were. I still think about it all the time. He was wrong, but by not playing, I was also wrong.

True, I didn't have to be on a team with him or even see him after that workshop. Still, my job is to make the scene work. **To play it as it is, not as I think it should be.**

You're probably thinking: I can't do that. This person is no good in any way and anything I do he/she will wreck. Maybe. I advise you at least to think of it in these terms: "I don't yet know how to make that good."

More: I asked someone who was on a great team if they ever sat down and had a big honest talk about what kind of improv they wanted to do. And this person said to me "We would never give each other notes, and even if we did, no one would take them." And that illuminated it for me. You can't worry about what the other person SHOULD do, because you don't know for sure, and you can't control it. You have to worry about your side of the street. Say yes. Add to it. You go to them. You make it work.

Even more! In some future group, you will worry that YOU are this person which everyone else dreads. At that time, you will be happy if you have discouraged the part of your brain that judges others so that it won't be so powerful when it turns in on you. I've done it to myself—judging harshly—it takes a lot of effort to undo.

DECEMBER 29TH, 2012 at 4:34PM

YOU MUST APPRECIATE THE GOOD IN WHAT YOU DO

Beating yourself up is easy and natural for an improviser. You must learn to see the good in the scenes you do and hold onto it. It is an essential tool of getting better and an emotional survival skill.

YOU WILL DO MANY SCENES LIKE THIS:

Suggestion: "dartboard." Already, you're panicking. *Should I just play darts? Is that too obvious?* No, you decide, it's okay that you're just in a bar. Phew. *Okay, I'm playing darts in a bar.* Quick, start playing darts—*oh my god, I've been standing here for too long*—you start playing darts, you throw an imaginary dart, fast, and set up to throw another one and you think: I'm playing darts.

Scene partner enters, and he's smoking a cigarette and taking a drag every two seconds and you think you have to say you're playing darts so he/she knows and you say "I'm playing darts." But before you're even done saying that the other person says "Aren't you supposed to be bartending?" and the other people in your class laugh. You want to say "yes" because that's what improv is, so you say "Yes, I'm bartending but first I'm paying darts. Would you like to play darts? Come on, play darts!" And this other person has started to play darts with you. And three seconds which feels like three hours go by and then you say "Good dart game."

Then the other person goes "You know what? We suck at darts" and maybe one person laughs and it's a relief, but part of your brain says *wait, no that's a denial* and then before you know it you say "I'm fucking your wife" and the other guy, who has been noted for fighting too much says, goes "Hey man, it's cool, I don't care about her, let's just play darts!" and the teacher says "Okay, two more, notes later."

And you won't remember the notes because your brain is full of this thought: "I am terrible."

—

Bad scene? Yeah. But actually, you did a lot correctly. Can you see it? You got a suggestion and made a clear who/what/where. You interacted with a scene partner and you agreed with each other's reality. You each said yes to the other at least once. You avoided a fight. You made decisions even though you weren't sure. You started to build a history together.

You got up out of your normal life and came to an improv class and got up in front of people and were brave and vulnerable. You put yourself out there. Your brain started to blaze trails of making choices, and those trails will be quicker to travel next time.

You did improv.

You must appreciate the good in what you do. No one else will ever pay as much attention to you as you will. So learn to be a genuine but generous audience for yourself.

You are good. You wouldn't have wanted to do this so badly if it wasn't a good fit for your brain. Keep going.

DECEMBER 31ST, 2012 at 1:41PM

Q: FICTIONAL CHARACTER HAROLD TEAM?

halphillips asked: What eight fictional characters would you like to see on a Harold team together?

Fun! Um,

- Sherlock Holmes—if-this-then-what,
- Ferris Bueller—acting,
- Delirium—randomness,
- Guadalupe (Love and Rockets)—voice of reason,
- Captain Jack Sparrow—yes-anding
- Henry V—passion, group game initiations
- Chaplin's Tramp—object work, reactions
- Darlene Conner—wit, sarcasm
- Alternate: Elektra Natchios—edits, assassinations

2013

JANUARY 10TH, 2013 at 11:46AM

WATCHING ZIP ZAP ZOP

I like watching people do zip zap zop.

See the real world slip away. See them smile despite themselves.

They transform each other. The teacher doesn't have to say anything. They start off tentative, giggling, apologetic. And after 30 seconds—which is nothing, that's NOTHING—they are more confident and brave. Maybe one time you say something. You say "MORE" or "COMMIT" and they just all lean forward and widen their eyes and lock in.

Fast and loose. I don't go for that "copy the last way someone said it" thing. I just want to see people get loose. Free and easy. Eye contact. Passing invisible bolts of energy to each other. Dropping the walls of the real world. Turning into actors and comedians.

JANUARY 11TH, 2013 at 9:23AM

THE BRAVE CHOICE

The right choice is often the brave choice. The character from the pattern game that you're scared of doing. The opinion you're worried the audience won't agree with. The object work you think that no one will understand. But you just commit and do it. You visualize your spine made of flexible steel. Improv shows have a way of rewarding bravery. Maybe it's pragmatic: brave things are difficult things or surprising things and therefore more enjoyable for the audience. Or maybe the audience can smell the bravery on you and they become fascinated. Or maybe there's just magic afoot, and some invisible energy exists all around us that will be at your beck and call once you tell the universe that you are not scared. For me this includes doing an accent or dancing but your mileage may vary.

JANUARY 20TH, 2013 at 10:11PM

Q: CRUSH ON A TEACHER

Anonymous asked: I have a crush on my improv teacher. He doesn't know. Have you experienced this? How do you handle it? Don't worry, it's not you. Tell the world your thoughts on this phenomenon. I'm staying anonymous to protect the innocent.

My thoughts: Do not act on this crush. Wait until this person is not your teacher and see if your feelings fade, which they almost definitely will. If after a little while you still like this person, interact with them outside of the comedy world. At a party, or at a bar. Remember this is a strange enough person that he made the life decisions necessary to be teaching improv comedy which generally requires a certain amount of narcissism and emotional distance. Without the shininess or the stage or the front of the classroom, this is a regular person so wait until you can see that.

Also, teachers at my school (and I would imagine, all) are forbidden from pursuing romantic agendas with their students. If you or anyone knows of a teacher that is pursuing one of his/her students, tell someone because that is some serious shit and they know better.

JANUARY 23RD, 2013 at 9:49AM

Q: WHY DO I ALWAYS SUGGEST A FOOD?

halphillips asked: Why is my instinct when giving a suggestion always to say some kind of food? (This is true regardless of whether or not I am hungry at the time.)

At least 50% of all suggestions are food-related. Separately, I like that you submit questions non-anonymously.

JANUARY 31ST, 2013 at 10:22PM

FOLLOW THE FOLLOWER

Let it transform quickly. It should feel silly but not embarrassing because you're all doing it together. Commit. Give over to it.

Follow the follower is a good metaphor of what happens in an improvised scene. Taking things from each other and making them stronger. Listening and observing from others is more valuable than thinking of awesome things.

Let yourself break out of the circle. Everyone should roam the classroom like dust particles, all mirroring each other. Be physical. If you hear a noise, you do it too, but MORE. MORE.

FEBRUARY 2ND, 2013 at 2:18PM

LYING, MEANNESS, STUPIDITY

This is about the second line of the scene. Maybe the fifth line. For people who are kinda newish—like two or three courses in, maybe.

When doing improv in front of an audience, and when you are starting with just a suggestion (as opposed to an opening which gives you more full ideas) you will feel a pressure to make SOMETHING HAPPEN. You'll feel the vagueness at the top and want to make a big choice to make the scene about something interesting. You'll feel this pressure a lot in the second line of the scene and then again at around the fifth line.

Beware at those moments of being a character who either LIES, or is MEAN or is STUPID. In most forms of comedy, those are fine vehicles for laughs but in improv they create more problems than they solve. And also: young improvisers do them relentlessly and arbitrarily.

You will feel it. Someone says "Hey, would you mind helping me with this sofa?" and you will feel the urge to just say "NO" in order to humorously be a jerk (mean). Or someone will start "Thanks for babysitting my kid!" and you'll look very nervous and say "Uh, oh, yeah... right! Your kid! Yeah, everything is fine with your kid! No problems with your kid!" (lying) Or someone will say "Jerry, you're the best man! Where's the ring?" and you'll say, with very little thought "Oh man, I had no idea that was your ring. I left it at home." (stupid)

Those could actually all be fine scenes. But when you are new to improv, you will hit LYING and never own up, you will be MEAN and never accept responsibility, you will be STUPID and block yourself into doing just one empty thing over and over.

You must find other ways to be funny.

A better way: advocate an unusual view. Champion it. Pick an unusual philosophy and fight for it. "I would help you move your couch, but I am opposed to couches. They promote laziness." Or "I am keeping your child. I am homeschooling your child without your consent." Or "I have the ring but I can't give it to you. I deserve to marry your wife."

In these cases, you have a philosophy we can use to build a whole world on, not just a knee-jerk funny moment that hurts the scene later.

This is where you become an improviser: when you can be funny without lying, being mean or being stupid. It's not natural or easy. But a big part of humor is surprise, right? Well, we live in a world where often the most surprising thing you can do is tell the truth, be compassionate or be smart. Improv is maybe the only form of comedy that will reward you MOST for doing that.

Sometimes I write these things and I think "am I going to read them a year later and think I'm a complete jackass?" This paragraph is technically not related to the rest of the piece.

Sometimes, you'll all do something rhythmic—like everyone slapping the sides of their legs and saying "baa." Don't get stuck there too long. You're not listening and reacting any more. It's okay for a bit—like 15 seconds—but let it transform out. Wake yourselves up.

Go easy on the floors.

FEBRUARY 4TH, 2013 at 10:49AM

THE RULES

A few thoughts on the appeal and danger of coming up with new "rules." Short version of this post: The rules are bad because they are not... quite... right. But they are great because they are memorable and they stick.

Talking about these:

- Don't ask questions
- Don't fight
- Don't deny
- Don't do teaching scenes
- Don't do transaction scenes
- Don't talk about the past or future
- Don't talk about people offstage
- Don't do talking heads scenes

I think about them a lot ever since I read Mick Napier's book "Improvise: Scene From the Inside Out." In that book, which is interesting and great, Mick writes that the rules are destructive. That they came about because people noticed things bad scenes had in common, and then worked backwards to invent rules. That's why they're worded in the negative—"don't do X." They take space in your head and don't actually directly improve scenes, he said (or something like that—just read the book).

Smart, I thought, when I read that. Yeah, forget these rules! They're dumb!

However, the rules have one really powerful thing on their side: **People really remember them.** If someone took an improv class 15 years ago, they'll remember "yes and" and then also "oh! and don't ask questions!"

These rules, they stick. I respect stickiness. I figure it means there's something about them primal and true.

Someone told me this metaphor: picture a college quad where there are paved sidewalks where the designers of the school expected you to walk. But then there's these dirt paths that show where the students ACTUALLY walk. The rules are the dirt paths. Our collective oral culture has selected them over the generations.

As a teacher I want to use things that students naturally remember.

Trouble is, as Mick noted—the rules are not really RIGHT. They are approximations at best. Training wheels to use until you get a feel for how to improvise in such a way that things move forward.

If only people didn't remember them forever, we could just ignore them.

A lot of improv writing and talking are attempts to come up with better rules. Some people are good at that. I think this was one of Del's most powerful talents: to pluck simple phrases that were easy to remember and made people better.

Ones I've liked:

- "You can go to crazytown, but take the local" and "Avoid common wisdom"—Neil Casey
- "Game is what WOULD happen. Story is what COULD happen."—Anthony King
- "Chill the fuck out"—Gethard
- "Let 'er rip."—Abra Tabak

I don't know. Lots.

Someone else good at it: Amy Poehler. (Sure, I'm name-dropping but I'm allowed because I work for her.) Anyway, Amy had a meeting with the teachers at UCB a few years ago and she said to us "we want these students to **'live life onstage'**—to say what they would say. Really drill that home." And "live life onstage" really stuck—many teachers say that now. I'm not even sure if it's something Amy came up with it or if it was something she's passing on, but at any rate, it worked.

I still teach the rules, but I try to remind people they're just training wheels and at some point they won't have to think about them.

FEBRUARY 5TH, 2013 at 2:18PM

KNOW, CARE, SAY

So i just wrote about the danger or people trying replace the famous **"improv rules."** The **"don't ask questions"** and **"avoid teaching scenes"** and **"don't be coy"** type of rules. It's tough because the one thing the rules have on their side is that everyone remembers them forever.

But here I go. I'm going to suggest replacements for the rules. Oh man, can you feel the electricity?

Ahem. Okay! So: the rules aren't quite right. There's too many. They don't work in enough cases. If I had to replace them, I would replace them with this:

- Know It
- Care About It
- Say Something About It

I say this because I basically don't follow the standard rules, or at least I don't really think about them. They rules say "**Avoid transaction scenes**." But I love transaction scenes and they are very often funny. The rules say "**don't ask questions**" but my characters ask lots of questions and it works out fine.

What I DO tell myself when I'm on stage is that I should to act like *I know this world, I'm invested in it, and I'm going to speak my mind about it.*

KNOW. CARE. SAY.

See, here's what happens: improv works best if you "**live life onstage**" and just say what you would normally say in a situation. Express the opinion you really have and such.

EXCEPT we have these annoying instincts that protect us in real life but make us boring on stage. I'm talking about: admitting when you don't know something (which in real life is often), not getting invested in things that aren't your business, and keeping your mouth shut about things that might get you in trouble.

Smart rules for life. Boring onstage.

We want you to "*say what you would say, assuming you know and care.*"

Know it. Care About It. Say Something About It

So you "**don't ask questions**" because *you already know*. You should "**be affected**" because *you care*. "**Don't be coy**" but rather rather *say what you're thinking*. If you're in a transaction scene then decide that you know the clerk and you care deeply about what you're buying. It doesn't happen in real life enough, but we need it to always happen that way on stage.

Is this anything? Would people remember this? It is a help? I guess we'll see.

Related but separate: I need a word for the effect that knowing, caring and saying has on a scene. Is it "activeness"—it makes the situation more active? Present? Stakes? Importance? Interesting? Open is a word I like. It keeps the scene open. Vulnerable? I'm really letting these final paragraphs just kinda ramble and hurtle forth. [edited to add: Michael Kayne suggests "engaged" sounds kinda good, maybe] [others are suggesting "invested" but I want this term to include the kind of move where someone says "the brownies will be ready in an hour" and then realizes that's too far away and follows it up with "actually, i forgot, they're done right now." That kinda move. IMPORTANCE?]

FEBRUARY 6TH, 2013 at 12:11PM

Q: GAME VS. PREMISE

weirdlessbeardo asked: In your opinion what's the difference between game and premise?

Premise is something one person comes up with. Game is what you have once you get another improviser's input.

Don't let these semantics make it harder. We distinguish "premise" from "game" just means to point out that even if you start with a funny idea (premise), you don't have a game until your scene partner has contributed/responded. Meaning: stay open. listen, react. Be ready for your idea to change because it ISN'T "your" idea, it's the group's scene. This is a group sport.

Oh wait, you LIKE semantics? Okay, well then...

After an opening I might initiate with "Is this the Park Ranger's office? I was hunting and I killed a panda." That's my premise. I'm saying that I think that's interesting or funny and might be the heart of a game.

Then the other person says "If you have a permit, then you are free to go!" or maybe "A panda? How did a panda get here? This is Florida!" or "I've told you before. This is a RESERVE, not a SAFARI." Now we're starting to get a sense of our game—each one a bit different depending on the response.

Sometimes the premise ends up being the whole idea and the response doesn't really change it. I saw Andy Secunda on The Swarm initiate with "Christmas Eve, kids. Tonight we catch the fat man." And everyone else cheered "YEAH!" The response didn't change the premise, just confirmed it.

A small initiation—like if the suggestion is "sunbeam" and I say "Warm day, right?" That's not a premise. It's too small. I'm just starting with a piece of who-what-where, giving us a place to start, and assuming we're going to yes-and our way to something interesting soon.

I never think of any of these words while I'm improvising, only when I'm analyzing it afterwards.

FEBRUARY 6TH, 2013 at 12:14PM

Q: JUSTCRAIG: CORRECT NAME FOR JAPANESE COMPANY?

justcraig asked: When you're in a scene where there's a meeting with Japanese businessmen, what is the correct name for the Japanese company they represent?

FEBRUARY 10TH, 2013 at 9:40AM

Q: SECOND GAME MOVE?

hotoscarsmattlaud-blog asked: I'm having trouble with second game moves in my scene work—I'm in a stage of my improv education where I'm getting better at labeling and making things clear, and after an opening, I am getting the hang of initiating with a clear game. The issue for me is executing on that second step. I've had coaches remind me to explore the scene, to keep "if this is true, what else is true" in mind, but somehow I still can't attack that second move.

A hunch: you're writing it too much. make that first move clearly—it's okay to kinda "write" that one—but then after that just commit and react and let the scene go. the second game move might come from somewhere else.

FEBRUARY 16TH, 2013 at 10:46PM

Q: BE THE BIRD OR JUST FLAP MY ARMS?

Anonymous asked: If a scene calls for a bird (like a pigeon) and I'm on the back line, should I just put my hands together and flap them, or should I be the bird with my whole body?

Is this not Craig Rowin?

FEBRUARY 16TH, 2013 at 10:48PM

MINI-RUT

(written months and months ago)

I don't want to do it anymore. I know I'll change my mind soon, maybe even after a single night's sleep but I want to capture what this feels like.

Did Stepfathers tonight and my goal going in was to be less ego-driven. Less concerned about how I was doing, how funny I was—because that makes my defenses go up and makes me mean for no good reason and makes me defensive. I wanted to just be in the moments and feel them and be confident and playful.

In a sense I was successful—I did not feel angry or defensive. I enjoyed the show. But I also felt toothless and out of ideas. Uninspired. Does one have to go with the other—serenity and and empty head? The Buddhists would say yes. But are Buddhists funny?

I could quit tonight. I could be done. I've had a blessed improv career and I could just stop and not perform again and focus on writing and maybe computer programming and who knows. Like maybe I've used up my last good idea.

Man I felt like a fraud a bunch tonight. Just with no idea of what to do or say, or what could be funny. How did I get on the Stepfathers? It feels like weeks since I've been in a groove there. I'm just someone who's good at obeying a system, it's why I succeeded at a hierarchal improv theatre rather than in the wilds of stand-up, scripted acting, etc. Learn enough people's names and they'll put you on a team. Lots of thoughts along these lines.

My teammates were good. I enjoyed watching them. I felt like a pillar of NO or else a brainless arbitrary scattershot of nice. Couldn't commit.

But YES I was serene! Really! I wasn't panicking or going into dumb rants or attacking people for no reason. I had philosophies, I could see the room around me my characters were in. I must remember that: I accomplished my goal.

I will wake up tomorrow and feel better. Or I'll see my brother or someone and feel funny again. But not now. Right now, I feel done.

ADDING NOW, MONTHS LATER: When I feel like I did that night I often think of times that I've heard people who I think are great express their doubt in themselves. I think "this person is crazy—he/she is really good! They have some weird self-defeating thing going on that they're giving into." When I think of that, then I can more easily cast off my own self-defeatism. "Someone else would look at me and think *I'M* crazy." So I put this here to make YOU forget your own self-defeatism. It happens to everyone; it's mostly pointless.

A separate thing I remember is all the people who quit before me. I've run into people I took classes with and they say "yeah, sometimes I wish I stuck with it. I saw you in that show and remember how we were in class..." and I think "Thank God I didn't quit."

I remember that, and then I don't quit. I shake that shit off. The universe will kick me out of this game when it's time for me to go.

FEBRUARY 17TH, 2013 at 2:13PM

Q: JUSTCRAIG: FUNNIER BIRD?

justcraig asked: That bird question earlier was not me. I do have a bird related improv question though: Which is the funnier bird to be talking about in an improv scene, "red-footed booby" or "squatter pigeon?" Thanks.

FEBRUARY 25TH, 2013 at 9:23PM

COACHING RATES

[ADDED AFTER POSTING: This post was aimed at warning away from newer coaches who haven't yet earned the right to demand a higher rate. PLEASE SEE MY NEXT POST about veteran coaching rates]

Coaches who charge a LOT are rarely the good coaches. You notice that yet? Yes, there's exceptions and stuff—you know it when there are exceptions, like if you get one of the very top people who is doing an occasional thing. But in general for your regular coaches: don't get played, young uns!

Sure, I'll put a number on it. I think $30 an hour is the top for a regular coach—that's for a senior coach that you KNOW is good. $20 an hour is probably more like it. Tell me if I'm way off, veterans, and I will post here if so.

But regardless of the numbers, if the only people you are talking to are charging a lot, get a less experienced coach who wants to do it. Contact me if you want some names of good people I bet you're not thinking of because they're not ROCKSTAR enough or whatever.

I don't mean to take money out of people's hands: it's still in the end a free market. I guess I say to indie teams and young teams: ask around and listen to your gut.

FEBRUARY 26TH, 2013 at 6:39AM

COACHING RATES, AMENDED

I'm sorry for posting my last post hastily. I've woken up to many vet coaches either gently or in a diplomatically irritated tone telling me I'm missing part of the picture: the veteran coach part of the picture. I can see their point. Let me elaborate:

A few qualifiers:

1. It's a free market. whatever you're paying, if you feel it's fair then it's fair. if you're paying a lot but the coach is good, then it's good. there's no hard, fast rules.

2. I run the UCB school but what i'm saying here is NOT official UCB opinion and I am not an active coach. What i express here is my personal opinion. My opinion in general is that *coaching should not be prohibitively expensive*, but yes that is a subjective term.

Okay, so what made me post my last post was thought of people who are in their third or fourth improv class EVER and they are FIRED UP on improv. Their eyes are aglow and they want to "DO IT RIGHT." I remember that feeling. You are in a state where you can watch someone do a sound and movement for two hours and rationalize that you saw a real work of art because you just love everything about improv. I worry that these people think they're doing it wrong if they're not paying TOP DOLLAR for a coach.

These are the same people that teachers like me tell, all the time, GET IN A PRACTICE GROUP. And we mean it, because you need reps.

NOW, I worry for those people that they are getting taken either by coaches who do not deserve a high rate OR coaches who DO deserve a high rate but maybe aren't a NECESSARY fit for what you need on a regular basis.

Let's say there's two general categories of coaches:

1. **COACHES.** The newer people. People who do the majority of the work out there. They're either never been on a team or they've been a team for around a year or less, and they've been coaching for a year, year-and-a-half. They have some experience, but not an overwhelming amount. These people do a lot of coaching. These are who I"m talking about in the previous post. They should be charging $20-$30 an hour, probably towards the low end of that. And if you're a new group, you can get a lot of mileage out of these people if they're devoted which a lot of them are. NOTE that this category is called COACHES not TEACHERS. They don't need to have the holy grail, they need to have a sense of what a good practice feels like, know the fundamentals, and know when it's time to say "buckle down on this one and take your time" or "time to just do a harold and get one in for practice." They're learning how to coach with the idea of being teachers someday and they know it, so they're not going to charge an exorbitant amount. They should be humble towards their craft of coaching like you are towards yours of doing improv.

2. **WORKSHOPPERS.** I don't have a term for this but it's for people who have indeed coached a shitload, and have been on a team for many years, like three or more and are really good and you know it. These people may charge more, and I can understand it. We're talking above $30 an hour. They deserve it, they've put the time in. Maybe they have a higher rate, but they come to shows? Coaching with them is kinda like an inexpensive informal class or workshop from someone who has been around.

   THREE THINGS FOR THIS GROUP
   - They should be good! You should be able to tell in the preciseness of their notes and their confidence and the confidence you feel during these practices that these people have been around the practice/coaching/teaching block. Even one practice should feel a higher quality. Without being hostile, you can expect more from these people. They should remember you from practice to practice and have sense of the individuals pretty early. They should be able to explain why they're assigning the exercises they are, they should know the general current scene of improv and be able to speak to examples from it. Know that there are more inexpensive options if these people fall short and be willing to expect more from this more expensive group. If it doesn't feel like this, go back to the first group.
   - Some of these people are not really coaching much but they're good and so they charge a higher rate because it's not worth their time unless they get paid a higher rate. They'll tell you that. They'll be like "i don't really coach, if you want to pay $150 i'll do a three hour thing." This case might be worth it once in awhile to work with someone you really admire, but you don't need this a lot if you're in that FERVOR of IMPROV I described above. You need reps and these are cool but maybe more-expensive-than-necessary reps. Except now and then, at your discretion.
   - If you're really just getting reps, and you're new—like a level 3 or 4 group who don't know each other well—you don't need to restrict yourself to this group ONLY. Not trying to bilk my deserving, veteran colleagues—but I believe they would agree with this: If you're a newer practice group who just needs reps to get more fluid and

relaxed don't restrict yourself ONLY to this group. That newer league of people can be great.

- Now, if you've formed an indie group and want a regular devoted coach, okay maybe you're looking for the "workshoppers" more. Bear in mind your own experience level when shopping around.

POSTSCRIPT—TWO/THREE HOURS

I had forgotten that lots of practice groups and teams have just two hour sessions as a regular thing. Three hours is better. But I know that with scheduling conflicts that sometimes it's two hours or nothing.

But here's another argument for three hours, especially if you're drawing from the more expensive coaching level which I'm calling "workshoppers": If it's two hours, the second more expensive group aren't going to come out for just their hourly rate times two. Like if a vet coach is charging $30 an hour or even $40 an hour, and it's just two hours and they factor in travel time—they'd rather stay home and pretend to work on their spec script (zing!). But for three hours, they'll keep a lower hourly rate AND your practice will be more effective. If you're going to pay a high rate for more experienced people—that third hour will add more quality maybe than you are appreciating. I know it's not always possible.

CONCLUSION

I do apologize for posting hastily last night. It's a more subtle issue than I gave it attention. Maybe if nothing else ask your teacher or other people about particular people if they think your coach is giving you a fair deal. I'm not saying this to create an atmosphere of suspicion. But it takes a while in this culture to get a feel for the "norm" and if you're paying money and investing time it's okay to get informed.

FEBRUARY 26TH, 2013 at 7:49AM

Q: JUSTCRAIG: COACHING QUESTION

justcraig asked: Coaching question: In improv, if you're playing a coach who is addressing a team at halftime, what name should you give to the one player who you will be yelling at the most? Thanks.

FEBRUARY 28TH, 2013 at 2:58PM

NEW CONTROVERSY

Not enough improv characters say "I gotta run this by the commish."

FEBRUARY 28TH, 2013 at 7:12PM

Q: GREG ROWAN

chriskula asked: Why come you never answer questions from Greg Rowan?

MARCH 9TH, 2013 at 11:31AM

HOW CAN I GET OUT OF MY HEAD?

Getting out of your head refers to the desire to be doing improv without having your head full of rules and thoughts and worries. It means you want to just... play... rather than be paralyzed by all the rules your improv teachers have told you. Getting out of your head also means that you want to stop feeling stuck on stage, that you have lost your instinct of what to do next, and that you are doubting yourself and worrying constantly. You feel that way and you're tired of it: what can you do?

Closely related to this question is the "I just had a terrible class/practice/show and I'm in a rut and what should I do?"

These are very common concerns. I would say it's the number one most frequent question I hear. Part of my job is picking which classes we put up at UCB-NY. If I ever want a class to sell out in zero seconds, I call it "Get Out Of Your Head!"

ZACH WOODS' ADVICE

Well the first and best set of advice I have to offer isn't even mine. It's from UCB Performer Zach Woods in an email he sent to then-UCB student (now teacher and performer) Achilles Stamatelakey about this very problem. In Achilles' words:

In May 2006, I had no confidence in my improv. After taking classes for a year-and-a-half, I felt like I was only getting worse at performing. I sent the following e-mail to some of the teachers and coaches I'd worked closely with at the time to seek their advice.

> I'm not feeling great about my improv and I hope you can give me some advice.
>
> I don't remember when I've felt this unconfident in my performance. For the past month or so, I've constantly felt indecisive in scenes (both in practices and performances). I also feel way in my head and tentative. I find myself making moves because they seem like the "right" move to make, not because they're best for the scene or the most fun. I'm making weak choices and end up in mediocre scenes because of it. In other words, I feel like I'm stuck "improvising" rather than "playing" a scene.
>
> Part of my lack of confidence might stem from having some really great rehearsals and shows in March, then having really high expectations of myself in April during Harold team auditions and not meeting those expectations. That I got rejected from two teacher-approved performance workshops hasn't helped my confidence either. It's a vicious cycle.
>
> What do you do when you feel like you're in a rut? I want to feel like I'm improving my skills as an improviser in some way, but I haven't felt confident in weeks. I don't see myself getting out of this slump anytime soon.
>
> Thanks again for all your help.
>
> —Achilles

I got a bunch of responses, all of which I am extremely grateful for. Here is one of those responses:

> Hey Achilles,
>
> I'm sorry you're feeling this way. Everyone gets in ruts from time to time, and I know how discouraging it feels. While there are some things you can do to help, I think the short (and probably disappointing) answer is you've just got to ride it out. Ruts always last longer than we want them to, but they don't last forever. So try to be patient....as impossible as that sounds.
>
> Here's some other stuff....

– I think sometimes people who care a great deal about improv can get so wrapped up in the improv community and improv itself that their self-esteem becomes dependent on the quality of their improv. This happens to me more often than I'd like, and it's always bad news for both my improv and my self-esteem. I think it's important to remember (especially when you're in a slump) that the qualities that make you valuable as a human being have nothing to do with group games or tag-outs. Whether or not you're a worthwhile person has nothing to do with improv. If you're doing awesome shows, you could still be an asshole, if you're doing bad shows you could still be a kind, generous guy. Hopefully you're not neurotic enough to be plagued by these issues, but, I know I am, so I figured I'd mention this stuff, just in case. So....

Remind yourself that your value as a person is in no way related to, or dependent on the quality of your improv.

– Another thing that can put people in their heads is a need to "achieve."

While it's great to get some validation in the form of recognition or approval, I think it's best not to put too much stock in external recognition. The warm, mushy feeling that comes from 'achieving' (getting put on a team, class, etc.) is fleeting, and soon you're back to worrying and working and trying to improve. I think it's good to be patient and to move at your own rate. Try not to measure your progress against other people's progress. I know that's hard (maybe impossible) but I think if you allow yourself to improve at your own rate, it liberates you from the self-conscious, insecure, self-flagellation that is anathema to good improv. Put your nose to the grindstone and do the work. It's important to have goals, but I think it's also important that those goals be rooted in personal progress rather than external achievement.

– Slumps are sometimes a result of improv-overkill. If you've been watching and doing improv constantly, it's possible that you're a bit burnt out. Good improv isn't inspired by other improv, it's inspired by life. If all you do is do/watch improv, you may have a deficit of life experiences to draw from. Take time to do the non-improv activities that you enjoy— things that have absolutely nothing to do with comedy. This will allow you to recharge. It will also put you back in touch with the things that make you unique and interesting as a person. That stuff is essential to good improv.

Improv isn't just about game and technique, it's also about personality. It's important to take time to do non-comedy things that make you who you are. Listen to the music you like, read a book, fly a kite, hang out with your non-improv friends, go swimming, walk a dog, do whatever you want as long as it doesn't require a coach. Just get away from improv.

In a weird way it's kind of like the game of a scene. If all you do in a scene is hit game, game, game, and you never play the reality of the scene, both the game and the scene will feel inorganic and contrived. Similarly, in life, if all you do is improv, improv, improv, and you don't do interesting, fun non-improv stuff, your improv will feel stiff, and your life won't feel so good either (in my experience).

– Get a new pair of shoes. I don't know if this works, but I was in a slump once and I asked Peter Gwinn what I should do. He told me to get new shoes and wear them during rehearsals/shows. Make sure they are significantly different from the shoes you currently wear to rehearsals/performances. This might be bullshit, but it might be a miracle cure.

– Eat healthy, sleep well, exercise. I find that this stuff makes a huge difference. Taking care of your body allows you to focus better, etc. You probably already do this, but if not, eat some soy and get 8 hours of REM.

– If you feel like a show/rehearsal went badly, don't beat yourself up. If you notice yourself moping or obsessing over the show, try to do something to take your mind off it. You are not helping your improv by mentally abusing yourself. Self-flagellation is just a way of indulging one's own insecurities and fears. Sometimes you can't help it, but try to avoid abusing yourself if you can.

– And remember, your slump is temporary. It's more in your own head than in reality.

Be patient, relax, and your slump will pass. Seriously.

You're going to be alright,

Zach

PS. I apologize if this email comes off as pedantic and/or convoluted.

Besides the great advice, my favorite part of this e-mail is that Zach apologizes at the end for having written it. Very Zach.

Yep, that's pretty good.

Here's some wordier, less helpful advice on the same subject.

WHAT I DO: REMEMBER SIMPLE MANTRAS

Expanding on Zach's "everyone gets in ruts from time to time," let me overtly state that I feel I am in my head on a fairly regular basis. I've done this for 12 years and have achieved some amount of success at least within the society of the UCB Theatre in NYC (perform on a weekly show on the weekend, am one of the senior teachers) and I'd say every 4 or 5 shows I walk off stage convinced, wholly, that I am a fraud, who snuck by everyone who is in charge of deciding who is good by keeping my head down and being quiet at signature moments.

And so here are the specific things I do when I am feeling "in my head"—and by that I mean when I am feeling doubtful, and unsure of my abilities and unfunny.

First I have a few different **mantras** I run through in my head. One is "**listen and react.**" I tell myself to forget everything else and just obey that rule. This is an effort to keep it simple, but to still be participatory.

Another one is I'll tell myself "**be playful.**" This was advice my brother gave me before we did a two-prov set. It was the first time we had performed at a particular theatre and we wanted to be good. He grabbed both of my shoulders and looked at me and said "be playful—you're good when you're playful" and it freed me of worrying about being "good" or doing it "right."

Another trick I will do is to **remember a particular improv class I had in which I always felt great**. For me it's my fourth improv class. For some reasons, whether it was the teacher or the people in that class I don't fully know, I always felt confident and capable in that class. When I'm backstage before a show and feeling lousy I will quietly invoke the feeling of being in the backline of that class. It helps me recall some muscle memory of that confidence.

A final trick I will do—and I bet this reveals some problem with intimacy or something but who gives a crap if it helps my show—is that I **pretend that I am performing with strangers**. Sometimes with people I know I get tentative and unsure and I will second guess myself. When playing strangers

I become a nice combination of decisive but polite. I listen more but I also make bold moves. It helps. So sometimes I'll tell myself that everyone I'm playing with are strangers.

Some other thoughts to consider if you're in your head:

THE LAST SHOW

Part of this phenomenon is that you only feel as good as your very last class/practice/show. You can have 1,000 great scenes in a row, but once you have a bad one, you walk away saying "maybe I'm terrible at this." It's easy to have a short memory when assessing yourself.

The good side of that is **it only take one "good" class/practice/show to feel better again**. Often the best way to get out of your head, is simply to do more of it, and increase the odds that you will do a scene where things go your way and you walk out feeling better.

BEWARE TRYING TO PLEASE JUST ONE PERSON (WHO ISN'T YOU)

Let's get some data here: is it ONE PERSON who is making you feel in your head? Like have you started taking a class, and the teacher doesn't seem to be impressed with you, or maybe even actively seems to be unimpressed with you? Are you "in your head" trying to please this one person? It's understandable to want to please your teacher but you should know that everyone who takes even a small number of improv teachers will invariably run into a class or teacher that they simply don't jibe with.

That doesn't mean that you're bad at this, it means you're in a particular context that is making you feel a bit out of sorts. **Do not get in the habit of letting your view of yourself be dependent on what someone else thinks of you.** Especially one particular person.

MARCH 25TH, 2013 at 7:52AM

YOU WILL NEVER FIGURE THIS OUT

I mean this as a consolation: you will never completely figure out improv. Not forever, anyhow. You have a grasp on it for a few weeks, maybe even a few months, and then it moves away from you. You stumble on a new exercise or a new mantra and can do no wrong. Decisive moves. Certain viewpoints. Audiences liking you right away. But then it just fades and you are lost again, searching for the next key.

Things that have given me the key to being good at this in the past:

- "listen and react"
- "find the game"
- "match energy"
- "accept every offer"
- "live life onstage"
- "justify"
- "point of view"
- "be brave and honest"
- "chill out"

Each one of those was like a booster rocket for a while, and then weirdly stopped working! I had to switch up my game and try something else. It's like improv is this invisible balloon that you cannot get your arms all the way around no matter what. You hold it, just barely, but it gives and starts to slip away you must adjust your arms, and find your grip again.

MARCH 26TH, 2013 at 11:48AM

"GOOD" FIGHTING?

This is my blog, right? So I can do something as shamelessly indulgent as just type out a scene I remember being in that made me laugh? This was in a Monkeydick (sorry yes, that was the team name) reunion show hosted by "The Lab" at Player's Theater in 2011 I think a week before DCM.

If it makes it any less indulgent, let me point out that I think it was my scene partner Matt DeCoster and John Gemberling on the backline who make this scene funny for me. It's also an example of "good" fighting, I think? At any rate, this made me laugh. If it's useless, you can all just summarily walk away, as that is the implied contracts you have with all blog entries.

Me: "Matt, could you proctor the SAT today? I'm supposed to do it but I accidentally made plans this weekend and can't do it."

Matt: "Sure, I'll do it. Doing anything fun?"

Me: "Linda and I are going to a B&B for our anniversary."

John Gemberling on backline makes a car honking noise.

Me: "Ah, there she is now."

Matt: "How do you know that's her?"

Me: "Excuse me?"

Matt: "How do you know that's Linda?"

Me: "You know, I don't know, I guess I just assumed."

Matt: "That seems pretty self-centered of you. Just any horn is the horn for you?"

Gemberling makes a different very distinctive old-timey cartoon car honking noise

Me: "Ah yes, THAT's her. I remember now, her car has that honking sound. Thanks for helping."

Matt: "No problem. Get to work on your narcissism!"

Something like that. I'm probably cleaning it up a bit, but this is close. Actually I think this scene ended with DeCoster coming with me and we got into an elevator and rode it in silence for a full minute, then the scene was edited? Improv is fun. NO RULES.

APRIL 10TH, 2013 at 2:15PM

Q: CAN ONE INITIATE WITH A GAME?

Anonymous asked: Is it possible to "initiate with a game?" from an opening? Sometimes I hear teachers talk about doing that, and then other teachers say you can't have a game until someone reacts.

Technically you "initiate with a premise" and you wait for a reaction to see what your scene partner's take is before you declare it a game. But I think this is besides the point. When someone says "initiate with a game"—even though that technically it's better to say "initiate with a premise"—the point is to try initiating with a pretty full idea rather than start with a smaller choice. It's not the only way to start a scene, it's not even necessarily the best way, but starting with a premise is a way that a seasoned improviser should feel comfortable with doing.

[EDITED TO ADD: I just think this kind of semantic parsing is kinda pointless? I mean for an improv blog it's okay, but if I said "initiate with a game" to a student and he/she was like "i don't know what you mean! do you mean initiate with a premise?" i'd want to say "never mind. two more up."]

APRIL 11TH, 2013 at 1:18PM

Q: STOP BEING CLEVER?

Anonymous asked: How do I stop trying to be clever? It's difficult to trust that things will work out into funny.

I don't know. Maybe the answer is to be MORE clever? Be smarter and funnier than everyone on stage and in the audience? It doesn't sound artful but I can't imagine how that wouldn't work. I would be interested in watching someone who was without-a-doubt the smartest funniest person in the room. Of course "clever" is subjective. I don't mean make the most clever "lines" since that's not really how improv works. But the most clever theatrical choice that puts us RIGHT AT THE START in an ironical, relatable, high-stakes situation? That sounds pretty awesome. I don't know how it is that words like "funny" and "smart" and "clever" get bad names to some people. I want the best, funniest, smartest people on the stages I'm watching. "Be undeniably better than everyone" is not a bad success strategy in any field, so I can't see how being clever is bad? Gethard wrote a great thing on how it's the TRYING that's bad. Like TRYING to be clever is lame, but I think even in that piece he doesn't say that the part where someone IS clever is bad? Go find that piece. Be clever enough to find Gethard's piece on trying to be funny—it's good. Take all this with a grain of salt. I honestly could be a fraud of a teacher who has "ascended" to his position at UCB through a weird combination of circumstance and luck and am actually a fountain of bad advice but no one has noticed. I mean I have this blog, but so what? The qualifications for starting this blog were 1) having an email address and 2) nothing else. Anyway, I can see what you're getting at in that trying to make jokes and be funny is usually something that goes along with bad listening and bad commitment. Then again, I can't think of a single good improviser that I wouldn't also describe as clever. Also funny smart interesting unpredictable and cool. Stop trying but also don't, like, undervalue being funny. Being funny is good! Being clever helps! I'm clever! I'm fucking super clever! Holy shit, you should see me! I'm all fast-thinking and shit and it's a big help. I recommend it. Yes, your teammates will support you when you're having off days or they should but then again it's not, like, BAD on the days that you are NOT OFF. Improv forgives off days but it's not like, EXCITED, that you're off either? Whatever happened in improv and in the world at large to the idea that we should celebrate superiority? I like people who are better. They are better. Can improvartvice put this whole thing on a t-shirt? I'll buy one for everyone in the City of New York.

APRIL 11TH, 2013 at 1:36PM

Q: WOULD YOU BLOW OFF SEMANTICS QUESTIONS IN CLASS?

Anonymous asked: Thanks for answering my question about game vs. premise. I have to ask, would you have blown off that question in class because it's an inappropriate question to ask, or because you don't want beginners getting bogged down in semantics? Semantics seem to really matter at UCB. Inventing vs. discovering, game vs. premise, on game, off game, yes and vs if this then what. I get so many notes related to these terms I'd feel strange if I asked about it in class and the teacher dismissed the question.

Yes, that's fair to say. I guess I think that NO semantics are perfect—they're all approximations and it's in the student's best interest to try and get the intention of the semantics rather than try to find the cases where the semantics fail. So I get upset when a student tries to think of hypothetical cases where the semantic seems to be indicating bad behavior, because it's a waste of time. And similarly any prolonged discussion of semantics quickly becomes just academic and not practical for the stage, in my opinion.

It's similar to a memory I have of Sunday School—like third grade—when a friend of mine would try to find cases where the ten commandments wouldn't make sense. "Honor your mother and father"—"what if you're adopted and your adopted father is abusive"—my friend (who was hilarious) wasn't trying to learn the lesson but just to see if there was a way to poke holes in the rule? And regardless of what your thoughts are of religion or sunday school—the phrase "honor your mother and father"—I mean, you get the point of it, right?

Game and premise are similar. They're both trying to articulate that improv scenes will often revolve around a single comedic idea or behavior or THING that comes up, and it's helpful to learn how to try and have that happen as early as possible sometimes. We make two different terms since one—premise—is something that a single person can bring up and the other—game—is something that is agreed upon by everyone in the scene, ideally.

But when someone says "initiate with a premise/game" I think what they're saying is "let's try the tricky thing of starting with an idea, which brings with a series of challenges as opposed to starting from just a suggestion which has a separate set of challenges." And whether they mean premise or game is almost immaterial in that context. What I hear when someone says "start with a premise/game" is roughly "start with something funny" where 'something funny' vaguely means something interesting/unusual/funny/intriguing right at the top.

And so I guess it would FEEL to me like the person who asked the question was trying to make the semantics these airtight formulas when they are best seen as principles?

It would depend on tone, level and context for me to determine if it were a topic that needed discussion in the moment.

APRIL 11TH, 2013 at 1:41PM

Q: WHY DO YOU LIKE PUTTING LIMITS ON SCENES?

dustindrury asked: Why do you like putting limits on scenes and seeing how people play them? Is it because art without limitation is more difficult to achieve greatness? Is part of it because giving us a rule puts us in on an inside joke/rule/game and gives an immediate meta subgame to play?I love watching and doing these scenes, just curious what your intent is.

You're talking about when I went into your class and made Alan Starzinski and Erik Tanouye come in and do a bunch of scenes with restrictions? I like seeing good people do hard things. And I was trying to pick things that I think improvisers find themselves wanting to do. "Start with a premise off a suggestion"—it's hard to do, and not essential, but it IS something that good improvisers can generally do. It's the equivalent of taking an NBA player and saying "make a three point shot with only 5 seconds left on the shot clock"—it's not the most important thing but it's fun to see a good athlete try. I'd like to make a battery of restrictions for people to try. Maybe like an improv obstacle course. "Think of 5 non-silly names for a family members. Now name 5 non-silly names that still sound Victorian." I just made that up. Hello Dustin!

APRIL 11TH, 2013 at 1:48PM

Q: JUSTCRAIG: HOW MUCH TONGUE?

justcraig asked: How much tongue should be used if you want to get a huge laugh by having two male improvisers make out in the last few seconds of a Cage Match show? Thanks in advance.

APRIL 11TH, 2013 at 3:04PM

Q: WHAT KIND OF SUPPORT WHEN I SEE NO WAY TO HELP?

Anonymous asked: Sometimes at the start of the scene, there will be some virtually impossible-to-resolve agreement problem between the 2 or more people who stepped out. Now, if I'm on the backline, and I can think of a clever line that helps create agreement, then I'll walk on and do that. But, my question is: if I'm on the backline, and I see no way to help create agreement, are there any other kind of support moves that can help the scene get back on track? Or are scenes like that just busted?

Sounds like you're walking on too early to me. Let the first two out deal with it. If you're thinking "but they're not dealing with it," be patient. Some scenes, especially first scenes, are like a car engine starting—sputtering a bit before it catches.

APRIL 11TH, 2013 at 3:16PM

Q: ADVICE FOR A SHOW TONIGHT?

weirdlessbeardo asked: I have a show tonight. Can you give me some advice?

Yes, try these initiations.

- "Why the bed?"
- "You are wearing all of my pants."
- "I think I'm making a new face."
- "Why SHOULD I put on clothes?"
- "I killed Freddie Mercury."
- (miming typing) "This tumblr post is hilarious."

And these responses (not for the above initiations, but to be used arbitrarily)"
- "Yes, that was me."
- "I know! It's terrible."
- "Too late."
- "God damn it!"
- "Cool if I leave now?"

Names for other characters:
- Landon
- Brill
- Sentry
- Johnnobbin
- Henries
- Shurtain
- Benson
- Jenly
- Bevers
- Georgous
- Viv
- Marion
- DeVoe

MAY 4TH, 2013 at 10:42PM

I live in the most northern area of Brooklyn where there are a bunch of warehouses (all slowly being converted into dumbly expensive lofts and headquarters for things like Kickstarter and weird ventures like community garden social networks and probably a permanent studio for the show *Girls*) and every now and then there is a for-real old-school RAVE in these warehouses.

And tonight is one of them. It's called "Into the Wormhole" which is hilariously rave-y and you can't buy tickets, you must be personally invited and I don't care because I am in my apartment hiding inside my Tumblr.

Anyway, my normally desolate street is jammed with cars and taxis filled with—there is no more fair term to say than this—*young people*—all filing into this warehouse on the East River. Here are some of the outfits I just saw on people as they walked in: Girl in an orchid-colored sparkly cocktail dress and heels, two guys in neon tank tops and shorts (matching), an impossibly thin dude carrying a skateboard, girl in welder mask and metal bikini, someone as a Mad Men-era stewardess (one can say stewardess when referring to that era) and a (i think) man dressed as Captain America holding a GLOW STICK.

And so I wanted to come to this improv blog and say that all the people going to this rave are very **on-game**.

That's it. Haven't typed anything here in a bit so here I am.

MAY 7TH, 2013 at 8:10PM

Q: ARE STRONG ACTING SKILLS NECESSARY?

Anonymous asked: I'm an improv student with zero acting experience prior to taking 101. I've noticed most of my classmates have a lot of experience with acting, or act for a living. For some reason I never drew a connection between acting and improv, but I'm now wondering if my underdeveloped acting skills are inhibiting my improv. What is your opinion—are strong acting skills needed to be a strong improviser?

I think acting skills are necessary to be a strong improviser but lots and lots of people start studying improv without any acting experience and without strong acting skills. You'll grow them; don't fret. To a certain degree, it just happens. Do enough improv and you just gain more comfort on stage, and that translates to acting skills. Get in touch with your opinions and feelings about things and you will make fast decisive reactions on stage and THAT translates to acting skills. As for the people around you who have done more acting: 1) they're aren't as many as you might fear/think and 2) their skills will rub off on you without you even knowing it.

I do not believe that improv can make someone's inherent sense of humor much better. But it can definitely make someone a better actor. I'd say that's the number one most reliable skill improvement one gets from doing a lot of improv. Number two is writing chops. Number three is awareness of dumb specifics from current geek cultures.

MAY 28TH, 2013 at 11:23PM

SMALL MEN DRAFTS: LIBERTY PLAZA

Thursday night (May 30) at 8pm Neil Casey and I present our sketch show "Small Men." It's been running a long time. We officially opened the show a year ago, and had workshopped it for four months before that, and had initially done it one time a year before THAT.

I recently looked back at the first drafts and was genuinely surprised to see how much the sketches had changed. I was also surprised to see that we didn't really know what the show was going to be like when we started working on it.

Our initial plan was to write a "2004 sketch show" since that was the last time Neil and I had written sketch together. I don't mean 2004 references, but that we'd do the kind of sketch show that one would have done at UCB-NY in 2004—not that much video, minimal tech. (The songs in the current show reflect this—they are all songs that were used a lot as transition music in the early 2000s.) It was going to be an unambitious show, something just to get Neil and I back on the sketch scene at UCB.

But in the course of writing and performing sketch that all faded and a different show emerged—one with long scenes and lots of dialogue and an unplanned recurring theme of celebrating people with minimal power, kind of.

I've never done a show with the long development period that Small Men has had, and so for the fun of it I want to show how one of the main sketches came to be. (consider this blog entry to be "sketchnonsense" not "improvnonsense")

So this is "Liberty Plaza" a sketch in which two employees of a small town argue about approving a left-hand turn lane into a shopping plaza. Here's a sample from the first draft:

DAVID

Shut your fucking face, Henry. Shut it the fuck up and tell me what it is you want. You want an awning permit for your brother-in-law's Einstein Brothers franchise?

HENRY

They are doing quite well without an awning.

DAVID

They are fucking dying, and you know it. Say the word, they'll get their awning and I get my traffic light at Liberty Goddamn Plaza.

HENRY

David, Liberty Plaza does not need a traffic light.

DAVID

Liberty Plaza is the FUTURE of this town! They've already got a Game Stop, they're got a sushi place and you didn't hear it from me but they're a goddamn cunt hair away from getting a Duchess in there. If you don't have a traffic light there's gonna be an apocalypse of traffic jams of consumers trying to get in its parking lot. It's the hottest strip mall in Wilmington!

This sketch came from me telling Neil about when I was a reporter and watched land use meetings in a small CT town and him talking about the strident dramatic tone of the Jane Jacobs book "The Death and Life of Great American Cities." We liked the idea of mid-level city employees passionately defending their issues, both because it could sound silly and because it was an example of real people doing real jobs that aren't normally celebrated.

We sat in a bar and improvised a bunch of dialogue, and wrote a "shitty first draft." It reads to me now like a clumsy Glengarry Glen Ross meets Parks and Rec. Lots of swearing. Specifics all over the place.

We met several more times over a few months. Each time we'd read what we wrote before and tweak it, and also improvise a bunch more stuff and write down our favorites. Certain lines were winning out and surviving these rewriting sessions.

We talked a LOT about the issues at play in this sketch. I'd describe the hammy and theatrical people from the zoning board I used to cover (a high-paid lawyer begrudgingly kissing the ass of a locally elected super-liberal guy in a turtleneck and a 'CCCP' hat). Neil made me read aloud from Jacobs' book—her diatribe against enclosed parks in housing projects was awesomely full of fire and brimstone.

We had a lot of discussions about the passion hidden in these town meetings, and how much they affected people's everyday lives much more than seemingly more grand things. We started getting protective of the sketch—we wanted our guys to come out looking good.

Over these meetings, we started to iron out the specifics. Replacing "Duchess" with the more recognizable "Friendly's." Neil's character was getting fussier, calling it a "turning lane" instead of a "turn lane."

DAVID
FUCK Bran Mar Plaza! Are you kidding me? What do you got in there, a SHOP RITE and a VIDEO STORE? It's an embarrassment! Liberty Plaza is the economic hub of the whole god damn Concord Pike if you don't count the mall! We got a sushi place, we got a Gold's Gym and you didn't hear this from me but we are one cunt hair away from getting a Friendly's in there!

HENRY
No way you'll get a Friendly's in there.

DAVID
Oh, it's coming.

HENRY
Look, David, you know darn well we can't just throw turning lanes in front of every shopping plaza that wants one. It takes planning, takes resources...

After we read it to our director Michael Delaney, he said that we were playing the "proper noun game" and so we should ramp that up. He also said to cut back the swearing. We decided we would never mention the town but that to us it was a mixture of Wilmington, Delaware (Brynn Marr Plaza) and Danbury, CT (Route 7 wetlands).

HENRY

Oh David, not now. Ann Gerratano was just in here demanding I finish up the survey of the Route 7 wetlands.

DAVID

Forget the wetlands survey, Henry! Need I remind you that I am chairman, interim, of the Chamber of Commerce...

HENRY

And I am Deputy Liaison to the Zoning Board of Appeals, David. But I have NO idea why you're so upset!

DAVID

Do not play dumb, Henry! Jack Cosgrove called me this morning, in TEARS, and told me that you revoked approval for the new left turn lane into Liberty Plaza. Please tell me he's joking!

HENRY

Yes, that's right. You know Eric Sprock did a traffic study that says there's no pressing need for a turning lane into Liberty Plaza.

We read it to Delaney, and then had a few meetings where we'd perform it. Each of these times we'd tweak the dialogue as we'd say it. Delaney would suggest phrases and veto others, or go to bat to protect others (I remember he loved when Neil would say "that's my wife's pet project and it's GD sacrosanct" and would remind us to keep it in).

Delaney also made our performances more specific. Neil was getting more buttoned-down. We decided he was a family man who would never really stand up to a superior. He developed a voice for it that sounded a mixture of mousey and rarefied. And I was someone who saw himself as a crusader, though in reality would not really have the power to change much. Delaney wanted me to be full of intensity without the profanity (though we kept in choice colorful swears like "one cunt hair away from replacing Computer City with a Friendly's").

The dialogue started getting very specific. This...

DAVID

You want an awning permit for your brother-in-law's Einstein Brothers franchise?

became this...

DAVID
I say you're still steamed that the chamber opposed the retractable awning permit for your sister's Einstein Brothers bagel place.

and this...

HENRY
David, Liberty Plaza will handle its capacity just fine. Look at Bryn Mar Plaza.

became this...

HENRY
Brynn Marr Plaza is an exquisite open-air shopping arcade that is doing very well.

The first few times we performed this sketch in front of an audience, it would start slow before doing well. We thought maybe because there wasn't a hard reveal where you introduce the game to the audience. The main "jokes" were proper nouns that seemed to imply a back story. So we added a line that was meant to be over-the-top even for this sketch, to sort of "teach" the audience that we meant the complicated mouthfuls of jargon to be the joke. This line:

DAVID
Eric SPROCK? You mean "used eminent domain to seize 2 acres of Tibbet's Farm to replace ONE traffic light with THREE roundabouts at the Augustine Cutoff to connect Falk and Weldin ROADS" Eric Sprock? Please.

HENRY
It's faster for me.

And there were jokes that we wanted to hit but weren't. So we framed more obviously. Like we loved this line but it never got any reaction:

DAVID
Liberty Plaza is going to the economic HUB of the town. If you don't count the mall.

So we started doing this:

> **DAVID**
> Liberty Plaza is going to be the economic HUB of the town.
>
> **DAVID / HENRY**
> If you don't count the mall.

Some of the jokes still don't hit the way we want. This line:

> **DAVID**
> What is this about, Henry? Are you mad that the Chamber hasn't featured you in our html newsletter?

"Html newsletter" makes us laugh—we imagine that it was an internal point of pride that they are able to send out newsletters in HTML. But I believe nary a person has reacted to that line? WE KEEP IT IN ANYWAY.

Each time we did it, we'd improvise small things differently, keeping some. This show existed primarily as stuff we say out loud to each other for fun rather than a script we have written down.

After doing the show a year we had to re-type the script because we were performing a much different version than what we'd written down. I just looked at the script and it's out of date again. It says this:

> **DAVID**
> I'll call Alicia Coen!
>
> **HENRY**
> I'll call Dave Luchese!
>
> **DAVID**
> I've got the number for Martha Finch on my speed dial!

When what we've been saying is (I think) this:

> **DAVID**
> Well, I'll call Alicia Coen! I've got her number written down at home!
>
> **HENRY**
> Then I'll call Dave Luchese! Or just talk to him when I see him at coffee and donuts after Mass!
>
> **DAVID**
> I'll call Martha Finch! Our kids are both second clarinet in concert band!

The ending changed dramatically. Here's the ending of our first draft.

DAVID
Fine, fuck face. You don't want to play ball today, then I'll leave. But I promise you this: that putt-putt will never get the signage it needs if you don't learn to take Don Kane's dick out of your mouth long enough to recognize Liberty Plaza for what it is: THE FUTURE ECONOMIC HUB OF WILMINGTON.

HENRY
Good bye.

Oof. But with the help of Delaney and putting it on its feet in rehearsal, we eventually got to this:

HENRY
Say, David?

TECH: PLAY U2 "WHERE THE STREETS HAVE NO NAME" start at :50.

HENRY
You really think Liberty Plaza's gonna get that Friendly's?

DAVID
We're gonna try like hell.

HENRY
My God. That'd be huge.

Very early in the process, we fell in love with this sketch and decided it would be the heart of the show. It's not the clearest game, or even the one with the strongest jokes. But soon after the first draft, the specifics all felt like they implied a bigger world. We could not revise this sketch without discussing the backstories of every character mentioned. It inspired the title of the show (Small Men). It also set the precedent of us following our own indulgences (complex deliberate dialogue in this case, long pauses, grand philosophizing in other sketches) and trying to find a way to make them work in a sketch. We agreed that even if it got zero laughs, we would not cut this sketch.

Come see! Thursday night 8pm UCB-Chelsea!

JUNE 2ND, 2013 at 8:40AM

SMALL MEN DRAFTS: SECURITY QUESTIONS

"Security Questions" is about a guy who is not able to answer any of the pre-set questions that guard his password. This is inspired by real life security questions like these:

- What was the name of my first pet?
- What was my first grade teacher's name?
- What was your childhood phone number including area code?
- What is your oldest cousin's first and last name?
- What is your maternal grandmother's maiden name?
- Who was your first employers?
- What are the last 5 digits of your favorite rewards card?

I think I can answer ONE of those with confidence?

If "Liberty Plaza" was our labor of love in which we wrote mostly to entertain each other, "Security Questions" was us trying to write a Proper Sketch, with a clear premise and overt jokes. It's the sketchiest sketch. If this show were an album, you could release this sketch as a single and it stands up.

The first draft was different: the questions are very presumptive...

SEAN (IT GUY)
"Who did you take to the senior prom?"

ALAN
No prom. I went to a fine arts magnet school.

SEAN
"First frat rushed."

ALAN
Never even thought about rushing a frat.

SEAN
"What position did you play for your varsity football team?"

ALAN
My acapella group competed.

And the IT guy asking the questions is very much in control.

SEAN
"Favorite ribs place?"

ALAN
Vegetarian.

SEAN
Hmm.

ALAN
Wait! Let the answer be "vegetarian." Anytime I'm answered that question I'd say "vegetarian."

SEAN
You might not be when you forget your password.

ALAN
I've been vegetarian for 10 years.

SEAN
You might get a taste for it.

When we read it out loud to each other and in front of our director Michael Delaney it didn't feel right. Delaney directed me to be happily oblivious that he did not fit in and for Neil to be increasingly frustrated.

BIFF CYCYK (IT GUY)
Make and model of current car?

JEFF STEIN
Don't need one. I walk or bike to light rail.

BIFF CYCYK
You did that today to come here?

JEFF STEIN
Yeah! There's a train station that's only 8 blocks from here.

BIFF CYCYK
That's pretty far.

JEFF STEIN
I don't mind!

(We also made the names be two characters who were offhandedly mentioned in Liberty Plaza. ALAN became JEFF STEIN and SEAN became BIFF CYCYK but I don't think we ever remember that.)

With the happy tone, little facts about the guy's life would get laughs in our first workouts of the show. This part has consistently gotten a laugh though I don't think we wrote it as a joke.

BIFF CYCYK
Never been married?

JEFF STEIN
No. I have a girlfriend. She's a poet!

Also, Neil had been a computer programmer for years and performed his part with the particular biting-one's-lip frustration of a tech guy dealing with a n00b:

Meaning this..

JEFF
What if you asked me "What is the name of the first short story collection you wrote in high school?"

BIFF CYCYK
That's too long.

became...

JEFF
How about "Of the short story collections you wrote in high school, which is the one with a gothic theme?"

BIFF CYCYK
Ah, this one's on me. That is actually too long a question: it has to be only 160 characters or less, and so that is MY bad, but if you could just...

Once we had that feel, everything fell into place quickly. Delaney instructed us to hit the game a lot so the three of us sat around a desk and wrote as many as we could. For most of the sketch, we cut stuff that was too silly. Like this passage got dropped for being too unreal—trying too hard to hit the jokes:

SEAN (IT GUY)

How about "Favorite fishing hole?"

ALAN

I never camped. How about "Pulitzer Prize winner I least agree with?"

SEAN

Ok, what's your answer?

ALAN

Actually, I disagree with many.

SEAN

How about "Favorite gun?"

But for the end, Delaney really wanted it heighten a lot. Fast, to keep up the pace, but silly to end the sketch with a bang. Though it's dangerous work to try and remember who came up with what in a collaborative brainstorming session, I believe Delaney said this in one unbroken riff:

"What's your girlfriend's name?"

"A glyph: a bird-man carrying a pot."

"What's your favorite fruit?"

"I'm allergic to pectin."

"What's your favorite type of air?"

"Not oxygen."

Right before we did the Spank (audition) performance for this show we recorded an audio version of this sketch to promote it and ended up revising it. We realized the the questions weren't in logical order, which made it harder to memorize, and that there were beats that were sort of redundant.

Specifically, we'd had this:

- who did you take to prom? (none, magnet school)
- dorm at college? (none)
- first car? (none)
- current car? (light rail)
- when disneyworld? (busch gardens)

- xmas: ham or goose? (jewish, non-practicing)
- name of neighbor? (don't know)
- first job? (you guys)
- astrological sign? (opihicus)

We moved "job" to be after "prom" and "college" (more logical progression), cut "xmas: ham or goose?" (too silly), cut neighbor (boring) and put in an ad lib we had done in a rehearsal about residence...

to get this:

- who did you take to prom? (none, magnet school)
- dorm at college? (none)
- first job? (you guys)
- first car? (none)
- current car? (light rail)
- when disneyworld? (busch gardens)
- rent or own? (unpaid housesitter)
- astrological sign? (opihicus)

I guess that seems subtle, but the sketch went better, heightened a bit more logically and was easier to remember.

During the recording Neil had his character challenge me on certain answers, and we kept these bits in the sketch going forward...

> **BIFF CYCYK**
> Astrological sign?
>
> **JEFF**
> Ophiuchus. It's a sign they just added. Turns out that's what I've been my whole life.
>
> **BIFF CYCYK**
> It only lets it be one of the 12. Do you remember which one you were before they added the 13th one?
>
> **JEFF**
> Nah, I wasn't interested until this sign was discovered.

BIFF CYCYK
You don't remember?

JEFF
Nope.

BIFF CYCYK
You have NO IDEA what your sign was?

JEFF
Not until I saw the Newsweek article on Ophicius and I was like "Hey! that's me!"

Delaney warned against how such "improvements" can bloat a sketch and in total honesty I must report we defied him and INVITED THE BLOAT.

Over rehearsing, improvising and brainstorming we probably had 40-50 ideas that winnowed down to 20. This sketch has what I think is the best single for-real joke in the show:

JEFF
What if you asked me "First literary magazine published in?"

BIFF CYCYK
Ok, great! "First magazine published..." And the name of that magazine?

JEFF
"Password."

BIFF CYCYK
Ok, "Password", great. Ah. That's... that's the one answer the system won't accept.

JEFF
Ach. Frustrating!

We'd tell each other that if UCB sketch students came to our show that this would prove we could still dot our i's and cross our t's with a "normal" sketch. I suppose it also boosted our sketch credibility when Neil got hired to write for Saturday Night Live.

JUNE 6TH, 2013 at 9:16AM

"RELATIONSHIP"

You tell young improvisers to "have a relationship" because it invokes all the right improv instincts: they suddenly choose to have knowledge of the situation, to be invested in it, to speak one's mind.

But once you learn to have those instincts in ALL improv scenes, you no longer need to worry about your characters' having relationships. If it's a scene where you are buying something at a Sears: you will choose to know about it, to care about it, to speak your mind.

So, no, I don't care if you have a relationship in your scene. I just want you to know, care and speak.

JUNE 7TH, 2013 at 11:31AM

MORE SPECIFIC?

What if you did a set and all you tried to do was make existing things more specific?

Someone says "nice day out"

And you go "Yep, bright blue sky."

Just that much more. A notch more specific. Every line.

"Pass me that basketball."

"The Spalding?"

I bet that'd be fun.

JUNE 7TH, 2013 at 12:44PM

SMALL MEN DRAFTS: YOUR SON'S BAND

"Son's Band" is about a man making the case to his co-worker that the co-worker's son is a lazy layabout. More than anything else in our show, this sketch was about rewriting. It was on the chopping block for the longest time, and had the most severe rewrites including a page one rewrite a few days before our Spank (try out).

It started with the idea that a man flyering at his office on behalf of his son would be funny. And then we got very excited about the idea of a sketch that championed the suburban Dad, since most sketch comedy that we see portrays suburban life as equal to failure and settling. We wanted to champion people who dedicate their lives to being the stable albeit uncelebrated rocks.

The early drafts of this were very long, with long passages meant to describe how lazy the son was:

> **GENE SHIELDS**
> He's not freeloading. Alex helps Ann and I around the house. He does chores.
>
> **DENNIS FORAKER**
> He does CHORES? What is he, making his bed every morning?
>
> **GENE SHIELDS**
> Most mornings.
>
> **DENNIS FORAKER**
> What rent do you charge him?
>
> **GENE SHIELDS**
> None right now. He's not really making money. He can't collect unemployment.
>
> **DENNIS FORAKER**
> Unemployment? Was he ever employed?
>
> **GENE SHIELDS**
> Well, no, after college he moved home. Needed some time to get his bearings. Hey, don't give me that look! I already told him. He's got six more months and then he's got to get his MBA.
>
> **DENNIS FORAKER**
> MBA?
>
> **GENE SHIELDS**
> Yeah, he was a business major.

DENNIS FORAKER

MBA?

GENE SHIELDS

He spent five years at the University of Pennsylvania.

DENNIS FORAKER

Gene, you're being had.

As well as passages which stand up for the dad.

DENNIS FORAKER

Your child? Your CHILD? GENE! Look, I'm not being disrespectful. I'm saying this because in every other area of your life, you're nobody's sucker. You served in Vietnam, and used the GI Bill to go to U of D, got an engineering degree and married a nice girl. You got a job for the city, and then bought a NICE home on Grand Avenue. GRAND AVENUE, just a block off of Prunett Street! The only time you let yourself go is at 19th Hole at Richter Park, a little bit.

We liked a lot of the bits, but overall it was rambling and long and didn't work.

Discouraged, we forced a "Sherlock Holmes" framework where the DENNIS characters uses powers of observation to deduce that the son is a jerk. This was very arbitrary! I was reading all the Sherlock Holmes stories and raving to Neil about how terrific they were and what a reliable formula they were for storytelling and he suggested giving it to Son's Band.

GENE

I wouldn't say it that way. With all due respect, Dennis, you don't know much about my son.

DENNIS starts talking like Sherlock Holmes.

DENNIS

I know enough. I know your son graduated college when he was 22, after five years as liberal arts undergraduate. He immediately moved back home with you and hasn't left. You don't see him in the mornings because he hasn't awoken. You don't see him in the evenings, because he's out. Only on the weekends, at noon when he emerges from the basement. He owes you at least 5000 dollars in cash loans, and that's generously not counting back rent which you never charged, tuition which you happily paid for and birthday and holiday gifts always checks written by your wife.

GENE
How could you know that...?

DENNIS
He joined this band within the past 2 years, around the same time you started politely suggesting that he find work. God, it's becoming so clear, Gene. The weekend trips with your wife to get away, you always browsing the classified looking for entry level jobs—your son: he's a freeloader.

We performed this version but ended up not being able to rehearse it and to my memory, it was kind of a mess. But it felt sharper so we wrote a version trying to REALLY ramp up the detective stuff ending in an Agatha Christie/Columbo style breakdown of the father:

DENNIS
What would your father say to you, Gene?

GENE
He wouldn't have to say anything! I just knew! I got out of the army and went to U of D on a scholarship, got an engineering degree!

DENNIS
A REAL degree!

GENE
Yes! Carol and I got married, we bought a house on Deer Hill ave!

DENNIS
Good neighborhood!

GENE
Good neighborhood! It never occurred to me to just.. DO NOTHING and wait!

DENNIS
But not Alex. He was content to just sit in your house, and eat your food while you look the other way and let him drop all responsibility. There's

been a murder, Gene, of your son's adulthood committed by his child self with his own father as an accomplice!

GENE

It's true! I did it! I ignored the pot smoke coming out of his bedroom when I knew he hadn't done anything all day. I didn't say anything when I heard him lying to get out job interviews that I'd set up for him! I bought him Call of Duty 3 for Christmas! Oh my God, what have I done?

We liked the story, but it was still long. We had backstories of the dad, son...

GENE

Look, you don't know how it is. Alex is a good kid. Gifted program in middle school, National Honor Society in high school—for Christ's sake he lived in the honors dorms the whole time he was at Hampshire—even after he switched majors! This is a talented boy! Music is what he wants, and he's got his mind set on it, and goddamn it I'm going to stand behind him!

...and even Dennis:

DENNIS

I know this scam. I lived with my father until I was 29 years old. But *I* was a poet. Did a weekly reading, sometimes a slam, in Bryn Marr, PA. Supposedly trying to get published while turning up my nose at copy editing jobs, much less teaching high school English.

When we did in rehearsal for our director Michael Delaney it felt weak and too long. I lobbied to cut it and find something else. But Delaney and I think Neil felt there was enough good stuff to make something out of it.

Sitting on the stage of UCB East less than a week before our audition show, Delaney said to throw it all out and write down only what was necessary. We got out pads and laid on the stage and wrote it out long-hand: short lines, only what was needed to communicate the sketch. "Pace pace pace" he kept saying. We did out best (on reflection this still isn't THAT short but it was short for us and cut a lot of stuff out from previous drafts):

DENNIS

(Putting on trench coat to head home)

Alright, Gene. I'm heading home. I'm gonna have to finish reviewing the annotations on this wetlands survey tomorrow. They're brutal!

GENE

(hands flyer to DENNIS)

Check out this show!

DENNIS

I didn't know you were in a band, Gene.

GENE

(Proud)

I'm not in a band. It's my son, Alex. He plays bass. His first professional gig.

DENNIS

How old is your son, Gene?

GENE

Twenty-six.

DENNIS

What does he do for a living?

GENE

He's a musician.

DENNIS

Kick him out of the house.

We cut almost all the backstory of Dennis and the Dad, and a lot of the detective stuff. We kept the final accusations and a muted version of the Dad breaking down and seeing that his son is a louse. We kept our favorite put-downs of the son.

DENNIS

What's their website?

GENE

myspace.com/planetflow

DENNIS

Disgusting.

We texted DC Pierson to get good specifics on music genres. He answered within five minutes.

Me to DC: Tell me the 4 dumbest music genres a band might be described as.

DC: Chillwave, Pigfuck (for real), Freak-folk, Gridcore. Sorry, grindcore. But gridcore sounds cool!

Neil and I still consider this the weakest sketch in terms of what's on the page and we deliberately put it in the middle of the lineup (following the "shit sandwich" theory of ordering sketches—start and end with big winners, putting more mild stuff in the middle when the audience almost WANTS a break).

But it works, maybe because of the relatable premise, some choice details and maybe the best button line in the show, which was a gift from Delaney:

He was directing me to be as overly dramatic as the ending of an episode of a tv drama when he said "You basically have to deliver this like 'i must murder my son'—actually, that should be the line."

And that gave us what has been one of the biggest laughs of our whole show:

> **GENE**
> My God. What do I do?
>
> **DENNIS**
> You know what you have to do. Do it tonight.

DENNIS leaves.

> **GENE**
> I have to murder my own son.

There are 9 full drafts of this sketch and these each have random remnants in the final version, including Neil wearing a long coat to evoke a "detective" figure, a reference to my character being in the army, and I guess a huge amount of details that only Neil and I know as we perform it.

JUNE 12TH, 2013 at 9:58AM

Q: JUSTCRAIG: SHOULD YOU SPEAK IN A LOWER VOICE WHEN YOU'RE SOMEONE'S FATHER?

justcraig asked: Quick question about relationships in scenes: If you're someone's father in a scene, should you speak in a lower voice and call your child "son?"

JUNE 20TH, 2013 at 9:10PM

Q: WHAT'S YOUR ADVICE IF NO GAME IS FOUND?

Anonymous asked: I know you said in an earlier answer to give the scene partner time, but if it's been several minutes in a first beat and no game has been found (or too many games have been passed up, I guess), what would your advice be for the back line? Walk-on? Sweep edit? Something else?

Probably sweep. You could also walk-on and make it more of whatever it already is. Add what's missing: the next step only. Make something more specific. Repeat something good. Make it more true. Make it more important. One of those? Pretend the scene has a color or a tone and make it more of that color or that tone. Join it and love it by making it MORE.

Don't "fix" or "help," okay? That's gross.

JULY 13TH, 2013 at 7:52AM

UNDERMINE YOURSELF

A useful skill: to be able undermine your own character without having your character change his/her mind. To have your character lose without ever having admitted he/she is losing.

To say things like "Oh, really? *I'm* the unreasonable employee? Just because I practice my trumpet at my desk during lunch and I happen to be working on fanfares? Give me a break: you just hate having true artists at your company!"

Like you paint the picture that you are indeed wrong, but your character is oblivious. That's often funnier than straight-up admitting it, and is definitely funnier than refusing to create any evidence that you might be wrong.

That sort of undermining is hard for a lot of people to do. For a lot of people, either their characters are right, and they stand up for themselves, or their characters are wrong and they admit it.

They say "well, that's not playing to the top of my intelligence." True, but it goes under the "one unusual thing" strategy—this character is oblivious to how his trumpet playing is ever inappropriate.

To watch someone unable to do this looks like a singer/guitarist who can't play the guitar a different volume that what he/she is singing.

If you can undermine yourself, you'll have an easier time when you're in a scene and someone yes-ands things in a way that make your character "lose"—you won't mind, you'll enjoy it and make it bigger and worse for yourself. It's fun to lose in improv, you get all the laughs.

JULY 26TH, 2013 at 10:14AM

LET IMPROV BE SMALL

Sometimes improv seems like a grand religion. It can be inspiring and overwhelming, and there's a lot to learn when you see improv like that. But other times it's just a set of best practices for brainstorming together on stage. It's a relief to remember that. Let improv be small: a handful of guidelines for working together to make some funny things.

AUGUST 14TH, 2013 at 3:11PM

UCB COMEDY IMPROVISATION MANUAL

If I wait until I write a whole proper review, I'll never say anything so I'm going to indulge myself in a blogger-like fashion to just list disparate thoughts without minding heightening or following through. This is an opening for a Harold-like review of the book that I will likely never write.

Short version: I love it for its ambitious scope, its directness and its earnest treatment of improv as craft worth doing well. There is no other book that explains as much, certainly not written by people with as much experience. A trade-off is that it's (perhaps necessarily) less inspiring and fun than other books. But that is in my opinion outweighed by the amount of thought and care that's gone into this, the first complete documentation of improv as a serious artform by one of the most experienced and talented groups in its history.

Long rambling post after the jump!

DISPARATE THOUGHTS

It's impressively, maybe even intimidatingly BIG. It's a college textbook, not a slim volume of inspirational essays. It covers how to do improv according to UCB style and it describes EVERYTHING, including basic scene work principles to finding game to longform structure with long sections on openings and even a chapter on running proper rehearsals and performances. There is no other long-form book that attempts this scope.

It's like the old school Gary Gygax Dungeon Master's Guide! For real! The book takes something you may have thought of as playtime and treats it with passionate thoroughness. Chris Scott compared it to an RPG manual (favorably) and I agree with that comparison!

It feels like workshops with Ian or Besser or Walsh. It has their directness and confidence, and also their clarity. Ian's voice in particular is clear, especially in analytical abstract descriptions of patterns when playing game. It puts as much a priority on finding comedy as it does simply cooperating and supporting. It makes improv feel teachable.

Despite the directness, *it's not saying this is the only way to do improv, just their way*. Although the completeness of the book's scope may imply the UCB wants to be the final word, I don't think that's the tone of the book. The tone is "here's how we do it" not "here's how YOU MUST do it."

The *drawings by David Kantrowitz* are beautiful and clear and add a lot to the book.

Joe Wengert, the editor, was in my opinion almost a co-author in that he wrote up the drafts based on the discussion and notes from the UCB. It's the UCB's book, but having someone as smart and funny as Joe—who has a masters in education and ran the UCB school for over 6 years—was an enormous boon to the quality of this book.

This book is more about how to do it than how to teach it. The art of teaching improv has a lot to do with running reps of exercises, of inspiring people to be confident and playful, of securing one set of skills before doing another, with keeping it simple. This book is not trying to fill you with the fire of improv. It assumes you have that fire, and is instead focused on the ambitious task of being awesome at it. Which is in itself inspiring, but not as directly as some well-chosen anecdotes about following the fear or the magic of group mind.

It's about making a beautiful watch, not being part of a fired-up congregation.

NO ARBITRARY CHOICES

If there's one consistent theme throughout, it's that improv should *avoid arbitrary choices*. From the second paragraph, which argues against the perception that improv is lazy, and then throughout the book, the UCB are declaring as their overall philosophy of improv (in my opinion) to always serve a larger purpose: either you're making a grounded reality, or you're serving the game. Anything done out of randomness or pure silliness is likely destructive, the book says again and again. From their philosophy of object work, to theory of what makes a good character, to avoiding ironic detachment, to whether or not to have your animals talk—the book goes back to instructing you to serve the larger purpose of the scene and not fall back on silliness.

That's a harder battle than it might seem to people who don't do improv. Improv can be silly. Audiences like silly, at least in the short term. And for the droves of non-actors drawn to study improv, it is very tempting to simply indulge in the joy and novelty of being on stage and making things up as enough to justify one's presence on stage. Many many people who do improv do little than go from moment to moment, indulging in arbitrary object work and barely-justified emotional reactions and pointless references. If there were one overall cause that the UCB would get behind, I think, it would be *a war on "crazytown."* You must have a point, a purpose when you make your improvised scenes.

GAME OF THE SCENE DEFENDED

The UCB's devotion to "game of the scene" has provoked many arguments from people. This book is *more practiced and savvy at anticipating those arguments.*Not that this book presents the discussion like an argument, but its descriptions contain within itself answers to common criticisms. Criticisms I've commonly heard from people who don't like seeing scenes as having games are things like "people just boss each other around" or "you're writing on your feet—not really building ideas with your scene partner." The book has repeated emphasis on listening, supporting, committing all throughout the game section ("Work together to play the game", page 148). Game as described in this book is still ultimately a cerebral approach that won't inspire everyone, but the book anticipates the initial misgivings and speaks to them.

Certainly, the themes of "listening" "committing" and "making your partner look good" are hit again and again and again.

Other examples of this: I'm looking at pages 78-92 right now—the "revisiting yes and" and "revisiting agreement" sections through "filtering through status" and finally "crazytown." These sections explain how commitment, listening, support are the fundamental skills of improv, even to these admittedly analytical, game-hungry improvisers.

SEMANTICS

Improv teaching is so much about semantics and phrases. The UCB have thought through all the semantics, changed some and redefined others.

I find that semantics is where most improv arguments are born. People have terms that work for themselves and get territorial about those. For some people the words "game of the scene" simplify their approach, for others it will muddy it but the phrase "point of view" will get them behaving almost the exact same way. For some "commitment" and "grounded reality" make them into better actors, and for others it will be "relationship and emotion." Improv is ultimately an art form and one person's internal experience will never be completely universal.

Having said that, the semantics in this book are fascinating, smart, comprehensive and do fairly represent how the three authors play. I could write a whole essay on these, but a few quick comments.

"Yes And" is slightly redefined, or maybe it's better to describe as "re-focused" as meaning the discovery and initial exploring part of the scene, and then once you have your game you switch to "if this unusual thing is true then what else is true." But I can easily imagine an improviser arguing that "if this is true" is simply a restatement of "yes-and." Sure, if you like. You're the boss of you, have at it. But the UCB are arguing that there is a switch in priority once you have a game, so let's reflect that in our terms. We "Yes-And" till we have a "game," then we "If-Then." It's not the final answer, it's AN answer.

Even the decision to say "if this unusual thing is true, then what else is true" is an evolution from "if this is true, what else is true" which is how it was said when I took classes.

"base reality" replaces "who, what, where."

"premise" vs "organic" improv is a UCB categorization, I believe.

"chaff, half-idea, and premise" as the three types of initiations off an opening is a UCB categorization.

CODIFICATION IN GENERAL

There will be many who think the whole purpose of that much codification is pointless. Improv is art, not a computer program, so why try to make a formula? I guess I would argue that the people who don't like this approach should and would select themselves out by not buying or reading the book. That is a non-offensive position to take, I think.

But in teaching improv, I have found that the right set of "rules" and principles and mantras can be a big help. They give the right mindset and posture. Later, when the improviser has developed his/her own voice he/she may find that certain mantras are important whereas others are not. But for the student who's learning, I'd think the UCB's suggested models would be a relief.

I mean if Ted Williams can write 96 pages on swinging a bat, I think the UCB is entitled to write 380 pages on the art of making up comedy on the fly.

Many people won't try to "solve" improv the way this book tries to. Many teachers, understandably, like to leave improv as a few principles—"play it real" "find an unusual thing" and "heighten" and pretty much leave it at that. It is interesting to see three people who have done it for years refuse to settle for that. When the book explains strategies of initiating—"on the nose" vs "one step beyond"—you may roll your eyes with how precise they are trying to be, or you can be impressed that they are tackling the intimidating job of trying to feel the rules of comedy!

Certainly anyone who reads this blog with any passion would love the book. Read three of the biggest improv nerds on the planet answer every question you could imagine on how to do it.

WHAT WILL LAST

I think there will be some evolution now that the book is out. Some things will stick, some will not. That's certainly happened with previous books. After "Improvise" by Mick Napier was published I heard many people using his descriptions of things like "your deal" as opposed to more formal terms. I've heard many of his specific examples from "The Perfect Actor" cited. But I haven't heard many people cite his analogy of thermodynamics as it relates to improv. The masses will eventually decide which of the UCB's semantics and ideas are lasting.

But let's remember the credentials of the authors. They studied with Del and Charna and every great teacher in Chicago in the early 90s, one of the most fertile and creative periods of improv comedy. They founded a theater and within just a few years had fostered it into a major player in the comedy scene. They have done improv, continuously, for over 20 years with the best people in the country. The points in this book have been developed in thousands of hours of shows. It's completely exciting to read the thoughts and beliefs of people who have done improv as well for as long.

SOME COOL PARTS

Page 108-109: "Responding" and "Give it Time" in relation to premise improv. Their discussion of the importance of responding (and not being in your head assuming you know the answer that's coming) and also the reassuring words of how hard premise stuff is at first show that these are guys who taught classes, and are not just casting down carved stones from mountains.

Page 137-147: The book gives a painstaking analysis, line by line, of a scene to explain which ones heighten, which ones explore and which ones are playing top of one's intelligence. Though I don't know, it feels like an Ian analysis. And to see Ian's insanely powerful and machinelike improv brain tackle a scene is, frankly, weirdly exciting? I'm sure it's intimidating to new students also, as in "shit, am i supposed to be analyzing scenes that much?" No, and the explanation says as much. But this section is like having The Chicago Bulls give commentary on how they scored ten points in two minutes.

Page 189: "Playing Animals and Inanimate Objects"—I just love that improv is such a medium where this is a reasonable topic to have an opinion on.

Page 253: The invocation of Del Close. For all of its analysis and textbook formatting, Del's hippie recklessness is still present in this book and the authors' respect for him and it is apparent.

Page 279: The "paint pouring over a sphere" drawing by Kantrowitz is pretty fucking cool.

Page 297: "What do you do when the game isn't clear" in regards to second beats, is a question every ucb 201 student asks. I like that they speak to it.

Page 304-309: They offer categories of group games, which is something we didn't do when I was taking classes. this is an area that students ask about a lot ("how do you do group games?") and here the UCB is offering an answer.

Page 362: Getting out of your head.

—

CONCLUSION

No book can substitute for experience on stage, and this book does not break that rule. Nor is this book the final word on the subject and it's not trying to be. But it IS a thorough, careful, honest expression of how best to perform an art form as seen by three of its best practitioners. It raises the bar in terms of thoroughness and scope. It's really cool and I'm excited to have it!

AUGUST 15TH, 2013 at 3:01PM

JUSTIFICATION: MAKE SURE SOMEONE'S HOME

"I hate justification. I don't care. If it's funny I want to hear more, and I don't need you to explain why."

Someone very smart and funny said that to me yesterday. I get where he was coming from, but I also know why we say "justification" in improv classes and it's to avoid ARBITRARY CHOICES.

It's very prevalent in improv: you do something, it gets a reaction, so you do it again but louder. You get more of a reaction. So you keep doing it. It can work. But it feels empty and has diminishing returns. And when I see it, it looks terribly boring. Or else someone is in a scene and the actor gets bored or panics and suddenly changes energy just because: usually to get louder and screamier.

What you want is the choices to come from some authentic place. I'm directing a sketch group and an actor pitched an idea where a guy goes to a shoe store, timidly tries on shoes and then does a bunch of aggressive karate kicks. It was hilarious. Then the rest of the team and I interviewed him about that character: how old was he? was he angry? was he good? how did he learn karate?

For most of these, the actor had SOME kind of answer. He had some sense of this guy even though he had not thought him through. And while it might not be necessary to know the answer to all the questions we asked, it was helpful to know that there was some organic wholeness underneath the silly action of kicking in the air. Our questions were sort of kicking the tires of this idea to see if it held together.

A phrase a fellow teacher uses is "someone's home in there." It's a good phrase to use for characters in sketch and improv. Or for anyone in an improv scene. Is someone home in that character?

If someone is not home, then the actor is just doing things arbitrarily—making noise, doing physical things, and it feels thin and false. In improv practice we say "have a why"—but what I think we mean is—"Be a full person even if we only see a tip of it."

We say "don't think" but we don't mean "be arbitrarily random," we mean "let the very bottom of your brain make the choices and everything will fit together into an organic whole that the top of your brain didn't see coming." We say "justify" or "have a why" but we just mean—"be connected to it, don't just pick random idea balls from the manatee pool."

AUGUST 16TH, 2013 at 6:10AM

Q: "THAT GUY" QUESTION

Anonymous asked: Hi Will, love your article on 'That Guy.' My team is dealing with one of those and I'm trying to impart your wisdom. Do you have any advice for directors/coaches for how to deal with That Guy? What notes are okay to give in front of the group and where can it cross the line into embarrassing singling-out/bullying? How is best to approach him privately if needed? and what can a good director do to manage the rest of the group's dealings with That Guy when complaints are received?

The 2700 words I wrote on this is all I have to say.

AUGUST 16TH, 2013 at 6:10AM

Q: "THAT GUY" QUESTION

Anonymous asked: One of the members of my team consistently struggles with the basics—not listening, not yes-anding, asking loads of questions, etc. And he's scene-hogs into every scene possible.

This is very frustrating for all. Now he says he can't afford to split our coaching fees and studio rental that we all share. Fair enough, I have been there. Problem is he still wants to perform with us, but not practice with us. I really don't think it's fair to the rest of the team to let him get away with this.

As to you assessing his improv, that's not productive:

http://improvnonsense.tumblr.com/thatguy

But if he won't practice or pay dues, kick him out for that.

AUGUST 16TH, 2013 at 6:12AM

Q: DIFFERENCE BETWEEN "RAISING THE STAKES" AND "HEIGHTENING?"

Anonymous asked: What's the difference between 'raising the stakes' and 'heightening'? I was asked this recently, and couldn't come up with a coherent answer. Help!

Semantic question. Whatever works for you. But to me: "Raising the stakes" seems to encourage only PLOT—which might be good but "heightening" means anything that makes the scene more absurd. "raising stakes" = people arbitrarily putting scenes in the white house, in space when that's not necessarily funny. "heightening" Is more open to mean "whatever it takes to make the scene more absurd." Heightening, in the way that I think of it, INCLUDES raising the stakes as one of many possibilities.

AUGUST 16TH, 2013 at 6:13AM

Q: THE GROUP MISSED THE BEST IDEA.

Anonymous asked: Group game question. Say a teammate has started with an interesting philosophy (obviously hoping to be matched), but

the majority of the group by-passes that first philosophy to latch on to less-interesting banter. If I want to recognize what that team mate started with: Is it too late to play that first, strong, idea? Or is it better to keep the banter going as a group and forget about that first move?

Better to go with what's first, but if only one person noticed it's kinda like it didn't happen so go with the group. EDITED LATER TO ADD: the judging you're doing in this example "Less-interesting banter" and "first, strong idea"—sounds like you are disagreeing with the majority of your group. You might be "right" in terms of a strong comedic choice but since improv works best when we are all on the same page, can you get on their page? Can you do the banter how they're doing it but have a specific contribution that makes the banter better? However you answer all these questions, I'd rather watch a group that is playing together than one guy trying to correct the group's decision from within.

AUGUST 16TH, 2013 at 6:14AM

Q: WHY SO MANY "J" NAMES?

halphillips asked: Why do you think people use generic fake-sounding names like "Jenkins" and "Janice"? Where does that come from? How do we make it never happen again? Am I the only one who gets infuriated when characters call their sons "son"?

People gravitate towards "J" names in improv, I don't know why. Also "K" sounds when making jokes? I dunno, I dunno. Saying "son" doesn't bother me.

AUGUST 16TH, 2013 at 3:00PM

OVER EMPHASIS

Students apologize for their bad scenes, classes, even the suggestions they give.

None of those things has enough of an impact to make it worth apologizing.

Do people go to the gym and apologize for bad reps? bad sets? Not as much I bet.

AUGUST 17TH, 2013 at 3:00PM

ALL ADVICE

Everything in every improv class is just tricking you into doing this:

1. do something inspired by a suggestion.
2. understand each other
3. move the scene forward
4. sense what's funny
5. do more of the funny thing

How you dress these up is your preferred semantics, but ultimately this is what you want out of a successful improvised funny scene.

AUGUST 18TH, 2013 at 3:00PM

NEW WORKSHOP: GET IN YOUR HEAD!

My new workshop—*Get In Your Head!*—is designed to put you solidly in your own head! Become aware of your own thought processes! Doubt all of your initial instincts! Wonder if there's a better way at all times! Exercises presented with a cold neutral air by a coach (me!) with a glassy-eyed stare! Validation in all forms withheld. Warm-ups skipped. Chit-chat omitted. Temperature of room hostile. Physical matching, arbitrary jumping and any screaming will be fined $1 an occurrence (no refunds). Exercises run: "Improv Is Hard," "Understand What Was Said," "Make Sense," "Be Able To Think of Things No Matter What" and if time, "Make This Funny." Despite the sarcastic tone of this description, please know that this is a workshop that I would actually like to run! No refunds given, and even if documentation of psychiatric damage is presented afterwards the workshop will assume no legal or medical liability (see Supreme Court Case #90874 *United States vs. Improv Teacher*, 2013). Spots available.

AUGUST 19TH, 2013 at 3:00PM

CONUNDRUM

For all their training in yes-and, get two improvisers in a bar and ask them to debate any improv theory. I don't know if I've ever seen two improvisers agree on theory for more than five seconds.

AUGUST 20TH, 2013 at 3:00PM

CHANGE THE LYRICS, KEEP THE MUSIC

If you make a big choice, and then you get thrown because your scene partner was making a different assumption about the who/what/where, it's helpful to keep acting in the same TONE of your initial choice, but switch up the specifics.

LIke you walk out and decide to be a nervous weatherman apologizing to his boss for having screwed up his broadcast. But your scene partner somehow thinks you're a detective. Okay, so you stay apologetic, still have a nervous energy, but you change your specifics from a weather report to a murder you're investigating. It's like you keep your music, but just change your lyrics.

AUGUST 21ST, 2013 at 3:00PM

IT'S YOURS

You decide if you're an improviser, not anyone else or any theater or any school. They can decide if they think you're interesting, or if they want to cast you in their shows or promote you into higher levels. But they can't tell you whether or not you identify with the term "improviser." To borrow language from 12-step programs, being an improviser is a self-diagnosed condition.

The mantras just have to ring true for you. You know it when you're excited in your first ever class or maybe at the first long-form show you see. You think "yes and" in your everyday life. You think "good heightening, world" when things get increasingly shitty.

Even if you leave this world and go off into a "normal" (shudder) career or lifestyle. You're in an office, getting a PhD, waiting tables, raising family, or even acting in scripted stuff. But you still get inspired by the mantras you learned in some dusty rehearsal space. Even (especially?) if you don't watch television or web series or read comedy blogs like this one: you're allowed to still love it.

Tell people you're an improviser. You feel it, right? Then you are.

AUGUST 22ND, 2013 at 3:00PM

NEW TERMS

I'd like simple terms for these moments in improv scenes. They each give me a palpable feeling of satisfaction when I see them happen.

- When you first feels that everyone on stage knows the same who / what / where. The moment of connection, I guess.
- A game proposed. ("I got the tickets. They only took my thumb.")
- A game accepted. ("That's good. I was expecting them to take the whole hand.")
- The move that gives a previously unfunny scene a funny context. But not in a way that's a denial, just in a way that makes you realize "yeah, well I guess this COULD have been 1967 the whole time."
- The move that implies a big juicy moment before that you now want to know about.
- When someone changes their viewpoint because of something their partner suggests.
- Object work with something you thought they had forgotten about.
- Naming someone.

AUGUST 23RD, 2013 at 7:44AM

Q: JUSTCRAIG: WHEN SOMEONE MENTIONS WILL SMITH?

justcraig asked: In a scene where there's mention of a celebrity, like Will Smith, is it better to say, "Did someone say 'Will Smith?'" while coming through the door or coming through the curtain? (In both instances the person saying "Did someone say 'Will Smith?'" would be acting like Will Smith)

AUGUST 23RD, 2013 at 3:00PM

THINGS THAT ARE HARD TO DO IN LONG-FORM IMPROV

Here are things in class that, when I see them, I think "this is getting good."

- having your character disagree with another character, but still yes-and each other
- resisting that urge to just say the word 'yes' all the time. meaning having your character say no when someone would almost definitely say no to, and still have the scene move forward
- being willing to let your character lose in order to make the scene funnier
- yes-and a specific reference to a tv/movie/person you know nothing about and never betray you are faking it
- justifying stuff in a way that makes your character look bad
- adding a context to scene that didn't have one which makes the scene have a game
- choosing to already have known things that were just confessed

AUGUST 24TH, 2013 at 3:00PM

THE JUDGE VS. THE HEART

The actor vs. the writer?

The committer vs. the commenter?

The Jack Kirby vs. the Stan Lee?

The lessons that we teach make people better actors:

- Habitually accept offers
- Support
- Trust
- Live life onstage
- React simply, naturally, follow cues

There's also the other side of the coin, the comedian's side:

- Question
- Attack
- Confront
- Examine

Well, wait—we need both don't we? We do, we do. I guess if you have a room of funny people, they'll already do the second group so you need to push the first set of things. And with a set of actors or touchy-feely people you need to push the second set of things.

But still, I get more mileage out of that top group. I push that and things get better. I don't know.

Not gonna edit or fix this post.

(edited: I wrote this post over 2 years ago, sometime in 2011).

AUGUST 25TH, 2013 at 3:00PM

NOTING A BAD HABIT

(For teachers. For MYSELF, God knows.)

Ideally, you don't just note a bad habit. You understand why the bad habit is happening and explain why the bad habit is not the best solution to the problem.

Like if you tell someone they are acting too broadly, you should understand that broad acting is often a well-intentioned desire to communicate your thoughts to the other players and audience. It just takes some experience to learn that you don't need to play that broadly—so that bad result (broad play) comes from a well-meant place ("understand me") and is rectified by experience (the realization that a smaller move is enough).

So I don't think it's enough usually to say "Don't play broadly—improv is better when you start small." I mean, you can say that but when the chips are down they're still gonna feel that insecurity of not being understood and will continue to play broadly until they have done X scenes and relax. OR you can say "you're worried about not being understood, but we see you—you can play smaller and we see what you're doing."

I certainly fall short of this all the time. But there's something improv-y to assume that the students are smart and have good reasons for doing what they're doing. Be good enough to know what those reasons are.

AUGUST 26TH, 2013 at 12:05PM

Q: WHY IS IT GOOD TO CHOOSE TO KNOW THINGS THAT HAVE BEEN CONFESSED?

Anonymous asked: Why is it a good thing to choose "to already have known things that were just confessed" ? It seems to just lower the impact of what has been confessed...

It's not ALWAYS good, but it's OFTEN good. From what I've observed, it doesn't lessen the impact, it enriches it. I guess if the person who is doing the confessing NEEDS the other person to be shocked, then it would lessen the impact.

"I'm leaving you."

"So? I knew that."

Though if you could be affected by it.

"I'm leaving you."

"I KNEW it!"

But in improv, confessions are often done not to shock but just to add in information that is personal and important.

"I need to tell you something: I want your job."

"Yes, I knew that. It's all about money to you."

Meaning the content of the new info is more important than that it was framed as a surprise. Choosing to know keeps it moving rather than:

"I need to tell you something: I want your job."

"What? Why? When? How come?"

And the point I was originally trying to make is that choosing to know something that's confessed is hard to do, or at least counter-intuitive, so once I see that the improvisers can do that I know that they're probably very capable.

I have posted about my feelings on this with better real-world examples from the group Outlook of the Poet.

AUGUST 26TH, 2013 at 3:00PM

YIN AND YANG

If you find yourself thinking of a group's style of comedy as "male" or "female"—try using the terms Yin and Yang instead. Yin is what you traditionally think of as female, Yang is what you think of as male. From wikipedia:

- Yin: slow, soft, yielding, diffuse, cold, wet, and passive.
- Yang: fast, hard, solid, focused, hot, dry, and aggressive

It works better than thinking male/female and it's more accurate. A show can be too Yin or too Yang, and that has nothing to do with the gender of the people in the show. Players, too, can emphasize too much of one of the energies.

It sounds annoying on-purpose hippie, but it nicely lets you talk about 'aggressive vs. passive' without falling into weird and untrue assumptions/arguments about gender.

EDITED TO ADD: Maybe I shouldn't have even brought up "male" and "female." Regardless of that, "yin" and "yang" are terms I find useful when thinking about the types of improv groups and types of scenes and types of players.

AUGUST 27TH, 2013 at 3:00PM

TRUE AND IMPORTANT

Try this: make everything your partner says either TRUE or IMPORTANT. No matter how small or big or whatever.

"Nice day."

"Yes, bright blue sky." (true)

"You're fired."

"Oh, no!" (true, important)

"What can I say? I got caught in traffic."

"Yeah, the construction on I-95, it's holding everyone up." (true)

"I need the cheese."

"Wow. You're really going for it." (important)

Fun, I bet.

Don't overdo it like this:

"You're fired!"

"You BASTARD! You are KILLING ME! OH MY GOD!"

That's too much, I think. Though it could work. But moderation is better. You don't want your performance to be too sweaty.

I DON'T KNOW.

AUGUST 28TH, 2013 at 3:01PM

FIGHTS

Fights are tricky. You will stop yes-anding the scene and start making it so your character wins. You won't even notice. Teachers will often forbid their newer students from having arguments in scenes. Even the most veteran team will check in with each other: "We're fighting too much." It is pervasive and, frankly, fascinating.

I think it's the hardest thing to do in improv: having characters disagree while the actors still agree.

But you can't just say "don't fight." Fighting well is essential to good improv. The characters must be able to disagree while still moving the scene forward. A whole set of character who just blindly agree with each other's opinions gets old.

More ramblings after the jump!

So you can't avoid it, but you have to respect that it's tricky and tread carefully.

A sign of a bad fight: an improviser who usually finds a way to say yes suddenly finds only reasons to say no.

A good improviser I had in a workshop lately was in a scene as the daughter of the other character. An early line of the scene was him saying "you're trying to sneak out" and she said "i am! i was just out the door" which is a good solid yes. Then they start disagreeing about whether or not he's being overly strict with her. And he says "every since your mother started dating that.. what's his name?" and the daughter character says "James" and he goes "james right. is she really happy In his double wide trailer?" and the daughter goes "well, no, he moved in with HER." and it felt like a denial.

I asked her afterward why she did that and she pointed out that very early in the scene she had said that the mom's boyfriend had just moved in, so she felt obligated to not overrule that. She's right, although it's telling to me that your brain finds reasons to say no when you're in a fight. I bet there'd be a way to agree with the father's character that she had moved into a double wide and still justify her earlier statement—which I couldn't even remember.

I've found no silver bullet piece of advice on this. Here's several good ones I've heard.

- **Accept the offer.** Remember something to support the accusation against you. You're being painted by it.
- Another version of that: **Make yourself wrong.**
- Make sure someone is **low status**. Be low status if no one is.
- Fights are **sand traps**, you will get caught in them, just be aware that's happening and drive on out.
- **YES AND** will get you out.
- Generally, you **don't** try to **WIN** the scene.
- **Confess something.**

AUGUST 29TH, 2013 at 3:00PM

TEAMS ARE VALUABLE BUT OVERRATED

Teams are weird. It is terrifically exciting and validating to get cast on a team. Then again, it's a roll of the dice, it seems, to see which teams really gel. It's tough for something to get cast/put together by an outside source and work.

Then AGAIN, it's not always great to put yourself together. You can get a lot of like-minded people with not enough variety that way. It helps to have an outside source tell you what you're missing.

But psychologically, we put too much on "being put on a team." There aren't enough spots, and it doesn't matter as much as you think. I know, I know. Easy to say. But it really doesn't matter as much as it feels and the anxiety people go through over it just isn't worth it.

Teams are valuable, but overrated.

You have to make your own thing. You will eventually realize this, and those who get put on teams often realize it later than everyone else.

AUGUST 29TH, 2013 at 11:57PM

Q: WHAT DOES "THERE AREN'T ENOUGH SPOTS" MEAN?

Anonymous asked: I liked your "Teams Are Valuable But Overrated" post, but you wrote something I always see and hear which I take issue with. What does "there aren't enough spots" mean and why does that sound like a half-hearted way of cheering up people not selected? Everyone knows there are limited spots. However some think they are good enough to have one of those available. It's not really adding any information nor is it acting as consolation to be considered perhaps the 105th best. Right? I don't know.

1. Nothing can cheer up people not selected.

2. Not enough spots means there's more qualified people than there are spots so some of the people not selected would be good enough to be good on a team. As opposed to, say, a classroom where theoretically everyone who does well could get an A. It's like a classroom where you're only allowed to give out three As. There's not enough As. So some people who do A-worthy stuff aren't getting As. Only the three highest As. So that's the frustration: people who feel that they are good enough and who probably are good enough not getting picked. LIke they have achieved enough compctency to be able to play, but then are not able to. It's different than being "Not good enough." You ARE good enough, but there are some who are MORE good enough and so you don't get picked. I feel for these people because it feels unjust to be turned down for a job you could theoretically do.

3. Some people aren't good enough and they think they are would feel the same as people that I just described. I have no idea what to do about these people. Could anyone ever be convinced that they're NOT good enough and that's why they didn't get picked? Maybe there should be an alternate dimension where everyone can visit and be on

a team for two months and then you come back with a videotape of it and people can watch it and be like "Hey, you were good!" or else "You weren't good!" I mean, if I tried out for the Olympic pole vaulting team I would fail at doing even one pole vault and then I would not question why I was not picked. But some people rarely do good shows yet still audition and still get mad when they're not picked.

AUGUST 30TH, 2013 at 3:00PM

EMPATHY AGAIN

It's interesting to see how often people in everyday life use their sense of humor to protect themselves or to mark territory around themselves. For example, I buy something from the deli near my office every day. But I go into work late—like at noon. Very often the cashier says to me "Starting late today!" Except that I work until 9 to 10, so it's not late. It's a regular time that starts after most people. But SHE starts work at 6:30am. So yes, to her, I am starting late. But not to me. Yet I am the one she is telling.

The doorman in my office's building—who is kinda crazy or at least conversationally reckless—generally makes jokes that only are funny from his point of view. "Maybe *I'LL* get to come in at noon, huh?" he says and then laughs out loud and how silly that idea is. It's not a joke really, but whatever it is is not from my point of view.

Freedy Johnston, a musician who is one of my favorites and who has a terrific voice is great to hear live. But the three times I've seen him—I've witnessed terrible in-between song banter. It's never from the audience's point of view. HE says "Took me forever to get this guitar tuned" which is something we haven't witnessed nor know anything about. Or "This water is warm!" Then he starts singing and everything is great. Still, bad chit-chat.

At any work function I've ever been at, when people have to gather somewhere that isn't their office, people generally enter the room and then comment on what they imagine everyone is noticing about them. "Sorry I'm so out of breath!" is one I've heard. Or "Here I am, last one again!" from someone presuming we have been keeping track of his ranking in arrivals.

It's not natural to think of things from the other person's point of view. It's hard to do.

I do acting for web videos, usually small parts. Often I'll be one of five or six actors in a scene. There will be one or two main parts and the rest have small jobs to do. Invariably the actors with the small parts will ask after "cut" is called. "How was I?" They were paying an inordinate amount of attention to their own performance and assume the director was too. If the director gives notes and doesn't mention them they'll say "And I'll just do the same thing?" and the director nods yes and the actors nods yes in agreement.

It's somehow the same thing that makes people go "woo" when someone on stage mentions their hometown.

To be good at improv is to see other points of view easily. It's the best superpower improv will give you.

AUGUST 31ST, 2013 at 3:00PM

TERRITORY

something about territory, the concern over what's YOURS or MINE and whose FAULT is it, and THIS PERSON is the problem, and ACCUSATIONS and INTERRUPTIONS. to be good at improv is to make strong choices but not take it personally when you need to switch things up. your character should have an agenda, but you should not become more interested in your character's agenda over that of the agenda of the scene. the scene is more important than your character. very very often, the scene's agenda is different than your character's. you will have to lose and be wrong and give up territory all the time, effortlessly. get used to losing, and when someone else is losing you can help them lose but don't get blinded by the joy of "winning." typed in lowercase to represent lack of thought.

SEPTEMBER 1ST, 2013 at 3:00PM

IT'S NOT A RULE BUT FOR MY TASTE DON'T SAY THE SUGGESTION IN A SCENE KINDA EVER

BUT CERTAINLY ONCE YOU'RE MORE THAN THREE MINUTES IN

It sounds like Darth Vader saying "I hereby declare STAR WARS."

SEPTEMBER 2ND, 2013 at 12:53PM

Q: WHAT IF I DON'T LIKE BEING FUNNY IN THE FIRST LINE?

Anonymous asked: I used to do short form, and I began studying long-form because I liked the idea of abandoning the pressure of "Be funny right away! Now!" However now that I've taken 201-301, I'm being told to be funny in 3 lines, or even 1 line by "initiating with a game." Even the short form I did rarely required being funny in the 1st line. If I don't like deciding what is funny about an improv scene before it starts, is UCB not the theater for me? That seems to be the dominant technique taught and performed.

Short answer: Trust your instincts.

Longer answer: I will say that it's not so much as "BE FUNNY IN THREE LINES" as "INITIATE WITH A PREMISE"—like, start in the middle of something. And that's not ALL we teach, but that is one of the main parts of improv 301 and it can be heady and tough.

I mean, I am in charge of the school at UCB so I'm perhaps unsurprisingly in favor of our curriculum and our approach. I will say that the goal is to teach both the intuition that comes from feeling-the-moment acting AND ALSO the patterns and heightening and specifics that come from good writing. I BELIEVE that these elements which are currently causing you distress are the "writing" portion of UCB (not really writing, but the "build an idea in the opening with your team and use it" part—it feels like writing at first) and that if you stick it out and learn what we are teaching that you will be a versatile comedy warrior. You'll honor the moment and your scene partner and the group mind, but you'll ALSO learn how to walk out of an opening with a starting point ready to go. Those two things are not exclusive, we believe, if you're doing them right.

But lots of talented people never study here, and lots of other talented people try it out and then go somewhere else. It's not for everyone. If what I'm saying doesn't sway you, let's just agree to disagree and maybe I'll see you someday and I imagine we would get along fine.

Trust your instincts.

FYI BTW OMG: This approach was great for me! I like it! I like initiating with premise! I also like starting with nothing! I LIKE IMPROV AND COMEDY AND SKETCH MORE MORE MORE MORE!

PPPPPS: Also, I might not agree that "longform" equals "abandon the pressure of be funny right away"—that implies to me a desire for things to be easy. Long form is not meant to be easy! If you're trying to entertain an audience, there SHOULD be pressure at some point, right?

SEPTEMBER 2ND, 2013 at 3:00PM

PRACTICE

You don't need a lot of theory, just reps. You are not going to be able to think or read or worry yourself into being a good improviser. This blog won't do it, that book won't do it.

You need to get up and find it on your feet. You need to practice.

Your scenes feel bad at first because you're still looking at the frets while you strum your chords. You're still looking at the ball while you dribble it. You're not dancing until the music has been playing for four bars. You're learning. It's okay.

Repeat, repeat, repeat. It is the most reliable method for getting better. More and more of your real self will be available to you.

SEPTEMBER 10TH, 2013 at 3:00PM

HOW CAN I GET BETTER AT GAME?

Okay, but can we first talk about what you mean by "game?" Because I find a lot of confusion with this comes from two different people thinking of the word "game" in different contexts. People will say "so and so didn't play game" and that phrase, all by itself, doesn't tell me a lot except that the person saying it didn't like a show.

ONE IDEA AT A TIME

At its very simplest, having a "game" means your scene is funny. And it has mostly just ONE funny thing that runs throughout it and probably heightens as it goes—meaning it becomes a more absurd version of itself. "Who's On First": the "game" is that Costello misunderstands that the name of the baseball players are also pronouns. That game goes throughout the scene.

So at its simplest, when you say "have a game" to improvisers, you mean for them to have their scenes settle on one idea and then stays centered around that idea.

For example, an improv scene which isn't worried about game might be about a number of ideas, only loosely related. Maybe the scene is about a couple moving into a new house, and we learn that the husband is a very nervous sort who has overly planned the move, and we spend a little time playing with that idea. Then we discover that the wife character has a very new age sensibility and has made alterations to the house to reflect her philosophy. A couple of moves there to confirm that funny bit. And along the way we learn that they had a honeymoon fraught with disasters that are funny but not really related to either of their basic personalities. There's games in here, but the improvisers aren't worried about sticking to just one, and they're not concerned with heightening any of them more than naturally happens in the flow of the scenes. This could be a rich and enjoyable scene, finding itself one step at a time. It also could be aimless and flat.

If you want to "play game," you'd stop at the first discovery that the husband was a nervous sort who had overly-planned everything—and try to expand just that idea into your whole scene. You'd learn that he alienated the realtor with questions; he booked three different sets of movers out of a fear that one would abandon them. That he is wearing a germ-resistant suit and that she had acquiesced to a honeymoon in the Arctic where diseases have trouble surviving. The scene would be more narrow in its focus, but it would heighten farther and faster. You could escalate to huge laughs, amazing your audience at how organized and pointed your scene is. You also might force it too much and get a scene that's too broad and rushed.

"Playing game" means turning "if this is true what else is true" into "if this ONE UNUSUAL THING is true, then what else is true?"

The idea of "game" turns improv from jazz explorations into tight pop songs. That can be good or bad news, depending on your goals, taste and ability.

So: is that what you mean by "getting better at game"—like just having one idea per scene? That's not really so hard to do once you've decided that what you want to do. Try to use the first funny idea you have more and more rather than switching.

HEIGHTENING

But some people, when they say "play game"—what they mean is that they want to see you hit a comedic idea several times in a way that obviously gets more absurd as you go. They want to see something REPEAT and to HEIGHTEN. If you don't do that, then to these people you did not play game.

This is where stuff starts to get confusing. Because maybe you had an improv scene that started slowly, then found something funny and then you just edited it. And then someone says "you didn't play game." But you DID, kind of, in that you arrived at a comedic idea. You just didn't stay with it.

Sticking with the "Who's on First" example—someone who prioritizes heightening wouldn't think Abbott & Costello were playing game until the conversation moved onto the subject of second base. Telling someone that the name of the first baseman is "Who"—well, that's not really playing game (to some people). But once you've revealed that the second baseman's name is "What"—ah! NOW you're playing game.

Okay, then what these people want is REPETITION and HEIGHTENING.

A CLEAR, EXPLAINABLE IDEA

And to yet ANOTHER group of people, playing "game" means that you are basing your comedy around an idea that you can explain. It's an absurd philosophy, or a clearly unusual thing as opposed to just a silly voice, or an absurd way of walking or something. If you're getting your laughs in a purely silly way, then to some people, you are not playing game.

I don't agree with this. If something is funny, it has a game. It just might not be the game you like. A silly voice is a game, it's just a silly one. The game is "say things in this silly voice." But there are people who dismiss silliness alone as being not enough.

So sometimes when people say "you're not playing game" they mean "you're just being silly."

UNUSUAL THING - REACTION - JUSTIFICATION

Finally, some people really love to break down what's funny about a scene into separate parts. A very common way to break down the comedy of a scene is the UNUSUAL THING, followed by a REACTION to that unusual thing, following soon by a JUSTIFICATION—or an explanation as to why this unusual thing and reaction is happening.

So, staying with "Who's On First"—the UNUSUAL THING is that the players have pronouns for names. The REACTION is Costello's blustery confusion. The justification is right at the top when Bud says "you know players these days have really unusual names." So I guess it's a sign of the times that baseball players have names so weird that they even have pronouns for names.

Breaking a game down into unusual thing, reaction, justification can be useful because that's the order that we generally discover our funny things in improv scenes. If you like thinking of scenes in this way, you can check to make sure you check the boxes. Do we have an unusual thing? Did someone react to it? Do we have an explanation for why this world is like this?

Another way to break this down is that the initial unusual thing is the PREMISE. And then the reaction and justification combine with that premise to give us a GAME. So the PREMISE of Who's On First is that "players on this team have pronouns for names" and the GAME is "every time we tell Costello this, he gets confused and mad."

This way is useful because it makes sure that more than one person was involved in making the game. Someone proposed a PREMISE, and then someone else reacted which gave us a GAME.

So some people will tell you that you can't play game unless you can express the comedy of your scene in these discernible parts. These people are no fun and write big long posts on their blogs about what's wrong with improv these days. Sometimes I am one of these people.

DEFINE YOUR TERMS

So if someone wants to get better at game, ask them what they mean. Or if they're trying to please a particular teacher or coach, they should ask that teacher/coach to be specific.

- Do you mean scenes should be about mostly one idea?
- Do you mean they should heighten more?
- Do you mean they should be about something that's an explainable idea and not just silly?
- Do you mean I should hit each of the separate components of a game, and in such a way that I can tell you what I consider those components to be?

GAME EQUALS TASTE

As a teacher, I don't like when I see the word "game" used simply to express disapproval of a show. "They don't play game," someone will say. That's not enough. What is it you don't like about the show? Until you've said that, I don't think you've said anything.

SAYING YOU DON'T LIKE GAME

Separately, I've seen students turn that strategy around. They'll take classes at UCB, audition for a Harold Team, not get a call back and then say "I don't like how the UCB focuses on game." Or maybe they'll have a class where the teacher doesn't think they are funny and the student will say "that teacher focuses too much on game." In both of those cases, the student has understandably had his or her feelings hurt, but these not truly disagreements about "game" or whether it's a useful philosophy. They're just upset they weren't picked.

SEPTEMBER 11TH, 2013 at 3:00PM

YEAH, BUT REALLY, HOW CAN I GET BETTER AT GAME?

Ok, well, "playing game" generally means you do improv a bit more like you're writing a sketch on your feet. It should feel like your scenes come up with a funny idea, and then once it finds its idea, uses that idea as the main theme.

Here some things you can work on.

1. MEMORY

So much of improv is about being in the moment and reacting to what just happened and trying not to plan ahead that it can be difficult to remember anything that happened earlier in the scene. But if you want your scenes to have a nice clean comedic shape, you have to. When someone funny happens, we are going to want to have that funny thing happen again, which means you have to remember it.

I've seen lots of players who are entertaining performers, and they have a knack for reacting to almost any move in a way that can get a laugh, but cannot seem to remember how they behaved just a few lines before. If your character gets a big laugh out of being pulled over and then telling the policeman "I don't trust cops" then it is weird if in a later scene that same character tells someone "I love cops." I would say that you are TOO in the moment, and that you need to hold onto the big moments of scenes or else your improv is going to be shapeless and rambly.

When someone funny or unusual happens, restate it. Right as you notice it.

Secondly, it helps if you are a reactive character—someone who is emotionally invested in the scene around them, and who reacts with their body and voice when something happens. If someone says "The name of the first baseman is who" and you get upset and snap back "I'm not asking you Who's on First!" you will remember that moment better than if you calmly answer in a robotic voice.

2. GIVE IT A TITLE

Games are generally simple, and if you want to show that you see the game, it helps to be able to name it. So practice naming scenes while you're watching them. Names of scenes should reflect the main funny part and be simple. Sample titles of scenes:

- "Break-up Talk With Blockbuster"
- "Dad Hates Commies"
- "Cake Equals Sex"

But I actually mean: give it a title while you're in the scene. Say a line of dialogue that summarizes the main point of what's funny.

On the backline, listen for a line of dialogue that seems to encapsulate what's funny about the scene. Generally there will be one. Something like:

- "I'll be honest, I'm using this job interview to get back together with you."
- "Oh no! That guy we pantsed is King."
- "Never trust the gym."

When I come around to a second beat, or if I'm deciding if I should enter a scene, I'll repeat that line in my head to inspire me—"never trust the gym"—and then start the second beat: "Okay, I've set up cameras in the stationary bikes. See what those bastards are up to after I leave the room."

The title—by which I mean the telltale line which summarizes the game.

3. JUSTIFY EVERYTHING

You can get laughs in an improv scene by just repeating a silly thing over and over again. But it's probably not a good game until there is a justification to explain why the character is doing that thing. Something simple, but something: The Wild And Crazy Guys are acting that way because they are from Europe. The Chicken Lady is the child of a farmer and a chicken. Penelope wants to one-up you because she is jealous in the way that we are all jealous, just more.

4. BE GOOD AT BEING WRONG

Justifying is no good if it explains away the absurdity. You must justify things so they make sense to the character but are still funny to the audience. Why is the boxing trainer advocating to stop throwing punches while in the ring? Because he read about Gandhi and now believes non-violence can beat anything.

Think about movie villains and masterminds. They have reasons for what they do, but we the audience know they are "wrong." They still have reasons, are smart and are compelling. As an improviser, it's more useful to be the bad guy. To be the Joker, not Batman. To be Alan Rickman, not Bruce Willis.

If someone says you are washing your car with a toothbrush, have a silly reason not a sensible one. That's being good at game.

5. LOOK FOR TWO THINGS

I feel like in general there's one funny thing—the unusual thing—that stands out as the funny part of a scene. But generally that one thing is only good when it's connected to something else. Like an old bit on a Conan O'Brien sketch was Mother Theresa tearing apart her hotel room in a fury over late room service. ANGRY MOTHER THERESA would stand out in your mind, but the context of TEARING APART A HOTEL ROOM is what really makes it funny. Those two things. Make sure you are taking both elements with you into second beats. Not that all the specifics have to stay the same, but remember there's two things playing off each other. So if you want to put your ANGRY MOTHER THERESA somewhere, it's got to be somewhere as mundane and everyday as a hotel room, like maybe she's having road rage at a stoplight or else screaming at a TSA agent in an airport.

Or another way to put it is think of your game having an UNUSUAL part and a particular BASE REALITY part. If it's a high school principal who seems to always mispronounce brand names—be aware that it's not just the mis-pronouncing that's funny, it's that it's coming from a principal—someone in a position of authority.

6. TAKE A SKETCH CLASS

Game tends to make your improvised scenes more like ones that were written ahead of time. So take a sketch writing class. You'll watch comedy sketches and analyze why they work. Your teacher will ask you to write sketches where there's one main idea that runs throughout your scene. You'll be working muscles that will come into play when you do improv again.

SEPTEMBER 12TH, 2013 at 3:00PM

I CAN'T REMEMBER ANYTHING FROM THE OPENING

An extremely common question I get is "how can I remember stuff from the opening?" or "I can't remember anything from the opening" or "once I finish the opening I can't remember anything from it."

The good news is: you are not alone. This is an extremely common problem that most improvisers go through. But they all get through it.

The bad news is: I was not one of those improvisers so I can't help you. I could always pretty much remember the opening. Not EVERYTHING, but I'd walk out with two or three ideas/subjects/themes that I could use to start a scene. Almost every other aspect of improv I had and sometimes still have trouble with: committing to a range of emotions, stage presence, finding a game and keeping it, using my real life, playing patiently, active listening. All difficult. But remembering stuff from the opening I could pretty much do.

Here's some advice I've heard from other people.

1. **Enjoy the opening.** If you like a movie, you will summarize it in great detail for your friends. Lots of images, lines of dialogue and story points just STICK in your brain. Partly because it was a well-organized story, maybe, but also because you loved it and were therefore immersed in it and fully concentrating on it. Enjoy your openings are you are in them: enjoy your teammates way of saying and doing things, be sensitive for moments that genuinely tickle you. You will remember those moments best.

   1a. **Feel it as you do it.** Get into it. Be expressive. Say it with tone. Once more with feeling. Use the bottom of your brain more than the top of your brain. Don't think so much, feel more. You remember stuff you feel more than stuff you logically arrived at. If it's a word-association pattern game, practice feeling your reactions to everything that is said.

2. **Practice it.** The openings that are hardest to remember are the ones

that are weirdest and most unlike real life. If your opening is just someone telling a monologue, well, that's pretty easy. You've heard lots of people tell stories in your life so your brain has practice absorbing information in that way. But if your opening is a pattern game of people using word association to create ideas—then that is a way you are not used to communicating. But after enough repetitions, your brain will be better at processing them and just naturally hold onto the information more easily. You're a human: you are good at learning things when you repeat them.

3. **Almonds.** My teammate Connor Ratliff was worried about remembering stuff from openings and he read somewhere that almonds improve memory so he started eating almonds every morning. He may still do that, I have no idea. I also have no idea if almonds have any real effect on memory. But he's a really good improviser so I thought that made his plan worth mentioning.

SEPTEMBER 14TH, 2013 at 3:00PM

FIGHTING ADVICE: MAYBE THIS?

If you're fighting in your improv scene, make sure both actors agree on who is going to lose.

Maybe that? Oh goddammit, I don't know. Still looking for some silver bullet piece of advice about FIGHTS.

OCTOBER 3RD, 2013 at 9:11PM

FUTURE TALK AND PAST TALK

I've said it before but it's so interesting I wanted to bring it up again.

When improvised characters are reminiscing they tend to agree. When they propose events for their future, they quibble.

Like, if someone says "Be great to see a game tomorrow, right?" the other person will automatically go "Well, I don't know, I'm not sure, maybe." But if the first person had said instead "Great game yesterday, right?" the other person will just automatically go "Yep!"

This has been my experience watching classes. People agree on past events, and equivocate on futures ones.

Here's the thing: THEY BOTH DON'T EXIST IN REAL LIFE. THEY ARE BOTH THE SAME, IMPROV-WISE.

It sort of doesn't matter since in either case they're not talking about the present and what they really need to do is talk about the present moment. But still, I think this is weird.

I guess a practical benefit of knowing this is that if you and your partner are not on the same page, one way to get on the same page is reminisce a bit. "Remember when we went to the bank?" will get you an automatic "yes" and that's something to start with.

OCTOBER 4TH, 2013 at 9:11AM

BROTHERS HINES

I get to do improv with my brother. It is one of the best things that has ever happened to me. We've had a weekly show at UCB east for just over a year (thank you Nate Dern), and for almost ten years before that we've done various indie shows and UCB sets (thank you Anthony King), and lots of Cagematches (thank you, Charlie Todd).

Doing an improv show is a very specific sort of intimacy. You're listening very closely to each other, you're trying hard to say yes to each other's impulses, you're obeying all the improv mantras that are directing you to make your scenes more specific, important and funny.

To do these things with someone from your family is intense. Kevin and I have always gotten along (I'm 5 years older than him—maybe that was enough of a difference that we weren't rivals growing up? Maybe our natures are just easy-going enough?). But doing improv has made us closer.

Separate from this, Kevin is an amazing improviser. He has built more tools for himself than maybe anyone I've seen. He'll play any style, any tempo, any form and make it work. There is nothing that throws him on an improv stage. In the above clip I get all the fun parts (which is probably on a subconscious level why I'm sharing it? no, not totally but yes partly), but it's Kevin who initiates, introduces the unusual thing, heightens it, edits and supports. He enters as a character and when I interrupt him, he drops his thing and uses that moment. He is both straight man and character in this. He endows me with everything I need and gives me other characters too. I am never more free than in these sets because I literally don't give a moment's thought to what Kevin can handle—he can handle everything.

If I were a student and wanted to figure out improv, I know what I'd do: go see Kevin Hines and write down his every move.

I am amazingly blessed in my improv career—I've gotten to do improv with the best people at the UCB theatre, sometimes for years. But these sets with my brother, both for personal reasons and for the fun of doing improv with someone with Kevin's range—are my favorite.

OCTOBER 9TH, 2013 at 10:04PM

Q: HOW CAN YOU BOTH KNOW SOMEONE AND FIND THEM UNUSUAL?

Anonymous asked: I've gotten the note to "know someone" in the scene and I was wondering how you can find someone's behavior unusual if you know them. Presumably if you knew someone then their mode of behavior would already be known to you so how could you point it out as unusual?

Good point! I guess improv can never work.

(In a later post I get correctly called out as being a bully here, and I apologize for it).

OCTOBER 10TH, 2013 at 9:29AM

Q: WHAT IF ONLY YOU GO TO THEM, AND THEY DON'T GO TO YOU?

Anonymous asked: Thinking about the idea of "Go to them." I think I play that a lot, but how do you identify the feeling when people are coming to you? It gets incredibly frustrating when you think you're the only one playing supportively. Always playing Go To Them can feel like you have to be a babysitter. I don't doubt that other people are also supporting, I guess I'd like to know when I can cut loose, not worry about everyone, and let people come to me instead.

If you're really going to them, it should be as satisfying as if they came to you. It's the connecting that's fun, it doesn't really matter who had to move more to make it happen.

OCTOBER 10TH, 2013 at 11:36AM

MADE-UP PROPER NOUN IMPROV

A fun exercise suggested to me by Ryan Karels, though I'm sure everyone has a version of this (I didn't):

A series of scenes where you try to use as many made-up proper nouns as possible. Not real ones like "The Matrix" or "Mayor Daley"—but made-ones like "Craig Bankowski" and "Return Of The Toad." Everyone has to decide to already have heard of everything.

- "Hey, I just got the Flogs album."
- "Oh great! I was going to borrow one from Candice Genellman."

I like to structure it: the initiation and the response each have to have one and then after that you just do whatever.

These are very fun. Something about the specificity of the names and then the subsequent decision to already have heard of it makes everything work like a charm.

OCTOBER 14TH, 2013 at 3:00PM

IMPROV AS RELIGION

A cult. A philosophy. A religion.

These are the terms people use to describe improv. The casual outsider would be amazed at how intensely some people view improv. It's just a way to make jokes, right? Or a some guidelines for brainstorming together in public? Well, yes, it is those things. And to some people that's all it is.

But something in the language of our culture communicates something grander. And so, those of us who really get into it, we automatically probe all of the advice we get for our scenes for something more.

There's the content of the advice—the practical usefulness of it—and then there's also the wording and tone which that advice is given in. And I think the genius of Del Close and other great improv teachers is that they know how to give genuinely good advice in such a way that it connects with actors and writers in a deep, personal way.

When Del said "say yes"—that could be seen as just practical advice for building scenes together. Del could have just said "cooperate" but that term wouldn't have the magic, alluring hint of something MORE that "say yes" does. When we hear "say yes" we hear something much deeper. We instinctively know that we're being asked to be fundamentally open-minded, to be brave, to be adventurous.

The most popular improv advice sounds like spiritual challenges. "Follow the fear"—without even considering if that's actually practical advice for an improvised comedy scene, you want to believe that. You've been hungry to have someone tell you to follow the fear. You find a way to make that advice true. "Choose to know each other." "Commit." "Why is this day important?"

You may come to improv because you like comedy, but if you stay, it's because all this advice challenges you in a way that you've been hungry for. You want this to be a more interesting world, and you want to be a braver person, and then in a dingy improv classroom someone is saying it to you.

It's why you don't mind not being paid (at first, and for a while), because you are learning. You're growing as a person, so it seems just that you pay for it. Your shows are not a place where you give your services, but are a place where you are being taught by an audience of how to be spiritually and philosophically more bold.

We believe that these improv classes are going to burn away the parts of our personality that we don't like and leave in its place a braver, more powerful person. There is no one more ready to flagellate than a newly excited improv student. "Call me out on my bullshit," they say. "I like this teacher because they didn't let me get away with shit." It's almost sadomasochistic, their desire to be corrected and fixed. But it's because they sense a spiritual perfection. The wording of improv lessons baited them into it, and now they want it.

At some point, ironically, you have to get cynical about this stuff to get good at it. Even though it's probably necessary to get starry-eyed and hypnotized by the promise of a grand philosophy for a while, you have to back off that kind of attitude to get funny. You have to simply examine the advice for its practical value.

You calm down and realize that "say yes" is really only useful in the beginning of a scene, and that once you realize the point of the scene—the game, the funny part—well, then saying yes isn't really a priority anymore. You realize that "follow the fear" speaks more to just a general attitude of bravery on the part of the actor, and that for the characters in the scene it's almost completely irrelevant how brave they are being. You realize that not every improv exercise is good. And that your improv teachers may be good actors and writers, but are not trying to fix your life. That an improv audition is not a referendum on you as a person. The advice gets simpler and smaller and more practical.

But I guarantee that if you do improv for years that you're still coming back because you think it's the Right Thing to Do—to pursue improv.

OCTOBER 14TH, 2013 at 10:09PM

Q: YOU ACTED LIKE A BULLY!

Anonymous asked: It seems like the person asking about knowing each other and unusual things had a real question, but you acted like a bully and made fun of them. Others then jumped on board in the comments. As a new student, I'd be crushed if I submitted a sincere question and got made fun of by UCB teachers. Maybe you should take down the "It's okay to ask questions" link, if you're going to be critical of the people who use it. I'd love to read an honest answer to this person's question if you are up for it.

This question is referring to this post in which I snarkily dismissed someone's question.

You're right. I apologize to the person who asked it.

The question irked me because it feels like a thing I see people do where they try to poke holes in advice being given to help them. That's probably not the intention.

My sincere answer is that the question "if you knew someone then their mode of behavior would already be known to you so how could you point it out as unusual" is in a sense true, but it's also just parsing the language in such a way as to avoid two simple lessons that generally help: 1) choose to know the person, because that makes your character able to make choices more easily and to be invested and be affected and 2) recognize unusual things, since those tend to be the center of the funny parts of scenes.

The term "unusual thing" gets argued with a lot by students. What's unusual? If something's unusual why should we let it happen? The thing the teacher describes as unusual isn't unusual to the person in the scene so what treat it that way?

And...I mean, yeah, that's all true. But we use the term unusual thing to refer to the part of the scene that seems to generally happen in funny scenes: something is different than normal. Think about it too much and it gets too hard. But in a funny scene, something is different than what we expect and it's the source of all the fun. So be sensitive for it and be affected by it and explore it. I can't be more specific than that since it depends what kind of unusual/funny thing it is.

If the term unusual doesn't feel right, how about the "funny" thing? Or the "interesting" thing? Or whatever word works for you that makes your character focus on the part of the scene that is interesting. Or "the turn" I've heard used?

And again, I apologize to the original poster. I should have answered politely or not answered at all.

NOVEMBER 3RD, 2013 at 7:04AM

Q: BEST TIME TO REVEAL YOU'RE NOT DEAD?

Anonymous asked: if you're in a class and playing the dead body in a funeral scene, when is the best time to reveal that you're not really dead and ruin the scene?

The moment there is any silence whatsoever.

NOVEMBER 3RD, 2013 at 9:55AM

Q: WHAT ABOUT BEING THE "REAL" DEAD BODY?

alexispereira asked: My go-to move in funeral scenes is to sit silently in the back of the room and then reveal myself as the "real" dead body. How cool is that?

That is some next level stuff, right there.

NOVEMBER 3RD, 2013 at 7:47PM

Q: WHAT IF THE ACTOR DIES?

Anonymous asked: If you're in a funeral scene and you think the person pretending to be the dead body might actually have died while pretending to be dead, what do you do? I don't mean MORALLY what is the right thing to do, I mean as an IMPROVISER what do you do? This has happened to me twice now.

Commit hard and bury your friend. Only after the scene has been swept, dig him up and call a doctor.

NOVEMBER 12TH, 2013 at 2:22PM

Q: INVENTORY

Anonymous asked: INVENTORY

You are carrying:

- a half-idea
- an accent you do when you're out of ideas
- a list of specials to say in case you're a waiter
- a mimed glass

NOVEMBER 14TH, 2013 at 7:48AM

OFFICE WORKERS ARGUING

So I'm in an office for month and being back in an office environment I have the following near-useless observation I need to share with someone, and you, dear readers, get to be this someone:

Here's a VERY COMMON template of office conversations:

- person A: (introduce a topic)
- person B: (declare a pro or con opinion on that topic)

- person A: (take the opposite view)
- person B: (argue the different sides)

The topics are generally menial, at least 50% of the time about food (what to eat for lunch, the best K-Cup to choose). People are not mad but they seem to like having "their" side. There's lots of "Well MY favorite flavor is Hazelnut Decaf. Not Hazelnut! The Decaf one is slightly more bitter!" And the people get loud and animated but they are not mad at each other.

There's (at least in this office) a very common category of phrases that ostensibly cede ground but don't:

- "**now i'm not saying** that I totally know everything..."
- or "**maybe** saying he's a cancer on the Panthers **is too much, but** the guy is definitely destructive."
- or "**all i'm saying is...(smile of satisfaction)** that's not a coffee."

It's polite to nod whenever someone uses those phrases as if you have actually been agreed with. But no one changes their mind because of these phrases. People have dug in early. But generally you get the feeling that no one cares.

I know that it's dumb and tread ground to talk about office small talk and how shallow it is. But it's interesting from the perspective of an improv teacher: people communicate to a large degree within the construct of fighting.

And they mark territory by taking opposite views. They can't have an opinion without first knocking down another. Their opinion exists IN ORDER to destroy another, not simply to exist.

It's weird. No wonder no one can yes-and in an improv scene. No one does it in real life.

I just witnessed a conversation amongst five people and these topics were discussed:

- was Terrell Owens a cancer for his football teams?
- better venue: MSG or Barclays
- best manner to eat chicken wings
- is one required to go to birthday parties you've been invited to?
- what's an appropriate topic to distract sports fans from talking about

sports (like what topics would successfully distract—not pop music but yes news of the day)

It isn't how trivial these topics are that strikes me, it's that everyone feels a need to own their own unique point of view. Can't MSG and Barclay's both be excellent venues? Do the strengths and weaknesses of one have anything to do with the strengths and weaknesses of the other? Do we humans want a hero and goat in all narratives, even office small talk?

I can see why Seinfeld was so popular. The characters on Seinfeld were masters of coining terms, marking territory and criticizing points of view on mundane things. They were the models that the office workers of today learned from. "He's a close-talker"—"I wouldn't say he's a close talker, *I* would say he's a FAST talker." etc. etc.

P.S. Got to write a whole other post about the appeal of correctly categorizing things—that's Seinfeld's (the show, and also the comedian) main superpower. Humans love labels, re-labelling, arguing about labels (see the recent article that divides America into 11 regions, or astrology, or Myers-Briggs tests, or which Sex in the City character are you, etc etc).

DECEMBER 2ND, 2013 at 6:25AM

you're on a stage, not on a screen. so stop taking inspiration from movies, where someone has controlled lighting and framing and sound design. see plays, where they are using the same tools you have available to you in your improv shows: real people, monologues, interplay between real humans, big choices, specific wordplay, emotional reactions, minimal costumes and props (more often than not at least), dramatic loaded pauses, movement up and down stage, facing forward, big deep exhales you can hear, etc.

and make fun of plays too. that's your medium.

Saturday Night Live, a tv show, makes fun of tv shows.

National Lampoon, a magazine, makes (made) fun of magazines.

So if you're doing improv on a stage, you should make fun of plays. watch plays. do parodies of plays. be happy forever.

DECEMBER 5TH, 2013 at 7:36AM

IMPORTANT UPDATE

Improv husbands, regardless of the gender of the actor playing them, often name their wives "Tracy."

DECEMBER 21ST, 2013 at 5:38PM

Q: SHOULD ONE START AT IO THEN GO TO UCB?

Anonymous asked: I have been reading through your blog, which is a fabulous source of information. I was wondering do you think it may hinder an improviser to take classes at iO and then try to transfer to UCB? I ask because iO focuses mainly on establishing relationships and doesn't care too much about game where at UCB they pound game into you. Would this make it harder to focus on game if you have other habits ingrained in you already? As my friend puts it, iO is like Jazz and UCB is Rock N Roll or Rap.

I've never studied at iO so despite my UCB experience I'm not the best person to ask. I know by reputation and by quality of improviser that iO is excellent, so I'm sure it's a great place. And I know firsthand that UCB is a great place. So I can't see how there's any hinderance in studying at one, then the other.

The idea that iO focuses mainly on establishing relationship and that at UCB pounds game into you—I think that it's not as simple as all that. We at UCB want your scenes to be about truthful and grounded characters, and we want our actors listening and affecting each other. And I believe that at iO they prefer your scenes to find a simple focus and for that focus to be funny? I mean, I've seen shows there and the scenes had games.

I bet there's way way more in common than different, and the idea that they're different is the kind of thing that makes for a good article summarizing different improv schools but in practice is not that accurate.

We DO focus on game a lot more than other places. But there is plenty of time in an improv class to focus on many things and I think by the end of our core classes you've been noted on lots of stuff including relating to each other and to game.

So even if we are "rock and roll" and iO is "jazz"—I mean, you want to play an instrument with other people right? And at this point you don't play anything? Neither one will hinder you for the other.

I understand it's helpful to abstract things down to a label—it's how we humans conquered the globe. But you're ultimately not fair to either place, I bet, to do that!

Good luck.

DECEMBER 21ST, 2013 at 5:40PM

Q: HOW TO "BE PLAYFUL?"

Anonymous asked: You said here once that you find it helpful to tell yourself "be playful". Do you have any advice on how to do that?

I don't. But I'll say that different mantras and sayings work well for different people. If simply saying the phrase "be playful" doesn't do it for you, then there's probably a simple piece of advice that gets you in the right mindset. Listen and react? Play it real? Yes, and? First unusual thing? Point of view? Follow the fun? Follow the fear? One of these will make everything easier for you in a way that won't require a ton more explanation.

DECEMBER 30TH, 2013 at 9:12AM

Q: HOW COME I'VE NEVER SEEN YOU ONCE PLAY A TALKING BEAR?

ferniecommaalex asked: If you know so much about improv, how come I've never ONCE seen you play a talking bear?

Hmm, good point! This blog is officially closed.

2014

JANUARY 2ND, 2014 at 9:13AM

SAYING "NO" TO OFFENSIVE THINGS

Q: Improv question! Do you have any advice for if someone makes an offer you don't agree with on a personal level (for example sexist, racist, offensive, in poor taste, etc), how to accept it and build on it and move the scene forward in a positive way supporting the improviser and keeping the fun going while also keeping integrity and not necessarily agreeing with or implying you condone/accept the nasty thing itself?

I think this is a really interesting question so I'm going to talk forever about it. Spoiler: My answer is that you should trust your gut and know it's okay to not do the thing you don't want to do.

A slightly more advanced answer is: trust your gut and push back, but say WHY you don't want to do the thing and then stay open to discussing it more, in character, for the sake of the scene.

I believe "accept the offer" means "tell me what your character truly thinks of this and why," not "you have to do this now."

But let's use many examples and get into this, it's a common and tricky thing.

When people are learning improv, they are told time and time again "say yes, say yes, say yes."

Students are also told, either directly or indirectly, to be skeptical of their first instinct in terms of things like learning how to speak your mind (as a character) in situations where you would normally not confront someone. or learning to try things that you might not try in real life ("Let's see what happens if you DO dance to this song," or something).

And teachers ask you to do interesting things in your improv scenes, in general, rather than look for excuses to do boring things—even if in real life you'd normally do the boring thing. Like "Quit stalling—just jump out of the plane" (there are high number of "two people about to jump out of plane" scenes in beginning improv classes—and students seem unaware of how emotionally transparent that is).

So it's confusing because you spend some time as your learn improv during which you basically don't trust your first instinct, especially when that instinct is to say "no."

And so—and this is extremely common—when you get into a situation when someone asks your character to do something you consider uncomfortable, maybe creepy, possibly sexist, racist or in poor taste—you seize up. You wonder "wait, SHOULD I do this? Am I being a bad improviser if I 'say no' to this? Am I being boring?"

Let me say clearly: You're definitely not being a bad improviser to 'say no'—in character—to something you don't want to do or just don't like or find in bad taste. You SHOULD, in character, say no to those things. That's you putting your true self in the scene, and that's essential to making your scenes unique and compelling. Trust that instinct. If your gut tells you something is weird or off, or just in poor taste, say no—in character.

A great follow-up to this, is that once you refuse to perform the action or say the thing—is to say why—the simple truthful reason why—you don't want to do it. This is a chance for a real truthful moment which makes a show great.

YOU CAN REFUSE THE LAP DANCE

I saw a scene in a level one improv class where a guy initiated to a girl "Honey, happy anniversary. Time for my annual lap dance," and he started doing a lapdance to her. This was maybe not as gross as it sounds—the guy was trying to play this for laughs, he seemed to be mindful of not being actually physically intrusive—the other student is the only person who can really say whether that's right, but it didn't feel creepy to me, maybe just lame?

Side note: I've actually seen a fair number of "lap dances" as initiations for scenes. People are drawn to them because, I guess, they're forbidden, they're physically silly, they feel funny to do? And I've seen it where the person receiving the lap dance immediately thinks it's funny and gets into it, and the whole class laughs at this physically bold lap dance thing. And I'm sure many students see that and are like "oh, great, so do I have to be into lap dances now? Am I going to have to grind up on someone or even just grind in anyway whatsoever? Ugh, I probably do."

No, trust your gut. Because in the example I'm citing, the female student said calmly what I think was a perfect response: "Sweetheart, I don't know how to tell you this, but I just don't like when you do this. It's really, I don't know, like... gross?" And it was so true and calm and not angry and great—everyone exploded with laughter. The guy was not insulted and they had this great scene. She said yes to the information—that it had happened before and was a regular thing—but she was changing her mind of how it was implied she felt about it (presumably her character had let it happen before).

THERE WILL ALWAYS BE THINGS THAT BOTHER YOU

I think you DO become more comfortable with offensive things as you do more improv. They don't shock you as much. Your boundaries get a bit looser. And so your gut won't say "no" as much. So I can understand how you might think that the mark of a great improviser is being willing to do offensive and outrageous things. But that's not really true. You always a have a personal boundary and improv scenes have a way of sniffing out what they are and bringing you right to them. It is not only OKAY to say no to stuff at your personal boundary, it's essential for the audience to believe you're being truthful with them.

Also, when you are starting out, it is sometime hard to know if you want to say "no" because you're fearful or because the thing presented is in poor taste or offensive. Don't worry about that. If you feel bummed or annoyed or grossed out, you can say "no" in character and decide later if that was the absolute best move.

Just push back (say "no" in character), say why you don't want to, and stay open to hear and consider the reaction.

SPECIFIC EXAMPLES

Getting a bit more improv nerdy about it, let me say that there are ways to "accept the offer" in an improv sense while still not doing the thing you think is offensive. I think this is really what you're asking.

I think the key is to not get angry, and to not outright dismiss or try to skip over the thing. Trust your gut but speak to it, and stay open to hear the reaction.

If a character is telling you to do something, **say the word no and then explain why**. "I need you to shoot this dog." Say "Uh, no. I don't shoot dogs. that's cruel."

If someone is implying that you always do something you can say **you've**

changed your mind—just agree that you've done it before. "Time to shoot the dog like we always do." You say "You know what? I think I've come to realize this is cruel. We've got to stop."

Here's a made-up example. Let's say someone initiates as a bully, and they're doing (what I'm now realizing is) a standard improv "bully voice" and they say "Good news, dude: I just beat up some girls and fags."

Actually, I think that's funny. It's so insane, I'd probably match it. But let's say that I didn't want to. Maybe it feels too far, too dumb. I think you should **match the tone and energy but say what you feel**. Use the same improv bully voice they're using (or your version of it, but use SOME voice so you're not breaking the tone) and say "Hey man, you ever think we go too far?" That's a pretty common improv tactic. Agree with the music and energy of the scene, but say the things you mean.

This is all for things that offend you. If it's purely a question of comedic taste, I think you should try to do it. Hard to say without real examples. But if someone for example initiates as a really dumb cartoonish chimney sweep, and they're doing the worst musical theater version of a cockney accent, crooked elbow—and it's just lame and dumb and you hate it, I still think you have to be YOUR version of a chimney sweep and you shouldn't call the person out. Be your version of it and move the scene along. You should never really "roll your eyes" on stage—though god knows I've done it literally hundreds of millions of times.

JANUARY 3RD, 2014 at 9:34AM

Anonymous asked: Is it ever too late to save a bad scene by going "this has to be the weirdest orgy I've ever been to"?

Always works. It's the "chimpanzee in a suit" of improv moves.

FEBRUARY 26TH, 2014 at 12:11PM

Q: WHAT ABOUT TEACHERS WHO SAY "DON'T MAKE JOKES?"

Anonymous asked: TJ Jagadowski is quoted in the NYT as saying UCB's style is "joke heavy" and "has a purpose and that is to get a laugh." I know this is comedy and not drama and yes we want it to be funny, but how does that square with what I heard in 101, specifically "don't make jokes" and generally don't do things just because you think they'll get a quick laugh?

Interesting question! TJ and your 101 teacher are talking about different things, I think.

1. When the 101 teacher says "don't make jokes" they mean: commit to the scene harder. Don't say or do things that make the scene feel less real. In most cases they mean: don't try to sound like you're a character on television, sound like the people who walk around the actual Earth.

2. But when TJ says UCB's style is "joke heavy" I think he means that the strategy of finding a game of the scene and hitting it can encourage fast play that has a lot of payoffs early.

   These "jokes" are not the same thing your 101 teacher is talking about. These are funny moments that can be very on-pattern and fit the scene in a committed way.

   What the NYT article is saying, I believe, is that some people like their improv very discovery-oriented and don't mind if that makes it include long stretches without a clear funny moment. And the UCB championed a more aggressive style: have a plan to get laughs, and then execute it.

   But neither camp likes it when improvisers aren't committed.

3. I've heard improv teachers say we shouldn't make "joke" a bad word. I agree. But we do need a word for the attempt to be funny by sounding like an uncommitted sitcom character. You aloofed? You detatched? you de-committed?

FEBRUARY 26TH, 2014 at 3:00PM

ACCUSATIONS: THREE EXERCISES

Okay! I present here for improv nerdy delight and judgment a series of exercises on handling accusations in a scene. Each one evolved out of the previous one, and I think they're each useful for different levels.

When I say "handling accusations" I mean treating accusations like gifts rather than an excuse to fight or to prove your character "right."

And when I say "accusations" I mean both:

- Actual *accusations*, like: "Hey, Jeremy, YOU were supposed to invite people to this party!"
- And the related *'explain this'* statement which is less angry but still makes the other person 'weird': "Jeremy, I hired you to be the clown for my son's birthday party, why are you discussing philosophy with them?"

Both of these things can bait people into either being defensive or deflecting or fighting, so it's good to practice responding to them.

(Also: great scene ideas in my examples, as always)

EXERCISE ONE: SUPER VILLAIN / MASTERMIND

Two people up. Person A makes an accusation. Person B deliberately acts like a super villain or mastermind in response. *Person A must then sympathetically disagree* (otherwise Person A will often get too angry).

Person A: Jeremy, did you use all the conditioner?

Person B: Bwa ha ha, yes I did! Now your hair will look stringy and flawed! AND I SHALL LOOK MORE BEAUTIFUL BY COMPARISON!

Person A: (sympathetically disagreeing) Look, I know that I can be arrogant about my hair but this is really going too far.

PROS: Person B practices being the "bad" character while still taking full ownership of the accusation. The sympathetic disagreement lets Person A practice giving his/her scene partner room to digest, since they are defending something they didn't think of. Exercise is silly and entertaining. As an exercise, it's clear and easy to measure if you've done it right.

CONS: Resulting scenes are kinda dumb.

EXERCISE TWO: OWN IT

Same thing, but now Person B must admit to the accusation and explain why as a "normal" person, not a super villain. Person A still sympathetically disagrees.

> Person A: Jeremy, did you forget to invite anyone to this party?
>
> Person B: I did it on purpose. I wanted the party to fail because I'm jealous of you having friends besides me.
>
> Person A: Yes, I know I've been ignoring you but you're acting like a child!

PROS: As an exercise, it's still easy to follow. It makes Person B use the accusation as a way of learning more about his or her character. In an improv scene, this strategy will actually work very often.

CONS: Although more natural than the super villain one, this one can still feel forced and contrived and the scenes all take on a similar feel.

EXERCISE THREE: THE REAL REASON

Same set up (two people up, Person A accuses) but this time Person B tries to feel why he/she would have done such a thing FOR REAL. Like, in real life. The only condition here is that you have to accept without argument that you REALLY have done the thing, you can't change it so you didn't do it, or even that you didn't do it on purpose.

> For example, if Person A says "Sir, we found these knives and excessive liquids in your luggage. Why were you sneaking these onto the plane?"
>
> If you were doing super villain approach you might say "So that I can take over the skies!"
>
> If you were doing the "own it" approach, you might say "Because I plan on using them to bully other passengers up there."

I actually think both of those responses could work.

But if you take a moment and try to feel why you might really have done it, I bet you'd take a moment to consider, then say something like this:

> "You know, I just was hoping you wouldn't check. I thought I could get

away with it. I think the TSA policies are kinda dumb, and I'm not planning anything bad and I just didn't care to follow your rules."

PROS: The answers are rich, specific and have the ring of truth that makes improv compelling. This is what the best improvisers often do when endowed with a strange situation. It is the best approach in actual scenes.

CONS: It's hard to measure, from the student's perspective, if you've done this right. They don't necessarily know what truth feels like on stage. And since there's so few restrictions on how you respond, many students will inadvertently deflect: ("I don't know! Someone else must have put them there!" or "Ach, I took the wrong bag by mistake!")

The exercise is basically just telling the students "be good actors and be interesting people" which is not the most helpful teaching exercise.

IMPROV IS LIKE MEMENTO AND/OR SPLIT-BRAIN EXPERIMENTS

Here's two stories I will tell to explain what it should feel like when you're accused of something in an improv scene:

a. In the movie *Memento*, the main character can not form new memories and thus is constantly in situations which are a surprise to him (and since the scenes are show in reverse chronological order—the audience also does not know what came before). At one point, he's being chased through a parking lot by someone shooting at him and you hear him thinking "Okay, so what's going on here?" And he has to guess what's going on with context clues. He generally assumes that whatever is going on is because of something he's done and that he meant for it to happen.

  That's how the improviser should approach scenes where they've been accused. They must assume it's true and they did something to create this situation kinda just sense why they would have done such a thing.

b. Split-Brain experiments. For a few decades, if someone suffered from epileptic seizures that were so intense the person could not function, doctors might perform surgery to separate the hemispheres of their brains! It would stop the seizures, but leave the patients with a "split brain," meaning the two halves of their brains could not communicate directly.

This relates, just give me a moment.

Doctors could then perform cool experiments like this: they'd cover the patient's eye and ear on one side of his head, tell him something which then only one side of his brain would perceive.

In one experiment, they made the patient cover his right eye and ear. Then they said "Okay, get up, switch to cover your other eye and ear and go to the next room." The man got up, switched to cover his other eye and ear and started to walk to the next room.

The doctors stopped him and said "Where are you going?" And he said "To go to the bathroom."

Because: he didn't really know why he was going. It was the other side of his brain that had made that decision. But in the heat of the moment he made his best guess as to why he was doing such a thing and convinced himself that was the reason.

That's what it's like to do improv. You're doing something, or you're being told that you're doing something and you don't really know, at first, why. But you have to explain it. If you're a good actor, and you're in the moment you will come up with a specific, true and interesting reason. It will be related on some level to why YOU would have done such a thing.

FEBRUARY 27TH, 2014 at 12:20PM

Q: JUSTCRAIG: WHAT'S FUNNIER IN A SUBWAY SCENE?

justcraig asked: In improv, what's funnier to do in a subway scene: pretending to be a guy who's selling candy to raise money for his basketball team, or starting to clap in rhythm while saying "ladies and gentlemen," in order to get other improvisers to break dance. Thanks in advance.

FEBRUARY 27TH, 2014 at 3:00PM

#

Something to be aware of when talking about a group is pace. Not pace in terms of how quickly people are talking or how high energy the scene is but the pace of the unusual things. When does the first unusual thing happen, and then how quickly does it heighten?

There's no right answer. Some groups are fast—they put an unusual thing in the first line, then a tag-out in the 5th line; and they've moved to a new scene inspired by that in the 7th line.

Other groups like to really wait. Set a slow pace. Unusual thing just hinted at, then confirmed, then really confirmed. Heightened maybe once and then edited.

Neither one is better than the other; it's just how the group plays.

Also, this "pace" is actually separate from the tempo of the scene. A scene can have two high energy characters adding lots of info—but if the funny/unusual part is advanced slowly—well, that's still a slow scene, improv comedy wise.

Lots of members of groups wish their group played at different paces. It's hard to DECIDE to play at a different pace than the group naturally falls at.

Here's where forms can help. A monoscene tends to encourage a slower heightening than a montage where you're allowed to tag-out. Or a decision to only have two person scenes for the first 3 or 4 scenes can slow down heightening.

Whatever happens, it's easier to speed up than it is to slow down. Slowing down takes confidence at first and then smart choices later when you want your scenes to actually heighten now that you've been slow for a while.

MARCH 1ST, 2014 at 11:27AM

Q: OFFENSIVE SUBJECT MATTER?

matthewalston asked: Hey Will, I was wondering what your view was on scenes with offensive subject matter. I usually thought these scenes should be avoided entirely, but every once in awhile, I get roped into a scene with a pedophile, or someone mentions AIDS and the room goes dead silent. But, I still feel the need to stick with it in that moment. Do you think there's an effective way of dealing with those kinds of scenes and making them good?

With a specific example, I'd have a more certain answer.

What it reminds me of is when someone blurts out a really powerful thing in a non-committed way in a non-committed scene, and it's too sad/mean/real to just ignore.

I'm going to risk trying to make up hypothetical situations and then honestly say what I think I would do, rather than come up with some proper-sounding teacher platitude.

1. Let's say a nervous actor is a priest, and even though the scene was mostly about how this priest is jealous he's not allowed in the choir, he then blurts out "Well, I'm just going to diddle an altar boy anyway" and the audience goes "ooooh."

    Same if a person accidentally makes a sexual innuendo, the audience notices it and then the person acts like they meant to make that innuendo. Like if that priest character said "When I need guidance I look to the children" and the crowd laughs, and only then the actor says "to molest them."

    I would either:

    a. React big, abandon the previous scene and focus entirely on that confession for the rest of the scene, and try to have it work through surprisingly intense commitment or

    b. Treat that confession like a sub game. Like I keep talking about the priest wanting to be in the choir and then now and then throw in "and of course we'll have to deal with your molesting at some point, also."

    c. If the actor REALLY just threw that away and it was clear he wasn't committed, I might just straight-up dismiss it. "You wouldn't have the balls, Father Klein. Now let's get back to this choir thing." That's lame but I might do it.

I wouldn't ignore it, and I wouldn't do politically correct scolding either. First is a cop out, second is no fun.

2. The case of over emphasis, like the very common case of a doctor's scene where the doctor is telling you that you are going to die in five minutes, or that you have AIDS or cancer. It's not the general situation that makes this tough, it's that the specific example used is so huge that it feels like there's nothing to do but scream.

What would I do?

    a. React big and scream and have the size of my reaction be the focus of the rest of the scene.

    b. React but react smaller than you really would, so that you can still have a conversation with the doctor. "Oh my God, ten minutes? I can't believe it!" Just choose to not be a screaming mess for the sake of having a scene.

3. The real best strategy is to be an amazingly good actor and make the situation true in your brain and also instantly realize how you would really feel and say that. I'm saying this in an overstated way, but there are performers who have such gravity in their voices and can process their feelings so quickly, that they would take either of the above cases and respond with such truth and specificity that it would turn what feels like a gaffe and make it an amazing scene. They do it in one line. They turn to the priest and say "We have to stop such things" and the room is thrilled.

P.S. I have one slightly bitchy thing to say, and I recognize that you're just sending a question to an improv blog and not parsing every word you're using but I think this is an important point so I'm going to make it anyway: be wary of the part of your brain that says "get roped into"—though I sympathize, it's not helpful. Your job as an improviser is to welcome being in situations that you weren't expecting. The audience enjoys it when you're thrown, you should enjoy it too. If you field it right, you got roped into the most interesting scene in the show.

MARCH 10TH, 2014 at 10:17PM

IRONY

Is there a way to practice being funnier? Generally, people say no. A sense of humor is so personal and subjective that we can't teach it, all we can do is tell you how to best express your sense of humor. You tell us what you think is funny, and then we'll tell you how to exaggerate that and heighten it.

Well, probably. But I'm trying to think of exercises and principles that might at least increase funniness. This feels sort of forbidden to even try. I might look back in a few months and think "Nope, you can't really teach it." But for now I'm trying.

This is one of those entries that should definitely be regarded as BETA.

So: One of the clearest ways to have something funny in your improv scene is to have something IRONIC. It's not the only way, but it's the clearest way. By ironic I mean something behaving in the opposite way that we expect it to.

A drill sergeant screaming nice things. A Mother Superior tearing apart her hotel room in a rage. A teacher burning a book. A bully cheering on the math team.

Could be the setting. A drill sergeant acting just like a drill sergeant but he's in a yoga class.

It's very close to simply being MEAN or STUPID—but it's not. It's something behaving in the opposite way. It's not someone acting arbitrarily random, it's opposite of their expected way. It's not a drill sergeant being really into dubstep. It's a drill sergeant being forgiving, or being against rules, or being soft-spoken.

Gilbert and Sullivan called this "the topsy-turvy."

I bring this up because I see a lot of improvisers do scenes where something weird is happening, but it really isn't funny.

UNUSUAL ISN'T NECESSARILY FUNNY

Example: Two improvisers establish that they're on a deserted island, and they're bemoaning how much they want to get rescued.

Then a third improviser enters and says he's flyering for Subway sandwiches. Would they like a flyer?

It feels funny. The rest of the class laughs, and everyone in the scene feels their eyebrows raise: hey, this is it! This is what our scene is going to be about!

But then the couple asks "Where did you come from?" And the guy passing out the flyers says "Just over the hill." And the couple says "There's a town over there?" And the flyers guy says "Oh yeah, there's a whole town." And then a fourth improviser comes on and invites them to a dance at the local club in the town. And I think a fifth one came on and said he was a doctor with food and he's got plane tickets to the mainland.

This is common in scenes! Something unusual happens, and everyone makes more of it but they lose what's funny.

Everything working out for the couple unusually well: not funny. A couple having been so dumb they didn't notice a city: not funny.

But if you're attuned to looking for irony, or something OPPOSITE, or topsy-turvy—the scene would go differently.

The first thing—the guy flyering. That's not just good luck for the couple, that's someone who is not where he belongs. FLYERING on a DESERTED ISLAND—that's irony. That's funny. You need someone to come on raising money for Greenpeace, and a census taker, and then a guy who sells traffic lights.

Or you don't need walk-ons: the guy with the flyers keeps trying to get people interested in Subway. He offers coupons, describes the nutritional value. He talks about how he needs to reach huge crowds of people. He offers group discounts for groups of 10 or more. The deserted island couple look around and see no one.

Other ways it could go and still be ironic:

- The guy fliers the couple and they are relieved because the only thing they missed from civilization is being fliered
- All those walk-ons I described happen and the couple STILL believes they won't be rescued; they've given up hope

Ultimately, you don't think—"what's ironic?"—while you're doing improv. That's too heady. But you feel something funny happen and you help make more of the funny thing. But for people learning about game of the scene, I think there's something to be gained by looking for who is acting differently than we expect.

MARCH 11TH, 2014 at 11:19AM

Q: WHEN IS IT APPROPRIATE TO HAVE A COACH AND WHEN NOT?

Anonymous asked: I'm v. new to improv (a little over 6 mos). I just started Improv 2 at Second City, but I've been taking classes at a different schools as well. The Second City group is basically all people 100% new to Improv, and they want to form a practice group. When I suggested we might want to get a coach for our practices, I got shut down and told "we want to keep it consistent Second City curriculum." It really felt like an insult directed at me. When is it appropriate to have a coach and when isn't it?

Appropriate to have a coach: in my UCB world, we always have coaches. But you know what? There's no universal right answer. Can you ask either of your teachers for their opinions? The Second City might have its own unofficial or even official protocol/tradition of how to do practice groups.

Regardless, try to treat this disagreement like you would an improv scene. Above almost all else, you want the scene to move forward, so maybe go with what the group wants and try it without a coach. If it works, it works. If someone is trying to boss everyone around and that person is wrong, the truth will bear you out and you guys will decide to get a coach. My very first practice group had 3 or 4 practices without a coach where we tried to just do the exercises we'd done in class that week and we soon decided we wanted someone there so that people weren't giving notes to each other, since it started arguments. So we went with a coach, but the coachless practices didn't hurt us either.

I've had many improv groups discuss different approaches—openings, priorities, general feel—and very often we just say "let's try it." A few hours of doing something will settle the discussion. "Find it on its feet" is a good mantra to remember.

It does sound like you got shut down, but your best move here is to not take it personally. Take the high road and try to sense where the group wants to go and go with that. Group negotiations are weird. You state your opinion, and then have to be ready to bend. There's often a squeaky wheels or wannabe-alphas who feel they know best. Sometimes those people are right, sometimes not. A "good" alpha will back down in the face of actual evidence that he/she is wrong. A "good" beta will quietly suggest alternatives and not get mad as the group try things. Most good improv groups have a mixture of personality types, who bump up against either other until they work it out.

Worst case: learning to not be defensive in a group talk—even if you're the only one following that practice—will serve you well in improv scenes, so you might as well practice it in real life for the sake of your improv performance.

There may also be benefits in real life from this approach. Those do not interest me.

MARCH 17TH, 2014 at 9:07PM

IRONY: EXERCISES

Last entry I talked about irony as a thing to look for in order to find strong games. It's hard to practice something that seems as subtle as irony. But here are two exercises that do it. They're very strictly structured and definitely meant to be exercises that demonstrate a point rather than be strong scenes all by themselves.

And they're meant to be simple! In each case, let's have a case of a type of person acting the opposite way than we expect!

They are also good if students are making unusual scenes that are more just random weird things rather good solid games.

EXERCISE 1: CHANGE THE SUBJECT

Two people up. Someone initiates as a character, preferably a bit broad and definitely with a distinctive tone in their speech. The other player matches so we have two peas in a pod. They start with a conversation we expect them to have and then partway through change the subject to something that feels like the exact opposite of what we expect.

Two fratty dudes are talking about homecoming, and then they start talking about the beauty of Keats poetry.

Two Latinas are on the corner complaining about their mothers when they change the subject to get very passionate about the latest Wes Anderson movie.

Two Buddhist monks begin by calming discussion meditation and then start worrying about how big their asses are getting.

Go ahead and play these characters a bit more broad and silly than we might normally want, so that the tone is very palpable.

Their tone should not change. If it's two people being Buddhist monks, and they are affecting that tone by speaking in a low, slow monotone and nodding towards each other in a humble, submissive way—they should keep doing that even after the subject changes. Someone who doesn't speak English shouldn't even be able to tell the subject was changed.

Another way to think of this is that the music stays the same, but the lyrics change. If that doesn't make sense, please ignore this paragraph.

EXERCISE 2: YOU WANTED TO SEE ME?

Two people in chairs. One says "You wanted to see me, OCCUPATION?" where occupation is anything from the very general "farmer" to "head chef at the best restaurant in town."

Then the other person has to make three EXPECTED requests and the a fourth one that is the exact opposite of what we'd expect. So it should go like this:

> Person A: You wanted to see me, farmer?

> Person B: Yes, thanks. We need to order more grain, we need to get the tractor fixed, I'd like to lay off some of the hired help for budget reasons and also, I'd like us to stop growing food.

Then Person A "straight mans" it, meaning he/she tries to respond like a rational person would. "Uh, but that's all we do is grow food. We're a farm."

Person B then has to come up with a reason why they want to do the weird thing. But for the purposes of this exercise, it doesn't even matter if they have a good reason. We're getting used to having an ironic agenda.

The straight man should ask why, and then the person with the occupation should come up with a reason why. Don't worry about this too much.

Although there are a lot of exercises that focus on the WHY, this one is actually more about enjoying it when there's someone behaving in the exact opposite way as we expect.

It shouldn't be random. This wouldn't be as good:

> Person A: You wanted to see me, farmer?
>
> Person B: Yes, thanks. We need to order more grain, we need to get the tractor fixed, I'd like to lay off some of the hired help for budget reasons and also, I'd like a pet dolphin living in my house.

That's kinda funny, but it's sloppy.

Once you'd done a few, you can broaden the occupation to be a short description of a character. Like this:

> Person A: You wanted to see me, guy going through a hostile divorce?
>
> Person B: Yes, come in. I'd like to make an appointment with my lawyer. I'd also like to set up some therapy for myself. Call me friends to see who wants to hang out with me for a drink. And then hire a poet to write a love sonnet about my marriage.

MOST IMPORTANT PART

Choosing the opposite of something reveals what you think the most important aspect of something is. For the "You wanted to see me?" exercise, I saw one like this:

> Person A: You wanted to see me, Stevie Wonder?
>
> Person B: (not worrying about doing a vocal impersonation, by the way) Yes, sit down. I'd like to have my piano cleaned for the upcoming concert, let's call the venue to make sure everything is in order. I'd like to hire some different session musicians to rehearse with. And then I want to start painting.

And this person was seizing on the fact that Stevie Wonder is blind. And yes, that' can work—it is well-known that Stevie is blind.

But is that Stevie Wonder's PRIMARY quality? Is he known PRIMARILY for being someone who is blind, in the way that, say, Louise Braille or Helen Keller was? No, he's known primarily for being a musician.

The student tried again, and did this:

Person B: Okay, have my piano cleaned. Let's get some studio time soon. I'd like a new tour manager. And then I'd like to talk to someone about getting my hands removed.

Person A: But you're a musician! You need your hands to play the piano, or anything!

Person B: Come on! People were impressed that I could be a recording star while being blind, think how impressed they'll be when I do it without hands!

It was better. And this isn't meant to be a lecture on political correctness, but it's pointing out the importance of being precise. Or at least, that the way you make something ironic reveals what you think the most important aspect of something is.

MARCH 21ST, 2014 at 1:02PM

EXERCISES FOR BETTER IMPROV

Try these exercises at your next improv practice.

EXERCISE 1: HAVE RICHER SOURCE MATERIAL

1. Two people up.
2. Leave the practice and go see a movie.
3. Talk about it together afterwards at a coffee shop.

Alternate versions: read a book, see a play, watch a concert. Something neither of your have seen/heard.

EXERCISE 2: BETTER LISTENING

1. One person up.
2. Leave the practice and find a friend or acquaintance and get into a conversation
3. See how little you can say without the person noticing.

Tips: Whenever you are asked a question, answer it quickly and then immediately ask it back to the person. Ask what they did that day (better than the more open ended 'How's it going' which is harder to answer). Complain about social media.

APRIL 22ND, 2014 at 6:02PM

IMPROV AS PRACTICAL ADVICE

When you ask people to think of reasons why someone took an improv class for the first time you get answers like "I wanted to do something fun" or "I'm a huge comedy fan" or "I wanted to be able to think on my feet more for my job."

(Side note: people often say "wanted to get better at public speaking" but only when they're guessing why OTHER people might be taking improv classes.)

Improv classes aren't as silly as you expect. Yes, they're fun but they're more like acting classes. Many big comedy fans don't know what long-form improv is, and they take a class because they've memorized the casts of SNL and see that many of them "did improv." They don't know what they're in for.

I don't really think it improves thinking on your feet. And no one speaks publicly ever, now that we have the internet.

So what practical skills DOES improv give you? These ones.

1. **Listening.** Deeper, fuller, more actively. Time will slow down during conversations and you will be able to hear them more accurately. This absolutely will happen to everyone who takes improv classes for any decent length of time.

2. **Brevity.** Improv rewards succinct, direct talk. You'll learn to do it because the audience laughs and listens to you more when you get to the point.

3. **Empathy.** You will more easily be able to see things from other people's points of view. You will be able to argue the other side of an argument better.

4. **Acting.** Improv is acting and writing but it's more acting. You become more reactive and emotive just through the sheer reps of playing make-believe in front of others.

5. **Clearer opinions.** You have opinions all the time but very often you don't pay attention to them as they're forming. Not the big ones, but the little ones. You see someone on the street eating an ice cream and lots of tiny versions of superiority, jealousy, gluttony will flit through

your brain, and then vanish. Improv makes you notice and then hold onto those opinions because in a scene you might need them.

6. **Saying yes.** You will at least consider saying yes to things and see the value in that option more often than you did before.
7. **Patterns.** Patterns are funny, and you will learn to see them early and often.
8. **Silliness.** You will get sillier. You'll walk funnier. You'll use dumb voices more. You'll make up better fake names for things.
9. **Knowledge.** You'll learn more since you'll run across so many scenes where someone mentions something you don't know. You'll find out what they were saying and remember it.
10. **Losing**. You'll learn the joy of losing arguments and fights.
11. **Bravery.** You will be more comfortable to have people see you and watch you.
12. **Being Present.** You'll worry less about the future, less about story, and more about what the moment feels like and what that implies.

Those are some skills you learn. AND NOTHING ELSE.

APRIL 26TH, 2014 at 10:16AM

Q: HAVE YOU EVER HAD TO KICK SOMEONE OUT?

Anonymous asked: Hi Will. I hate to ask this anonymously, but it could result in hurt feelings otherwise. My question: have you ever had to kick anyone out of a practice group, and do you know of any way to do it without burning in hell for being a dick? The issue here is that there is someone in my group who just plain doesn't understand improv and who has a history of frustrating coaches until they quit. That person, however, is the most dedicated and reliable member of the group. I don't know what to do!

1. First, please know that it is an extremely common thing for a group to think there's one person holding everything up. So much so that you should make sure this person is being as bad as you say. Once you all get more seasoned, you might look back and realize that it was unfair to pin this all on one person. Like, have you tried saying something directly and asking him/her to change behavior? "Take the coach's note," or "Take a class" or "Don't walk on so much" or "Don't get drunk for shows" or "Show up to practice" can sometimes go a long way. I wrote a huge amount on this phenomenon at this link: What Do We Do About 'That Guy?'

2. If you're sure, I think the fairest way is someone to tell this person honestly what's up. That you think he/she and the group are on different pages and you're going to try it with a different lineup. It's like a break-up. Yes, there will be hurt feelings, but some non-angry honesty is respectful and the person should realize that. I suggest doing this in person or on the phone, not over email where hastily written words can be scrutinized over and over again.

3. You could also try to just break up and the quietly reform without him, which I can understand and some people do. But I've done this, and you'll regret not just being honest and direct.

APRIL 26TH, 2014 at 10:32AM

Q: WHAT ABOUT LOW-ENERGY BORED STUDENTS?

Anonymous asked: How do you handle teaching students who come across low-energy, bored, or disinterested? Even at advanced levels, some students seem as though they don't want to be there and they're running out the clock. What can you do about that as a teacher?

You could ask the student after class is everything's all right and saying what you've observed. You could try, once, to give him/her that note after an exercise. "You aren't reacting and you don't seem to be committing. This is an acting class, so commit." I think the word "commit" is good in these situations; it's less judgmental than "care more" or "don't be bored" which inadvertently puts people on the defensive.

If those don't work, you could also just stop giving the person notes and attention. I had a guy in a lower level class once who argued every note, so I stopped giving them to him. He'd do the exercise in the the most emotionally safe, non-original way, barely obeying the spirit of the exercise and I'd just tell the other person what THEY did right or could work on, and move on. It gave me more time to spend with the students who were interested.

Now you're thinking: "Is that fair to the other students?" It depends. In general, in a class, I don't like saying that one person is really hurting the whole class. Playing with people who are off their game for whatever reason is part of learning. The strong students will see that you're just moving on to the others and appreciate it.

If it's an advanced class, you could recommend that this person be dropped a level. If you're going to do that, it's most helpful if you are able to warn the student that you're going to make that recommendation. I know that's no fun, but I used to run an improv school, and when teachers would tell me that a student needed to be dropped a level, and then I'd go talk to the students, they seemed genuinely surprised that anything had been wrong.

And finally: be careful of falling into an "appalled" tone as a teacher. This situation you're describing is frustrating, but I think improv teachers (myself included) too often become appalled at scenes they don't like, which isn't helpful. No one consciously intends to hurt a scene, so being upset will just feel from the student's perspective like personal dislike.

Special case: If this person is really an actively disrespectful jerk to others in class, then you can note them hard once in a punitive way. Just don't go to that well often, it's like a nuclear bomb option.

General qualifier here of me not being able to see this student, not knowing you, me just being one teacher, etc.

APRIL 26TH, 2014 at 10:34AM

Q: WHAT ABOUT A RELUCTANT PERSON?

Anonymous asked: I'm on a strong team of seasoned performers. We brought someone new on, and a month in, I see reluctance to enter scenes with him, myself included. The throw-everything-at-it, kitchen-sink improv is frustrating. What do we do?

1. Make sure you're not unfairly falling for the "that guy" syndrome. (What Do We Do About 'That Guy?')
2. Try telling him/her honestly what you think in person and in confidence.
3. Kick him/her out. If this is the second or third time you're doing that, re-examine your tolerance level.

APRIL 26TH, 2014 at 10:34AM

Q: WHAT ABOUT PEOPLE WHO WANT TO BE "THE STAR?"

Anonymous asked: I am taking my first performance-level improv class. Unlike my previous classes, there are several improvisors who really want to be "the star" of the scene. A few individuals always say the opening lines, "jump in" disproportionately, do not acknowledge gifts from their scene partners, and every time literally dictate the scene. What is the best way to work with these improvisers and still have fun?

1. Make sure you're not unfairly falling for the "that guy" syndrome. (What Do We Do About 'That Guy?')
2. Try telling him/her honestly what you think in person and in confidence.
3. Kick him/her out. If this is the second or third time you're doing that, re-examine your tolerance level.

APRIL 26TH, 2014 at 10:37AM

Q: AWKWARD / UNCOMFORTABLE STUDENTS?

dustindrury asked: Any suggestions on how to help students that are so uncomfortable/awkward they can't tell a true story or have an honest conversation in rehearsal?

Hello Dustin! You mean, like for a monologue? Or just when you're trying to discuss improv with them? It sounds frustrating. Maybe try backing off any discussion and just run exercises. Just let exercises do all the work. Restrict notes to pointing out where they broke the rules of the exercise? See if that gives them confidence to withstand discussion? If they're telling fictional monologues when you're asking for true stories, and they won't stop doing that—I mean, that's crazy. Don't coach them, that's a weird coven who are posing as humans and want to immerse you in a skin-harvester.

APRIL 26TH, 2014 at 10:40AM

Q: WHAT ABOUT PEOPLE WHO LOOK TO THE BACK LINE FOR AN EDIT?

Anonymous asked: when a scene progresses to the point where both characters say "well, uh... okay" and then shake hands and the two actors look to the backline like 'why are you all just standing there.' what's the best thing to do next?

Teacher/coach should gently remind them that giving up is not allowed, that commitment is maybe the most important thing after listening to each other. Here's a name-droppy anecdote: Three years ago Amy Poehler met with the UCB-NY teachers and one of her main pieces of advice was to nip all quitting/bailing in the bud, starting from day 1 of 101. Not that you have to be mean about it, but make it clear that giving up is not an option.

Give them permission to do whatever they have to to not quit. Talk about what clothes the other character is wearing, add in something crazy, restate things you already know in the scene. The audience smells fear, and quitting is fear.

If you're on the backline, then walk on and help your scene partners.

If you're one of the two people shaking hands, then don't quit.

APRIL 26TH, 2014 at 10:42AM

Q: I'M CONFIDENT IN CLASS BUT VERY NERVOUS IN SHOWS.

martinmaidrite asked: Here's a question I have trouble asking most people: I feel like I really excel in and am among the best in my various groups while in practice/class. However, when it comes to actual (indy) performances, I find myself getting very, very nervous and flat-lining during the shows. I'm not nearly as playful while I'm out there in front of even a small, insignificant amount of people. When you were starting out, did you have any issue with that? And if so, any advice on how to get over it?

I did have this issue. I was terrified in front of crowds, and felt for sure that I was a stiff and boring person who was ruining the scenes I was in. Short answer: it's common but you have to get over it. Try to give yourself a small do-able goal. For my level 2 and 3 grad shows, I told myself to just "listen and react" and not worry about anything else. Like just "hear and understand what's going on, then do something" and let everything else go. If you want to do improv, you've gotta beat this one. And you can do it. And lots of people who are extremely comfortable now have been in that same spot. Reps, bravery.

APRIL 26TH, 2014 at 10:47AM

Q: HOW ABOUT JEALOUSY / ANXIETY OVER YOUR CAREER?

Anonymous asked: Hey Will, apologies if you've addressed this before, but I'm curious about another side of comedy, which is: how does one not get bogged down in jealousy and anxiety over their career? Surely you've been in a position to see someone you don't have a high opinion of rise fast in the business? How do you avoid rooting for someone else's downfall (bc this behavior can't be good for one's own mental health). It's an ugly subject, but career anxiety and jealousy are real. Thank you for your time.

Yeah, that's a huge one. Comparing yourself to other people is a huge source of insecurity at all levels of the performing arena. And within improv theaters, which usually have a very clear hierarchy in which you can easily see that some people are marked as "higher" than you: it's hard to not be totally obsessed by this.

Everyone struggles with this and it's impossible to totally escape it. But you can mitigate it. You have to get zen about this, like real buddhist and just remind yourself that jealousy is toxic and hurts you, YOU, way more than it will ever affect whoever you are jealous of. Learn to be your own generous and sympathetic audience. Like actually build a voice in your head that likes the things you are doing, regardless of external reward. Picture how you feel about your best friends' efforts and point that energy at yourself. I would get as hippie and new age about this as you can stomach. Measure yourself only against things that you can control. Did you practice? Were you brave? Did you give a shit?

A word about auditions: your goal should just be to avoid the thing where after the audition you're wishing you did it differently. If you can walk out and YOU feel good about what you did, then you did it. A word about shows: Have a specific goal before the show, and measure yourself only against that goal after the show, regardless of what the audience thought.

Not easy.

APRIL 26TH, 2014 at 10:47AM

Q: ADVICE ON PLAYING CHARACTERS?

Anonymous asked: Advice on playing characters when you're someone that doesn't come easily to, or who just never even thinks to?

Peas in a pod or mirroring exercises with people who are good at it. Steal their powers.

APRIL 26TH, 2014 at 10:48AM

Q: WHEN SOMEONE PIMPS YOU INTO AN ACCENT?

Anonymous asked: What the fuck do you do when someone pimps you into an accent or an impression and you can't come even close and you just sound retarded?

Enthusiasm and effort matter more than accuracy in improv. And even though the word "retarded" has become dated and juvenile, this question did make me laugh.

APRIL 26TH, 2014 at 10:50AM

Q: I'M YESSING AND NOT ANDING.

Anonymous asked: Lately I've been "yessing" but not "anding" and it's driving me nuts. It really sucks 'cause my scenes just die right then and there.

It's that you're judging yourself so harshly, that's what's killing you. You want to be able to know exactly how well you're doing, and there's no way to know, and so you're condemning yourself just for the certainty of the condemnation. Listen to your coach/teacher, even the audience, instead of your worries. You don't know if you're yessing/not anding. If it were that simple you'd do it. You're doubting and fearing. It's very common to do this. You've got to be nicer to yourself, give yourself the benefit of the doubt and assume that someone will tell you when you're off and that you are good enough that you will notice when someone is telling you. It's all gonna be okay!

APRIL 26TH, 2014 at 10:56AM

Q: OBJECT-WORK A WALKER OR USE A CHAIR?

Anonymous asked: When playing a person using a walker, is it funnier to use an object-work walker or to use a chair?

I think this is a joke question? But I have a real opinion: object-work walker is funnier, just.

APRIL 26TH, 2014 at 10:57AM

Q: WHAT IS "NO ACTION" BY ELVIS COSTELLO ABOUT?

Anonymous asked: Is 'No Action' about a guy who doesn't really want to get back with an ex but is still really bothered that she's with someone else now? or does he really miss her and the first verse isn't genuine? something else?

I choose to interpret it as a guy who misses her but is too proud to admit it. A terrific song best listened to/discovered when around the age of 16 and feeling rejected, while studying for an AP test, which is how I first heard it.

APRIL 26TH, 2014 at 11:07AM

Q: SHOULD A TEAM ACKNOWLEDGE A SHOW WAS BAD?

Anonymous asked: Should a team acknowledge that a set was bad, and how?

I find this to be a fascination question, and I don't actually know a rock-solid answer. I would like to hear veteran improvisers' opinions on this.

I know that if a team refuses to acknowledge anything bad at all, then that can be nerve-wracking and frustrating. Like if some members of the team are irritated if anyone dares say anything bad about the show, then that's not good.

But I also know that some people will wallow forever, and will always dislike the show no matter what. And their long drawn-out discussions with a self-punishing tone are unproductive.

I don't know how you get to this place, but in my personal experience, the best type of post-show discussion is when the team stands in a circle, (after having gotten notes from a coach if they're not a veteran team, i.e. 3 years or more) and assess the show to each other in a non-angry, concise way. And then tries to remember the key moments to each other. "X was good" or "I felt like we maybe lost steam at Y" or "We killed the first scene." Being complimentary of each other in an honest way is helpful here and is contagious in a good way. "I loved when you did A" and such, or "Thank you for matching me at point B." Never note each other, but bring up the scene that bothered you and what you should have done differently. "I felt us losing steam here, and was thinking of editing; maybe I should have." And then someone says "I don't think so, it wasn't until later that we were in trouble" or "Yes, I was thinking that too." Use past shows to explain yourself "Last week we were so good at labeling things, I missed that" or "we did the same thing as that show where we were all trying to be bears but no one knew that, and we bailed." Be honest with a generous amount of agreeing to disagree.

You want a balance: you should feel like there's a sense of being honest but generous of how it played out, and seeing which parts stick out in each other's mind as high and low points. You're making educated guesses and staying open that your own view is likely distorted to some degree.

After around 10 minutes max, everyone should have been able to have a moment of feeling honest, and after that these discussions are no longer helpful. On to the next show.

MAY 5TH, 2014 at 4:00AM

HOW DO YOU MAKE A LIVING?

I had a level 1 student in a button-down shirt who had a mortgage come up to me after class recently and say "Man, I love this. I'd really love to be paid to do comedy."

I believe he was thinking: *I'd love my current paycheck and stability in exchange for coming to this class*. That doesn't ever happen.

But it's maybe the second most common question/comment I get from people, right after "how do I get out of my head?" Some variety of "how do you make a living?" or "How could I quit my job and do improv/comedy full time?"

Short answer: You don't get paid to do improv. You can get paid to teach/coach it, making a solid notch or two below what you'd make at a low level cubicle job.

And "getting paid to do COMEDY," practically speaking, means living the life of a freelancer in which you hustle lots of little gigs all the time, hoping for a bigger one. And then even a bigger gig like writing for a TV show is something you get hired for just a few months at a time.

In this life, you get a lot of your time returned to you and a lot of freedom, but you get stomach-dropping insecurity when you think about: children, vacations, property, the future or even just paying rent. That's the trade-off.

Most people I know who are "doing comedy" have either a part-time job (teaching, usually), or a night-time restaurant job, or a flexible retail job, or possibly a spouse/family who bails them out once a year or so (though I hear people WISH for that more than actually having that). They sit in audition rooms and talk about real estate licenses, babysitting gigs, tutoring opportunities.

Once you make yourself available for creative stuff full-time, you WILL find a lot of small gigs some of which might lead one day to bigger gigs. Small gigs: teaching things, web videos, short films, auditions. Bigger things: TV and movie things that pay SAG rates and residuals that make your financial life temporarily easier.

CASE STUDY: ME

NOTE: The following answer is based on my experience. Everyone's is unique. I'd love to hear others, actually, if anyone cares to send theirs to me (how do you make a living, those without day jobs?). If I get enough I'll publish them (with permission, of course!. Send to whines atsign gmail dot com if you'd like).

What I did: From when I was 26 until 32 I was a full-time computer programmer making okay money. I socked a lot of it away because I was responsible and also boring.

At 33, after having done improv for 3 years I quit my full-time job and tried to do computer programming part time along with improv coaching/teaching to let me write and audition for commercials. Turns out I did very little writing/auditioning and instead ran out of money and had to get a full-time job programming again when I was 35.

I programmed computers for 1.5 more years, while teaching/coaching on the side and auditioning at lunch, i.e. not that often. I also started dabbling in stand-up where I could (not often: once every two weeks).

Then at 36 I got a job producing videos for AOL (thank you Sara Schaefer, i.e. a friend I'd made via NYC comedy world), which felt much more creative, though this was still a full-time "show up for your job" job. I learned to shoot and edit. I did that for 2 years, while teaching and auditioning on the side and writing some stuff and making web videos.

Then at 38 I got a job running the UCB school in NYC (thank you, UCB friends) which paid a small steady amount with huge time flexibility. This was essentially like having a steady part-time job. I taught more and aggressively auditioned, which I could do because I'd at this point spent several years doing it and getting known in the NYC scene.

Now I'm in LA: a "professional" improv teacher and, gulp, commercial "actor"(?) who's trying to get acting/writing work.

What I got paid for last year, very roughly in order of amount: teaching improv, residuals for two commercials, running UCB school, writing puzzles and appearing on NPR quiz show, writing for a soft-scripted reality show, acting in web videos and one TV part, plus very small computer programming gigs.

Which all added up to about as much as I made when I was 27 and wrote javascript for a computer programming company full-time. Though now I spend most of my waking hours doing fun things. I'll take that deal!

I certainly don't mean this as bragging, I hope that's obvious. Nor do I feel that this is a "poor me" situation. I am being specific because I think people who are not doing comedy seem to sometimes "flatten" the comedy world and think that "guy teaching my improv class" is very close to "person who is on SNL" and also "guy who is in this commercial playing all the time on my Hulu" is close to "guy who's been in 5 movies this year."

"Doing comedy" = "being free lance" = lots of freedom and time but less money and less consistency.

If you're trying to get the most talented actor you personally know to be in your short film that requires several long days of shooting, try offering him/her $100!

P.S. To even have a chance of this freelance life, now that you can maybe picture what it's like, you need a network of friends who know and like you. Stand-ups rely on the people they've come up with, improv people need their former fellow students and teammates. Unless you're so amazingly talented or a direct blood relation of an established person, I don't know of another way in.

JUNE 11TH, 2014 at 1:33PM

THE FUTURE VANISHES!

This post is about how improv trains you to see the present moment and not worry, as much, about the future.

In a level 1 class, two students were doing a scene and one looked stuck. A bit more than I usually see.

"What are you thinking about?" I asked.

The student said, "I'm trying to think of what's going to happen."

"You don't have to worry about what's going to happen," I said.

"But then, how do I know what to do?"

It was such a reasonable answer that I was stunned. I haven't thought about *what is going to happen* in an improv scene in years.

But—of course—people who are making up scenes for the first time must constantly be worried about *what is going to happen*.

When you watch a TV show, you try and guess the ending. When a character is introduced in a movie, you try and figure out what that person will end up doing LATER. There's so much setup NOW and payoff LATER in TV and movies and plays.

So it's only natural that if you tell someone to improvise a scene they're gonna try and and play it like a 22 minute story heading for an ending.

Like this: A new improv student looks at their scene partner and thinks: Maybe my character is going to fall in love with this other character. Okay, that's my choice. I'll start planting seeds now that we will someday be in love. And they say out loud, warmly, "Nice day, isn't it?"

That's not how it works. You should instead see what is already happening and either react to it, or even just say it. Like this:

You're sitting down at a table, so you decide must be at a restaurant. Your partner is smiling at you, so you must be on a date. You notice that you feel kindly to this other character, so you think, maybe I'm in love with this person. And out loud you say "I love you" so that your scene partner knows what you're thinking, and because your scene partner was watching your eyes, he/she knows where your character is at, and looks down and takes the moment in, then looks up and says "I wish I felt the same way."

You work backwards from what is happening. Which means you have to assume something is happening.

You shrink your scope down. Instead of thinking ahead 22 minutes, or even two minutes, you look around you at the current moment.

"Now" gets bigger and slower and richer and more evident.

You turn into a Sherlock Holmes of observing the present instant. From a snapshot of a moment, you can make decisions about what you feel, what the other person must be feeling, what must have happened to get us here.

It's not where you're driving to, but what the car ride feels like NOW. It's not the whole mathematical function of a curve, it's a single point and which way it's pointing (math analogies are cool, you like them).

You're constantly waking up into worlds that already exist and trying to fake it. You say what you see as soon as you see it. This gets you out of your head because there's no need to plan because everything is constantly changing.

You observe and react—honestly and directly—and wait for your partner to do the same, and then you'll have something else to observe and react to.

The future vanishes! It's weird and cool and oddly soothing.

I didn't know how to say this to the student. So I just said "If you're stuck, try confessing something. That usually gets it going. Okay, two more up."

JUNE 25TH, 2014 at 11:10PM

Q: GREY AREA BETWEEN OFFERS AND DENIALS?

maxsitt asked: Do you ever see a grey area between offers and denials? For example, someone initiates organically by saying, "Edwin, I didn't think I'd ever see you again." And they did this in a heightened Medieval tone while miming a sword. Then the other person replies, "Ok Ron, just put the copy toner down I don't want to fight right now." That denies the implicit reality, but also gifts the initiator with a playable absurdity. I've also seen it button a scene, or re-contextualize the base reality.

It's a denial! The initiator has to take it as an offer, but it is a denial and should be punished by the universe.

JUNE 25TH, 2014 at 11:29PM

Q: ABOUT "REACT HONESTLY?"

Anonymous asked: I am confused about how to use the notes "react honestly" and "how would you really feel if this happened to you"? They sound simple, but I've gotten those notes when I was reacting honestly and how I would in real life. It really sucks to get that note about how I play traumatic experiences I've really been through. It feels like a judgement on how I handled that in real life. I'm quiet, big and loud is not my honest or realistic reaction. How should I take that note in cases like that?

Take the note as if it were "don't be coy." You don't have to be big and loud, but you have to be forthcoming.

In improv, we act like real life with one BIG BIG exception: we speak our mind honestly.

We want the scene where the waiter speaks his or her mind honestly to the pushy customer. In real life, a waiter would never do that. In an improv scene, we want to see it. "You shouldn't treat people like that. It's mean and unnecessary." And then the customer speaks his or her honest opinion back. "You're my waiter. It's your job to take my crap no matter what."

It takes practice. You have to get good at catching your real reaction in your head—the one you rarely say—and then expressing it. How you express it is up to you in terms of volume or emotion—but it has to be honest and direct. That is your job as an actor. To speak the truth we rarely get to hear.

JUNE 29TH, 2014 at 10:45PM

Q: JUSTCRAIG: EATING MARIJUANA AT DCM?

justcraig asked: DCM related improv question: What's better improv, eating so much edible marijuana that you wander on stage during a show and do nothing OR showing your dick at a late night bit show?

#dcm16

JULY 1ST, 2014 at 6:34PM

Q: HOW'D YOU GUYS COME UP WITH THE BEER COMMERCIALS GUYS?

Anonymous asked: Small men question. I'm wondering how you found the game for your opening introduction, the beer commercial guys and how you figured that would be a good lead in?

I love Small Men questions. (Small Men being the sketch show Neil Casey and I wrote/performed 2012-2013).

"Beer Commercial" is the opening sketch and it features two guys who were in tons of beer commercials in the 1980s and are no longer getting booked. They complain to the audience that this is because beer commercials these days are whiny emo passive aggressive ads that make their heroes look like self-effacing dopes, and it's time to make the ads a celebration of machismo and partying.

We didn't write it for Small Men. We wrote it for a UCB Industry Showcase in December 2011. The first line of the scene is the cowboys coming out and saying "Hello, industry!" They talk about their experience at a series of real NY casting offices (they characters are careful to say nice things, since people from those offices were in the crowd and they are hoping to get cast).

After we did it, we realized it would be a good opener for Small Men. It reminded of us of sketches that Rob Huebel and Rob Riggle used to do in the old days of UCB-NY: two aggressive peas in a pod yelling at the audience. We liked starting our show with a presentational piece and it was a good contrast to the rest of the show which was very verbal and passive.

So we just plopped it on the top of our show. Even though there was no reason for it, they still come out and address the "industry" in the crowd. They still mentioned NY casting offices. We liked the idea that these guys just go from sketch show to sketch show hoping to catch some industry in the crowd pleading their case. And we liked that they begin the sketch as ridiculous people but end up making a pretty good case for themselves. I think we could have done a half hour just as these guys!

Neil and director Michael Delaney always referred to it as separate from the show. They called it the "Crimson Permanent Assurance" short before the real feature (referring to the Terry Gilliam short film that opens the tonally much different *Monty Python's Meaning of Life*, which I pretended to remember until I could go home and re-watch it).

That's it! I don't know where the original idea came from. I think I said I missed the dumb beer commercials from the 80s (really just one Budweiser commercial featuring NASCAR star Richard Petty—hence our pronounced mustaches) and Neil improvised a bunch of philosophy... I honestly can't remember.

JULY 7TH, 2014 at 11:53PM

SOME SUGGESTIONS FOR LEVEL ONE CLASS ETIQUETTE

Without a good teacher monitoring, most improv exercises favor bold, aggressive students. Whoever either thinks faster or at least acts fastest tends to affect the scenes more and therefore have more chances for feeling validated that they are doing well. While there's a place for boldness (and certain exercises explicitly focus on being more bold), any good improv team has a mixture of aggressive types with more patient and calm energies.

Believing that, here are five simple rules of conduct which I think help the less aggressive students find their footing in lower level improv classes. These are also just common sense policies for fair play. They're not meant to leave out aggressive students. And I never state them as being "for the students who are bit more hesitant." They're just good etiquette for improv scenes which happen to also help the non-alphas find themselves in the scene.

Merely my opinion: Take 'em or leave 'em, fellow teachers!

Initiation Etiquette / "Be Comfortable With Silence". Students should not interrupt or finish someone else's initiation: very commonly done by eager alpha bulldogs in lower levels. Teach that whoever moves first gets focus and a generous amount of time to make their move. The person who responds also gets a lot of time before they have to answer. Discourage the very common practice of talking until you are interrupted. "Be comfortable with silence" I will say a lot.

It's Okay To Not Know Cultural References. After the first scene in class that happens to mention a movie/book/song/TV show—I point out that they're not expected to know every movie, book or current event that gets brought up. They SHOULD try to fake it based on context or else admit in character that they don't know it. And if they are the one who is bringing up a reference and their scene partner doesn't know it, then it's their job to help. This affects younger students' confidence far more than I had appreciated—teach them how this works. (The other side of this coin is that after you've taught them how to handle references, no one is allowed to bail on a scene because they don't know something.)

Protect Decisions To Play Against Type. Gently point out when someone misses their scene partner's attempt to play against type (gender, age, etc). It's bad listening and invariably happens to people already feeling left out. Correct whoever misheard as a casual note, not a lecture. "He's being your mother, not your father." Or "That's a teenager talking, not a mom." Be vigilant for this in the first few sessions especially.

Set Boundaries. This is a class, not a team. Students see very physical and intrusive things on stage at shows. They need you to make clear and enforce that that's not for class, where people don't know each other well. Though everyone would assume this is probably true, many will be relieved to have the teacher explicitly say it.

You Are Allowed To Say No. You are always allowed to "say no" in a scene to ANYTHING that your character wouldn't want to do. Like if someone starts a scene by asking if you want a lap dance or maybe wants to steal someone's baby from a hospital nursery, and your character wouldn't want to, you can say "no" and you're not being a bad improviser, (best way is to add a simple truthful reason why, and then stay open to discussing it in character). Even if you immediately realize you are saying "no" to something out of nervousness and you wish you had said yes, it's okay because it's important to get practice saying "no" properly in a scene. The take-away here is that you need to play your characters to the top of their intelligence, not trapped by what you think you "should" do because of "yes-and." They forget this a lot so you remind them.

SEPTEMBER 2ND, 2014 at 6:03PM

YOU ALREADY KNOW THE REAL "WHY"

In improv, you always need a good "why."

The trick is realizing that you often already know why, deep down, even when the things you're doing happened instinctively. Don't fix it to what you think the why SHOULD be.

Like you're doing a two person scene and the other person says "I want to run with the bulls in Spain" and you have a gut reaction that makes you shake your head with a little bit of disgust and you say "Ugh, not that."

You didn't sit there and plan that out. You're not in your head, you're just reacting—which is good—but NOW you need to decide why you just did that.

The teacher stops the scene and asks you "I see you don't like that idea, why not?"

And you feel guilty at first that you "said no," so you hurriedly correct yourself: "I mean, I LOVE RUNNING WITH THE BULLS."

And the teacher says "No, I didn't want you to change your mind. It's okay you didn't like it. I just wanted to know why your character didn't like it."

And you think back and try to think of a logical explanation and glom it onto to the scene. "Maybe his father was killed by bulls?"

"No, " says the teacher. "That's not what they reason was. You HAD a reason—there's something you didn't like about the idea on a gut level, I'm just asking what that reason was. The one you already had."

And you remember what it felt like when you had that reaction and realize the honest answer is something like "Because that's something douchey frat jerks do?" or "Ugh, that's what EVERYONE wants, let's do something different" or "You're just trying to show off, don't be a jerk."

That's it. That's the real reason. The one the audience could sense and the one they will laugh at when they see you able to realize it and articulate it.

I think when you have an instinctual visceral reaction to something—it's probably the honest and true one. You have to be able to just say what you're honest reaction is.

Being able to stop, hold and articulate your natural feelings is a hugely necessary skill in improv. There are many people out there who can't do that. The moment you make them think about what they're saying or feeling and ask them why—all their awareness vanishes. Can you imagine your co-worker, after they say something like how they "hate French Vanilla coffee" being asked "why?" They'd look at you and just say "what do you mean WHY? I just DO."

Not enough in improv. You must be an honest reporter of your natural unaffected feelings. Tricky. But it's way more important than doing a great accent, or being able to think of 20 movies from the forties, or even being able to emote a huge range of feeling.

Don't think about it, don't fix it—just say what you felt.

SEPTEMBER 2ND, 2014 at 6:15PM

Q: DIRECTING MY FIRST IMPROV SHOW.

Anonymous asked: Hello. For the first time ever I'm going to be directing an improv show. Any wisdom for me?

Someone told me that a good director should focus first and more often on saying what the show already is, not what he/she thinks it should be. Assess what it is, what it feels like and report back. As an enthusiastic, sympathetic, educated, attentive but honest audience.

SEPTEMBER 2ND, 2014 at 6:18PM

Q: MY IMPROV IS TOO DEFERENTIAL.

Anonymous asked: My improv's too deferential. I'm good at reacting, but bad at being bold or making big moves, and I feel like I'm not carrying my weight. I feel like I should "just have fun" or "do whatever the fuck I want", but I'm not sure where to pull that from. What do I do?

Yeah, that's a tough one. "Just have fun" as an ORDER is a tough one. First of all, are you sure this is what you should be doing? I find giving notes to oneself to be a very unreliable process. Ask a coach or teacher you trust. Also, ask yourself why you are giving yourself that note. Why is it you want to hear that so much? You're thinking too much, maybe, and your brain is rebelling and saying 'I need someone to tell me to do whatever the fuck I want?' Maybe you need fewer notes right now.

To your point: I think the best way to just have fun is to focus on moments rather than the whole scene or show. Shrink your scope down to just the last line. Hear it, react to it. Make it specific. Repeat the part you liked best. After you have fully digested it, say what you really think, regardless of what it does to the scene. If you are greeted with silence, don't be scared. Stay still for a moment and let that silence rush over you and turn you into a unbeatable actor made of steel and a moment later, you'll think of what to do.

SEPTEMBER 3RD, 2014 at 6:50PM

Q: WHAT IF THE HOUSE TEAM AT YOUR THEATER SUCKS?

Anonymous asked: The improv company I'm in has a team of 7-8 who are responsible for festival shows and a big monthly show at one of my city's biggest theatres. Half of them are selfish, ungenerous performers but are consistently given stage time because they're the senior members. It's really demoralizing as a newer performer (5 years) to

see terrible, under-rehearsed work rewarded, especially when attendance at our shows has flagged over the last few years, but how do you tell the house team that they suck?

You don't. Worry about your own work and move on when there's a chance. It's not your show, so don't try to direct it from your head.

Do the people on the team share your opinion? Probably not, so don't worry about them. Does the audience like the shows? If not, the show won't survive. But if the audience does—which I suspect they do—then try and figure out what the show is doing right.

You sound like people who complain that SNL is a bad show. It's easy to find people who wonder out loud "How can that show be rewarded with its long term success when it (pick one: focuses so much on dumb pop culture, caters to a young audience, runs popular characters into the ground with little variation)?" Rather than figuring out why it is that SNL is the most successful sketch show in American (world?) history (ah, it focuses on the pop culture everyone is talking about, it's one of the few shows with talent catering to a young audience, it repeats its popular characters).

What I'm saying: You're being too harsh. The judge who lives in your brain is being given too much power. It will turn on you in times of low confidence and you won't be able to recover and you'll quit. Practice compassion and empathy. This paragraph is perhaps too new agey to be accepted at face value, but I suggest you take this advice if you want to be happy doing creative things.

POST SCRIPT (added a few hours after posting): Ugh, I jumped on this in too hostile a manner, which is hypocritical. Though I mean what I say above I want to add that I am sympathetic with the frustration this person expresses. It is frustrating to see people take for granted a good show or a good time slot, etc. I do understand that. But the "judge" thing I speak of—I know this from experience. If you indulge the part of your brain that is scanning someone else's show and demanding that it be improved or fixed and wanting to punish those who fall short—that part of your brain will get stronger and turn on you in ways you do not realize. This is the same point but I wanted to add that I also have the feelings you express but I've learned they are a red flag to be dealt with in my head for my own sake!

SEPTEMBER 26TH, 2014 at 8:09PM

DEFENSIVENESS

This is an essay about the natural defensiveness that rises up in improv and can hold us back. But to get there, I want to talk about a very common way to start a scene, and that's the "explain this" method.

EXPLAIN THIS FUNNY THING

"Hey, Bill, you want to tell me why you brought a ten course buffet to eat on your desk at work?"

(Newer improvisers: don't worry that this is a question—it's adding information so it's not a the kind of question we worry about.)

It's the "I'm giving you an unusual thing, now you explain it" initiation. You're expecting that the other person will give some fun reason for what you endowed them with, and then you've got a game.

Maybe the person answers: "Yeah, man, I don't want to get up. Working for that promotion, so I don't have time to go to nice restaurants so I'm bringing the nice restaurants to ME."

[Some people, by the way, feel that that initiator should maybe supply the explanation also—something like "I know you're trying to treat yourself better, but could you not bring a ten course buffet to work for your lunch?" That's got its problems too (too much information, your 'why' might be too inorganic and forced)—and I don't want to debate it here. Right way or not, lots of people do the "First person gives a weird thing, second explains why" approach.]

EXPLAIN THIS CRITICISM

But an interesting side effect with the "explain this" beginning is when the gift in the initiation is not clearly funny and maybe just a sort of criticism.

"Hey, Randy, did you eat my sandwich from the fridge?"

Often, you can see the other person start to just say "No, I didn't." But then they remember that they are supposed to yes-and and so instead they DEFLECT it, by just having a reasonable explanation.

"Yeah, I thought we said all the food is up for grabs."

> or "I didn't know that was yours."
>
> or even "Yeah, I'm sorry, I screwed up."

You can hear in their voice ALREADY that things are starting to go astray. They're not sure why they're being given that gift—it doesn't seem funny, what are they supposed to do? Am I screwing up, they worry? The actor is shifting into defensive mode.

And then, the initiator is also getting just a bit thrown. He wanted his gift of "you ate my sandwich" to be treated like a funny thing, like a gift. And it's been deflected. Very often, the initiator will double down on his accusation.

> "Look, you know that was my favorite sandwich. I told you."

And the other person, who is not sure what her/his role is, will flail back.

> "Favorite sandwich? You say EVERYTHING'S your favorite sandwich! Not everything can be your favorite sandwich."

This is the beginning of what Alex Berg calls a wizard battle—where the improvisers are using their powers over the reality of the scene to make themselves right.

Unsure of where the real comedy was, the improvisers have started to feed on each other! Gruesome!

Worse, the audience will start to laugh. With nowhere else to settle their attention, the audience decides this must be a competition scene—who can come up with the most clever defense? Who will zing each other the best? That IS a viable comedy scene, but not a good one to improvise. It's hard and it feels mean.

SAY YES

A common note coaches will give here is for the person responding to the initiation to "YES AND"—agree that you are a jerk and ate the sandwich. If possible, treat that like it's a funny idea and make it funny with a good "why."

Problem: This is harder than you think! The initiation doesn't seem that funny to them—they can't think of how to give it a good why.

Another common note is to tell the initiator to be less coy: say what you think is going on, why it's funny.

Problem: the initiator might not even know why he thought it was funny. They expected it to be like lots of other "explain this" scenes—he throws out what he thinks is an unusual thing and the OTHER person comes up with the reason why it's funny.

I am sympathetic to the responder. It's hard to simply say yes to a mundane criticism; it doesn't feel that fun. And lots of people use the "explain this" format to simply say "you are being a jerk to me, isn't that funny?" In some strange way, they're not after comedy, they're after JUSTICE!

BE SUSPICIOUS OF ANGER

Rather than wonder what should or shouldn't be done with a particular idea, the most useful universal lesson to take away is:

Be suspicious when your character gets angry, especially when they were not angry at the start of the scene.

If the anger is your character genuinely reacting to the events of the scene, then it's good.

But defensive anger is the dark side. It feels good, it gets laughs, but it's not coming from the scene, it's coming from your insecurities.

It's got its own flavor, separate from the anger you feel from good acting. Defensive anger has a wavering, genuinely uncertain tone. It's got a bit of a desperate edge. It's a little bit more pointed than necessary.

It's the anger that wants to PROTECT YOURSELF as opposed to BE FUNNY. It is primal and dangerously satisfying.

Another Alex Berg essay talks about this—the instinctive defensive responses of the mammal brain. They are rooted deeply.

To do improv is such a vulnerable thing! You get up in front of people without a script and promise to be funny. You are often intimidated by your scene partner, or your teacher/coach, or someone in the audience, or even just an imagined audience in your head! It's VERY easy for insecurities to rise up and start making decisions for you.

Defensiveness is a type of anger that you learn should be let go. You learn that it is a sign that someone is getting confused in the scene. Rather than fight, you need to relax and speak candidly until you regain your footing.

TAKE A BREATH AND MAKE THE DECISION

You'll see seasoned improvisers sidestep their anger. Someone snaps and says something a bit pointed and angry: then they both slow down, speak very directly, make a decision and then move on. They'll kind of negotiate who is being "weird" and then plunge forward.

"Hey, Randy, did you eat my sandwich from the fridge?"

(unsure if this supposed to be weird, the responder answers small)

"Uh, yeah, I did."

(doubling down on the accusation for clarity)

"I had my name on it. You know it was important to me."

And then here—in this moment—without letting defensive anger cloud their judgment—the two improvisers feel it out and decide what is the truth of the situation. They either do this, where the person asking about his sandwich is the "weird" one:

"Hey man, you gotta chill out about food. You know? Like, I screwed up but... what are you doing?"

"MY FAMILY IS ONE OF GREAT SANDWICH MAKERS."

Or they make the guy who ate the sandwich the strange one:

"Yeah, I ate. You make.. You make great sandwiches, man. I can't control myself. I'm gonna keep doing it."

LET DEFENSIVENESS GO

They've learned to not let defensiveness make their decisions for them!

Your mammal brain is a genius   you need its simple instincts to be a good actor. But it is also scared of everything. When it tells you to fight back, you have to be a zen master and just wait for that wave of fear to pass.

SEPTEMBER 30TH, 2014 at 9:52AM

IS IT COMING FROM FEAR?

There's lots of rules that contradict each other. Play it real or don't be coy? Play yourself or take the endowment? Edit now or give the scene more time?

A good way to resolve if you're doing it right: is your decision coming from fear? If it is coming from fear, then try waiting.

> "My character wouldn't dance so I'm not dancing"

> "I have to label this right now or the audience is going to turn on us"

> "I have to call out that mistake or else everyone is going to be focusing on it for the rest of the scene"

> "I don't know anything about that movie/doing that accent/miming that thing—so I have to justify and not do it."

It's scary doing improv, nonetheless: don't be scared.

OCTOBER 2ND, 2014 at 12:55PM

EXERCISES: THE SAMURAI

(This is an intended series on exercises I like to do. I say intended because who knows if I'll do another one!)

An exercise: "The Samurai." It's a bit complicated but it's fun. It's where classmates reward each other for fulfilling specific improv goals.

4-6 people up on the back line. They are the "samurai." They will be doing the scenes.

Another 4-6 people along the side walls. They are the "sensei." ("Sensei" isn't the historical accurate term, but I find it more palatable than "master" and also more cool to say.) The sensei will only be watching the improv, not doing it.

Give each of the sensei 5 playing cards and assign to them one of the samurai.

So if Erik is one of the samurai on the back line, you assign Gwen who is one of the side lines and is holding 5 playing cards to be his sensei.

The samurai get a suggestion and do an improv set. Normal improv set: they edit, they tag-out, the do walk-ons.

But before they start, you give the samurai a mission (examples below). They can all have the same one or maybe they have separate ones. Whenever they accomplish their mission—the sensei steps out right then and hands their samurai a card.

Sensei should err on the side of being generous.

Keep going until all cards have gone out.

FIRST ROUND: ACCEPT OFFERS

First time I do this, all the samurai have the same mission: ACCEPT OFFERS. Every time they explicitly yes-and something that was just said, their sensei steps out and gives them a card.

So if Sam says to Erik "Sergeant, I'm exhausted."

And then Erik says "You LOOK exhausted."—then Erik's sensei Gwen steps forward right then and hands him a card.

And THEN if Erik keeps going and says "You should be having been on watch all night." And Sam says "I was out there but I'm not sure I did a great job"—he gets a card because he's acknowledging he was on watch.

It gets tricky/helpful/funny when people make accusations and the recipient has to make them true.

If Arnie steps out and says "Clarissa, you jerk!" and then Clarissa goes "Shut up, asshole!"—Clarissa would get a card.

It is somewhat subjective what merits a card. The teacher should confirm or deny the first few times cards are given out—"yep, that's right" or "no, he's not confirming anything" or even "Where's the card on that?" but then try to back off.

Once the cards are all out, switch sensei and samurai.

SECOND ROUND: SPECIFIC MISSIONS

Once everyone's had a chance to do the "accept offers" round, do one where each samurai has separate tasks.

FUN TASKS TO ASSIGN:

Emotional reaction: get a card whenever you make a pronounced emotional reaction.

Toys: when someone uses an object that you created, you get a card.

Made-up proper nouns: anytime you make a specific reference to something that is made up ("you guys seen the new Jules Candy film?"), you get a card.

Justification: anytime you explain something that was contradictory, you get a card

Playing against type: anytime you play someone who is not your gender/age/race/general energy—you get a card

And you can still give "accept offers" as a mission here too.

These missions are supposed to be easy fun things that an audience enjoys. They're not heady logical things like "playing game" or "taking an idea from the opening." They are things the audience likes THE MOMENT THEY HAPPEN and also generally enrich a scene.

THIRD ROUND: GROUP MISSIONS

In addition to the sensei who are up on the side walls, you can assign students watching to be sensei, and give them missions which anyone in the group can accomplish. These are optional missions that are not any one samurai's responsibility.

When the group sensei see their mission accomplished they should throw a playing card in the air and shout the name of the mission, to indicate it was just accomplished.

Stage picture: Whenever the group strikes a good stage picture, this sensei throws a card in the air and declares "Stage picture!"

Truthful moment: Whenever someone in the group says something that is surprisingly truthful, this sensei throws a card in the air and says "Truthful moment!"

Moment of silence: There's so much frantic talking in improv that an audience appreciates committed silence. Whenever there's a nice pregnant moment of pause, this sensei throws a card in air and says "Moment of silence!" (ironically both celebrating and ruining it)

True love: Improv also has so much scattershot meanness and snarkiness, that any time there's a moment of genuine vulnerable sweetness—someone saying I love you, a father complimenting his son, a friend helping a friend—this sensei throws a card in the air and says "True love!"

These mission don't all have to be completed. Meaning these sensei don't need to get rid of all their cards for the round to be over—it would take too long.

POSTSCRIPT

This can be a chaotic exercise. But if you build up from the first simple "accept offers" version it can be a fun celebration of the types of moments that make improv shows fun.

The sensei are watching more closely than they are maybe used to.

The samurai focus their awareness down to just one useful task.

The businesslike action of handing a card to someone is an oddly pleasing punch line for otherwise mundane improv moments.

YEP I LIKE IT

OCTOBER 7TH, 2014 at 10:00AM

EXERCISES: YOU WANTED TO SEE ME?

I've been using this one to teach game. It is a structured exercise, not a scene. (I've written about this one before, yes)

Start with one person in a chair. This person is in an office. A second person mimes entering, saying "You wanted to see me, OCCUPATION?" where occupation is anything from the very general "farmer" to "head chef at the best restaurant in town."

This second person is the assistant to the first person. Even if it doesn't make sense for someone of the named occupation to have an office and assistant ("You wanted to see me coal miner?") we just pretend they have one for the sake of the exercise.

Then the seated person has to make three EXPECTED requests and the a fourth one that is the exact OPPOSITE of what we'd expect. So it should go like this:

> Person A: You wanted to see me, farmer?
>
> Person B: Yes, thanks. We need to order more grain, we need to get the tractor fixed, I'd like to lay off some of the hired help for budget reasons and also, I'd like us to stop growing food.

Then Person A "straight mans" it, meaning he/she tries to respond like a rational person would. "Uh, but that's all we do is grow food. We're a farm."

> Person B then has to come up with a reason why they want to do the weird thing.

Your fourth request shouldn't just be random. This wouldn't be as good:

> Person A: You wanted to see me, farmer?
>
> Person B: *[three expected requests and then]*... I'd like a pet dolphin living in my house.

That's kinda funny, but it's sloppy. Better for the fourth thing to be somehow the opposite of what we expect.

Once you'd done a few, you can broaden the occupation to be a short description of a character. Like this:

> Person A: You wanted to see me, guy going through a hostile divorce?
>
> Person B: Yes, come in. I'd like to make an appointment with my lawyer. I'd also like to set up some therapy for myself. Call me friends to see who wants to hang out with me for a drink. And then hire a poet to write a love sonnet about my marriage.

THINGS TO NOTICE

This is a useful exercise because without a lot of coaching, people tend to do the following things well during it:

- People tend to say "yes" to whatever job they are assigned and come up with three pretty specific "expected" requests. In other words, they play the reality well without saying "Oh, this is my first day" or "I don't really know anything about this job"—people just agree, and it is funny.

- The straight man supports the first three items even if they are inadvertently a bit silly.
- The straight man questions the fourth one in a polite, non-angry way.
- The reason "why" that the seated person comes up with for their strange request: it's almost always funny, and the person doesn't have to work that hard to come with it.
- The straight man notices and pays direct attention to whatever is weird about the fourth thing. Good "framing" is what you call that.
- Opposite of what we expect is better than simply arbitrarily different than what we expect

If you do this exercise early in a course or a workshop, you can refer to it when they do free-form scenes. You can tell someone "your scene partner just dropped a '4th thing' and you didn't respond to it"—or "they're just trying to give you an expected thing, don't quibble with it"—or "where's the why? you need a why for that weird thing."

OCTOBER 8TH, 2014 at 5:28PM

Q: GIVING TOO MANY HEADY NOTES

jennysaint asked: As a new coach I find myself giving a lot of technical heady notes about things to keep in mind in a scene. It is inevitably getting people in their heads. How do I keep the fun alive and also work on some of the more technical aspects of improv?

Oof, yeah, I relate to this. Very often I'll walk out of a practice I coached and think "Well, I just put those people in their heads for the rest of their lives." To show that I never learn, I will now answer YOUR question with too much analysis and put YOU in YOUR head. Get ready!

The goal is to have more reps with shorter notes.

1. **The rules:** Over the past year or so, I've re-discovered the power of the

old standby notes—meaning the classic improv rules/mantras like "avoid teaching scenes" and "don't be coy" and "start in the middle."

Like if a scene ends in a bad fight, I could talk forever. I could analyze how the actors were acting defensive, or denying the accusation, or were overly concerned about their own territory—I mean, I could go deep as to the exact moment and mechanics of what probably went wrong.

But it's likely just as good to say "don't fight so much" and move on.

2. **Say what it feels like.** Instead of analyzing the scene, just describe what it felt like. Something like "Felt a bit like we're all just trying to do the right thing, not have fun." or "Felt like we were super excited to be with each other but never made a decision." This is kinda going macro instead of micro. If you can really nail it, they might be able to make an adjustment to correct whatever it was you noticed.

3. **Admit when you don't know.** You might not know what went wrong. Or you know it has something to do with how they refused to get out of the car, but you don't know how to translate that into a general rule. Just say "Probably should've got out of the car, but I'm not sure. I'm not sure! let's try another one."

4. **Think of it as an exercise class, not a lecture.** People need reps more than theory a lot. So just think of the practice as something analogous to a yoga session. A yoga teacher COULD get very philosophical about the meaning of all the poses and the effect on one's mindset on the body. But just as often, especially with beginners, they're just trying to get basic poses down. You're just there to correct form and be forgiving.

What I do lately is try to keep track of how long I've been quiet so I can "earn" a chance to yap about whatever anecdote/larger point I'm dying to tell. I'm not always successful in managing myself, but I try.

OCTOBER 9TH, 2014 at 7:00AM

EXERCISES: WORDS SLASH FOLLOW (WARMUP)

A simple warm up I like to do has two parts.

Everyone up in a circle.

First part is "word association"—teacher picks someone to start. That person points at someone else in the circle and says any word or phrase ("traffic light", "stone", "acceptance"). That person then points at someone else and says whatever that term makes them think of.

Specific ("suitable match", "ferocious appearance", "south of france") is better than general, but it's more important to just keep it moving.

Second part is follow the follower. After like 20 seconds of the word association, someone in the group makes a big physical move—preferably in reaction to whatever was just said at that moment but it's more important to just do it when it needs to be done. Once the person has made a physical move—everyone switches into a non-verbal "follow the follower." That means everyone just physically copies each other so the whole group is repeating a physical actions which is morphing.

They can make non-verbal noises, meaning no words. Commitment is good! Big physical commitment. The group can break out of the circle if it happens, though it doesn't have to.

THEN after like 20 seconds of physical movement, someone stands up straight and points and says a word or phrase. The whole group snaps back into a circle and does words.

After 20 seconds, someone makes a big physical move: back to follow the follower.

Alternate "words" mode with "physical" mode for like 4 minutes.

What's good: You're alternating left-brain verbal analytical stuff with physical animal stuff. The two sides inform each other. When the group finishes their first physical round and returns to words they will be energized and the choices will be coming easier. After they come back to physical after doing words, they will be more specific with their physical choices.

OCTOBER 20TH, 2014 at 2:46PM

EXERCISES: WHO'S UNUSUAL?

An exercise for deeper listening and for being aware that the audience is waiting for someone to be unusual.

Two people up. They get a suggestion and then they take a starting position, look at each other and wait. The starting positions don't have to take into account the suggestion, and they should be small choices: sitting in a chair with a slight slump; standing up straight, or maybe hands on hips.

The teacher timeout 30 seconds. The students do not start the scene. They must be able to see each other. During that time the students just regard each other. Again, the scene does not being. No object work, no starting. Just this initial position, looking.

After 30 seconds, before starting the scene, the teacher asks the class to vote on "Who's Unusual?". There are four choices.

1. Person A is unusual
2. Person B is unusual
3. They both are.
4. Neither one is.

There is no right answer. But the interesting thing is that people will have opinions. Just based on how you stand, how you look at each other—the audience is starting to see and feel things. The actors should also be in tune with this.

Now, let the actors do two lines. An initiation and a response. The initiation should take the suggestion into account, and should also take into account how they are standing and facing each other. The initiation doesn't HAVE to address how they're standing, but if it feels like someone is an authority figure and someone is being submissive, the initiator should take that into account with how and what they say.

After these two lines, the teacher takes a vote again. Same four choices. People will be more unified now.

Now, make the two actors do 4 or 5 more lines. Then take the vote again.

The point here is that the scene begins as soon as the actors leave the backline. The scene is much more than what you say in your first line. It's in the way you walk, the tenor of your voice, the expression on your face—even the plain base expression when you think you're not doing anything. These things are all part of the scene.

I was lucky enough to be on a Harold team with a group of people with very pronounced personalities. Everyone brought such a distinct energy—before the scene even started—that it was impossible to not let that affect what you were going to say. Our scenes got going very quickly. We felt funny, even when we didn't have good ideas.

This exercise is to get in tune with that—the intangible hard-to-describe vibe which exists beneath and around the words that you say.

OCTOBER 23RD, 2014 at 12:19AM

Q: AN EXERCISE FOR FOCUSING ON THE OTHER CHARACTER?

Anonymous asked: I've been having trouble with putting focus on my scene partner. I tend to endow myself with a lot and focus inward with details about myself and the scene—everything as it relates to my character and usually not the other. Do you have any tricks/exercises to make your scene partner more important and focus on helping to define them more acutely instead of just myself? Thanks!!!

EXERCISES: PASS THE CARD (COREY BROWN)

I think I DO have an exercise for this. Or rather my friend/teacher from UCB-NY Corey Brown does. He's got an exercise that I call "Pass the Card" and it goes... like... this!

Two people up. One holds a playing card (or business card or whatever). Teacher gives a suggestion. Either person can initiate (doesn't have to be the one holding the card).

As soon as the person holding the card says anything about the other character—they hand the card over as they say their line.

So if Person 2 is holding the card, and the suggestion is "hurricane."

> Person 1: I think we're prepared for the storm.
>
> Person 2: You really deal well with emergencies (as he/she hands the card)

As the other person takes the card, he/she must confirm right then what was just gifted.

> Person 1: (taking the card) Yeah, I like to be prepared. Easier than dealing with feelings—I'd rather just DO.

Then you keep the scene going until Person 1, who now has the card, says something about Person 2—at which point Person 1 hands the card over.

You keep going—and you can see from who has the card longer who is not talking about the other character. You also practice explicitly accepting offers as they happen.

So there. That's an exercise to address what you're saying.

OCTOBER 24TH, 2014 at 10:46AM

Q: HOW USEFUL TO NOTE A SCENE'S PROBLEMS WHEN IT WENT WELL?

Anonymous asked: When coaching, how useful is it to note a scene that had one or two small problems, but ultimately went well? I'm thinking specifically of instances where an early offer is missed, or there was a small denial when there should have been agreement, but the performers found something else in the scene and played it well.

I think you're answering your question in your question which is to say: probably just let it go.

Especially if the bad part was right at the top, but then they righted the ship: don't worry about the missteps. I think that's really common, especially in class. It feels like an engine sputtering to life—just ignore the sputter. Winning teaches you how to win, so focus on the good part. Or maybe just say "we started a little shaky, but then from this part we got it " and you explain why the rest worked.

OCTOBER 24TH, 2014 at 11:56AM

Q: IS THE PATTERN GAME GOOD FOR A PERFORMANCE?

Anonymous asked: What is your defense of the pattern game? Is it appropriate for a performance setting?

I have complicated feelings about this.

SHORT ANSWER: No, it's generally not appropriate for a performance. Too stilted, too obtuse. There's other options that are easier to make entertaining.

LONGER ANSWER: It's often not worth the work. But if you're for real, you do it.

Don't underestimate the audience's tolerance for a weird arty thing at the top of your long-form show. IF you make it clear how the suggestion is informing the opening, and IF you make it clear how the following scenes derive from the opening—the audience will generally like it. People know what an overture is, and the pattern game can be like an overture.

I have vivid memories of seeing a Harold for the first time. Solo Arts Theatre, 1998—UCB Harold Night, before the UCB's comedy central show started, before they had a theater. The NY Times did an article on the UCB4, and I wanted to see them. I had only seen improv at college short form shows, and a few other theaters in New York.

I found Harold Night listed on a student (Ed Snible)'s web site, and climbed up 6 flights to wait in line to sit in a small rehearsal studio to watch.

But it wasn't the UCB, it was Harold Night. I had no idea what that meant, or why they were saying "UCB" when there weren't any members of UCB there. I didn't know why the performers all looked 20, or how anyone else in the 30-person audience knew to be there.

The show started. I watched 4 harolds. Each time, the opening was bizarre. One was like a hot spot of monologues, one was a sort of scenic sound-and-movement, one was two lines of people shouting declarations at each other, and then one which I now know is a pattern game. The harolds themselves were—like many (most?) harolds—very up and down. Lots of things didn't pay off. Some things very much did.

But when it was over, I was solidly convinced that I had just seen the coolest improv I could ever conceive of.

Every other improv show I'd ever seen was short-form, or medium-form at best ("give us first and last lines") . It was desperate and gimmicky, usually done by older tired people for an audience of six. Hammy and self-effacing.

But Harold Night—in large part because it was so obtuse and weird—looked more confident and ambitious and cool. It seemed like it had taste. No one was playing with big hammy expressions. Many people spoke in their natural voices. They seemed into it, and possessed with passion.

I say this even though the performers were clearly amateurs. The form looked bad ass. They looked like they were unapologetically if clumsily performing a ritual.

All other improv was like a lame tired arena rock cover band, and now I was seeing Nirvana.

So, I don't know. I've seen the pattern game tear down shows and groups. It's difficult and obtuse. You have to really practice it and decide how your team is going to do it. You have to make it clear to the audience how your scenes come from it so they don't feel left out. It's not as important as being able to do good scenes. I understand why it's not worth it to many people.

But there really is something magical and ritualistic in it that comes through. It sends a signal to the audience: we are doing something weird and artistic and deep now, so watch closely.

OCTOBER 24TH, 2014 at 12:07PM

Q: JUSTCRAIG: BETTER TO LEAN ANGRILY IN AN INTERROGATION SCENE?

justcraig asked: In improv, if you're in an interrogation scene, is it better for the cop to lean angrily on the back of the criminal's chair, or to sit backwards in a different chair on stage (also angrily)?

OCTOBER 30TH, 2014 at 11:14AM

EXERCISE: COMPLIMENT/BOAST

This is an exercise to boost the confidence and vulnerability between members of a group. WARNING: This is a touchy-feely actorly sort of thing, so improvisers have to get over their smirkiness to do this, which is partly the point.

I recommend it for the last session of an eight week course, or for teams who are a bit burnt out / in their heads. Either at the top of class, or after the break.

DIRECTIONS

Split up into pairs. If there's an odd number, the teacher should join a pair.

PHASE ONE: COMPLIMENTS

When the teacher says go, one person in the pair starts complimenting the other one on their improv. What they do, the way they do it, anything.

At 45 seconds the teacher says "switch" and now the person who had been getting complimented does the complimenting.

Then everyone should switch into a new pair.

PHASE TWO: BOASTING

This is the harder part. When the teacher says go, one person boasts about his/her own strengths in improv to the other person. Like, you say what you're good at. Boast about the version of yourself on a good day; it's okay if you don't ALWAYS do the thing you're bragging about. The person who's listening can help by nodding.

The teacher should tell the class that they are being given permission to boast. And also: being on stage requires a bit of an ego, so boosting your own ego before you act is not an indulgent thing, it's a necessary thing. The audience and your team and also you all want the confident version of you on stage, so boosting yourself up is actually helpful to everyone. It is also good to practice bolstering your own view of yourself.

At 45 seconds, the teacher says "switch" and the other member of the pair boasts.

It's not nearly as hard as it sounds and leaves the class feeling pretty great.

BACKGROUND

I learned this when I took a monologue study workshop in the fall of 2001. I had been put on a Harold team shortly before this and was terrified of not being up to the task. So I started going to an acting class: A drop-in monologue study workshop run by a guy (Rob McCaskill) from whom I'd taken an improv course a few years before.

Doing "real" acting was terrifying. I was a computer programmer, and everyone else in this monologue drop-in class were these very emotive actorly actors. The first day, I performed the monologue from the end of "Cool Hand Luke," feeling silly and scared as I did it.

(It is odd how improv courses and teams will make people do things they would never consider doing. People who refused to dance at their own high school proms will still swing their hips when coming on stage with their improv teams.)

I liked Rob a lot. He gave generous pragmatic advice that was easy to do and didn't make me feel terrible. (Ranging from very direct things like "try a longer pause after each period" and "Pick a specific person you're addressing." to more general stuff like "Let this get simpler, do less.") Just the act of going to this course made me feel more brave, and the actual advice also improved my performance.

Rob would often have us start the workshops with this compliment/boast exercise. It reminded me that the other actors didn't see me as someone who wasn't up to the task, but instead as someone who was being brave and going for it. We were all rooting for each other and focusing on what was working. Which, when you're doing it right, is any improv class or show.

NOVEMBER 2ND, 2014 at 10:46PM

SUGGESTED PRACTICES FOR BETTER LISTENING AT TOP OF SCENES

I'm using the word "suggested" very deliberately. These are hardly rules. But I see a lot of scenes get tripped up because people are throwing too much out in the first three lines. These suggestions are meant to combat that.

All of these are just saying listen to each other, and don't assume you know the next line. But this is hardest to do at the top when we are all feeling enormous pressure to HAVE an IDEA.

1. Have a short beat of silence after every reveal. And keep eye contact.

    A lot of people do: "Also, I threw out your favorite toy (spins to face away) Anyway, how was your day? I hope…" Isn't that odd? A lot. They make a (usually mean) reveal, then spin 180 degrees and keep talking. It's like a 1930s stage version of being catty or zinging someone or something. The practical effect is you miss the nonverbal information your scene partner is giving off about your reveal.

    So try "I threw out your favorite toy." Then stop talking for just a moment and keep looking at the person. Just a dollop of silence.

2. If you initiate by walking downstage and getting immersed in object work, which happens a lot, don't get so immersed that you forget to look up and see your partner. Check in early. Just a quick glance. Your object work isn't going to get better by you bathing it in an unbroken stare.

3. If your scene partner was out first and she/he walks downstage and gets immersed in object work, stay quiet. They are not listening to you yet, maybe, so stay neutral until they check in. Don't label their object work for them, which takes away their idea and confuses them. Unless they're quiet a while, then it's okay. But assume they've got something.
4. Don't interrupt the initiation.
5. Don't interrupt the response to the initiation. Happens a lot, because the initiator didn't get all their thoughts out, and it all comes spilling out right after the responder starts talking.
6. If there's an opening, assume the initiation has a pretty full thought in it. They might need more than one line. So, responder, don't AND it too much. Make sure they got their idea out. They won't really be listening to you until they do get it out. Very often a good second line (if there was an opening) is a YES with only a little AND.

EXAMPLE!

(some opening happens)

First person: "Man, these dishes really pile up after Thanksgiving."

Second person: "Yeah. Phew, there is a ton!" -> *just a YES, assuming there's more coming.*

First person: "I bought an elephant." -> *There it is! They were waiting to say this, and now you didn't throw them off.*

After which the first person stops talking to give the other person a little quarter-beat to absorb it.

If the first person really didn't have an idea beyond "we're doing dishes after Thanksgiving" then you can put a big AND after the third line if you like.

Disagreements welcome! Or at least, I will silently sympathize with all disagreements though I might not respond.

NOVEMBER 6TH, 2014 at 11:22AM

Q: HOW TO GET RID OF FIGHTING?

Anonymous asked: One of the best notes I've ever gotten was don't just make a scene a fight or an argument because someone will always be trying to win the scene. It seems so obvious yet I think it's one of the most difficult things to do. So I guess I'm just wondering how do you replace fighting and one upping with a more constructive and interesting game?

This question opens a huge maelstrom of thoughts and feelings in my brain. I have to answer far more than you're asking so I don't explode. My apologies.

First off, fighting is okay and even essential. Don't think fights are bad. A good improv set has plenty of disagreements between characters. You just have to learn to fight WELL.

Fighting well amounts to:

- saying yes to accusations,
- while holding on to your character's opinions,
- while not getting so angry that you lock up and quibble on unimportant things.

First key of fighting well, and this is what answers your question: **accusations are generally gifts.** Adjust your view of your character so the accusations are true. That's your way out of the unproductive argument.

Second key: **Don't win.** This is different than actively losing. Just don't win. You're arguing to explore, not to dominate.

Third key: **No deal making on the funny thing!** You can agree to do something you don't want to do in order to move forward, but don't admit to changing your mind. You can make accusations true while still holding on to your opinion. However DO make deals and move on from unimportant bullshit.

Too much, I know. I'm sorry. Wait, more!

Style tips about arguing in improv:

- If you feel yourself defeating another character with quips and zings and meanness -> you went down the wrong path.
- If the scene is about something, don't turn it into a scene where everyone is against you. Like halfway through a group game, don't say "Wait a minute, are you all saying this because of ME?" They weren't, and this is akin to a denial/invention.
- If your character is always critical of everything by default, like right away you're folding your arms before the other person is even done talking—that's the actor being defensive. Relax so you don't obsess on unimportant stuff.

Another way of saying all of this: **Always agree on the facts, but you don't have to agree on opinions.** That's how you give notes on a fight, too. Don't say "fights are bad" but instead find the moment when someone denied or rejected a FACT. That's where the listening failed.

NOVEMBER 6TH, 2014 at 12:49PM

NO BULLSHIT HAROLDS

I'm trying to run an exercise in classes lately of what I'm calling "no bullshit" Harolds. It's tricky, mostly because I'm working out how to describe what I'm looking for.

(I think every teacher has a version of this. I'd like to hear how other people achieve this in class! What do you call it? What do you say?)

It's roughly that I want to see scenes where people are not worried about making a game, or making a pattern, or doing anything at all where it seems like they're doing it because they think they SHOULD. No shoulds. This is slightly different in my mind than the related "don't be funny" exercises. I just mean, forget the rules of what you think you SHOULD do, and instead just be in the scene for real and tell me what the person would really say.

It's okay if it breaks the scene, or if you leave, or if you fight, or if you ask questions, or if it's not funny, or if you walk away from a chance to repeat a pattern. We're going for reality.

GET BACK YOUR INSTINCTS

Improv students have so many rules thrown at them, and the Harold is such a demanding structure that by the time you see people in an Advanced class, they no longer sound like real people. They're being so diligent, to an impressive degree, to make active choices and say yes to every offer and find a game and to be specific, that everything sounds false and fake. Usually in the manner of some old 1940s move where everyone is hammy and big and everyone is speaking exposition in every line.

I mean, I know this happens for a good reason. Level one students are so scared of improv that the only choices they can ever think of are to say no, to reject, to run away. So we spend all this time forcing them to overrun those instincts that improv students inevitably enter a phase where they've stopped paying attention to their natural instincts at ALL.

So I'm trying to run "no bullshit" Harolds, meaning no SHOULDS. These are not true Harolds by anyone's definition. There's no games, there's lots of indecisiveness. Inevitably some scene is brought to a standstill. BUT if they are done right they achieve something that has been sorely lacking: a world that feels real. Which is ingredient number one of compelling improv.

Overly detailed examples after the jump!

WHAT WOULD YOU SAY?

To try and explain what I'm looking for, I'll have a discussion with the class where I give them a scenario and ask what they would say.

1. Like "Okay, you're in a scene where you and your boyfriend/girlfriend are in a hot air balloon ride, which you're doing for your anniversary. What are you talking about in this scene?"

    The first bunch of ideas are generally high-stakes, highly emotional problems. "I'm too scared to go up." "I'm mad at the person for making me do it." "I realize I left the dog in the car."

    All high stakes, active. Also all very fake and contrived.

    So I say to assume that there are no problems. You're a bit nervous but you can handle it. You both wanted to go on this ride and your relationship is in a generally good place. And then again: "What are you talking about in this scene?"

So then the students start saying things like "We get philosophical about the view and our lives." "I tell her how much I love her."

Better, but I still don't buy it. Still feels forced. Feels like people who know they are being watched talking about what they think they SHOULD talk about.

So I say. "No, picture it happening. What would YOU be talking about. Ten minutes into the ride, after you've exclaimed how beautiful it is, What would you talk about?"

Last time I did this, someone said at this point "We'd talk about the last episode of Game of Thrones." And I laughed. THAT feels true.

Other suggestions: Talking about where you're eating later. Talking about a mutual friend. Checking your phone for messages.

That's what I want. What you would really do. That's where we need to start in scenes. You have to be in touch, right away, with what would REALLY happen, so that things don't sound fake.

WHAT WOULD YOU SAY, ASSUMING YOU WANT TO BE THERE?

2. Then I say: Okay, new situation. The scene starts and the other person in the scene tells you that you're in a scuba suit and you're about to dive in the water for your first solo swim with the tanks. What are you thinking about?

   First bunch of answers: I'm terrified! I'm don't want to go! I refuse to do it!

   And I say no, that's not what you would do. And the students argue: YES. We are picturing it, and that's what we would do.

   But you have to assume that you took this class on purpose, and you want to, and you finished the class and you're ready. Given all that, what are you thinking about?

   Last time I did this, a student said "Well, I'd be checking over my equipment and making sure I remembered what I was about to do." I agreed with that. And then someone else said "I'd be excited to do it." And then someone said "I'd just jump in the water and go."

   Those all feel true. You'd probably just take a beat to consider, then jump in the water and go.

A WHOLE HAROLD LIKE THAT

I run a whole Harold like this. No opening. Anytime anyone does anything that feels to me in the audience like they're just doing it to do it, I say: "Would you really do that?"

A few admittedly confusing constraints:

1. Make a few choices before going into "no bullshit" mode. Say yes to the first few choices so that some world can come into being.//
2. Still try to make things happen, as long as it doesn't break the "no bullshit" rule. But when in doubt on any decision, side with "no bullshit."

The second beats aren't true second beats, though it's interesting to see what the students bring back! And they are funnier than people expect. They DO find certain realistic behaviors which naturally repeat.

The scenes tend to be passive and a bit obstructionist. But not too bad. And they are more interesting. The people look and sound real. I trust them to be good judges of what is worth paying attention to.

I'LL TAKE THE COTTON CANDY

I am reminded of a scene that happened in my level 3 grad show. My classmates John Gemberling and Rob Lathan were playing two guys who heckled people, based on something in the opening. Specifically, they were two guys heckling a tightrope walker at a circus.

They were saying things like "Come on, fall!" "You can't do it! Get over yourself!"

Then someone from the backline walked on to the scene as a concession worker, saying "Cotton Candy! Slingshots!"

And Gemberling went "Uh, I'll have a cotton candy."

Some would say that was a denial of the intention of the walk-on. But I think it was just that Gemberling was respecting reality, and very in touch with what he would really do. He doesn't want to kill this guy on the tightrope, just heckle him. And he likes cotton candy.

A whole Harold like that.

NOVEMBER 7TH, 2014 at 10:52AM

EXERCISE: OBJECT INTO POV

Everyone up in a circle.

Person who starts mimes an object, says what it is, and gives it to someone else in the circle. "Stapler" they say, and they give it to someone.

Whoever receives it does this to create a POV from the object.

- This is a OBJECT
- It stands for IDEA
- IDEA is important to me because (does 3-4 sentences as a character who really values IDEA).
- Then they cap it by holding up their mimed object and saying IDEA.

They make a new object and give it to someone else. Like this!

- This is a STAPLER.
- It stands for HOLDING THINGS TOGETHER.
- HOLDING THINGS TOGETHER is important to me because, well, I guess I think there's nothing as important as family. Keep your money, your power, your everything. All I care about is family.
- HOLDING THINGS TOGETHER.

For the 3-4 sentences, it should be done in character, and the reasons why they think the thing is important should be a philosophy, not external circumstances.

Practices the useful tool of taking a mundane detail and inferring a point of view from it!

NOVEMBER 11TH, 2014 at 11:44AM

AN UNFAIR LIST OF PET PEEVES AND PERSONAL PREFERENCES

Emphasis on "unfair." This list is dumb.

PET PEEVES
No high-fiving.

Long-form improv has more unnecessary high-fiving than you'd ever imagine. Two characters agree to get ice cream and then high-five. They get each other's name wrong, then correct it, then high-five. It looks really weird, though I must admit no one seems to notice it. But I notice it. Even "bros" in improv high-five way more than regular bros. Only time a high-five is okay is when a character in improv just hit a homerun.

No J names, especially "Janice"

This isn't a pet peeve as much as a phenomenon: The most common name given in improv is "Janice." By far. i'd say 50% of female characters in improv scenes are named Janice. And then the other J-names make up another 25% of characters. J-names feel funny and interesting to people, I guess? "The Jenkins report" is another phenomenon, but I think people know about that one. "Janice" is everywhere but unnoticed. *Disclaimer:* I once belonged to a harold team that used Janice so much we changed our name to Janice. No one liked it.

Edited to add: most common male name is "Gary."

Minimal pop culture references

Hearing the current movie du jour dropped into an improv scene starts to sound really clunky a few years into watching improv. I prefer made-up proper nouns. I remember an improv scene classmates of mine did about two people trying to guess the stars of the film "Two Jerks And A Stick." And an old UCB tourco show where they talked about guys named Paul Boston and Ed Grapes.

"That's not what you said on your (dating website) profile"
Come on.

"That's the last time I get something from Craigslist."
You can do better.

No bowling alleys, dentist appointments.
I could guess why (bowling means not looking at each other? Dentist requires someone to have their mouth full?) but for whatever reason, these scenes are often nightmares.

No board games
It's usually Monopoly or Battleship. That's weird right? I mean, Monopoly I get but who plays Battleship? Anyway, no one ever knows the rules and the scene doesn't start for like five minutes. Weird exception: building houses of cards and Jenga seems to work.

No pitch meetings/spitballing/ad guys
Right? "Guys, we need to come up with a new slogan for..."

Audiences giving as a suggestion whatever they see on stage, or a food
50% of all suggestions are foods, that we have realized. But another 40% are whatever the audience can see right in front of them. If half the guys are wearing plaid, they say "plaid." (seen that multiple times, including last night). If someone has "Wildcats" on a shirt, they say "Wildcats." If more than 2 people have glasses, they say "glasses." It baffles me. You get one thing to do, audience, and you're already out of ideas? I guess this is also an argument against everyone wearing plaid and such, but still. The remaining 10% are pop culture references. Everyone is dumb, including me.

PERSONAL PREFERENCES

Use names of friends from middle school
Advice I'll give to anyone who will listen: when you need a name, grab the actual first and last name of someone you knew in middle school. They're always specific and weird while still sounding true, since they are! Mark Chisholm. Chris Chamberlin. Paula Kubisek. Regina Glynn.

Everyone stand one half-step closer to each other
That makes it funnier. Another half-step is funnier still. For maximum funniness, use the Charlie Sanders "close eye" move where you stand so your

right eye is directly in front of the other person's left eye. It is intensely creepy and weirdly funny. Not for strangers.

Specify a not-that-long-ago year
Explicitly set your scenes in a specific but non-notable year. "Hey, what do you want? It's 1997." Sort of like how "The Big Lebowski" came out in 1998 and made a big (largely unnecessary?) deal about being set in 1991. My favorite years for this are (inexplicably) 1974, 1987, 1995.

Set your scenes in the third-most populated cities from any state
- Eugene, Oregon
- Rochester, New York
- Cincinnati, Ohio
- Tampa, Florida

Scenes where people are constantly preparing more and different foods in the kitchen while never addressing it or talking about it
I only saw this once, but I loved it.

Scenes where at least one person is holding their eyes 10% more open than normal.
Yep.

These words and terms, I love them: The commish. Dog war. Lock load and explode. Hewn. Brutal. Catbird seat. Not catbird seat, that's too much.
That's it.

NOVEMBER 18TH, 2014 at 11:16AM

DIFFICULT PEOPLE

There's no hard rule on difficult people. Here's some contradictory thoughts that explains how I feel about them.

Don't put up with jerks offstage. If they make you feel bad about yourself, find ways to avoid them.

But DO celebrate and enjoy weird and eccentric approaches ON stage. Don't try and tell other people how to improvise; you just react honestly as your character and let them do as they do. Be the improviser who can work with any style.

There will very often be one person on the team that you want to kick off, and you'll think that will solve all your problems. It's very common. But get rid of "the guy" and they'll be another "the guy." Sit on the impulse and see if it goes away.

Exception: if someone is missing rehearsals or not paying dues a LOT—that's disrespectful and they need to take a break or move on, no hard feelings. They'll agree and will understand.

Still, remember that almost every very talented person is a bit of trouble. Be good at picking who's worth the trouble. Some are always late. Some are always broke. Some wallow after every show. Some drink a troubling amount. Some will want to change openings and coaches every week. Some will post the most annoying things possible on every social media platform. Be patient, look for windows where you can be honest with them and the meantime enjoy the chaos of having interesting people in your life. Work with them so you can steal their powers. If they're good, they're worth it.

How to deal with stand-up comedians when they talk about improv: just nod your head and tell them they're right.

NOVEMBER 19TH, 2014 at 9:57AM

Q: CAN I CHERRY PICK WHO I WANT TO FORM A TEAM WITH?

Anonymous asked: Can I cherry pick who I want to form a team with? I just finished a class and there were a few people I felt strong chemistry with. Is it okay to reach out to them and say we should form a group, without opening it up to the rest of my class? If so, is there a most respectful way to approach it?

Yes, you can pick.

It is okay to reach out to a small group and make a practice/performance group.

My general advice as to how to do this is that if you don't make it a big deal, it won't be a big deal. Be direct, honest and concise when people ask. You say "Yeah, we're doing this thing, trying to keep it small, see how it goes." If you're direct and casual about it—it communicates "this is just a thing we're doing, it doesn't mean that we can't all be friends or do something in the future." Being honest and direct is respectful, even if what you're saying is "yeah, we're doing something without you right now."

If the OTHER people choose to take that very personally and take great offense to that, that is on them.

I've generally been pretty good about this, and I've been on both sides of it. I had a very passionate level 1 practice group—it was a group of 12 or so people. I'd contact them each week and some subset would show up. But of that group, there were 6 of us that felt like we were more into it and clicked better.

So mid-way through level 2, I just shut the old group down and started a new one just with the 6 of us. People were a little bummed, but it was fine. Of the people left out, some stayed in improv and MOST DID NOT. Within six months they kinda faded away! Some of them never even knew another group was happening.

THEN after a few months, my group of six fell apart because half of US quietly stopped showing up! They were writing their own sketch show and getting asked to do a bunch of other shows in the community. It had the feeling of your middle school friends "moving up" to a more popular group once you make high school.

But rather than make a big deal about it or focusing on being hurt, I called one of them and confirmed "so you guys are out, right?" And the guy I called was like yeah, we're doing this thing, and we don't have time and sorry, man. And I agreed it was cool, good luck, no big deal.

And then the 3 of us left grabbed another 3 from classes and kept going. These new three were more into it, and it was a better group for it. We eventually got made into a UCB Harold Team, which is insane and a story for another day! Point is none of this made any of us lose touch with each other or become enemies.

There's gonna be a lot of switching around, so try to be cool and sympathetic and not take stuff personally NOR make yourself the self-appointed guardian of everyone's feelings. In fact, it's VERY common for people to end up being asked to join a group that they were initially left out of. It's like the universe corrects those things that were mistakes, as long as the people don't let pride and ego get in the way.

I could keep going on this: that Harold Team which emerged from that practice group—Monkeydick (sorry for the name) went through many cast changes, and then after several years it got broken up. But half of the group immediately re-formed as a new weekly team: Death by Roo Roo, one of the best teams in UCB history! Those of us not included were not hurt, because we knew that it made sense—those guys clicked, it was time to make a change. Channel 101 (monthly video contest from LA) started in NYC and we all helped each other make videos, and would be in each other's sketch shows.

THEN: when I moved to LA this past January, I got asked to be on Your Effed Up family, which is a direct descendant of Death By Roo Roo. I did my first scene with a guy named John Gemberling, who was in my ORIGINAL GROUP OF 6 PEOPLE 15 years before. We had never stopped being friends during any of this. People are gonna play in different bands; you have to just be cool about it.

Making a practice group does not mean you are not all part of the same larger community of people who love improv. It's going to be fine.

NOVEMBER 21ST, 2014 at 12:30PM

GENERAL QUALIFIER

It would get redundant and boring, but any time I post an "advice" post, please understand that I don't see myself as the end-all be-all teacher. I always look back one year, two years, three years and see these things I wasn't really doing as well as I know now. These advice things are meant to be more like "here's stuff I'm thinking about, as an improv nerd just like you." I sometimes write in very simple declarative sentences but that's for efficiency and clarity in writing, not to say THIS IS THE ONLY WAY or I HAVE THIS ALL FIGURED OUT.

Okay, here comes another one.

NOVEMBER 21ST, 2014 at 12:32PM
GIVING POSITIVE NOTES

In my level 1 classes, I felt I was putting the students in their heads by talking too much and delving too deeply into the reasons behind the improv principles. Hard to imagine that a guy who keeps an IMPROV BLOG would talk too much, I know, but somehow I did it.

So I asked another teacher for advice on keeping level 1 classes confident. He had what in retrospect seems like obvious advice but I found it so helpful I want to pass it on: **Give mostly positive notes for the first half of the course.** Obvious, perhaps, but it was a helpful reminder and I'm seeing good results with the adjustment.

Things you say: "Great job of yes-anding in the first few lines," "Nice job speaking truthfully in the middle," "Great specifics." "I love how you chose to know exactly what she was referring to—helped us feel like we're starting in the middle." Be specific and true.

You don't point out how they started with three lines of fighting before they yes-anded, or that all of their object work disappeared once they got into it, or that they missed a chance to really bring home a game move, or that they changed each other's names twice.

This isn't coddling, this is letting them get reps in until they are more confident.

My own observation after focusing on this: **Be especially lenient with their first four of five lines.** Very often scenes in level 1 classes start with questions or confrontational statements and if you just keep your mouth shut, they get better. I won't even mention whatever they did "wrong" in the start of their scene—to me it was just their scene engine sputtering to life and should be discounted.

You DO give a note if the whole class senses a scene was particularly off. If everyone sat in stony silence and the students in the scene are rattled it will sound false if you go "Great scene!" So you focus the class' attention on something helpful. "You know what we needed there? The characters needed to already have known each other. So instead of 'Can I help you, sir?' you could go 'Your usual table, sir?' Then all those other moves would have had more importance. Okay, next two."

You're not trying to solve these scenes. You're trying to emphasize good habits and move on.

Also, **the more you talk, the more negative the note feels regardless of whether or not it IS negative.** This is boldfaced to remind myself. You want to give inspiring speeches about how cool the improv mantra is, you want to point out all the things you're noticing, but that can just make students feel weighed down. Practice saying a lot with a little. There isn't an improv teacher on Earth, this author certainly included, who couldn't benefit from saying less.

DECEMBER 6TH, 2014 at 10:34AM

Q: I'M IN MY HEAD IN UCB 401

Anonymous asked: I'm currently in UCB 401 Class and I feel completely in my head because all I can think about is getting the teacher's recommendation to move on to Advanced Study. I'm having trouble just having fun. Any advice how to just forget about the class stuff and just do the comedy I came to do with everyone in the class?

This is a very common happening. Being in your head during 401 (at UCB—and the same goes for any theater's class where you need approval to advance) because you're worried about how every class is an audition—yeah, that's rough.

Here's the simple answer, which is true although maybe not immediately helpful: you have to just put the approval out of your mind and enjoy the class. You TRYING to be good will ironically make you less good. You will do your best when you just let yourself be yourself: that includes sometimes being bad, sometimes being good and sometimes not even really knowing how you're doing.

Use this level to get in touch with your own approval of what you are doing. Do YOU like what you're doing? Forget what the teacher thinks. Were YOU happy with it? Knowing how you feel, without letting your instincts getting gummed up by trying to please an outside observer, is very key to being good at improv. The best people bring a lot of their own viewpoint and their own personality into every scene. Knowing how you feel is part of that.

You still take notes, but every time you're wondering "how I am doing?" make sure you separate "how does the teacher think I'm doing" from "how do *I* think I'm doing?"

Even better, is if you stop thinking about it in terms of good and bad. Like don't even evaluate YOUR performance and just try to enjoy each scene, each exercise, each class. But if this level of zen-whatever is impossible for you (it was impossible for me) then at least make sure you regard yourself as important an audience member as anyone else.

There's another, longer essay I could write about whether an improv school should have levels where you need approval to move on. The short answer is: yes, when the school is big enough you absolutely need a level where you can't go on without approval. And the fourth level in, with 8 sessions of observation—is as fair a way as there likely is.

DECEMBER 9TH, 2014 at 2:41PM

Q: HOW DO I AVOID "ME-FIRST" MOVES?

Anonymous asked: I feel like a lot of the time in scenes I think "what can I do to make this scene better" which leads me to think of what "I" should be doing yet I know that as a good scene partner my goal should be to make the other person in the scene look good.—So I guess my question is, How do I improve the scene for my scene partner instead of making "me-first" moves?

I like this question but I don't agree with the assumptions you're making. So prepare yourself, for we are about to enter a (hear this in a deep reverberation, please) SEMANTIC DISCUSSION.

So come into my debating chamber. Have a seat in the cold metal chair. I will sit upon the oak cube. Please help yourself to some ionized water. There are some notebooks and pencils for all of us to scribble our terms down. The blue fluorescent orbs should give us plenty of light. Now, let us talk TERMS.

I do not think your main trouble is that you tend to think "me-first." Me-first isn't necessarily bad, and it's often great. I don't agree that we should always

always be trying to think of what our scene partner needs or wants. You do need to be LISTENING, fully and deeply, to your scene partner(s) at all times. But that doesn't mean they need anything from you. YOU may be the one who needs something. Or the environment. Or just an idea that's been talked about. So this isn't a case, in my opinion, of ME vs PARTNER.

I think the problematic term here is "make this scene better" specifically the terms SCENE and BETTER.

Would you like any dry crackers, by the way? Or celery? There's nothing more flavorful here, I'm afraid. Pleasures of any kind detract from the semantic debate.

BETTER: This word BETTER presumes the scene is bad and needs to be fixed, and needs to be fixed by you. This is is the self-centeredness that you detected might be problem when you said you needed to focus less on yourself. The word BETTER means you're assuming that the scene is in a state of BADNESS and needs to get to GOODNESS and you are the person to do it. Even though this is sometimes TRUE, it's not helpful to think of things like that. Don't think about BAD or GOOD, at least not by default. Maybe the scene is great and all you need to do is give a nice YES to something that's already working, or to heighten something that's been fun. Or maybe you could just be quiet and things will be great.

SCENE: I'm really picking nits here, but I also don't think you should put responsibility for the whole SCENE on you or any one person. I would replace this word SCENE with LAST THING THAT HAPPENED. Your job, primarily, is to respond helpfully to the LAST THING THAT HAPPENED. I like to think of this as the OFFER. What is the current OFFER which needs answering or confirming? What just happened, and what is important about that? React to it, confirm it, remember things that relate to it (i.e. add things to the world which confirm what was just said), make it more specific. If the scene is working at all, you should be mid-volley at almost all times.

But I really don't think it's helpful to assume that we must always be doing something with the other person. LISTENING to them, yes absolutely. But the focus might need to be elsewhere.

If the scene is at a plateau—meaning there's nothing to volley back, well then you have to make choice. Here's some high percentage shots:

1. Add something specific.

2. Add something from your real life or your real interests or the real interests of a real person you know and add it to the scene—in reaction to the last thing that happened. These will tend to be specific and have a nice pleasing ring of truth

3. Repeat whatever the most interesting thing that has happened thus far.

4. Have your character confess something.

5. Give a specific gift to the other person.

Well, I'm rambling now. That's all I have. I have to go transport myself back to Improv Central where we're all arguing over the right way to do an Invocation. Deacon Qualls feels the "you are" section should be personal, but Headmistresses Edmonton is solely concerned about making the "thou art" section more full of callbacks. And Prefect Fordly is, frankly, ignoring everyone and just trying to do bits, which we must tolerate but is exhausting. I expect the discussion will take all day. See yourself out. Leave your robe on the hook, please. Thank you.

DECEMBER 23RD, 2014 at 10:00AM

JIMMY AND WILL: WORRYING ABOUT BEING SMART ENOUGH

Welcome, ladies and gentlemen, to a new feature. As you know, I get a fair amount of questions at this blog. A new thing I'm going to do is that every now and then, I'll team up to answer them with Jimmy Carrane. Jimmy, as many of you know, is a well-known improv teacher in Chicago. He teaches The Art of Slow Comedy in Chicago and around the country, and he's also the co-author of Improvising Better and author of Improv Therapy. You can check out his popular improv blog at jimmycarrane.com.

Here goes...

Q: I have a severe insecurity over my intelligence level. I was a terrible student, dyslexic and barely graduated high school. I work now in comedic TV shows and commercials, but I'm scared to death of improvising.

My agent asks me why I'm not at UCB or The Groundlings. I always make up some excuse, but really it's because I don't feel smart enough! I walked through my fear recently at The Groundlings but quit after Level 2 because I felt incapable. Is there hope? Suggestions? Thank you!

Will: I think this is a really brave and honest question. I wish my answer was as brave, but I get a little technical and wordy and I apologize in advance.

Insecurity over intelligence: This is a tough but very common fear. I think a lot of people have it. I think it's totally natural when you take an improv class to feel that you have to be unbelievably brilliant or else the class and teacher are going to think you're no good. I notice it most in Level 1 classes when two people are in a scene, and one person brings up a movie or TV show or worst of all, a book, that the other person has not heard of. You can see the other person be overcome with fear: oh no! I don't know what the movie is, and everyone else knows it, and I look dumb! It's a genuinely scary moment!

But the reality is that you can never know about every single thing that gets brought up in an improv scene, and that you just have to learn to be calm and do a combination of kinda faking that you know, and being willing to just calmly admit it when you don't. If you watch seasoned improviser do improv, you will definitely see countless moments where someone either doesn't know something or doesn't understand something. They never let it rattle them because they know it's just part of the deal when you don't have a script.

Here's the main dirty secret when it comes to being smart in improv: it doesn't really matter. It's way more about emotional intelligence than witty knowledge. Really. People who don't do improv assume that improv is about being brilliantly witty, meaning SAYING FUNNY AND SMART THINGS. It's not. I mean, funny and smart things do get said—but the ability to come up with a brilliant phrase is low on the priority list for a good improviser. I'd say the main skill of a good improviser is something much close to just emotional intelligence: being in the moment, and reporting very honestly how your character feels. That is a much more valuable skill. If you can calm your fears down (not always easy) and just hear what's being said and then report back honestly—you will be a great improviser.

Jimmy: Yes, there is hope, and I hope we are not going to lose you because you think you are not smart enough to improvise. There is a misconception in improv that you need to be some sort of brainiac or have some incredible reference level to be good at it. Intelligence can be overrated in improv. It doesn't matter what your IQ is or what your SAT scores were in high school. If you can listen, agree, emotionally react to your partner, find the game, and not be an asshole you will do just fine. I have seen smart people be terrible at improv and people who weren't that smart soar. It's your life experience that matters. Being a terrible student, having dyslexic and barely graduating from high school is your life experience. You just need to embrace that and use it in your improv. Here are my suggestions to get your butt back into class:

First ask yourself why are taking these classes. My guess is that you are an actor who wants to book more on-camera work. You may be taking classes at The Groundlings to eventually be on SNL, I don't know, but I think to be honest with why you are taking the classes will take some of the pressure off yourself. This is important because when you study at places with such famous alumni as The Groundling, you can sometimes be intimated and have a huge expectation for yourself, which can make it weird and competitive. Once you are clear about why you are taking classes, such as because your agent thought it would be a good skill to have for auditions, then you can focus on learning and having fun.

The second thing I would suggest, which you may think is crazy, is to admit to the entire class that you are scared to improvise because you don't think you are smart enough. You are not looking for the teacher or the students to fix you or say, "Of course, you're smart enough." You just want to admit it.

When you go back to take Level 3 at The Groundlings, you could say, "I am back taking Level 3, and I am terrified that I am not smart enough to take improv." We don't have to hear your life story, just your fear. You may or may not get a reaction from the students or teacher. That doesn't matter. You just need to say it to get out of your own way. I cannot tell you how freeing it is when my students get an opportunity to speak about their fears out loud. I have had people wanted to quit the class before they gave themselves permission to speak their truth. Also, usually at least one person in class will speak up and say they can relate.

DECEMBER 29TH, 2014 at 11:03PM

Q: DOES "CLEVER" IMPROV LEAD TO IRONIC DETACHMENT?

Anonymous asked: It seems that a lot of improv teachers tend to marginalize "clever" improv in relation to emotional based play, do you believe this comes from a belief that overly clever and smart improv will lead to play with ironic detachment?

That sounds right.

2015

JANUARY 10TH, 2015 at 12:09AM

RIP JASON CHIN

No, I didn't know him. I never met him. I came up in UCB NY, not Chicago or iO. But I have known for years and years that Jason Chin was a true blue improv nerd who loved improv for the right reasons and with all his being and he spread that enthusiasm around to anyone who was open to it. You couldn't miss that. in the early 2000s, the Chicago guys would talk about Jason Chin as if he were a friendly bar that everyone went to—a comfortable familiar place to hang out at where you were welcome and liked. They'd tell a story about some show they did with him. Sometimes they'd make fun of him but warmly, usually about how enthusiastically he liked so many show ideas, I think? I like that he wrote an earnest book on improv. When NYC improv harold team went to iO for a cross-theater Cagematch championship, Jason Chin is the guy who gave them a tour of the place. He was part of the landscape—you knew that from another city! I relate to him as a guy who through improv found a way to relate to himself and the whole world! When I saw yesterday that he died I was stunned and sat in my room looking around and missed him. He was so young and, god damn it is just really sad.

Came so close to not releasing this because I am suspicious of internet eulogies because they are so often self-indulgent but I believe that he would have encouraged me to do it, since it's the improvy move to say yes and publish it. Raise your glasses to the guy I never met but I feel like I knew: RIP Jason Chin, a for-real improv dude.

JANUARY 20TH, 2015 at 10:45AM

Q: I GOT WORSE AT THE THINGS I WAS "GOOD" AT?

Anonymous asked: i think I'm pretty good at some of the headier stuff in improv but I used to have really bad nerves that kept me glued to the back line. I started stepping out more to fight that and it actually worked. However it seems like I got worse at the things I thought I was

"good" at. Any tips on striking a balance between playing with reckless abandon but also making sure nothing else suffers in the process?

Congrats on getting off that back line! I think that's hard to do; you did it.

What an interesting observation that you think you're worse at what you thought you were good at.

I remember feeling that way. I think of myself as a very logical, writerly sort but really, once I started doing improv a LOT a lot, I realized that I was actually a much sillier player at heart, and not so great at the logical part. The game, and the heightening—it escapes me a lot. And on the other hand, I can command a room more than I ever assumed I'd be able to. I am not the improviser I once envisioned myself as.

Maybe something like that is happening to you? It sounds exciting. Don't get stuck trying to box yourself in. Try to just BE and figure out later what that is. Get zen about it, I think.

An analogous thought: I think TEAMS also want to be certain kinds of teams, but then have to just accept that they are a different kind of team. Maybe a team loves the patient actorly troupes, but they are a zanier bunch. Or maybe a team loves the reckless abandon of fast loud teams, but when they step out they are rule-followers. To some degree you have to just let yourself be what you are.

I'm reminded of George Saunders' "author's note" that he wrote about his short story collection "CivilWarLand In Bad Decline." The whole note is terrific, but here's the relevant part:

> When a young person first decides he wants to write, a number of mountains spring up around him, labeled with the names of his heroes.
>
> Hemingway Mountain, let's say.
>
> He heads up it, armed with his love for Hemingway.
>
> At some point, he starts to get tired. Tired of imitating. Tired of the low-ceiling feeling of trying to express his reality in someone else's voice. Tired of the way that, by trying to sound and think like someone else, he is falsifying: selling his own experience of life short, omitting things he knows are true, adding in things he knows aren't.

If he's lucky enough to realize this, he trudges back down off Hemingway Mountain and starts over again.

Ah, look: Toni Morrison Mountain. That's more like it.

Rinse, lather, repeat.

Then one day—maybe age has something to do with it, or something difficult happens that brings him to a boil—he snaps. No more imitation. That's it. Something breaks. He starts sounding … like himself. Or at least he doesn't sound like anyone else, exactly. A new mountain has appeared; he can actually see it, his name on it.

But wow, is it ever small.

It's not even really a mountain. It's like … it's like a little dung heap or something.

Okay, okay, he thinks and goes over and stands on it.

The work he does there is not the work of his masters. It is less. It is more modest; it is messier. It is small and minor.

But at least it's his.

Goddamn George Saunders is good at words, is what he is.

JANUARY 20TH, 2015 at 10:46AM

THE APPALLED TONE

When I was a student, I did plenty of bad scenes in class. But if if it was a good class, I did not feel badly about it. There was permission to screw up.

For teachers, including myself: try to run that kind of class, one where it's okay to screw up. One of the keys to this is: beware adopting an appalled tone. When you're irritated and annoyed that they are not doing it right. Unless someone is being overtly rude to you or other people—assume they're trying.

If they're doing it totally wrong, be a good enough teacher to have a decent guess why. Maybe you want very natural realism, but their last teacher was all about a BIG reaction to the FIRST thing, no matter what. Maybe you want heightening, but the last teacher enforced patience. Maybe you want them to say yes to everything, no matter what—but their last class had them trying to say "no" to things their character wouldn't do. Maybe they have decided for themselves that they need to play game, and you want them to act more.

A great antidote to this is to take a workshop. Or get notes after your show if you're not currently getting notes from anyone. Remember how unnerving it is to not be 100% sure what the teacher/coach wants. That teachers are rarely as clear as they think they are being. That you want an example. That you don't mind hard notes, as long as it's specific, but they rarely are. That you are trying and willing to do whatever you're asked, and if you don't do it—it's because you can't picture what the teacher is asking for.

Don't be dismayed when they do a scene you've seen a million times (jumping out of a plane? two guys about to do a presentation and they have not prepared? a guy trying on a tie and asking his wife how it looks?)—it's THEIR first time doing that, so let them.

Now I'M being appalled. See? It's such a trap. My favorite classes had teachers who had a good sense of when to let us go through a scene to live in our bad decisions, and when to just cut it off and let us do another.

FEBRUARY 3RD, 2015 at 1:39PM

Q: I FELT BAD STARTING OUT WITH OUR CHARACTERS HATING EACH OTHER

spacecowboyblevins asked: In improv we were always taught to start out the scene positive, and indeed it gets kind of tiring to see so many people start out with arguments. Yesterday I was in a scene and our suggestion was "nemeses in art school". I felt bad starting out with our characters hating each other, but I couldn't think of any way to start out positively without betraying the suggestion. What's a good way to still have a positive beginning with a negative suggestion?

Yeah, this is a tricky one. Here's the thing: "Positive beginning" simply means you and the other actors are on the same page. The characters can still have different points of view.

BUT it is TRUE that many beginning students simply cannot play a disagreeing character without making their character win. That's what Alex Berg calls a "wizard battle."

The key, I think, is that you have to disagree without worrying about winning. You, the actor, cannot be focused on making your character win. And you can't be distressed when your character is losing. The scene does not move forward when one person wins or loses. It moves forward when we learn more about the world.

In your example, if both art students want to win the Henry L. Stiles Grant For Distinguished Painting, you say what is so important about that award, what it stands for, what they both value, etc. It doesn't matter who actually gets it.

But it's hard for some people, many people, especially beginners, to play someone who WANTS something and not become wholly obsessed with making choices that get your character that thing.

Improv is hard. I sleepy. Drink coffee now, water too. Read something, talk to friends.

FEBRUARY 4TH, 2015 at 6:50PM

ASK JIMMY, ASK WILL: SHORT-FORM GROUP TRYING LONG-FORM

Now and then Jimmy Carrane of the great improv blog "Improv Nerd" and myself (go there to see photos of us, it looks like we are evolving into the same person) will both give answers to questions one of us has gotten at his blog. THIS IS ONE OF THOSE TIMES.

Q: What steps do you recommend for a troupe that does almost exclusively short-form/game-y improv, but is looking to add a bit of Harold

or other long-form work into their repertoire? Is there a certain form that is a natural starting point?

Jimmy: When making the transition from short form to long form, it's more import to focus on scene work, especially two-person scenes, than form. That is the foundation for most long-form: good, solid scene work. Don't ever lose sight of this. I see way too many improvisers when they are first starting out worrying about form before they have their scene work down. It is very frustrating to watch. NO form is a substitute for good scene work.

The other skill you'll need to work on besides doing good scene work will be editing. This can be a bit tricky since you are going from more structured short-form games to a more unstructured long-form piece. My suggestion is to keep it super simple at first, and I think "Montage" would be a very safe place to start before going into the Harold. Montage can be played in various ways. Most ways I am familiar with feature a series of unrelated scenes that you edit from the back line or from the sides with a sweep edit. You have the option to bring characters back, but I would not concern yourself at the beginning with trying to get to fancy. If that happens organically, by all means take advantage of it.

Once you get comfortable with "Montage" and you feel you have your scene work down and your editing is up to speed, then I would move on to the complex forms.

Will: I'm spoiled since I learned improv at a long-form theatre that already had a pretty big audience (UCB Theatre in NY). So I've never done short-form, or had to build a long-form audience.

But another UCB teacher named Brandon Gardner has thoughts on this because his alma mater's improv troupe is trying to get into more long-form. Here's the article:

http://collegeimprovadviser.tumblr.com/post/109552369613/transitioning

FEBRUARY 21ST, 2015 at 11:23PM

PHRASES FOR DESCRIBING THE GAME OF THE SCENE

You've got a funny idea. Are you able to explain it? Or maybe a scene was actually funny, thank god, but can you describe what the funny part was? You've got to do better than just saying "the part where everyone screamed" or "the way Bert did the thing."

Try these helpful phrases to accurately describe what made it funny:

WHAT IF: Title the game with a "What If"—"what if the top clique at a high school were scientists?" (via Fernie via Matt Walsh). That makes you isolate the main funny part.

INSTEAD OF: Say "instead of" to clarify: "So, a version of the show Cops but instead of domestic violence and drug deals they bust people who play sex games." This forces you to say the "normal" version which makes the "funny" part pop.

AS IF: "A guy who tries to wow his date with a fried egg as if it were caviar / champagne." This is direction for the actors/performers (even if the actors/performers are YOU); this gives an example of how to play the funny part.

That's good. Right? I mean, there's probably others but don't get nuts this is good.

FEBRUARY 24TH, 2015 at 10:00AM

EMOTIONAL PRIORITIES

Some advice worth remembering now and then: Don't get so obsessed you get unhealthy. Value real friends over status. Don't drink too much too often. Avoid toxic people and groups. Take breaks. Miss things (the show everyone says you HAVE to watch, the workshop everyone's dying to get into, even your own show) now and then so you can re-charge. If your friend is getting married during the weekend that there are auditions for house teams, skip the audition.

FEBRUARY 26TH, 2015 at 10:00AM

EXERCISE: THE "STATIONS" PATTERN GAME

This entry is aimed at people outside of LA and NYC who have bought UCB book and tried to do the pattern game and had trouble with it. Maybe even people IN LA and NYC, I don't know. It's an exercise which is a training wheels version of the pattern game. Let's call it the "stations" pattern game.

And as you can probably already tell, this entry will be the most improv-y improv entry ever. Holy shit, is this one ever nerdy. If you read this, you are in DEEP, my friend. But it'll be worth it! I've been running this exercise a lot lately and it's killing! You gotta try it!

WHAT IS THE PATTERN GAME AGAIN?

The pattern game is an opening. It's basically a ritual where a group uses word association to turn a suggestion into a bunch of ideas. You then use the ideas to start scenes. At the UCB, as championed by Matt Besser, we use this ritual to aggressively develop and pitch very full comedy ideas at the very top of our show. You've heard of "game of the scene"—in the pattern game we almost build the entire game BEFORE the scene. Whoa, right?

Perhaps you've tried to learn the pattern game, which means you've become totally confused by the pattern game. I mean, it IS crazy. A bunch of people stand like robots in a semi-circle and blurt terms at each other. It puts everyone in their heads, and there's no way to remember everything people say, and everyone's eyes glaze over and looks down at each others shoes and it's REALLY WEIRD. Right?

And to make it worse, everyone—EVERYONE—seems to do the pattern game a bit differently. Everyone likes their own way of doing it and turns their noses up at the way everyone ELSE does it.

Well, I like my way of doing it and I am looking down my nose at the way YOU do it.

Not really, but this exercise will help make the pattern game work. And once you get comfortable with it, you'll see the pattern game is a powerful tool, and if you get good at it you will be able to do something that only a small percentage of improvisers can do: realize the game of the scene as you are doing it.

You should shudder with anticipation here, because that's some major shit I just said.

THE PATTERN GAME IS WRITING

Okay, first off, give over to the idea that the pattern game is about writing. It just is. It's pitching ideas to each other. You can try to liven it up with a lot of physicality and emoting, but you're just delaying the root issue: you're writing. That's partly why this is hard. You're using a different set of mental muscles than you do for the rest of improv.

There are people who think that anything that feels like writing is cheating in improv. Don't be like that. Improv is acting AND writing. It's MORE acting, yes, but it's also writing and you should accept that.

I mean, the writerly types need to get over themselves and commit to abstract sound-and-movement stuff. And so the actorly types should get over themselves and do some thinky verbal stuff. Let's all meet in the middle and use each others powers to become a huge comedy machine.

TELL ME THE EXERCISE ALREADY

Here we go! It's a bit awkward to write out so stay with me, here.

6-8 people up. Could even be more. Whatever. Break into three groups of at least 2 people each. We're going to call those groups "stations."

STATION ONE: TERMS

Coach gives a suggestion to station 1, like "birdhouse." Someone in the group says something which "birdhouse" reminds them of, like "hummingbirds" and then everyone word associates off the last term. Words or very short phrases. "sugar diet" "atkins diet" "fooling yourself" "lies" "the dog went to a farm."

The group should try NOT to be funny. Just do terms. Rich specific ones are better than simple boring ones.

STATION TWO: PITCHING AND CONFIRMING

As station 1 does their word association, the people in station 2 are listening and trying to think of funny ideas for scenes. When someone thinks of one, they go "stop"—and station 1 stops—and then the person in station 2 says their idea to the other people in station 2.

They just say it like a human being. They say "Okay, so maybe it's a dad telling his kid about how the Atkins diet is not a real thing."

That's the pitch. Maybe that's not funny. Maybe it is. The people in station 2 shouldn't be too fussy. Be aggressive and say ideas even if you're not sure of them.

Okay, so once a pitch has been said—SOMEONE ELSE IN STATION 2 HAS TO CONFIRM IT. They have to say back what is funny about the idea. They can clarify it, but they shouldn't change it.

Something like "So it's like a birds-and-the-bees talk, but instead they're telling the truth about the Atkins diet, and that it's a sham?"

That confirmation part is important. Because a lot of people will accidentally completely change the idea. They'll say something like "So this is a world where Atkins is a huge conspiracy and you get in trouble if you're not on Atkins?" In that case, the person who pitched it would say "no, not like that." THAT'S RIGHT, IT IS OKAY IN THIS EXERCISE FOR THE PERSON WHO PITCHED THE IDEA TO SAY NO. Then someone else tries to confirm it, or that person who already tries keeps trying. Maybe the person who pitched it has to re-explain. They are talking like normal human beings here.

If the person who is confirming says something that amounts to a different idea, and the pitcher likes the new idea better—you should still stick with the original idea. For right now, being able to understand someone else's idea is more important than pitching around.

Phrases that help to clarify a game: "instead of" and "as if"—instead of birds-and-the-bees, it's about Atkins. Or it's as if the Atkins Diet was the story of Santa Claus and kids have to find out.

Once the pitch has been clarified, station 2 is done.

STATION 3: EXAMPLES AND TITLING

The people in station 3 will then give three examples of things that might be said in the scene that station 2 pitched. Either lines of dialogue that would be said at some point in the scene, or just things that might happen.

"Son, it's time to talk. Put down that bacon strip."

"Johnny, when a person loves his body very much, he stops shoveling crap into it just because of a fad diet book."

"My parents were pretty progressive. We never did the Atkins diet, they were big on telling me the truth when I was like 3. Yeah, it was intense."

Really hilarious, right? Okay, it's not great. But you can see how these examples fit the scene that was pitched. And if there was any doubt as to what this idea really was, we will now know. You'll be able to feel it: AH, yes, that's what the idea is.

After there's been 3 ideas, then someone in station 3 gives a title. The title is not really a title but a phrase that describes what the game is. This part may be redundant with something that was said in the station 2 portion, but do it anyway.

So maybe someone titles this scene "If the Atkins Diet was like the Santa Claus story."

Then the coach gives a new suggestion to station 1 and you do it again. Do it a bunch. Everyone take turns being in different stations.

What happens very quickly is people learn how to communicate their ideas to each other. And they see that even the weaker ideas can be very fun once station 3 tries to come up with examples for it. You learn how to talk to each other about games.

NEXT STEP: EVERYONE IS IN ALL STATIONS

For the next phase, everyone stands in a semi-circle and there are no stations. Anyone can do any part. But you still go through the same phase. People are saying words, then someone pitches an idea, then someone confirms, then 3 examples, a title and start over. So the same person might say a term, and then later give an example.

FINAL STEP: NO STATION 2, NO TITLING

And the last step is to skip what station 2 was doing, and you also don't bother titling it because it sounds lame.

You do terms, and then instead of pitching an idea with full words—you just give an example when you think you've got something funny. And then the group does two or three other examples until you feel like you all get it, and then you go back to doing terms.

So it'd be like…

birdhouse, hummingbird, sugar diet, atkins diet, fooling yourself, "son it's time we had a talk—you're too old to be avoiding carbs anymore."

And then you're doing something very close to the pattern game. At the very least you will have a common language for describing the games of the scene.

And as you do this more and more, try to use fewer and fewer words. Brevity is the soul of wit and all that shit.

Wait, who am I to talk about brevity? This entry is… oh my god, 1500 words. This is insane.

But wait, more!

HISTORY

I did a version of this in a class at UCB in New York, and one of the students was Shaun Diston. Then years later when I hired Shaun to be a teacher I saw him doing a stations pattern game in a practice of his I was observing. I was like "hey, I love that exercise" and he said "I got that from your class!" But he had improved it greatly. Then I took the way he was doing it and tweaked it again to the version I described above. I'm sure Shaun has tweaked his and it's probably better than mine again. What I'm saying is that Shaun and I are at war.

Ok, that's it! If you have read the UCB book and are interesting in learning the mad ritual that is the pattern game I recommend this training wheels version! Also if you want a way to practice naming the game of the scene!

Whew.

MARCH 3RD, 2015 at 7:16AM

Avoid doing things just because you think you SHOULD do them. Sometimes you NEED to break the rules, just to remind them who's boss. You are a co-writer and co-director at all times during an improv scene and you should speak your mind. Yes, it's good form to take endowments as gifts ("you always said you loved this place"), but not at the expense of YOU not being in the scene ("I have said that but I'm realizing this is a terrible place.") The key here is to agree with facts, but make up your own mind in regard to opinions. Listen, commit and then filter everything through you. Put a lot of yourself into every character you play so it's easier to do.

I'm talking about improv. Don't, like, steal stuff.

MARCH 10TH, 2015 at 2:08AM

A NIGHT I REMEMBER FROM MY LEVEL 1 PRACTICE GROUP

Frankie from my level 1 improv class at UCB was the first person to get me stoned. I was 29 years old and when he, 20, found out I'd never smoked pot he became obsessed. "I'm gonna smoke you up, man. Oh man, it's gonna be great!" People who love pot love introducing other people to pot.

So one night after our improv practice group met, Frankie and I stood in the same office where I made my living programming computers and smoked pot. Then we all walked over to the Bull Moose Tavern on 44th street.

Frankie, Brett and Josh asked me every three minutes how I felt. I felt not that different.

"Does this do anything?" asked Josh, shoving his face close to mine and then yanking it away. "How about THIS?" waving his hands an inch away from my eyes. "THIS?" He got up from our table and did a small Irish dance. It kind of was weird, but not that much.

Brett shut him down. "None of that has anything to do with being high. (pause) But THIS does—" and then Brett freestyle rapped a bit.

Then I remember Frankie interrupting: "You know what the best invention is of the 20th century? Sandwiches."

"They're from before the 20th century Frankie, " I said.

And he said "Well, whenever. They're amazing. Everyone loves them. Literally everyone loves sandwiches. It has something for everyone!"

If a wizard appeared at that moment and said "You know, you're gonna be doing improv for the next 16 years" I would have said "good."

MARCH 17TH, 2015 at 10:00AM

"RELATIONSHIP" AND "GAME"

So what about the words "relationship" and "game?" They are both what I think of as magic words, meaning they have a disproportionate and powerful effect on people studying improv.

If I were to ask "what's your RELATIONSHIP?" to two students after a scene—all I'm asking for is for them to confirm the general who/what/where. Yet, when they do their next scene, with the word "relationship" in their heads, so much gets better. They listen more deeply, play more realistically, focus on each other rather than the past, future or pop culture. For young students with little to no acting experience, saying the word "relationship", almost without any context, seems to turn them into better actors.

Similarly, if I say "What was the GAME of that scene?, what I'm asking on the surface is "what was the funny part to you?" Yet, when the students who were asked about game do their next scene—with the word "game" floating between their ears—everything changes. They are more aggressive, their patterns pop, they repeat things earlier and more often, they are more ironic and yes, they are funnier.

I can barely take any credit as a teacher. Those words carry some magic aura that communicates far more than the actual meaning of the words.

Making it one versus the other seems to miss the point. And if you tell a teacher who is currently running a workshop on game that you "prefer to play the relationship" you are just asking for a fight, whether you know it or not.

MARCH 19TH, 2015 at 7:30PM

Q: WHY ARE THERE LESS WOMEN ON HAROLD TEAMS THAN MEN?

Anonymous asked: Why are there less woman on Harold Teams than men? My classes seem pretty even, gender wise. Is there an unconscious bias that favors men? How can I address this issue without sounding like a jerk? Do I have to be pretty to get on a Harold or Maude Team? I see a lot of scrubby older guys and younger cute girls. Is my thinking fixed and somewhat paranoid? Possibly!

FULL DISCLOSURE RIGHT AT THE TOP: I is a white dude from New England whose family had enough cash to send him to college. Got it? Okay.

EDITED TO ADD: The most interesting answer would come from getting all female performers from the UCB in a room—no men allowed—and ask them. That would be interesting. I would want to hear the answer.

Okay, onto this long ramble.

WORTH TALKING ABOUT

"Women vs. men" stuff is always interesting, though also always fraught with personal bias, anecdotal evidence and kneejerk reactions. That doesn't mean it shouldn't be talked about. It should be discussed without apology. But if you want to have a productive discussion that will change things, it is best approached in a calm, non-scolding manner. I like the tone of your question, for example. It feels curious and honest without being accusatory—which is the most helpful posture.

The way to talk about it without sounding like a jerk is to just take a breath and do it as honestly as you can. And be cool when people get a bit huffy. People get huffy. Just stay cool and nod your head that you understand and hope that your calmness calms them down.

Try to have empathy that no one gets up in the morning and says "Today I will be biased." Artists like good art, and the people who put house teams together want good teams above all. That is for real true. But bias does happen anyway! It's mysterious how it happens.

Honesty, empathy, patience and experimentation are the answer, somehow.

WARNING: STATISTICS AHEAD
In December of 2011, while I was running the school at UCB in NYC I was talking with then Artistic Director Nate Dern about male-female ratios. He asked what the ratios were in the classes, and I was stunned to realize I had no idea.

So, Erik Tanouye and I started looking at male-female ratios in the classes. It was tough because we hadn't been recording people's gender. So I had an intern go over 6 months worth of improv classes (first 6 months of 2011) and GUESS the gender of the students based on name. I know. Not a great system. I also got some teachers to indicate some of the names we weren't sure about. Some teachers didn't want to do it, others were just disorganized and never got around to it. Hardly an exact science, but it was a start. We got numbers on about 2000 registrations.

What we found in was that for that 6 month period—the male/female ratio was about 1 man for every 1 woman in level 1, and it steadily became more men until it was about 1.3 men for every 1 woman in level 4. Not even as bad as I had feared.

BUT: You had to be approved to get to level 5. And what we found was that in level 5 the ratio was *2.2 MEN FOR EVERY ONE WOMAN in the advanced level*. More than two to one!

WHOA. I was stunned. Were we approving men at a higher rate than women? We checked that—and no. We were approving just about the same percentage of men as we were women. There were slightly more men than women to pick from, but there was no reason that we shouldn't at least have the same ratio in level 5 as we did in level 4.

Women were just way less interested in level 5 than the men. I had no idea why.

I also looked for the first time at the gender ratios of the teachers and discovered to my horror that in two years I had only ever assigned one female teacher to teach the level two classes—44 of the 47 level 2 sessions had been taught by men. What disturbed me was I didn't even realize that. It wasn't a conscious decision. But it had happened! Weird.

I reported this all to the teachers, and everyone immediately had guesses as to why all this was. But they were just guesses.

COLBY INITIATIVE

So we started something called the Colby Initiative (named by Shannon O'Neill after the Amy Poehler character on the UCB Show). Our mission: increase the number of women in level 5 improv classes. More informally: would Amy Poehler have taken level 5 at our school?

I liked it because it was specific and measurable.

We threw a lot of things against the wall: Shannon started the Lady Jam and started teaching free workshops for female improvisers. We told the level 4 teachers to specifically recommend level 5 for the strong female improvisers. I promoted more female teachers into higher levels, gave more classes to existing female teachers, and hired female teachers first.

We all had different opinions on which of these things mattered. But rather than argue about it, we tried whatever we could. Find it on its feet, like good improvisers do.

People who worked on the Colby Initiative got a little money for their time and we got teachers working on it in their spare time. Chelsea Clarke led a group of teachers in calling female students who were given the highest rating from their level 4 teachers but who never took another class. Chelsea and others called them and basically asked "why did you never take another class?"

(They didn't ask that directly. They just took a general survey of their experience at the school. We didn't say "we are trying to figure out why women are less interested in level 5." But in the general survey we asked why they had started taking classes, and if they planned on taking more.)

WHY DID YOU STOP TAKING CLASSES?

I wish I could give you a hard answer here. But we're not experts in data analysis or methodology. And there was no one single overpowering answer. These people in general had really good things to say about their experience at UCB, but they also said they felt they were done. Common things said: classes were too expensive, the good teachers' classes sold out too frustratingly fast and that they had gotten what they wanted out of UCB classes and were trying other things.

What we suspected—and it was just a suspicion—was that they didn't think they had enough of a chance to get on a UCB house team to make it worth the time/money/trouble of taking more classes unless it was a great teacher.

Maybe it was just a vicious cycle: more men on the stage makes the men in the classes try harder makes for more men on stage? That is just a guess.

I will say that one year later the ratio of men to women had evened a bit to be 1.5 men for every woman. Better, at least. Moving in the right direction.

What I was most happy about was that we tried stuff. You can theorize all day (and post rants, and re-tumblr things that make you and others outraged), but in the end the only way to really learn anything is to try it. There was also no finger-pointing within the ranks. It wasn't like "you did X wrong" and instead it was like "what if we tried X?" Our years of performing together gave us respect for each other, and we focused on results rather than arguing.

LIKE BEGETS LIKE

My personal feeling is that LIKE BEGETS LIKE. If you want more women in the classes, get more talented women on stage. People take classes if they identify with the people on stage. Gender and race are powerful factors when people relate to each other.

Though of course they're not the only ones. Comedy nerds like other comedy nerds regardless of gender or race, of course.

But it comes down to this: If you feel like you belong on the stage, you'll take the classes and stick with it.

I think that demographics and diversity is something worth worrying about and trying to consciously improve. I also think that you have to be sensitive to the fact that communities form organically and that you CAN'T really meddle beyond a certain degree. You can nudge and push but there has to be a natural momentum which you are accelerating. You try stuff and then try to figure: is that working? It's like an improv scene—you know it when you feel it if it's working.

As far as your question about wondering if you have to be pretty to get on a team: I think there IS a bias towards attractive people but I think it's there for both men and women. Especially if you look at percentages. There is a much higher percentage of attractive male improvisers on the stage than in the community in general! That's just my impression. I see attractive men and women doing better than their less attractive counterparts in ALL AREAS OF LIFE UGH.

POSTSCRIPT: added April 23, 2015. I've gotten a few messages asking why we didn't devote the same energy to other diversity issues, like for example black improvisers, gay improvisers. Two part answer. Part One: we do have the diversity program which has scholarships and workshops and jams and stuff. So we were/are worrying about that. But I recognize that doesn't seem like the same level of intensity as the Colby initiative. That's because of Part Two: note that we had fifty-fifty male/female in level one and LOST the women after level four. Trying to hold onto a group of people who started but left seemed like something that was CLOSE. Like a solvable doable thing. So we bore down on it. Figuring maybe we could learn something about the weird world of trying to change demographics in the process. Also, we're idiots who are just trying stuff as we go.

MARCH 20TH, 2015 at 9:47AM

Q: JUSTCRAIG: PLOPPING DOWN A PILE OF PAPERS OR SAYING "JOHNSON FILES?"

justcraig asked: In improv, what's better improv, plopping down a pile of paper (using object work) and calling them "the quarterly reports" or calling them "the Johnson files?"

Another great question.

MARCH 24TH, 2015 at 10:00AM

WOULD YOU RATHER

A fun game: When we were all on 1985 together, Charlie went through a phase of playing "would you rather" games, but with only horrible options.

This would be at McManus after Harold Night usually.

Charlie would think for a second and offer "Would you rather that you have a stream of jelly donut filling ooze out of your rectum FOREVER ... OR that you have to roll everywhere."

"Charlie, do you mean you couldn't walk at all? You roll on the ground instead?"

"Yes."

"Could you take a car?"

"Hmmm. Yes, but when you got out you'd have to roll."

"Does the jelly donut filling hurt?"

"No, but you have to clean it up."

"Can you eat it?"

"Yes, and it tastes good but you get full."

And everyone would vote.

Another good one: would you rather only be able to speak in a shriek or, whenever you have a sexual thought a tiny man in a tuxedo would come in and say 'ta-da' and you would have to explain what that meant?

MARCH 31ST, 2015 at 11:07AM

Q: WHAT ABOUT PEOPLE WHO SAY "GENDER/RACE SHOULDN'T EVEN BE THOUGHT ABOUT?"

Anonymous asked: what do you say when people go "gender (or race) shouldn't even be thought about. it should just be about whoever is the best/funniest!" how do you explain that it's basically impossible for things to not be influenced by gender/race? that it's something

we have to consciously account for? it can be very hard to convince these people. thanks for the great post.

I don't try to convince them. People who make statements like that, especially on line, aren't looking for a discussion. They're looking to be proven right. I worry about areas I have authority over (even if the only such area is just my own performing) rather than convincing people who aren't even listening to me.

FLATTENING

If I DID believe the person was listening to me, here's my argument against that statement. The problem with "it should be about whoever is funniest" is that it FLATTENS the situation. It implies that being mindful of diversity is mutually exclusive with picking the best people.

If you had to pick someone for an improv team, and you could only pick either Will Ferrell (straight white comedy genius) or an untalented not-funny person who happened to be a black Asian jewish transgender deaf woman. And a diversity directive made you pick the latter case, that would be a bad choice. You should have picked Will Ferrell.

UNDENIABLE...

But that never happens.

In my experience, when it comes time to pick people for an artistic job, there are always a few candidates who are UNDENIABLE. That's a term I'd like us to remember. UNDENIABLE. The people who are UNDENIABLE—meaning they are pretty universally regarded as great and perfect for the job—well, they should get picked.

Spoiler: the undeniables pretty much DO get picked. If they're white, black, male, female, whatever. They get a shot, often more than one.

I remember an interview with Fran Lebowitz about bias in America and she put racial progress in a hilariously cynical perspective by saying something like "Yeah, we are now doing okay with the black geniuses. Good for us."

(This is why, by the way, that the best way to beat unfairness in an artistic system is simply to be undeniably great. It transcends bias.)

...AND THE PROMISING

The other thing that some people may not realize, is that there are almost always spots left over after you pick the undeniable people. I think people don't like to admit this. But it's true.

Maybe you'll like it better if I put it like this: People get hired for creative jobs who are less than undeniably great. All the time. Every writer's room. Every cast. Every set of directors.

Because after the undeniables, you go to the ones who are PROMISING. They are talented, good, but they have some drawback. Maybe it's that they're not consistent. Or they don't have the range you'd like. Or they don't have as much experience. There may be something about their personality that seems worrisome. Or their work ethic seems shaky. Maybe they're just weird. Something.

But they're good. Among them are the future undeniables who just need a break.

So you do some internal gut check and pick who you think is best.

That's where it happens. That's where bias sneaks up on you. You will unconsciously forgive things in people you identify with when you're picking the people who are merely promising.

This is bigger than gender and race, though gender and race are two hugely powerful factors. Whoever you identify with, that's who you'll make a case for.

ONLY GOOD PEOPLE ON THE LIST

I used to hire the teachers for the improv/sketch classes for UCB in New York City. Often, there would be a very small number of people who I'd consider undeniably ready for the job. Them I'd hire.

Then I'd need a couple more. Because the undeniables were often busy doing a million other things. Or I'd just need more.

So I'd make a list of likely contenders. I'd rank them in a few admittedly subjective categories. I think it was experience, credibility, force of personality, technical knowledge/articulation and work ethic—all of which I was basically guessing at. I'd run the list by Director of Student Affairs Erik Tanouye: was I mis-rating someone in an obvious way? Anyone I'm forgetting? Then I'd also ask the other teachers and the senior students for their recommendations.

Nobody bad got on this list. They weren't undeniable, but they were really good. They were promising.

GUT CHECK AND ADJUSTMENT

And then I would do this—and this is where the hypothetical arguers would get upset—if I didn't have strong feelings, I'd bump up the people who were in demographic categories: women, non-white, non-straight. I'd hire the highest-ranked promising woman or non-white person before the other promising straight white dudes ranked slightly ahead of her.

But that's different than not hiring Will Ferrell. I would already have hired him. That's taking people who are all good, whom all have something to learn, whom I really don't know for sure who is the "right" choice, and making adjustment for some internal bias of myself and the system.

LIKE BEGETS LIKE

If there's all men on your improv stage, then few women will take classes. And the law of averages will make it so that you have way more promising men than women. So you need to make an adjustment—after you hire the undeniables which you definitely will—to plant seeds for the future.

No one means for bias to happen. But it does. So you have to consciously break that cycle. It's worth it. And it's possible to do without sacrificing any quality.

GIVE ME AN EXAMPLE

Another interesting but probably useless way to respond to "it should just be about who's the best" is to say "give me an example of when someone was given a job just because they were a certain demographic category."

This will not help you convince that person. Because they definitely will have a great example. Confirmation bias means we hold onto and over-emphasize the examples which prove our own point. So the person will undoubtedly have an example which completely suits their point.

But you ask them for an example so that YOU can learn. The example will reveal exactly what is rankling this person. They picked an example because it supports their case. They're giving it disproportionate importance in their brain. So you can work backwards: what is it that pissed this person off to make them blame an entire gender for something?

And that one case has made them FLATTEN the whole of human existence so that they can be right about their one case.

Humans are dumb. Do not try and reason with them. But you can figure them out for your own sake.

SMUGNESS

One more thing! I don't like the internet's tendency to make everyone sound righteous and smug, especially in the area of bias. People get really upset and then start stridently posting things that back up the view they have. I don't see the point. You're mobilizing your base, I suppose, but only your choir will listen to you preach.

Maybe what I wish is for everyone to think about what they DO have power over and to do something about that? I get upset about the alpha jerk-ness of many stand-up comedians I see on late night TV, for example, but I don't pick those people. But I did pick improv teachers. So I did something. And I do pick people to do indie shows with. I do something with that. And what tweets to retweet. I do something with that. And who to talk to and work with. Who to praise, who to pay attention to, who to welcome.

I don't care for preaching. I do care for doing things differently in the real world where we all walk around with our meat bodies provoking feelings in each other.

APRIL 1ST, 2015 at 5:30PM

ASK JIMMY/ASK WILL: AM I FUNNY ENOUGH?

When you get to be an improv teacher who has been around for a while, you get flooded with questions from improvisers all around the country. Recently, I got a question from an improviser and I decided to answer it and ask my friend and well-known improv teacher Jimmy Carrane, to give his take on it, as well. (By the way, check out Jimmy's blog at http://jimmycarrane.com/blog/)

If you have a question for either of us, please let us know!

Q: I've recently become interested in doing improv, but my issue is that I'm not the funniest person, nor am I super quick on my feet. I know that when my friends and I joke around with each other and go into all these scenarios I'm the straight man because I can't think of things quick enough to say to keep up with them. This scares me because I know improv is about reacting so you can move things along, and I wouldn't want to hold my group/partner back because I can't react well/quickly.

Will Hines: Hmm. The short answer is that you should just try improv and see if it feels good. Like, don't worry about how you are it if you're never even tried it. A longer thought: Your question also reminds me of something I hear people who have not done improv say when they talk about improv: "How do they come up with all those things to say?" They seem to imagine that improv is about being the fastest, wittiest person. It implies that everyone in a scene is racing against each other to win.

A surprising thing about improv is that you don't really HAVE to be the WITTIEST person to do it. You do have to be quick on your feet, but not impossibly so. You have to listen and be able to be truthful and be able to pretend to have opinions that you don't really have in a realistic way. But there are very few times when the pressure comes down to come up with something amazing FAST. It happens, but not on a regular basis. Given a choice between a witty person, and a person who listens and understands deeply—I'd take the second kind of person every time.

Jimmy Carrane: I love that you don't think you are the funniest person and not quick on your feet. Actually, this is an asset, not to mention the fact that you are very comfortable being the straight man. I hate to tell you this, but you are built to improvise. Here's why.

Some people start taking classes in improv because they were the funniest person at their fraternity or at their office and someone said to them they should take an improv class. The funniest person usually ends up relying on their wit and cleverness and ends up cheating themselves out of an improv education. They are scared to be real because they are afraid that being real isn't funny, and they think improv is all about being funny. As long as they are getting the laughs they are fine. Nobody is going to tell them what to do. They start out strong and then fade quickly. Oh, sure, it may work for them for a while and then people who they started out in class with them pass them by, because they are learning what improv is really about it—building a scene and listening and agreeing.

Now the funniest person from the frat or the office has hit a wall and they are either going to go over the wall and become a serious student of improv or they will quit. My experience is that 90 percent of them quit.* (*Totally made up statistic.) By admitting that you aren't that quick or funny, which I question, you have just saved yourself at least two years. The other thing that is important is that one of the skills we teach people in improv is to think on your feet. If you listen and respond to the last thing that was said by your partner, you will be naturally quicker. You still may not be able to come up with zingers or one-liners, but you will be quicker in being able to respond, trust me.

One more thing: It's been my experience that some of the best improvisers are not always the funniest people in the room, but rather the most serious people. And sometimes the funniest people in the room can be lousy improvisers. So, for God's sake, please take an improv class. My guess is that you will be pretty damn good at it.

APRIL 6TH, 2015 at 11:01PM

IMPROVISING IN OFFICES AFTER WORK

For the first year I did improv, a practice group would meet in my office after everyone else went home. 3 to 12 people just... do improv. No audience. Sometimes no coach. Just the weirdly quiet and awkward sounds of a small group who did not know what they were doing trying to practice making funny things up with no real way to gauge how we were doing at it.

There's a unique intimacy that you feel with people you practice with. It's very vulnerable to be on stage in front of an audience, but it's somehow even more strange to stand in the middle of a vacated office at night with 5 of your not-yet-friends watching you clumsily pretend to be traffic cop or the King of England or whatever while you're still wearing your work clothes.

APRIL 14TH, 2015 at 9:32AM

"THEMES" PATTERN GAME

This is an alternate to the "stations" pattern game exercise. Instead of trying to come up with clear premises for scenes, this exercise has you riff on themes and pieces of dialogue and scene painting specifics which you would use in the harold. It's an actor's opening instead of a writer's. You don't ever come back to the suggestion unless it happens organically. You don't worry about how you're going to convert things into funny premises.

(No one calls them "stations" or "themes." I'm just using those terms to describe different ways to approach the pattern game.)

OBVIOUS DISCLAIMER: This is another way-insidery super-long improv post. Normal humans, avert your eyes.

EVOLUTION OF PATTERN GAME

The pattern game has been through an interesting evolution at UCB. When I was a student circa 2000, the pattern game was a vague and difficult ritual. You would A-to-C away from the suggestion onto some number of ideas, and then return to the suggestion three times. It would go all over the place. When you started scenes you would do some intense mental gymnastics to try remember anything at all and then bend it into an initiation.

Sometime in the mid-2000s, the top teachers started teaching workshops where they advocated using the pattern game to aggressively pitch ideas to each other. A common quote was "pretend that Lorne Michaels gives you three minutes to come up with ideas to pitch to Saturday Night Live, how would you use that three minutes?"

With this focus, the pattern game suddenly became overtly useful. We all started pitching sketch ideas instead of riffing on abstract notions. It was still difficult, but it had clear goals. Overall, things were better.

However, something was lost. While doing it, you reflexively reduced everything to a simple sketch idea immediately, instead of letting it get mixed up with other ideas and coming back in surprising ways. The new way discouraged contributing ideas just because they were interesting or atmospheric or emotionally true. People started basically just having conversations while standing in a circle, speaking so casually that they seemed completely detached from the moment. Yes, we got more pointed and clear. But our acting got worse.

I do like the clarity of the current "pitch strong premises" pattern game at UCB. But I also think we can work in some actorly theme-riffing.

OKAY SO WHAT IS THIS EXERCISE ALREADY?
Right, okay.

OVERALL DESCRIPTION
5-12 people up in a semi circle. You get a suggestion. You start doing word association off that suggestion. When you get onto something interesting, you all stay on that a bit, riffing ideas around that concept. You try to have lots of short patterns and repetitions—sometimes it'll be funny, sometimes not.

You don't worry about going back to the suggestion unless that happens naturally. Yeah, you should kinda keep the suggestion in mind as a backdrop to everything you say, but don't worry too much about it.

The word association should have the feel of going from general to riffing around a specific idea, and then resetting to a general thing again.

As you go, you *call things back frequently and aggressively*. If there's a riff where everyone is talking like snobby fashionistas declaring that "oh this is SO 1990s" and then later people are riffing on people coming into Ellis Island, you might say "Darling you are SO 1810s." Don't worry about figuring out how this adds up to a scene, just riff, call back and go.

You build to what feels like an ending. The ending will have higher energy, faster pace and more callbacks.

The whole thing should take 3-4 minutes.

TIPS

Be actors, not writers. Get emotive. Be expressive. Do not ever say anything like you're pitching an idea. Be actors who are summoning ideas and characters. Instead of saying "maybe a principal who's scared of all his students?" you would say, in a principal-ish voice: "I'm too scared to give you a detention."

You don't have to only go off the last term. Go off of anything that was said somewhat recently. If you were all riffing on a circus thing, and then someone tries to A-C away to "permission slips" but you still want to say a circus thing, say a circus thing.

Get a flow going. Go fast. No long pauses between terms. You can backtrack or race ahead. The good stuff will get riffed on and will stick in your head, and the rest you can and will forget about.

Lots of patterns and repetition. If someone says "Get it together KEVIN" then the next person might go "Clean up your room KEVIN" and then the next might say "Get into a fulfilling relationship KEVIN." There should be lots of little patterns that heighten like that in a nice easy way.

Go for themes. Be grand and poetic. If someone says "icicle" you might follow it up with "mortality."

And yeah, go for funny. If something makes you laugh, do more of it. If someone does the voice of the serial killer Buffalo Bill in Silence of the Lambs ordering a cheeseburger, and that makes you laugh then by all means do a Buffalo Bill voice saying something similarly mundane.

Patterns, patterns.

Snippets of dialogue. You never have a conversation, but you can say things that characters who are associated with whatever topic you're on might say. Generally, you don't ever do two people talking to each other—just single, out-of-context snippets. Brief is better than long.

Rich specifics. Mixed in with dialogue you describe objects and people inspired by whatever topic you're on. If someone says "Cruise ship" you can have a quick string of things like "buffets" and "swimming pools" and "largest floating library" to flesh things out. Brief is better.

PROS AND CONS

Compared to the "stations" pattern game, this is much less structured. It's hard to measure if you're doing it RIGHT or not. You don't necessarily know what the focus of your scenes are going to be.

But it's easier to just flow and go. You are warming up your ability to entertain each other with short patterns and riffs, and your ability to remember and callback each other's stuff. You should be warming up yourselves as actors and theater people. It's less bossy and directed.

Ideally—I think a group would do this version, but now and then do a quick round of pitching hard on an idea within it. Like sometimes you'd be pitching an idea, and other times you'd just be riffing on something abstract like "Americana."

Okay. Yeah. Anyone still reading? Sheesh, right?

EXAMPLES

I don't have any full examples. I just coached a group so here's my rough memory of how one went.

> Suggestion was "redecoration"
>
> A few specific things of a redecorated room "couch moves" and "new lamp" and "feng shui"
>
> Then dialogue of people complimenting a room, including a bunch of "oh it's SO (a year)"
>
> Then to wanting a houseboat, to being on a cruise, and then things on a cruise (buffets, singers, pools) and people indulging themselves on too much food, too much drink
>
> to someone drowning, and things you might shout to someone drowning "We'll come around" "we'll come back"
>
> swimming to ellis island
>
> Then people changing their name to be more catchy, and examples of catchy names
>
> Then people trying to get into a club
>
> Then bounces at ellis island, saying bouncer-y things to immigrants
>
> Then the "oh you're SO 1890" etc
>
> Then riffs on some other things for a while, including thanksgiving, with people indulging themselves on too much food, too much drink.

Like that. Does that help? Of course not. I'll try to write one down later, maybe, and type it out.

This is the end of this post.

APRIL 14TH, 2015 at 9:44AM

Q: I'M SELF-CONSCIOUS BEING OLDER THAN EVERYONE ELSE.

Anonymous asked: Dear Improv Nonsense, i am about to start the third level of an improv program and am excited to do so. I can't help thinking how young everyone else in in the improv scene is. I am feeling very self conscious at 36 just starting out. Am I too old? What would you say is the typical timeline career of an improviser? I know this could be viewed as a facetious query, but in your experience have there been others that have started this late? thanks in advance! Auld in Improv Years

Oh my friend, I feel you on this one. I took my first improv class at 29 and felt as old as a tree compared to everyone at the UCBT (who all seemed to be in their early 20s), and so I'm sure you're feeling the same way perhaps more intensely. Since I've started improv, I've consistently been about 10 years older than all of my peers, and it's always felt weird.

Another wrinkle (pun intended?): I won't shut up about being older than everyone. I feel like I bring it up every day. Being older than most people in the room feels like wearing a t-shirt to a wedding: you keep wanting to apologize to everyone for having broken some protocol. And everyone else just wants you to not worry about it and enjoy the wedding. But there you are, hiding from the cameras, trying to explain to the bride and groom that you are not weird, you just mis-read the invitation.

A funny thing and I'm sure every single human being observes this—is when someone much younger than you complains about feeling old. Like when 24 year olds complain about it. Although even as I type that I can relate to that feeling too. Being 24 is the first time you're no longer "college aged." You see people your age—especially in the entertainment field but really in all fields—who have surpassed you so finally. In your late 20s you're no longer a kid. Early 30s is so definitely not "young." Late 30s is when you realize that most of pop culture has stopped paying any attention to you. Early 40s you're a punch line in so many jokes. And it just keeps going.

Have I depressed you yet?

The perspective I have to offer is this: while everyone is constantly obsessing about how old THEY are, most people don't give a shit how old someone ELSE is. I have been trying over the last year to stop mentioning all the time how old I feel because no one gives a shit. Yes, the overall culture of our society seems to look down on being older, but day-to-day, person-to-person, no one cares. If you can get over it, no one else will even notice it. Occasionally some bitchy / judgmental person will make a crack. But that's rare, and of course those people are being much harder on themselves than on you.

I'm ten years older than you. Right now I'm wishing you were older so I could make a *War Games* reference and know that you'd get it.

So: I hear you, big time, but you and I both have to just get over it and move on.

APRIL 22ND, 2015 at 12:08PM

WHAT MADE THE UCBT WORK?

So many people start improv theaters, schools, workshops. One of those people was a 4-person group from Chicago called the Upright Citizens Brigade who started their theater in NYC circa 1998 (pending how you decide when they officially started). Their theatre worked, but like REALLY worked. Holy jeebs it worked. So why?

There's better people than me to answer, but I'm gonna take a fast shot at it anyway. In a perfect world, this provokes better people than me to answer this.

Great people on the stage. Like, amazing people. The UCB4 doing improv, Andy Richter and Tina Fey sitting in. During the week it was Swarm, Respecto, Mother and Feature Feature. This is the gold that backs the currency of the theatre community: great people up on that stage. There's still great people now. Sheesh.

Creative people at the top. The owners are comedians, and really great ones.

Community. Lots of cheap shows. And students see shows for free. And even if you're not a student they're just five bucks so don't be weird about it, just go and see shows. After one class you're aware of a whole city of people that you could be a part of.

Be funny. Very early in classes it was "why do you think that scene was funny?" and "what is the game? Is that funny?" Funny was not a dirty word. Funny was overtly valued. Funny let you skip the line.

Throw you right in. You do scenes on day 1. Also a limited nostalgia for the past. We didn't talk about Chicago that much; we talked about shows we saw THAT WEEK.

Good teachers. The UCB4 themselves and that first batch of teachers were goddamn good. They were performers, they taught without ego, they knew what they were talking about. Practical advice, not empty theatrical artsy fartsy lectures. No coddling, move fast.

Find it on its feet. Just put it up. Don't be precious. Break rules, because maybe the rules have changed. Change it, do it again. Let's see it. In class, in indie shows, in spanks. More reps, more reps, more reps.

Word of mouth and personal referrals. People telling people who is good. Funny people get talked about; they get to do more faster. A lot of the right people—meaning the best people—got moved up fast.

Notes. But no matter how good you were, you got notes and were expected to take them. Almost every show, every class, every practice: someone more senior than you watched and gave you notes.

Weirdos. Good ones.

Give keys to everyone. Or it felt like it, anyway. If you were good, you were a coach pretty quickly and then a teacher. Or you were a tech, or you directed. You were asked for your opinion. You were given authority and you got invested. The theatre was partly YOURS very early.

The iO Theatre. Having a great theatre to learn from, in terms of its culture. Harold Night. Coaches. Not too many levels. Del Del Del Del Del.

Competition. Teeth. Meanness. People get cut. Shows get ended. Cagematch means improv is ACTUALLY a popularity contest. And rather than complain about that, just be good and WIN. Everyone. EVERYONE! WIIIIIIINNNNN.

Somewhere in there.

APRIL 27TH, 2015 at 1:29PM

PING PONG TABLE METAPHOR

A metaphor for playing it real.

Okay, so think about an improv scene like a ping pong table. In ping pong, you are required to hit the table on each volley. If you don't, you lose a point. You ALSO generally want to hit the ball as fast as you can so it's hard to return. But you can't hit it so hard that it doesn't come down and bounce off the table.

In a scene, you want interesting, fun, even crazy things to happen. You want to "say yes" to the thing that might not happen on a regular day. But you still have to hit the table on every move.

"Not hitting the table" means not playing it real, which means you're doing something that feels false and weird and forced.

EXAMPLES TAKE SO LONG TO EXPLAIN BUT HERE'S ONE ANYWAY

So let's say you're a cop and you've pulled someone over for a speeding ticket, and the person asks you to get in the car for a ride.

If you just say "Sure!" with no justification and no regard for how weird that question is—then you didn't hit the table. Sure, you "said yes" but you just hit it back as hard as you could and it seems false and weird.

Better to do one of these:

You just say "no, sir, I'm not getting into your car."—that is realistic. That's hitting the table. Younger students may feel like this is wrong—but think of it instead as just a slow return. It's okay and even essential for your characters to say "no" without guilt. If it turns out you need to get in that car, you can change your mind a bit later in the scene. But for now: you preserved the integrity of the scene. You hit the table, so the volley can continue.

Another option: maybe you're quick enough that you can say yes and you also provide a reason why. You say "Well, I don't normally do this, but I'm really mad at my boss." or "I guess this is my one chance to ride in a Lamborghini." You hit the table and you gave a very fast return.

OR—maybe you're a good enough actor that you can say yes with a sense of gravity and mischief. Without even explaining it, the audience can feel that your policeman has made some internal decision. The driver says "Wanna get in?" and the policeman takes a beat, lets the question soak in, looks over his shoulder to see if anyone is watching, then says "Yes." I would count THAT as hitting the table too.

I see newer improvisers who say no to everything in order to keep it real, and they don't seem to develop the skills necessary to "hit it back faster" (make fun stuff happen). And I see people who make fun stuff happen with no regard for reality.

My point here is that ideally you have to hit the table pretty much every time, and also have the skills to—not everytime, but at opportune times—hit the ball fast. When in doubt, hit the table. But also look for ways to hit it back with some speed.

That works, right? This is a good one!

APRIL 30TH, 2015 at 12:03AM

Q: ADVICE FOR SOMEONE GOING INTO COLLEGE WHO WANTS TO PURSUE COMEDY?

Anonymous asked: Any advice for someone going into college that wants to pursue comedy as a career?

Be a healthy person, make stuff and make friends. And know that you've gotta get to NYC, Chicago or LA at some point.

Advice I would give my own freshman in college self: You are good enough to do comedy by a whole lot so don't worry. Get real new agey about happiness and shit: be healthy (physically and emotionally), get to know yourself, practice being nice to yourself and your friends. As far as comedy stuff: Practice finishing things—don't worry about being awesome just do stuff. Don't wait 20 years to discover: The Smiths, Twin Peaks, Janis Joplin, Nichols and May.

MAY 11TH, 2015 at 11:30AM

FIRST IMPROV CLASSES

First improv classes can be fearful things, in which you are painfully aware of every line you say because you have done so little and each of those lines is therefore such a high percentage of your Complete Career In Comedy. Every new class, you are waiting until you get a chance to say something even remotely funny—which means other people in your class and hopefully your teacher laugh—so that you can be reassured that you haven't made a horribly wrong assessment of your own talents. Once you get that first laugh, a veil of nervousness lifts and you start hearing your teacher for the first time.

Teachers tell you to not worry about being funny, but that is all you worry about.

MAY 20TH, 2015 at 2:04AM

Q: WHAT DOES IT MEAN FOR YOUR CHARACTER TO HAVE A PHILOSOPHY?

Anonymous asked: What does it mean for your character to have a philosophy? At what point in the scene does this happen? Do you enter a scene with one? How does this idea intersect with game?

Usually "philosophy" means "point of view" means "have an opinion about the current situation" because a good philosophy/point of view means you can apply it to many things and maybe this will become a game.

OR even if your philosophy doesn't become a game, then it'll mean at least that your character is a more full person, and you're not just doing things to do them.

Philosophy often becomes a game, but even if not, it usually means you're acting better.

Philosophy and justification and "give a good why" and are just different ways of saying "be in the scene. be in it and react like some combination of YOU and the CHARACTER would."

It's late and I saw Mad Max today, so pretend that I wrote this while playing an electric guitar on the back of a truck to inspire my tribe's troops.

MAY 20TH, 2015 at 11:53AM

Q: JUSTCRAIG: WHAT'S BETTER? RE: JOB INTERVIEWS

justcraig asked: In improv, what's better improv, to be a job interviewer saying, "You don't need to stand," or to be a job interviewer saying, "You can sit down," if there isn't a chair on stage yet.

JUNE 2ND, 2015 at 5:05PM

INBOUND PASS

A metaphor for the very top of scenes.

Top of the scene should be like inbounding the ball in basketball. Routine, without much problem. The action is coming a few moments later.

Yes, that's a sports metaphor. So I'll explain the sport.

WHAT IS AN INBOUND PASS
In basketball, at the start of a play you've got one player standing just outside the bounds of the court. A member of his team waits on the court. The first player throws the ball to the second player who catches it. They both then turn and run up the court. It's the "inbound pass."

Usually, this initial inbound pass is a no-big-deal part of the play. Maybe the defending team has one person waving their arms in front of the inbounder, but they don't try that hard. The real action is going to happen when they get the ball closer to the basket.

SECOND LINE: NICE AND SIMPLE "YES"
Okay, so the top of your scene—the first two lines—should be like this

inbound pass. Make it easy and no big deal, and assume that the real action is going to happen a bit later.

This is especially important for the second line. Whoever is responding to the initiation—your primary job here is to just catch the inbounding pass. Let the other person know that you've caught the ball. Focus on the YES, don't worry too much about the AND.

>Player A: MaryAnn, would you step into my office?

>Player B: Sure Bill, is everything alright?

No big deal, just catching the pass. Nod your head a lot, repeat phrases, fit into the tone. You're just catching the pass.

DON'T RUN TOO FAST

THIS IS IMPORTANT because if you DON'T catch the pass nice and firmly, it will often make the first half of your scene a PROBLEM.

>Player A: MaryAnn, would you step into my office?

>Player B: (trying to do too much, changing things) Is this about the flood in the breakroom!?

Big choices are great normally. But it's bad form to do it before you've caught the ball. It throws the first player off, and often the characters will start fighting—a false fight, one that comes from the actors being thrown off, not from the characters.

>Player A: Flood? I told you to ... uh, to... watch out for floods!

>Player B: Well! You wouldn't approve the budget for... (whatever, whatever, connection lost, scene destroyed).

CATCH AND THEN CHOOSE IN ONE MOVE

If you're burning to make a big move in the second line, then explicitly catch the pass FIRST.

>Player B: Sure I'll come into your office. But I've got to get back to the breakroom. There's a flood in there.

This reassures the first player that you heard them. It also makes clear to everyone that you are making a switch away from what the initiation was going to focus on. Which is a bad idea. But it presents your not-great-move in a cooperative, clearly communicated way.

Catch the pass.

A GOOD METAPHOR

This is a good metaphor to use.

JUNE 3RD, 2015 at 11:58AM

HANDSHAKE

Forget what I said yesterday. A better metaphor for the top of scenes is a handshake.

Shake hands with the initiation. The initial offer. Before you worry about whatever it is you are going to contribute, whatever your twist is—shake hands with what was offered. Be in the same tone, nod your head, acknowledge the same beautiful sky, agree that you were just an asshole, have the same accent, know what they are talking about.

It can and should be fast and done in a simple, no-big-deal way. People shouldn't even necessarily notice it. But if you totally skip the handshake and make some big move, the other player will be insulted and thrown off and you will find your characters in an unearned dumb fight.

Yep, that's what I meant!

JUNE 3RD, 2015 at 12:13PM

Q: WHY DOES IRONIC DETACHMENT GET LAUGHS?

Anonymous asked: Why does ironic detachment get laughs in improv? In one of my classes one player constantly uses this style and it almost always gets a laugh. Is it effective or will his luck run out eventually?

Ironic detachment gets laughs because it's a denial, and denials are funny because they are a surprise. But they cause so much damage they are not worth that short-term joy.

But this guy in your class: Either his luck will run out or what he's doing is something better than ironic detachment. It's possible he's doing low-energy honesty. It's possible that what he's doing is just committing to the scene very well, as his own low energy self, and he is saying what his real self would say. My hunch is that's what's going on.

Ironic detachment is when your character is speaking to the audience, rather than to the other people in the scene. It's not just that you're unaffected but that you're not really in the scene.

>**Friend in a bar:** I need you to promise that if I start a fight with this guy you'll have my back.
>
>**Ironically detached player:** Uh, yeah, sure, THAT'S what I'll do.

That won't play. But this one could:

>**Friend in a bar:** I need you to promise that if I start a fight with this guy you'll have my back.
>
>**Low-energy but committed player:** I can't promise you that. No.

Honesty is always welcome and if it's surprising, the audience will reward it. So maybe that's what's happening?

JUNE 5TH, 2015 at 2:23PM

Q: HOW DO YOU FEEL ABOUT ALL THE BULLYING?

Anonymous asked: How do you feel about all the bullying towards the students in the UCB community?

I'm in favor of it. Big time. Especially towards people with passive aggressive conversational techniques! They need it the most. Yay for bullies!

JULY 2ND, 2015 at 11:26AM

Q: MBTI PERSONALITY TYPES IN IMPROV?

Anonymous asked: Do you know anything about MBTI personality types? If so, have you ever thought about how they might be related to the way we improvise? I'm thinking about specific types that might be more inclined to take improv classes to begin with, and whether certain types more easily fall into either the robot, pirate, or ninja camps.

MBTI is "myers-briggs" yes? I've heard of them but am not an expert. A quick look through the types (extrovert vs introvert, sensing vs intuition, thinking vs feeling, judging vs perceiving) tells me you need all of that, so I don't know.

I'd put "extrovert, intuition, feeling and perceiving" very roughly in an 'actor' camp, then "introvert, sensing, thinking, judging" in the 'writer' camp and say you need equal portions of both, favoring the actor side a bit more.

Grouchy point: I kinda think Myers-Briggs is really just a glorified Buzzfeed-type "what harry potter character are you" kinda thing. It's fun, but ultimately oversimplified and wrong!

JULY 2ND, 2015 at 12:19PM

Q: TRANSPHOBIC JOKES IN IMPROV

Anonymous asked: Do you have any advice for when a scene partner takes the scene in a direction that's offensive not just in a "that guy" way but that really makes you feel gross? I've been doing improv for a year and am trans but not out to many people. I've had some classes where someone has made a really not great transphobic joke and it took me so off guard the rest of the scene bombed & I felt pretty off the rest of the class. Do you have any tips to like power through in a show when you can't bail?

QUALIFIER

I am in every possible demographic majority (white male etc) and thus don't have a lot of direct experience with being the target of such jokes. But I do have a lot of improv experience, and have some advice about how things work in that arena.

ANSWER

Yeah, that's a tough one. I find this a really interesting and tough question, since it deals with boundaries, respect, comedic targets and potentially, playing characters.

My first instinct is that this counts as mean off-stage behavior and you should not do improv with those kind of people. It happened on-stage but it's coming from the person, not the character. Thus it's their off-stage self coming through.

If you're in a class and you kind of HAVE to deal, then, yeah, power through. Play your feelings out through your character. Not in an angry "trying to win the scene" just in an honest reaction "this is what i think about that" kind of way.

A trickier question: should you say anything?

A good thing to test might be "what is the target of the joke?"

If you ever want to say anything to anyone—a teacher, a fellow improviser, that's how I'd bring it up. "What is the target of that joke?" or "I'm not comfortable with the target of that scene." It's easier to find agreement this way than saying "I don't like that term/joke/character."

(Though some people will immediately want to argue that you are being politically correct, and that you are infringing on artistic freedom. It's a very tedious discussion, which many people—especially young angry people—love to have. If they try to shift the conversation this way, DISENGAGE. They are not listening).

Examples are so hard, but I'll try. I remember a million years ago seeing someone play a bully on stage. The character was recounting his day "There I was, bench-pressing a fag with one hand and hitting a girl with the other." It was a ridiculous image, and really funny. And the target is clearly the character of a bully: he's making himself a parody of a bully.

A more subtle case: I saw a good actor playing someone in NYC in the

1950s. He said "I only get tuna from Chinamen, they've got the best stuff." It was a bit shocking, but was it wrong? I'd say the target is the era: it's how people spoke, it's a time when someone would have said it, an assumption they would have made. Maybe I'm not portraying it right, but it didn't feel mean or even gratuitous.

But I've also seen (and unfortunately, done!) scenes where someone just drops the word fag like "are there gonna be a bunch of fags there?"—just thrown in for no reason. The target is the idea that homosexual people might be somewhere, or maybe the spectacle and forbidden nature of the term. Not the right target, and you can FEEL the meanness.

At one point, I was in a practice and a coach said "fag jokes are the black-face of our day." No one had used that term that day; he was just sort of pontificating about comedy in general. But all at once I saw how the casual use of these mean terms WAS getting laughs, but in the wrong way. And that in the very near future it was going to be an obvious embarrassment, blatant evidence of being out of touch, not to mention mean. I got the point.

Trans is not homosexuality, but I unfortunately have more examples of people using "fag" jokes!

Good improvisers don't like being jerks, don't like picking the wrong targets, and like updating their terms to fit with the times. The longer you stay in this world the more you're around only those kinds of people. Be patient, try not to get angry—jerks don't last in a group sport.

JULY 2ND, 2015 at 2:10PM

Q: WHAT ABOUT "THAT GUY" WHO GIVES NOTES?

Anonymous asked: There's someone on a team of mine that has had weird attitude lately towards the rest of us, giving me and other team members personal notes, doesn't seem to care too much about the team, and also doesn't seem to want to hang out with us outside of practice. Should we open up a dialogue about it or leave it alone? It's

been going on for a while now and I don't know what to do.

Push back on him/her giving individual notes; that's not cool. Forget the rest of it.

Remember the "that guy" phenomenon where there's always one person on a team who seems to be a scapegoat and that if you get rid of this person someone else will likely become "that guy."

JULY 5TH, 2015 at 11:47PM

Q: HOW TO COME UP WITH A SECOND BEAT WITHOUT IGNORING CURRENT SCENE?

Anonymous asked: When do you take the time after a first beat to come up with your second beat or maybe at least think about the first beat and distill it down to a game? Is there a time, I find it difficult to know what to go with into the second beat but everytime i think about it i lose pace of an ongoing scene and feel like a non supportive player.

I had a teacher (Armando Diaz) who said "If your first beat was you going BOO! and then someone else going AAAAH!, then your second beat should still be you going BOO! and them going AAAAAH!"

Basically: think of your first beat as a series of actions and reactions. One person does something, and the other reacts. Now pick the moment which was most representative of the scene. Or just pick the best part. Start with the best part. Re-create the signature moment right at the top of your second beat. You go BOO! and the other person goes AAAH! and then you can fill in the rest as you go.

Yeah, this is reductive. It doesn't always work. BUT IT WORKS A LOT. And if you're in your head, it's a good approach until you've had more practice.

JULY 7TH, 2015 at 11:52AM

Q: YOU DROPPED A QUARTER.

Anonymous asked: Not really a question, but during today's monoscene in The Smokes show, where you as Steve Largent got knocked out with a football, a quarter fell out of your pocket. I didn't have the courage to tell you or anyone on your team after blackout. the quarter remained there on the stage. It's likely someone else picked it up already and it's gone. But in my heart, it's still there. the dark secret I hold onto. The burning symbol of my cowardice—the constant reminder of my craven nature. FORGIVE ME.

I picked it up! Thank you.

JULY 7TH, 2015 at 11:56AM

Q: HOW TO DISCUSS YOUR SHOW WITH THE OTHER PLAYERS?

Anonymous asked: Just finished 401 so I want to preface by saying I know this may seem like a rookie question. How do you talk about your show with other players? I left the grad show not feeling great about my performance and I just wanted to get others perception but I didn't know how to go about asking. What is casual protocol, anytime after a shows usually feels awkward up till now.

Ask how they felt first. Address them by name. "Sean, what did you think of the show?" Then when you say your piece talk in terms of feelings, not notes. Don't say "We needed to initiate harder." Say "I felt all over the place" or "I was so excited at the first group game." Recognize that some people are wired to always hate every show, no matter what, and you may be one of them, so beware of wallowing. Others are wired to refuse to acknowledge any badness or else they think the world will crumble—let the conversation end if it reaches one of those points. Give lots of compliments—don't be so specific that it sounds like you're giving notes. Say "You were great" not "Great character work." After everyone has said their piece once or twice, never speak of it again.

JULY 7TH, 2015 at 12:01PM

Q: WHAT IF YOU ARE "THAT GUY?"

Anonymous asked: Will I think I'm 'that guy'. I don't feel very good after shows even if I've made good moves. I focus on how I've hurt other players, not in a personal way but more of an asshole improv way if that makes sense . I have days where I think I'm a really strong player and days where I think I'm the worst one. If I have a hard time jelling with certain people I question whether this is a good fit even though I love getting up there. But it's hard because I don't know how I'm actually being perceived.

I relate to this feeling. I have felt like the worst player on many teams I've been on. Truth is, there are some days where you probably ARE. Most players are like that. Only a precious few are good right away. But you're not that guy every show, either. On some days, you're a great player.

Probably you need to stop thinking about yourself so much. Compliment other people on the good stuff they do. Compliment the good part of the show as a whole. Shake it off. To yourself, compliment the good things you did, even if it didn't really work. Beating yourself up, even though it feels humble, is really a way of being focused on yourself. I do it every day, and I am trying to do it less.

JULY 7TH, 2015 at 12:02PM

Q: HOW TO PICK WHERE TO TAKE CLASSES?

lasirenamuerta asked: So I took an improv class in college and love came instantly. It started with short form but now I want to progress and get out there a little more. How did you go about picking UCB,

compared to other groups like groundlings or io? I've got the money saved up now but I can't decide where to go! I just don't know where I'd fit in I guess.. Also I'm terrified haha any advice helps!

I didn't pick. I took classes at a few, and I made friends with the people in my level 1 class at UCB and we all started hanging out and watching shows. If the other places had had a community where I fit in I would have stayed there. Try a place, don't fuss over which one, and see if it fits. Go with the flow more than deliberately choose.

JULY 8TH, 2015 at 5:20PM

WITCHES

There are great performers who are difficult people. I treat them like witches. I respect their power. I am careful to not unlock their wrath. I am nice to them. But I am guarded. I don't reveal any personal secrets. I get still and careful. I give them nothing. I talk about what they want to talk about. I compliment their shows, which is genuine since these people I'm talking about are awesome. I make them feel safe so they don't lash out. I also have their back and don't talk shit about them because I don't want to get cursed. My respect is true, it's just cautious. Then on-stage I say yes to them and commit hard and ride with them as they use their weird power to take us to great and terrifying heights.

JULY 8TH, 2015 at 7:11PM

Q: I CAN'T AFFORD CLASSES.

Anonymous asked: for many years, ucb has been my dream. the truth of the matter is that ucb is apologetically expensive and remains a privilege to those who are able to pay the fees to take classes. i have applied for diversity and jobs in the past and am unable to intern as i am supporting myself. what advice do you have for those of us who just aren't able to learn improv the traditional way?

I dislike when people answer money questions in a cagey manner so I will answer directly: There isn't really an alternate way in. You have to pay for and take the classes to be in the improv world. It IS a privilege and it leaves people out and it's a bummer, but it's also just the fact of a place being a business as well as a theater.

How much are we talking? At UCB it's currently $400 a class. You could take one class for that. But I hear you: it takes two or three to meet enough people to where you could make your own indie team—that would be $1200. And it takes four to six to have enough to get a shot at auditioning for a house team. That would be $2400. I think that's a real number for what it costs to get a full improv education. Some people take many more classes, but for $2400 you would have taken the full gamut of classes (four core classes, and two advanced levels) and know people and be IN it. It's hardly the $60,000 you pay for a year at a fine arts graduate school, but for someone on their own in their early 20s—it is a lot.

(Side note: Having to pay for classes is not limited to UCB. It's true at every improv theater/company: You have to take the classes. Shows are cheap/free, classes cost money. Note that the teachers are paid, and the performers are not.)

One idea: the UCB released a book. It's $25. And it is a very faithful description of the first four classes of UCB. You could buy it, read it, possibly even get a group of friends together and try the exercises in it to see what it feels like. It's not the same as a class, but it's the closest that a book could be to it. Maybe that's worth a shot.

Besides that, the only kind of comedy that I think you can start for basically nothing is stand-up. You can find free open mikes and try to make a name for yourself in a local community. There's problems there too: many open mics charge; it's hard to find a good mike, etc. But with devotion and legwork it's possible. There's not really an equivalent in the improv world.

I am sorry I don't have a more helpful answer!

P.S. EDITED TO ADD: People in the comments are suggesting indie nights and jams. It is true that there are jams that would welcome you to jump for a set. Tell the hosts your situation and they'll make sure you're welcome. That is true! But I still believe that if you really want to be in the community, the classes are the only way in.

JULY 8TH, 2015 at 10:53PM

Q: IS IT FUNNY TO FART IN A SCENE?

toyns asked: Is it funny to fart in a scene? Like a real fart, not an improv fart. Also, you're on the backline, not in the scene. And it's not your team, but you ran onstage anyway because you had this funny fart saved up. Let me know by tomorrow night please.

I'd laugh.

JULY 10TH, 2015 at 9:53AM

Q: CAN I TELL SOMEONE TO CHILL OUT IN A SCENE?

Anonymous asked: What do you think is the best way to react when someone is acting kinda crazy right from the initiation? Or not crazy, more like excessive. Like their initiation is "OH MY GOD I'M SO EXCITED WE'RE GOING TO DISNEYLAND AAAAAAAHHHHHHH!!!!!!!!!" and it feels too big and over-the-top to be realistic? My gut says you don't have to match the crazy; you can be like "okay, geez man, chill out!". But that feels like a denial.

Depends on your tone and how committed you are. Also how well you know the person.

You don't have to match the energy but at the very top of the scene, connection is paramount. If you say "chill out" and it sounds like the actor (you) is giving a note to the other actor, it may buzzkill the scene and lead to a false fight between the characters. If you are committed and your character says "hey man, calm down you're freaking me out" then it can be fine. I know it when I hear it: if one actor is telling the other one what to do it kills the scene; but if a character is reacting honestly then it's cool.

I think in line one, especially if you don't know the actor well, you'll do better by yes-anding the intention of the line as if it were said in its best possible way. If it were a mash-up and I didn't know the person I'd respond as if it were delivered with the best taste. I would choose to not be freaked out by their manner and would just react to the intention of the line.

If it were a team where I know the person well, I'd feel it out: is it true to my character to be turned off? Maybe, maybe.

After a connection has been made and the scene has existed for like 3 lines you're more free to start reacting completely freely no matter how well you know the person. You've shown the person you're listening and now you can do things like saying "hey man calm down." It's like you've built some scaffolding between the two of you so now you can walk on it.

If you DO say "hey man calm down" they may then choose NOT to calm down, which will also be fine! Assuming you guys have been reassured by the initial connection, assuming you have the presence of mind and self-confidence to turn your character's disagreement into a philosophical debate with clear points of view instead of just bossing each other around and feeling like you need the other person's permission to express yourself and oh my god, improv is hard.

AUGUST 3RD, 2015 at 5:07PM

SOME NOTES I'VE BEEN GIVING

I'm having good results giving these notes lately, all pertaining to better acting/listening/reacting at the tops of scenes. General qualifier here about how I'm sure these notes are not anything fundamentally new; but I like these phrasings.

1. **Don't be freaked out by the base reality.** You gotta be instantly comfortable in the world of the scene, no matter how confusing / surprising / weird it is. If you start off playing ping pong (which is not that weird but IS something that might take up more mental space than you were ready to spend), talk about something besides the fact that you're playing ping pong. Too many scenes start off with characters allergic to the very world around them.

2. **Be comfortable with silence, especially right after a reveal.** Lots of people talk until they are interrupted; better to make a point and let there be a quarter-beat of silence after. Especially if you make a big reveal/change to the scene. "You didn't know? The store is going out of business." (quiet).

3. **See it land.** After you make a move, make sure to see the move land in your scene partner's expression. Don't keep talking or walk away or leave or do some other move until you see it land. Someone told me this is a note Christina Gausas gives and I think it's great.

The fun thing about having an improv blog is you can just say stuff.

AUGUST 6TH, 2015 at 10:55AM

Q: WHAT IF I LIKE TO BE PATIENT, BUT EVERYONE KEEPS DOING EVERY IDEA "NOW?"

Anonymous asked: I believe that more often than not, if an idea for a walk-on/tag/etc. comes up in an early scene, it's better to put it on your back pocket and do it later as a callback or second beat. (Not always, obviously it's situational and subjective, but grant me the premise.) Frequently, I'll have an idea like this, and then a teammate will jump in and do it NOW instead of later. Any advice? Should I accept that this team works that way and just be less patient? Am I trying to "write" my shows too much?

Eventually this will be decided by the question "does it work?" That's different than "do these shows fit what you want them to be?" Just: are the shows working? If so, enjoy it. Are they not working? Then when the discussion comes around to "what should we try differently" then bring up "let's try holding off on tags." That's a common thing to try.

(Walk-ons are a lot less disruptive than tag-outs. I'd only worry about tags.)

If some people think it IS working and you don't, then leave the team. If you don't have other options, then enjoy the almost completely universal improv experience of being in a show/team/dynamic you never planned on being in.

EDITED LATER TO ADD: Generally you don't want tags in the first scene but I don't believe in a hard rule about it. Hard rules like "no tags in the first beat" are essentially training wheels and should not be followed blindly. Some shows will want tags right away. The test "does it work?" is a better thing to pay attention to.

AUGUST 6TH, 2015 at 11:16AM

CONSIDER EVERY OFFER (DON'T ACCEPT BLINDLY)

It shouldn't be accept offers (which is a phrase I have previously championed a lot) but instead should be consider offers. You don't HAVE to accept them, you just have to consider them.

This is because you can't do anything in the scene just because you think you SHOULD, that ruins it.

This falls under the principle of be present.

EXAMPLE: CONSIDERING AN OFFER, THEN DECLINING

In my third-ever improv class I saw a scene with two guys John and Rob as hecklers at a circus. They were talking trash to a tightrope walker—"you suck!" "fall down you bum" (something better than that). Then Vadim walked on as a concessions guy saying "Cotton Candy! Slingshots!" And John turned around and said to him "I'll take a cotton candy."

Afterwards in notes the teacher asked "Why didn't you take the slingshot?" and John said "I was more interested in the cotton candy. And I didn't want to hurt the tightrope walker, I just wanted to make fun of him."

Now John was a notorious wise-ass who liked doing what he wasn't supposed to. But on the other hand there was something very real and compelling about that moment. He considered it, and decided against the offer of the slingshot. I don't think that was bad.

I mean, all things equal, you should tend to accept offers. You shouldn't say "no" to something just for the joy of shooting something down. But if you've considered it and your character wants to decline that is a-okay.

EXAMPLE: ACCEPTING AN OFFER WITHOUT CONSIDERING

I think saying "yes" without considering is also bad!

I saw a scene with a (very good) improviser who established herself as an introvert, who wanted to skip a really cool party and instead stay home. Then someone tags in and says "Hey, there's two bald eagles mating in the air outside, want to see?" And the introvert said right away "Eh, shut the window."

They played a pattern, they said yes to an offer, which are good things, but the scene still felt off. And I realized it was just that I hadn't seen the introvert consider the offer enough. Two bald eagles mating? Really? You don't want to see that, even an introvert like you? I (the audience) need to see you really feel that moment and consider it. Maybe you still say "shut the window" (probably the right way to go as it keeps you consistent) or maybe you decide "hey, that's worth seeing." As long as you gave that offer its due consideration.

What I need is to believe that you are playing every moment fully, that you don't go on autopilot. I need to believe that there's a possibility I'm going to be surprised.

AUGUST 17TH, 2015 at 1:08AM

Q: I'M PLAYING WITH A BAD PARTNER WHO LIKES TO CALL OUT EVERYTHING

Anonymous asked: I'd like to learn to play better with someone who doesn't feel like a partner in scenes. They call out everything, inc. choices made in an attempt to build the world (eg. making up the

name of a chess move, if they know it's not a real one), and they don't feel like they're pitching in to build the scene. When they do call out the scene's unusual thing, it's as though they're there as an improviser rather than a character. Can you suggest an approach to avoid stalling out in scenes with them?

1. http://improvnonsense.tumblr.com/thatguy
2. Probably don't do improv with someone you feel that way about. if you're just mentally tallying all the things they're doing wrong, it's not worth it. You can't judge that much while you're doing improv, it distances you from the show. The audience can probably sense it. It's uncomfortable to watch. And you'll end up judging yourself just as harshly. Play with who you want.
3. If you have to or want to make it work then make it work. Stop focusing on what he/she is doing wrong, and connect with the good parts. Calling stuff out: maybe they want an unusual thing right away? That's not necessarily bad. I agree it's no fun to play with someone who just calls everything out, but as a show it can work.

SO: Make fun justifications for everything he/she calls out, play low status so he/she gets to be in a comfy high status. You make all the scene choices (who/what/where) and let him/her make fun of them, then agree with and commit to all the things they bring up.

Suggestion: airplane

> YOU: I got us tickets to Hawaii for our honeymoon.
>
> PARTNER: We've been married for 5 years—you're getting tickets NOW?
>
> YOU: Yeah. I decided it was time.
>
> PARTNER: But you've always said you hated Hawaii.
>
> YOU: I know. I panicked. I screwed up.
>
> PARTNER: Well, I guess we're going. Did you get us tickets to visit a volcano?
>
> YOU: Yes, a tour of the volcano (made-up name).
>
> PARTNER: That's not a volcano.

YOU (staying low status): Oh. Then, no, I didn't get any tickets for a volcano.

PARTNER: Where are we going to stay? Please tell me you got a hotel.

YOU: No. I thought we could befriend locals.

PARTNER: Great. This is the dumbest idea I've ever heard.

YOU: Why?

PARTNER: Because you haven't planned anything!

YOU: I know. We leave in an hour.

PARTNER: Do you hate me? Is that why you're doing all this so badly?

YOU: I might. I might hate you. I'm sorry.

PARTNER: That's just really rude.

YOU: It's hard to be a good person. Luckily you find me adorable.

PARTNER: I don't.

YOU: You dooooooooooooooo.

It can work as a show and even be mildly fun. You just have to get over the idea of being right, of trying to fix them, and try to have fun by connecting with someone. Connecting is fun, even with a jerk who is hogging all the good parts. Being fluid and adapting is fun.

Or don't do it! Life is short.

AUGUST 17TH, 2015 at 8:35PM

Q: HOW MANY QUESTIONS DO YOU GET?

Anonymous asked: How many questions does this site get daily? Weekly? This is the best improv tumblr ever.

Thanks! And: not too many. When I answer one I'll get 3 or 4 otherwise only one every two weeks.

There's 18K subscribers but those are mostly from when this was a featured blog on the "comedy" tumblrs. I can't imagine many of those folks are regular readers.

AUGUST 17TH, 2015 at 8:36PM

Q: YOU GET LABELED AS HAVING AN ACCENT BUT YOU HAVEN'T HAD ONE

Anonymous asked: this is not a joke question: you enter a scene using your normal American accent. after a few lines you're labeled as Julia Child or Sean Connery or whatever, do you adopt the accent of that person? do you even call attention to it ("i was pretending i was American because…")?

Improv is insane that such a specific question is … Actually a common occurrence! Personally I'd definitely start doing the voice (just to not be scared of doing it) and I'd justify why I didn't have it earlier only if I felt it would be distracting not to. If I get labeled early enough (like maybe I just said one unimportant line) I might not even bother explaining.

AUGUST 18TH, 2015 at 8:52AM

Q: JUSTCRAIG: WHEN IS TOO LATE TO PUT UP X-RAYS?

justcraig asked: Hi, this is a question about improv that I have about improv. When doing improv, if you're playing a doctor giving a diagnosis, how long into the scene is too late to put up x-rays (using improv object work)? Keep in mind that the diagnosis is probably elephantiasis of the nuts, or something equivalent.

AUGUST 20TH, 2015 at 12:02PM

Q: MORE ADVICE ON HOW TO DISCUSS SHOWS WITH YOUR FELLOW PLAYERS?

Anonymous asked: You touched on a few times how groups should talk to each other and about their feelings in a way that doesn't make other improvisors feel judged or shitty when discussing a show or how a jam felt. Do you have any more advice for how to do this? How specific about things that happened in a show can we get without making someone feel like something is their fault?

I wish I had this figured out enough to give a for-sure bulleted list. I don't. But you know what, I'm gonna try. Here's a first draft of some general principles.

Sit on impulses, especially angry ones. If you are thinking that you have THE ANSWER to your group's problems, or that you know that THIS PERSON is the whole problem: wait for a show or two. Do you still think that? Those thoughts often pass.

Make sure you've taken the note you want to give. I can't tell you how many times that the person who is the most upset about a certain improv crime is the one doing the crime the most. The person who insists that the team must play it real is the FIRST one to make it cartoony in a show. The person who wants big decisions will not make ANY decisions.

Don't do it over email. Huge long email manifestos are unclear and come off as indulgent.

When you want to say something, don't be polite. Be direct. You don't need to apologize 10 times before you say something. Just say "I think we're tagging too early."

Can you talk right to the person who is bothering you in an honest non-angry way? Can you say to the person "please stop tagging me out so early." Think of how you'd want to be told if you were bothering someone—say it that way. All business. One pro to another.

Offer a specific not-that-binding constraint. No tag-outs in the first 3 scenes. Don't heighten the first unusual thing. No starting scenes in chairs. A beat of silence at the top of scenes. Or: no silence at the top of scenes. A different opening. A different form.

Be honest. Think of how you describe your feelings to your best friend who is not in your improv group. Are you as direct with the people in your improv group? Would they be surprised to hear what you think?

Is the show working? Here's a tricky one: are you sure there IS a problem? Just because it's not going how YOU want doesn't mean it's wrong. Are you trying to be the group's director from within the group? Improv doesn't work so well like that. Might be time to move on to sketch where you can write the script for actors to do what you want, which is not a bad thing to realize if that's where you're at.

But here's my hesitation about all of this. You ultimately cannot control other people. If you're only going to be happy if other people do certain things, you will never be happy in your improv shows. Improv is about being surprised and reacting to it. If people are listening and not denying the FACTS of what you are saying, there's not much room to complain.

I asked a member of a very prominent and successful improv team if my team should have an honest session of giving each other notes and he said "I wouldn't give anyone on my team a note, and if I did, they wouldn't take it."

The best teams I've been on are people who are capable of taking care of themselves. This is assuming they do listen to and then don't deny the facts of what each other says on stage. Everyone is ready to react and deal with whatever.

Anyway, just give it a shot and let me know how it goes!

AUGUST 20TH, 2015 at 12:06PM

HOW DOES YOUR TEAM TALK TO EACH OTHER?

The second most common question I get is "how do i tell my team i don't like something?" (The most common one is "how do i get out my head/a rut").

I'm pessimistic about the good that can come out of group hand-wringing. But I'm likely too cynical about it.

So I put it to you, readers: tell me how your teams talk to each other about your shows. Answer below. Or use the "ask" function (tell me if I can quote you if you do that). I'm looking for success stories. How can it work?

AUGUST 24TH, 2015 at 12:27PM

Q: DO YOU READ ANY NEW-AGE TYPE BOOKS THAT CORRELATE TO IMPROV?

Anonymous asked: Do you read new-Age type books? I feel they have good correlation to improv, is there any you'd recommend specifically either for improv or life in general?

The Four Agreements. Amazing Fantasy #15. The story decisions of the movie Teen Wolf. I don't know.

AUGUST 24TH, 2015 at 12:48PM

Q: WHY IS "BROAD" BAD?

Anonymous asked: You use the term "broad" a lot to describe a certain kind of bad improv. Can you elaborate on what exactly you mean when you use the term "broad"?

Hammy and unrealistic. Big faces designed to get the attention of unfunny people and three year olds. Silly voices that have zero correspondence to real life. Unspecific choices. The kind of body language on movie posters that have RED CAPITAL LETTERS on a WHITE BACKGROUND.

Sweaty, desperate. Gross. Gross! I've done it.

Broad is different than genuinely funny people being physical and silly. The difference is that the good people are specific and generally calm. Kristen Wiig, Peter Sellers.

AUGUST 27TH, 2015 at 10:58AM

NO ONE HERE WANTS TO BE FUNNY?

One of my favorite moments at an improv workshop was one that Matt Besser taught in the summer of 2005, when he reminded us that it was okay to want to be funny.

It was in the UCB offices which at that time were three rooms over the Malibu Diner on 23rd street. The main office, where the artistic director and school supervisor and others sat, were in the middle. There were classrooms on either side to the north and south. The northern classroom stored all the costumes used for the UCB's sketch show and had a cot where Besser would sometimes crash when he was in town from LA, like he was at this time. The southern room was smaller, a bit neater, and had what I remember as about fourteen radiators which pumped full blast year round including the middle of July. We were in that one.

This was during the Del Close marathon, the annual festival/homecoming at UCB where there are improv shows and workshops 24 hours a day for 3 days to honor Del, legendary improv director/teacher and patron saint of the UCB. It meant that the workshop had a mixture of UCB superfans, out-of-town newbies and a few teachers, of which I was one. We were all exhausted from having been up all night, many of us hungover.

Besser walked in, presumably having just grabbed a few hours of nap on his cot two rooms away. We all sat up a bit straighter, intimidated to face one of the UCB himself, a founder of our theater and a notoriously hard-to-impress teacher. He'd moved to LA so few of us had had him for a class.

Besser sat in a chair and lounged way back. He had on an Arkansas Razorbacks basketball team t-shirt, baggy jeans and beat-up sneakers, loosely tied. He looked tired and his expression seemed skeptical by default. Though he was technically facing the class, he seemed to be gazing at a spot on the floor just a few feet in front of him. It wasn't clear class had started until he started talking.

"So why do you guys want to do improv?"

Silence, then someone timidly raised their hand. "I want to learn how to be in the moment."

Besser nodded. "Be in the moment, okay. Anyone else?"

Answers started coming a bit more confidently. "To learn how to play it real." "To support my scene partner." "To have a group mind." "To find truth in comedy."

Besser nodded at all of them. After the answers stopped coming, he raised his eyebrows and said "No one here wants to be funny?"

We paused and stared back, then at each other, then back again. Besser seemed irritated. Were we in trouble?

"Nobody likes… comedy? Nobody was a fan of comedy and then saw an improv show and thought it was funny and said 'I want to be funny?'"

We slowly nodded. Yes, we wanted to be funny. We liked funny things.

"I bet you all, before you wanted any of those things you just said, just wanted to be funny. It's good. You should want to be funny. Improv is funny. Right? Okay, two people up."

And we proceeded to have a Matt Besser workshop, which is an exciting, educational, inspirational and only sometimes terrifying experience. It was one of my favorites ever.

And it was the first time an improv teacher ever told me directly that it was okay to want to be funny.

Why Is Improv Teaching So Serious?

And that's what I love about my time at the UCB theater: I was told that improv should be funny. Very explicitly. Along with all the notes about committing and listening and honoring group mind and supporting your scene partner was the very explicit directive: your show didn't work if it wasn't funny. This is a comedy theater. BE FUNNY.

I understand how the culture came to abhor the words "joke" and "funny." That's because improv is first and foremost an actor's medium. It requires listening, agreement and commitment before all else. And since many people who get into improv have very little acting background, you must emphasize these things—listening, agreement, commitment—many, many times before your students can really start to do it.

And students who try to make jokes and who seem to want badly to be funny—well, at first they can only do those things by breaking reality, by selling out their scene partner, by making jokes that insult the integrity of the scene itself.

So you coach away from that and say "don't worry about being funny, just support. Be truthful: say what you would really say, not some joke."

But we go too far! We forget the ultimate goal: to come back from your time practicing good acting and to make a comedy show! To make a show that's funny! Our favorite improv shows are, regardless of what tone they strike or what pace they set, FUNNY. Even if there are truly amazing and gifted acting chops afoot, the part you remember when you walk out of the theater is the funny part.

You can get there however you want. Fast or slow. In one scene or in forty-five of them. Use tag-outs, or keep it a monoscene. Have an opening or don't. Two people, or twenty people. There's lots of ways, all fascinating.

But if you're putting a show up in a comedy theater, the audience should laugh or you didn't do it right. That's not heresy, that's respect. Respect for the audience that came to see a show. Respect for how hard it is to make something that's funny. Respect for the tradition of theater and writing and comedy in LA and NY and Chicago and every other place where someone put up a sign that said "improv show tonight."

AUGUST 28TH, 2015 at 12:42AM

Q: HOW LONG BEFORE YOU STOPPED BOMBING?

Anonymous asked: Do you remember how long you had been doing improv before the probability of completely bombing (I mean really eating it) was close to 0%?

Hmmm. Maybe like 8 years? But long before that I just got comfortable when shows were really bad. Spoiler: I am not a model for doing things in a successful way.

AUGUST 28TH, 2015 at 1:25PM

BE UNNECESSARILY SPECIFIC

They say you can't teach funny, and they're probably right but I can't help trying.

This is based on my highfalutin post yesterday, where I said that improvisers need to remember that it's okay to be funny.

I wonder if it's okay for improv teachers to specifically teach being funny?

Obviously you can't, really, just teach funny. It's more about creating an environment where people feel excited and free so that they can be playful and that funny stuff that they naturally have in them just sort of happens. You're assuming that the people who are taking an improv class have a built-in desire to be funny and ability to be funny of course, which is not always true. But anyway, that's how you normally teach funny. You get out of the way of the funny.

But say that I'm a robot, and always want stuff to be a system of rules. What are some ways to be funny? Goddamnit, just tell me.

Okay, number one I'd say is to be unnecessarily specific. Be more specific than a situation calls for.

That's usually pretty funny and pretty easy to do!

Especially in the ten million scenes you will do where you have to order dinner. Be fast enough to order an incredibly specific dish. Don't think of it beforehand, just look up and say the most specific meal you can: "Grilled tilapia and chilled white wine."

I don't even know if tilapia can be grilled. And isn't white wine always chilled? And doesn't my answer sound just a bit forced and jokey? Yeah, I guess, but get off my back—because it'll also work. It'll be pretty funny!

So yeah. Do that all the time. That'll help!

AUGUST 28TH, 2015 at 6:00PM

ARGUE THAT THE WORLD IS FLAT

Another way to be funny: argue the dumb side of any discussion.

I've written so much about arguments. Too much. Fights in improv fascinate me and I love analyzing them and trying to think about what they say about our natural defensiveness and mammal brains.

But all that analysis probably doesn't help you get better at improv. Improv advice is best served in small bites: mantras and tips.

Okay, so how about this: argue the wrong side. Argue that the world is flat.

Anytime any kind of discussion starts, take the wrong side, the side that is obviously wrong. And defend it the best you can.

That's usually really fun!

If two characters are arguing whether the world is flat or round (great scene, such a great example, great job), which is more fun? More fun to argue that the world is flat, obviously.

So anytime you find yourself in a fight, make sure that at least one of you or possibly both are arguing something dumb. Or else end the fight.

If your scene partner accuses your character of being lazy, and you defend yourself that your job is just too hard, and they come up with a reason why you're still lazy—realize that you are in a non-funny fight, so you make it funny by arguing a dumb point.

You (deliberately making your side a "dumb" stance): "I'm not lazy, I just do better work if I don't go in until after lunch."

Other person: "But you work at a law firm."

You: "So what? The mornings there just stress me out."

Doesn't this break the "top of your intelligence" rule, you ask? No, because you will argue the dumb thing as smart as possible. That's practically the definition of a joke: argue a dumb thing in a smart way.

This is another way to be funny! Yeah! Do this!

AUGUST 31ST, 2015 at 12:08PM

Q: 2-3 YEARS IN, I'M SUDDENLY ANXIOUS.

Anonymous asked: Hey! So I've only been practicing improv for 2-3 years, so this may be completely natural, but lately, I've been feeling very anxious again and just all tangled up inside when doing improv. Like I have this little ball of yarn at my diaphragm. I keep messing up even basic skills, that I thought I had nailed down. I've had a lot of successes, so I don't know where this is coming from. Any tips on going all gordian knot on that? And just achieving a state of calmness? Thanks!

See Zach's email in an entry I wrote up called *How Can I Get Out My Head*?

I relate completely to this feeling as does everyone. Being good at improv means knowing how to manage doubt and anxiety. They never totally go away but they can be handled.

I'm in favor of touchy-feely new agey things LIKE visualizations (before doing shows, I'll imagine the audience filled with people I know like me, or else I'll pretend the show is actually a class where I felt comfortable) or having internal conversations with yourself (I have told myself "i'll go out there with you" and I have addressed my negative thoughts with things like "I'll take that into consideration.")

Just be comfortable with where you're at, and know that you are united with everyone who's ever done improv when you are in a rut. That's not a solution but maybe it's a comfort.

AUGUST 31ST, 2015 at 12:09PM

GIVE A SHIT

Another way to be funny: give more of a shit about what's happening than we expect.

Caring is funny. It's unexpected.

"Have you thought about what you want for dinner?"

"Deeply."

Don't go too nuts or it'll feel false. Just give about 20% more of a shit than we expect you too. But still, err on the side of caring more than we thought you would.

"For this year's musical, we are producing West Side Story."

"Fuck yes!"

Hey, that's pretty funny! So yeah, do that. Give just a bit more of a shit more than we expect.

SEPTEMBER 2ND, 2015 at 10:36AM

Q: HOW TO IMPROVE TIMIDITY?

Anonymous asked: I've been told a few times to speak up more bc I'm funny, but I find it hard to do so bc I find myself in scenes with dominant players who won't let me speak and I never want to talk over people or unnecessarily interject if in a group game. If they initiate I

always wait till they're done talking and by the time I've taken a quick moment to think of a response it's too late. Do you have advice on how to improve timidity and find a stronger voice especially in scenes with more dominant players?

This is a common and big problem. There are just a ton of people in improv who won't shut up.

Eventually you will be with people good enough to tell you've got something to say and they will listen.

But before then you've got two main options:

1. **Speak up, cut them off, and GRAB THE FOCUS**. Give it as hard as they are. It's not polite, but it's the way it goes. Yes, it's not your natural way of being. It will change your tone. Do it anyway. Improv in the lower levels is like street basketball and you have to kinda play tough. Throw some elbows and make space for yourself. It's not elegant but it's part of getting better.

2. **Be in the moment SO HARD that all eyes fall on you**. Be completely in the moment, fully hearing and feeling everything, and letting all of your feelings be on your face and body. The audience—and everyone on stage—will see that you are the only one who is authentically there—and they WILL PAY ATTENTION TO YOU. People will magically give you space. Yep. It happens.

I saw a show a million years ago with a (surprise) bulldogging nervous guy and a quiet confident girl. He started the scene as a husband on a fishing trip with his wife (there's no way this guy was capable enough to imagine actors could play opposite gender, whatever) and he's complaining about the weather and demanding a beer and asking her why she picked this day to do fishing, but not giving her time to answer. There was basically no time for her to really answer, except for short phrases like "no" and "yes" and "boy, it shore is rainy!"

In his defense, the guy was more nervous than actually bullying. He was trying to play a character of a jerk husband more than he seemed to truly be a jerk. I felt a bit bad for him. But, still, the effect was that his scene partner couldn't get a word out.

But she was so much more confident an actor! She did everything physically. Her eyebrows popped up when he revealed that the weather was bad. She looked a bit sad when he said the fish weren't gonna bite. When he asked for a beer, she leaned over into a cooler and plucked a beer up in sharp funny movements. I remember she clutched the can just with her fingertips from the top, letting the imaginary can dangle as if it were a gross thing that she didn't want to touch. And she handed it over to him, which he absent-mindedly took as he rambled, and the audience laughed.

She was in the scene. She was funnier. She was a specific character. She was cool and calm and confident and making decisions and reactions. She was having fun. We were all just watching her.

That girl? MERYL STREEP. No, I'm kidding. I don't know who she was. But I remember thinking: *that's the way to play with a stage hog: you roll with it and just kinda surf the wave.*

But the first way is also important: get in there and get your time.

SEPTEMBER 3RD, 2015 at 9:42AM

IMPROV FOR PEOPLE NOT THAT GOOD

Hi! I'm Will Hines and I am not that good at improv. At least not naturally. I'm very naturally good at computer programming, memorizing lists and being fussy about things like fonts. But in the very basic improv skills of being comfortable on stage and staying present and being charismatic and doing fun characters: I am very much not natural at those things.

Yet, here I am, one of the best goddamn improvisers in the world. How the fuck did I do it? This is how:

- be brave
- never be freaked out/preoccupied by any base reality
- always do the scary thing (accents, dancing, stepping out, or NOT stepping out, being emotional, being honest)
- be authentic
- react, a bit more, in a fun way

- let things in the scene change you
- play with difficult people
- bad people
- people who are funny but seem to do it wrong
- (the trick: you assume they mean well)
- be funny
- keep patterns going, until they're used up
- be unnecessarily specific
- make the surprising choice, then explain yourself
- pick the wrong side of every argument

That is my current guess.

SEPTEMBER 12TH, 2015 at 6:11PM

Q: IS IT CRAZY TO THINK SOMEONE SHOULD BE ON A LLOYD TEAM BEFORE COACHING?

Anonymous asked: Is it crazy that I think people should at least be on a Lloyd team in order to claim that they can coach aptly? I ask because recently I noticed that an acquaintance who finished their 401 within the last 6 months has been actively advertising that they coach. And this isn't the first—it seems to be somewhat of an epidemic, at least in the current NYC scene, that many people claiming that they can coach are also just starting their advanced study levels. It feels scammy to me. Is that crazy?

I think your reaction is understandable though I doubt it's anything new. I've seen lots of cases of inexperienced people trying to offer themselves as coaches. Way back in 2001, one of the members of my practice group offered himself as a coach ONE HOUR after we got made a Harold team. It was gross.

But setting a hard RULE like "on a Lloyd team" (house teams at UCB NY that are more junior than Harold teams) is also too restrictive. There's plenty of good coaches who haven't been able to run the gauntlet of the audition process.

And there's also people who are good improvisers but are not great coaches.

In LA there's an "approved coaches" list. I believe NYC has one like this? Though these are hard to get on, being on it is probably a safe bet that one is a good coach.

Ultimately word of mouth settles the issue. Ask around who the good coaches are and you hear the same names. I think the truth comes out pretty soon.

Like: your friend who finished 401. Who's hiring him/her? People in advanced (level 5) or higher? Doubt it. So level 2 and 3 groups, then? How many: 1, maybe 2? The principle of the thing may bother you but the magnitude of the sin probably isn't that big. AND: if this friend IS getting hired repeatedly and by many groups: he/she might be good! (I doubt it too, but you never know).

SEPTEMBER 16TH, 2015 at 11:39AM

Q: HOW MUCH MONEY DO YOU MAKE AS A WORKING ACTOR?

Anonymous asked: You've spoken before about earning money as an improviser/actor with coaching and a day/freelance job. I'm curious what it's like to be a consistently working actor who only does a few bit parts every now and then. I'm curious how much money you can make doing this. Can this be a sole source of income? I know people don't like talking about money but it'd be very helpful to have an idea of what something like this would earn. Thank you.

Ah, money talk! I find the best way to avoid confusion on this topic is to not be cagey, speak in real amounts, and qualify that this is just what I've seen and maybe others have vastly different experiences:

For small parts you get $800 or $900 for the day, and some piddling amount on residuals months later. Non-union web videos usually pay, if anything, $100-$300 for a day (there are some rare exceptions that will pay $1000, which probably means they should just be union but if you're broke you might not care).

Big national network commercials can pay a shitload like $30K to even $50K over a year and a half. If you book one of those you don't need to work for a year, assuming you live like an actor which means you live small and weak.

Smaller regional commercials pay a one-time fee of 2-5 thousand. Sometimes those regional ones will run for a while and can pay you another grand or two in residuals over a year or so, sometimes five or six grand.

Besides the big national network spots, none of them are money you can live on for any time. And even the big spots you can't count on getting. So you generally need something small that is steady that you can count on. Common solutions: teach improv/acting/writing classes. Tutor kids. Walk a shit ton of dogs. Babysit. Be a realtor (barely ever works). Free lance computer programming. Freelance graphic design (barely ever works).

SEPTEMBER 17TH, 2015 at 3:40PM

Q: HAVE YOU EVER QUIT A DUO TEAM?

Anonymous asked: Have you ever quit a duo team? I feel like it's much harder to give the soft and vague answers you can fall back on for leaving a larger team. Any advice?

i don't know of any formula. You probably know the right way to do this for this particular person. My instinct tells me to keep it in person, direct and honest.

SEPTEMBER 17TH, 2015 at 4:49PM

Q: JUSTCRAIG: IN IMPROV...

justcraig asked: In improv, what's better improv, improv or improv?

DECEMBER 13TH, 2015 at 4:38PM

NOTES I GOT

Notes I've gotten and how/when I got them.

"IT'S LIKE YOU'RE WATCHING THE SCENE INSTEAD OF BEING IN IT."

1997. Chicago City Limits level 2. My teacher John is explaining to me why the scene I did stalled.

"BRING YOUR WHOLE SELF WITH YOU"

McManus, early 2000s. My classmates and I are talking with Rob about how amazing The Swarm are. Rob says he noticed that when the people from The Swarm step into a scene, they "bring their whole selves with them"—their opinions, their memories, their temperaments.

"IF YOU DON'T KNOW THE GAME, DON'T PLAY IT."

I first heard this from my level one teacher Kevin Mullaney. Not sure if it's his, but I like it.

"WE WOULDN'T GIVE A NOTE AND IF ANYONE DID WE WOULDN'T HAVE TAKEN IT"

McManus, early 2000s. I'm having trouble with my new Harold team. Everyone is going in different directions and the cool people seem to be kinda over it. I see my level 4 teacher Ali, sitting in a booth. Ali was on The Family, which is famously one of the greatest improv teams to have been at the iO Theatre in Chicago. I sit down and ask him if The Family ever did something like have a meeting where everyone goes around and is very honest about what they want. Ali responded **"We wouldn't give a note and if anyone did we wouldn't have taken it."**

"IF A GUY CAME IN THE FIRST BEAT AND GOES HONK, MAYBE A GUY DOES THAT IN THE SECOND BEAT."

Harold Team practice, our long-time coach Billy is trying to get us out of our heads and less scared of the Harold. **"If a guy came in the first beat and goes HONK, maybe a guy does that in the second beat."** He didn't mean that was a hard rule, just a rule of thumb. It helps us keep some patterns going when we don't know the game.

"AAAAH! EEEEEK!"

Level 3, my second time taking it. Armando is telling us to keep second beats simple. "If the first beat is someone going AAAAAH! and you go EEEEK! then the second beat should be that someone going AAAAH! and you going EEEEK! again." It doesn't always work but it demystifies second beats a lot.

"DOES IT HAVE TO BE $80,000?"

Level 3, I'm making up a session in a Secunda class. James and I are doing a scene as two guys talking about a boat we own, it's not going well. Amidst that I say "That light right there cost $80,000" and Secunda shouts from the side **"does it have to be $80,000?"** And I correct down to a more realistic amount. Don't over-swing, I think.

"IMPROV RULES ARE LIFE RULES"

Class with Ian, 2002. He's telling us that the improv "rules" are there to make us be more lifelife. "Improv rules are life rules." Do what you would do, say what you would say. He ends every class doing a scene. His characters say "no," they are not easily fooled but the scenes are always committed, always funny.

"PARTICIPATE"

Harold team practice, 2003-ish. James is coaching. We get into a group game where everyone is crotched down and digging in the dirt for something—one of the scenes where no one has yet decided what's going on. I step back and turn myself into a photographer taking pictures. "Will—**PARTICIPATE**," says James, sharply. And I realize I'm removing myself from the action out of fear. I dive into the group.

"THIS IS DISPOSABLE"

Workshop with Walsh. He's trying to get us to play with more of a spirit of fun. Remember "how ephemeral this all is, **this is disposable,** just PLAY, just TRY stuff."

"YOU'VE EATEN A BOWL OF CEREAL A THOUSAND TIMES, JUST EAT IT."

Harold practice, early 2000s and Owen is going over object work. Let's say you're miming eating a bowl of cereal. He says there's two basic approaches: you can get very precise and practice while looking in the mirror and make it perfect OR just realize that you've eaten a bowl of cereal a million times in your life, and just... do it. "just eat the bowl of cereal." He mimes doing it casually and easily, not making a big deal out of it.

MEISNER'S "COUNT THE CEILING TILES."

From Sanford Meisner's book "Sanford Meisner on Acting." (It seems weird to reference a book when most of these are anecdotes of getting notes personally but this is a note I think about all the time, so...)

The first chapter describes Meisner telling the class to count how many ceiling tiles there are. When they are all doing it, he stops them. He tells them **they look like people counting tiles**. And he asks them to consider how fake it would be if there were trying to just ACT LIKE they were counting tiles.

MEISNER'S "OUCH"

Also from Meisner's book, when he asks the class what the best way to help your scene partner do an authentic reaction. What if they need to say ouch? What's the best way to make someone say ouch? And **he pinches someone**, kinda hard, and they yelp "ouch!" It's not about physically hurting someone—it's about really provoking someone. You want a reaction? You can provoke it out of someone.

SHURTLEFF'S "FIND THE LOVE"

Another book one, this time Michael Shurtleff's book "Audition." He says that no matter how dry the audition piece seems, you can **find the love** between the characters. Even if it's angry, that anger comes from love. It's on the actor to find it.

"I'M NOT HERE TO BABYSIT PEOPLE"

I'm telling my coach Jackie about some internal politics going on in the group right before she coaches us. She stops me mid-sentence and says "**I'm not here to babysit people**." And went to the rehearsal room where everyone was waiting and we had a great rehearsal!

"YOU'VE GOT TWO MINUTES TO COME UP WITH A SKETCH FOR LORNE MICHAELS. DO YOU DO A SOUND AND MOVEMENT?"

Besser is teaching us about openings, and that openings should give us good ideas for scenes. We had been doing openings, but more like vaguely artistic overtures from which we'd pull a few random specifics. Besser says **"You've got two minutes to come up with a sketch for Lorne Michaels. Do you do a sound and movement?"** And it changes our minds: our openings should give us good ideas, or it's not worth doing.

"NO ONE HERE WANTS TO BE FUNNY?"

Mid-2000s, Del Close Marathon. Besser is teaching a workshop. He starts by asking us why we like improv. It rewards saying yes, someone says. Group mind, says someone else. Playing to the top of your intelligence, says someone else. **"No one here wants to be funny?"** he asks. We do, we realize. Of course we do!

GETHARD'S TEACHING ESSAY

Everything Chris says in this interview on teaching improv.

"MORE ABSURD"

Joe is coaching my group, which is a really veteran one, so it's been awhile since we've gotten notes. I do a tag-out and make a move, and Joe points it was less absurd than what came before. He says once we have a game, the moves should get "**as absurd or more absurd**" as we go. I had known the word "heighten" but "more absurd" really brought home for me a way to measure if the scene was going UP.

"DO NOT BAIL."

Amy is meeting with all the teachers. One of her most emphatic pieces of advice is to not let students quit. They don't have to be funny or good, but right from the first day of level 1, we can't let them quit. No bailing. Nip that in the bud, she says.

"AVOID COMMON WISDOM."

Neil is talking about political sketches. It doesn't matter if the point of view is liberal or conservative, it just has to say something we didn't think of. "Avoid common wisdom" is a good way to avoid the most boring and obvious political sketches.

"IS SOMEONE HOME"

What's the difference between a character that seems fake and forced, and one that seems great? Neil says that in the good ones, you can "**tell someone is home.**" There's a chunk of the person's real self in there, maybe, or something real.

IF IT'S FROM REAL LIFE, YOU DON'T NEED TO EXPLAIN.

A second-hand one. Patrick took a workshop from Joe, and what he got from it was a thing on justifying. If the thing you're doing is just a heightened version of something that happens in real life—you don't need to explain it. But if it's a weird thing that just kinda evolved out of the improv weirdness, then you need to explain it out loud.

"WHAT IF?"

Fernie tells me a good way to title the game of the scene is something he got from Walsh, and that is to phrase it like "what if?" So the name of a game of the scene might be "What if a sea captain was into sailing just for the telescopes?"

THE HAND THING

Berg tells me about his hand metaphor for explaining things in improv scenes. "If the first unusual thing is the thumb, the justification is the palm, and further instances of the game are the fingers." Oh, just read his explanation of it.

"SEE IT LAND"

Gardner is telling me how good Gausas classes were. One of his favorite notes is "see it land," meaning to make sure you see your partner react to the move you made before you even think about moving on.

2016

JANUARY 2ND, 2016 at 9:40PM

Q: I'M STARTING 101 IN 2 WEEKS AND FEELING ANTSY.

Anonymous asked: I'm starting 101 at UCB in 2 weeks. i'm kinda antsy about it, is there anything I can / should be doing to prep for the class?

You're gonna do great!

JANUARY 2ND, 2016 at 9:41PM

Q: "WIZARD FIGHTING" VS. "GIVING A GIFT?"

Anonymous asked: Hi, Will. What is the difference between "wizard fighting" and "giving a gift"?

Wizard fighting is changing the reality of the world so that your character wins when that's not what the scene needs.

Giving a gift is changing reality so that the scene is better.

JANUARY 8TH, 2016 at 1:22PM

BE A GREAT STRAIGHT MAN

The "straight man" is the voice of reason. It's the person (woman or man, despite the probably soon-to-be-insanely-dated term straight 'man') who is confused by the unusual thing in the scene. He doesn't agree that the weird thing is the way to go because is a voice of reason!

Someone says to you "Honey, we've talked about how our marriage is getting a little, well, stagnant. So starting this evening, in order to spice things up, I am going to hunt you."

And you say "I do not want to be hunted, sweetheart. That's dangerous!"

Aha! You are taking the "straight man" role. You're pushing back against the funny idea in order to call attention to how weird it is. That's called "framing" the unusual thing or else "calling it out."

PROBLEM: if straight men get too forceful or dominant or fussy they can ruin a scene.

Luckily for you I am the *greatest straight man on the face of the planet*. For real. It's my jam. I'm not as charismatic or as clever or as fun as almost anyone I've been on stage with. But there is no one—NO ONE—who can stare a silly idea in the face with as much delightful befuddlement as yours truly. I crush it as the straight man.

So here's how to be a good one.

Be Curious: The straight man should always want to know more. "Why do you want to hunt me?" And if the other person is stuck for a reason, you have enough empathy to suggest one. "Sweetheart, is this because the guys at work say you're not manly enough?"

Be Almost Convinced: The funniest posture for a straight man is to sit right on the brink of being convinced. No matter how insane the idea, you are almost ready to give it a shot. Better than a hard "NO" is a careful "I don't THINK so...." I did a two-person improv team with a friend who like me was often a straight man in scenes and we called ourselves "The Furrowed Brows" because that was such a common expression when dealing with an insane idea.

Point Out The Funniest Dumb Consequences: Writers and analytical people make great straight men because they quickly see the funniest consequences of a funny idea. The ones that are true, but that we the audience have not yet considered. In response to the above "I'm going to hunt you" you could say "You don't want to do that, you would be such a terrible widower." Or "And you'll clean up my body? I doubt it." Or "You couldn't defend yourself against a murder charge, you're a terrible liar."

Challenge Them: This is a more aggressive version of the previous tip: you challenge the silliness of the idea. "You want to murder me? Then what will do you when you're charged? Won't you be lonely?" Gauge the responses. If the other person isn't coming up with great reasons, back off. In fact, let's make that a tip on its own.

If You're Ever "Winning," Back Off: Generally speaking, if the voices of reason win, the scene feels smug and boring. We don't want you to "win" the scene. We just want you to explore and challenge the idea to get more fun out of it. So be ready to take your foot off the brakes and let the other person get their way in order for the scene to continue.

One of three basic tones you want to strike as a straight man:

Be As Dry As Toast: Just adopt a reasonable, moderate tone and engage the insanity with a disarming voice of reason, OR

Have Just A Small Stick Up Your Rear: Be perturbed, prissy and put off by the crazy person. OR

Be Insanely Freaked Out: Be completely taken apart by the craziness! Scream! This is the nuttiest idea you have ever heard of! This will ruin everything!

Regardless of your tone, you will STILL be ALMOST CONVINCED, you will still be CURIOUS, you will REMAIN ENGAGED and CHANGEABLE.

Being a good straight man is so much fun. Get good at it and enjoy it.

JANUARY 21ST, 2016 at 10:53PM

Q: ANY A-TO-C EXERCISES TO DO ALONE?

Anonymous asked: Are there any A to C practice suggestions that a person can do alone? Or things anyone has done that worked those improv muscles when they only had themselves to practice with?

I've sometimes practices word associations on my own. Like I'd be on a long subway ride, and I'd give myself a suggestion, and I'd just do a word association on it. Trying to make A to C jumps.

Like I'd give myself "apple" and then do "apple—sin—Massachusetts—boy bands—tailored suits—glass slipper—Aesop—morals—apple"

Or I'll give myself suggestions and try to think of initiations.

ROCK AND ROLL

JANUARY 24TH, 2016 at 3:43PM

Q: HOW TO COACH SOMEONE'S AGGRESSIVELY SEXUAL BEHAVIOR?

Anonymous asked: I have been coaching a team and am trying to determine how best to address one performer's aggressively sexual behavior. He seems to cognitively understand why these things are tricky, but seems to be having a hard time practicing it. I am maybe nervous about it because I'm a relatively new coach and also am a woman and they are all men about 15-20 years older than me and I do feel a little nervous alone in a room with just men in general. This is maybe a weird question! Apologies for that.

I think this is an interesting question, but since there's gender dynamics at play I asked some improv teachers I know who happen to be women to answer this:

FROM SUZI BARRETT (UCB-LA):

This is something i've dealt with as a coach, and it should be an easy fix. Send him an email, and don't get personal about your critique. I realize his behavior probably inspires a lot of opinions and judgments about his personal character, but all of that is beside the point as there are plenty of elements you can address from a purely comedic standpoint. So give him the benefit of the doubt (he has the newbie improv jitters, poor impulse control, he's trying to be funny by doing something shocking, etc.), and give the improv-related notes in a way that won't make things tense or put him on the defensive.

Here are those notes, as i see them...

This is becoming a go-to for you, and go-to's are the enemy of good comedy! Yes, sex and violence are automatic heightening devices, but i want you to challenge yourself to come up with other ways to heighten. If you don't, you're just copy/pasting scenes and robbing yourself and the audience of one of the main joys of improv which is discovery!

Also, be aware that physicalized sexual moves in improv scenes are a big pimp for your scene partners. Sure, they happen, and yes, you can make them, but be sparing about it. Why? Because when you make moves like that, you are being the guy on the team that forces your teammates to fill a very tall order. There are only so many times in an improv career someone wants to be pimped into miming a blowjob or getting bent over and mime-rammed in the butt. You know what i mean?

The same goes for the audience. know that when you make choices like this, you have more work cut out for yourself... you've got to find a way to make yourself likable and watchable even though you're doing something which (on the surface) looks violating. again, can you do it? Of course, you *can* do anything. But you shouldn't *want* to rush towards moves like this anymore than you would *want* to play a bunch of scenes as a character who is racist.

Audiences don't know your offstage life. all they know is what you show them. And if you show them extremely dark and gritty stuff, or stuff that appears to put your teammates in a compromising position, they will rally against you with clammed-up silence until you can earn their trust and respect again.

A great example of this happened at a Sentimental Lady show at DCM a few years ago. Mid-show, Berg's character called my character a "dumb slit", and the audience fell into an icy silence that continued whenever berg spoke for the rest of the show. It was almost scientific!

(note from the editor: Sentimental Lady is Suzi's improv team, DCM is an annual improv festival in NYC, and Berg is one of her male teammates)

FROM CHELSEA CLARKE, UCB-NY:

I'm not exactly sure what the situation you are dealing with here, so I'm gonna make some assumptions.

It sounds like you're dealing with someone who's making some "panic moves". Always humping in scenes, things that feel forced and out of nowhere, saying sexist fakey bro stuff, something like that?

I gather from your question you've already started to address it. That's really great, and not always the easiest thing to call out! Good! We have a foundation for dealing with him from here on out. But before we get to that:

Do not be intimidated by any group you coach. You can do this. I mean if you are legitimately physically concerned for your safety ok fine don't go teach them, but I'm gonna assume that that isn't what's happening.

The team wants you there to help guide them to the funniest ways of play with their ideas. You can be firm. Your guidance makes them funnier and they see that. You're funny, don't worry about giving harsh notes. You can do it in a funny way. Or in a mean way! Whatever you like. You are the leader, they will or should trust your instinct.

You are partially the voice of the audience when you are coaching. It's not just that YOU don't like how he's behaving. He needs to understand that the audience is going to be more engaged by good improv. The side effect of being a bad listener, bad supporter, stereotype aggressive yeller is that the audience won't laugh and have fun the way they will when you improvise well. Stop every single scene that be bails on with a panic move. Amy Poehler (no big deal no big deal) watched me teach a class where I let a struggling student bail on a scene, and I was gentle on him. Amy made sure to let me know that's not ok, even in level 101. And now I pass this info to you. Have a zero tolerance policy on bailing. Those panic moves hang his partners out to dry. You're coaching this team, it's important to teach him and support them all.

Anyway, back to practical steps for the next time you coach this group:

You may have to be creative in how you are going to get through to this person!

There's a shock value of those big choices that might feel fun and funny to him. He probably needs exercises that focus on working the muscles of playing realer moments and/or realer choices in crazy moments. These scenes may eventually heighten to the energy he's getting with those aggressive panic moves. But he doesn't get to start there. Put him in exercises where he has to commit.

Think of what you do to push through panic moments and make an exercise for him. Can we get him into some successful scenes where he's playing himself? What's your favorite exercise for characters that are different from you but still naturalistic? Can he only think shock yes ands? Maybe use Ian Robert's "Flash Scenes" exercise to hear his thought process and help brainstorm better ways to use his ideas.

Again, I don't know exactly what you are dealing with but I'm psychic and here is the solution: Give him an approach to "big" characters that doesn't allow stereotypes. So instead of "bro let's go bang some chicks" have him access *real things* he's *really* heard dudes say to each other or that he's *really* said to friends.

The details are foggy, but at an ASSSSCAT many years ago, there was a scene where a couple was complaining about their mother/ mother-in-law coming over and what a nag she was. Amy Poehler (I'm invoking her twice?!?) entered, kissed them on the cheeks and said "it's so good to see you my darlings I've just come back from Africa and really truly you MUST go, you must." It felt real and it killed. I was not an improv student at that point and I still appreciated how great that was.

He's going to feel how funny it is to play specifics from his own personal observations and experiences, and hopefully he won't want to continue regurgitating stereotypes. Get him to do that. And if it doesn't work fuck him in the butt forever til he dies and has to leave the group.

MORGAN JARRETT, UCB-NY:
The first part of my answer is this: Stop coaching these guys! If you feel uncomfortable and they/one of them continue to play aggressive sexual topics and they are not taking your notes, stop coaching them. You don't even have to say why, you can just say you have a conflict, b/c you do have a conflict, you're uncomfortable in a room with all men 20 years older than you, you're the only woman and they are playing aggressively sexual!?!? ARGH!!! This makes me mad, b/c of course you're uncomfortable who wouldn't be! It sounds like you have normal instincts!! And yes, they should be adult men and adjust and realize they are making a situation weird but they are clearly lacking the awareness or are in the mind set that in Improv/Comedy anything goes, which is not true. Hopefully, one day society and culture will shift but until then we as women still have to be the ones to make the choice to LEAVE a situation that makes us feel icky and not feel bad about it.

The second part of my answer, as I know the first part may seem a little rash.

Limit how much you acknowledge the sexual stuff. For example you could say as you're noting a scene, "Hey Brad, I don't think the blow job joke was needed since the game was clearly blank." And then move on to the next note.

Another tip, let him know he's going blue in every scene and not stretching as a performer. "Hey Brad, you're going blue in almost every scene, try something new, you have to get out of your comfort zone to stretch yourself as a performer." Another tactic, make the session a focus on challenges "Today Brad as soon as you make a blue joke in a scene you get tagged out, Erik as soon as you straight man you get tagged out, Hank as soon as you say Did I Do That? in your Urkel voice, you get tagged out. We're going to focus today on changing our habits!"

I would only use the second part of my answer if you feel like you want to keep spending time on this group. Since you're newer to coaching this sounds like a hard group to wrangle, make it a little easier on yourself in the beginning!

Coach a group that wants to practice their 101 show, a mix of men & women and ages. Give yourself time to find you're coaching sea legs with groups you feel comfortable with. Honestly, I would just stop coaching them. No need to put yourself through that when you feel nervous, they sound like creeps!

FROM MARY SASSON (UCB-LA):

If I understand this question, a man is being too sexually aggressive in scene work, and it makes you uncomfortable to give the note? I can understand why that could be weird. When you begin coaching in general, giving notes to people can seem awkward. But I would say that you are the one in charge, even if you are younger, so I would say give him the note that he needs to be less sexually aggressive. If he continues the behavior, stay on him, and remind him like any other note. I think speaking frankly, but not scoldingly, will help alleviate the embarrassment from giving a note that is sexual in nature. If you give the note and he doesn't like it and reacts negatively, then know that there are plenty of other teams to coach with performers who are eager to learn and take notes.

As to the other issue, if a room of grown men feels weird, and I could see coaching a group of men at night could feel weird, don't do it. I think you're well within your rights to ask groups before you coach what the breakdown of the group is and choose accordingly. In general, this is a made up economy and I think you can do what makes you feel most comfortable.

FEBRUARY 8TH, 2016 at 12:53PM

LGBTQ CHARACTERS IN IMPROV

I was on Matt Besser's Improv4Humans podcast and Besser read a question from a gay improviser asking why there weren't more gay characters in improv scenes. It was an interesting and thoughtful question, but no one on that episode of I4H was gay. We answered it. Then afterwards Besser suggested I write about it on my improv blog.

So I wanted to print answers on my improv blog from queer/bi improvisers.

The full question is here on reddit. Here's an excerpt:

"I can't help but notice a surprising lack of improvised gay characters on your show. What I mean by this, is that when you and the performers are in a scene, and the characters are in a relationship they are almost always in a heterosexual relationship. This is particularly noticeable when you have LGBTQ improvisers on your show and when they are in a scene they are almost always put into heterosexual relationships as well."

Answers from queer/bi improvisers after the jump!

SUZI BARRETT, UCB-LA

my first thought was "we play gay characters and relationships all the time". i spent half of our sentimental lady show on saturday playing a gay character. (johnny meeks played my wife) so... i'm not sure i'm seeing this through the same lens as the writer of the question. but here are my other thoughts...

a lot of the relationships portrayed on stage are totally open to interp, because the sex of the characters we play isn't always labeled. when it is labeled, i think the tendency is to label something according to your own experience... so if the sex of the characters (and hence whether the relationship is gay or hetero) is being named by a straight person, they're probably going to tend towards making it a straight relationship. that's their experience, that's what's in the front of their brain, and unless something else is called for by the show– they're going to keep things as "normal" (read: close to their own life experience) as possible. given that 90 percent of the population is straight, that's a healthy majority of improv scenes. and that's ok. it doesn't mean gay relationships aren't EVER portrayed– they are. they're just not always go-to's for straight folks... the same way african american characters aren't my go-to, because why would they be? you know?

and sometimes things just get lost in translation. everyone plays everything in improv. men play women, women play men, we all play pirates and animals and applesauce machines. so unless an actor is doing an over-the-top gender bend, or using corny dialogue like "as your girlfriend", their scene partner might just "cast" them as whatever they see them as. that means sometimes a gay relationship might be what one improviser sees, but not what the other one sees. again, it's ok.

everything is going to be ok.

JEFF HILLER, UCB-NY

I think the deal is that straight improvisers often feel that if they play gay, it will seem like THAT is the game of the scene. I'm sure if Gabrus started out as a gay man, even I might think that was the first unusual thing (and yet I see him at auditions for gay guys all the time...). So, consequently, I think straight improvisers want to be cool about the gay thing and so they don't make themselves gay, and then weirdly, no gay scenes ever happen. When I taught that queer improv class at UCB NY a few years ago, that was the main thing the students talked about. They loved being able to just be a gay guy and have it seem normal. And they loved that when they started the scene as a neutral character, they weren't automatically labeled as women (the class was mainly white gay dudes, so let's all check our privilege here). The (three!) women in the class liked playing in the queer class primarily because they weren't constantly made to be wives. They were allowed to play men occasionally. And ironically, that's how the guys felt too. I notice I will often just be playing myself in a scene and I will be labeled as a woman which I often sort of blanch at because I am surprised that I am such a swisher that my neutral tone is projected as boldly female.

Here is what I will also say though. While I love playing in all gay groups and getting to play a gay couple, I wouldn't want all of The Curfew to suddenly do lots of scenes where they play gay men. For some reason, it often DOES come across as a little bit homophobic to me when straight people play gay people. I would imagine it's similar when you (very rarely) see a white person declare that they are a person of color. EVEN in scenes where that fact is not being played for laughs, doesn't it feel just a little bit weird? Maybe it's just that it points out how very straight and very white our improv community is, but I often get uncomfortable in those situations. I don't know that this is right, or normal, it's just how I feel. Like you don't want to co-opt someone else's experience. When I am pimped into playing a famous person of color (ahem, my old team Police Chief Rumble) or just like a Jamaican guy on the street, always feel like I am doing something inappropriate.

And I think what it REALLY boils down to, is that the improv gets muddy. You are searching for that ONE unusual thing, and so you want everything else to be really neutral around that. If a (known) straight dude introduces that he is gay, it might add to THAT being the unusual thing, even if that straight improviser wasn't trying to do that.

Also, I just really love playing ladies. Ladies with purses and hair that I twirl and accessories that I put on and take off through brilliant object work. And so if a man introduces himself, I kind of WANT to be his wife instead of his husband sometimes. Because of all those object work possibilities!

This is so stream of consciousness, I am really sorry about that, but here is another thought that I sometimes have. I tend to worry that if I started playing a gay man to a straight guy's gay man, it might feel uncomfortable for them. I worry that they would think I was hitting on them, or that I suspected that they were gay or that I was doing some sort of weird gay magic. I would play two gay men with a straight woman without blinking, but I would totally make myself into a lady on purpose to avoid playing gay with a straight guy. Even though straight guys at the UCB are almost uniformly nice liberal dudes, I just have a hang up after being bullied all through childhood and I would rather leave that stuff at the door.

BRIAN FAAS, UCB-NY

My first thought is—Why assume the only way to show a character is gay is by putting him or her in a relationship? I feel like I play plenty of gay guys—which is my base reality—but it might not come up because it's not the point of the scene. These characters could be single, or not with their boyfriend at that exact moment, or a priest... who knows! Gay people are all around us, but especially in restaurants, shopping malls, and on airplanes.

Jokes aside, I do remember one time when I first started doing improv, I tried to play a gay guy, as a specific game move, and then got labeled a woman. It was a bummer. Over the years, I've learned to adjust my acting to make super clear—surprisingly, I found lowering my voice actually reads "gayer."

It also help to give yourself a name. Might I suggest Topher or Trevor? I'll never forget the time I was watching Harold Night and Will Hines introduced himself as "Bruce San Francisco." Zero confusion there.

Love you, Will!

xo, Brian

OSCAR MONTOYA, UCB-LA

I'm of two minds here. I always tend to be on the defensive whenever people label me as gay or of color right away without context because in my experience, they usually make that the focus of the scene and most of the time they CANNOT get away from it. I remember the first time I auditioned for a Harold team like in 2009, and being fairly new to the experience I had a scene partner who commented that he's "never dated anyone like me before." Instead of taking it to a place that was playable (different political affiliations, hobbies, etc) I distinctly remember him saying "Well, I guess I do like my coffee like I like my women: black." The improviser in me internally rolled his eyes (because I've been arbitrarily labelled as Carlos or Jermaine or some other "ethnic" name like that. And I still do!!). I tried to "yes and" that but I was so furious about it, and he would just not let it go, that I felt so defeated from improvising for a while.

Looking back at this experience, I do sometimes wonder why he didn't label me as a guy and instead immediately labelled me as a woman. Was it because he didn't feel comfortable being a gay dude, even in an improv scene? Did he feel like the "game" was him freaking out that I was black and that adding being gay would dilute the game? Did he not even consider being gay in a scene possible at all? I'm not sure what the answer is, and I probably won't ever know. I won't ever know what it's like to do improv from the perspective of a straight white male, and that's fine, because there's a lot of them out there.

What I will say is that I do feel a little trepidatious when establishing a homosexual relationship because I don't want my scene partner to think that's the focus of the scene, which has happened many, many, many times. I tend to avoid that fact altogether and just say I'm female because I just don't want to deal with it. I do have to make clear that in that prior statement I'm referring to doing scenes with people I don't know, or don't feel comfortable with yet. When it comes to playing with a team of my friends, I feel liberated to do anything I want. For example, I'm on an all gay team and I don't think we've ever had a scene where a couple was heterosexual, but that's only because for us a homosexual relationship is the "norm."

Maybe just having the balls to establish a homosexual relationship in a group of improvisers is what I should be doing. I should be able to trust that these people that I do scenes with won't take that as a gift of labeling "the unusual thing." I also think the community is getting much much much better about stuff like this, but I know we have a ways to go.

FEBRUARY 9TH, 2016 at 2:33PM

Q: "LONG DISTANCE RUNAROUND" BY YES OR "SPACE TRUCKIN" BY DEEP PURPLE?

Anonymous asked: In an improv scene if you turn on a radio which song should be playing- "Long Distance Runaround" by Yes or "Space Truckin" by Deep Purple?

"Space Truckin'" is my pick.

And: you're joking but I find the very best songs to have be playing on improv radios are ones that were in the zeitgeist exactly 15 years before the performance.

So "Hey Ya!" isn't a bad pick for right now.

FEBRUARY 21ST, 2016 at 11:36AM

Q: WHAT PROMPTED YOU TO MOVE TO LA?

Anonymous asked: On the heels of the Gethard article, I suddenly have a huge fear that I'm wasting my time in New York, and I'll wind up in LA eventually. You were in New York forever and finally moved to LA. What prompted you to? Is this sort of thing cyclical or is New York comedy just dying?

A fascinating question. The article you refer to is this one:

http://www.vulture.com/2016/02/comedian-chris-gethard-new-york-los-angeles.html

I love this article. Gethard is such a terrific writer and so funny. He paints these clear specific pictures and the dude is just GOOD AT WORDS.

But the truth is that the decision as to whether or not to move is not so dramatic as it might seem.

Okay: the answer is It's cyclical. People come up and ripen and move.

But much more important than what city you're in is where you are personally in your own growth. Where you live is far more fluid that people say. You don't have to pick a side: New York or LA. Even in that article, Gethard admits he could be in LA, even soonish, if his career takes him there.

New Yorkers love talking about New York. I lived there 17 years and I adored it and I loved talking about it and still love talking about it and am talking about it with this very paragraph. I have never felt cooler in my whole life then when I first moved to NYC when I was 26 and I walked out of my new apartment, locked the door, and strutted on down West 92nd street to Riverside Park and went for a run down the Hudson River. I was the coolest person in the universe to my mind, just for being in that city. It's great.

BUT really, it's not permanent. Get Buddhist about this: the only constant is change. Think pieces and good writing want us to make decisions and to assign specific meaning to things but in your actual everyday life you will change and move and evolve constantly. That may or may not involve a move to another city, and may or may not take you back.

I moved because I wanted the challenge of getting more professional work and I wanted to admit to myself that I was really "going for it" to be an actor and a writer. And the UCB was about to expand greatly (new training center in NYC, new stage and training center in LA), and so it seemed like a good crossroads to let a new person into running the school. It felt like the next natural move.

It's funny Gethard's article made you write this because three weeks before I moved out of NYC I completely panicked and wanted to back out. I was talking to Chris, in fact, and told him I was thinking of not going. We'd already had a goodbye show with my improv team and I'd told everyone I was going and I'd hired a moving company. But I was like "fuck it, maybe I'll just stay." And Chris said something like "You CAN'T back out now! Everyone will ... I mean, you will be humiliated" or something like that. It was funny, how he said it. "At LEAST go for six months, and THEN come back." He and I also agreed that if I were indeed on the verge of a nervous breakdown, which was something I posited, then it would probably be nicer to have that breakdown in sunny LA than loud crowded New York. So I went. And I loved it right away.

The changes in size of the UCB community mean more to the UCB world than the city each community is in. Meaning the fact that the UCB world was so much bigger in 2015 than it was in 2005 had more effect on my life than moving from NYC to LA.

The stand-up community: I can't really speak to it. I'm going to guess that it's cyclical. A bunch of vets come up in NYC, ripen and move. Some seem to never move: Eugene Mirman, Todd Barry, etc.

I've made no decisions in this post. It makes me a less entertaining writer. But I think I'm speaking the truth. YOU make your world, it doesn't matter that much what city you're in.

That said, there's 100 times as much work in LA, and many more KINDS of work. It's not just BE ON SATURDAY NIGHT LIVE or NOTHING out here.

The pizza and bagels are FINE out here. I don't know why people like to make that a thing. They're very good! Ugh, humans like to keep score.

MARCH 8TH, 2016 at 7:13PM

Q: MY 201 TEACHER IS "BRUTALLY" HONEST.

Anonymous asked: This blog is such a great resource for improv & life—thanks! Anyways, question: I'm in a 201 with a pretty experienced teacher who has a habit of being "brutally" honest (in a jokingly way). I personally love the way he teaches because he so aptly identifies what I need to improve but there are a lot of students who are so uncomfortable that it's not working for them. Without changing the teaching, how can I help the rest of the class get out of their head and rid of the jitters?

Are you one of my current students? I'm sorry, truly.

MARCH 17TH, 2016 at 3:56PM

TRUTHFUL AT ALL COSTS

I've had luck lately setting up exercises like this.

Two people up. Whoever initiates much make a big choice. Something unusual, fantastical or strange. The responder simply has to act exactly as they would.

That may sound obvious. But I find that students need to be reminded explicitly to do this. Two students did this.

> Player 1: I gotta tell you something. Last night I was abducted by aliens. It was a classic silver thing like you see in the movies. It pulled me right up into the spaceship from my bed. Performed weird acts on me.
>
> Player 2: (deeply concerned) Oh man, are you... are you okay?

I stopped the scene. That's not what you would say if a friend told you they were kidnapped by aliens. That's what an improvisers says who is under pressure to "say yes." But I'm asking for a truthful response.

> Player 1: They took me up there, they laid me on a bed. They performed,

Player 2: Wait a minute. Sit down. (Player 1 sits.) Dude, I'm, like, worried about you, man.

Player 1: I'm kinda worried about ME! It's like I'm the only one who saw it, so I like, I feel insane! I saw them! They were grey! They had the big eyes. And they were small! like this big, and they walked around me, and they poked and they looked and you're just like "What's going on?" And I was like, is this how my life ends? IS this life?

Player 1: Dude, um, maybe we should go, like, talk to a specialist. Someone who can help you with this?

You can dismiss opinions that people try to pin on you, and you can ask questions, and you can refuse to believe things and you can choose not to care! You also do not HAVE to find the initiation unusual if you don't.

Child: Mom, I've decided I'm never going to school again!

Mom: Oh, honey. You'll learn to like school.

The actor playing the mom doesn't find it weird for her child to say that. Great! No problem.

A few caveats you'll have to point out: The responder cannot leave and must engage the person.

And you cannot change any facts. If the weird thing is evident, you should believe it, although have a truthful reaction.

Player 1: (shoots gun at player) Did that bullet just bounce off of you man?

Player 2: Don't tell anybody!

Player 1: What the fuck? Stay the hell away from me!

Player 2: Don't tell anybody! I come from the planet Nangongongon! I come in peace don't tell anyone!

Think of improv like a bicycle. "Saying yes" to the weird thing is pedaling, and expressing skepticism and "saying no" is like hitting the brakes. True, we need to be pedaling MORE than braking, but you also need to brake.

Wife: So babe, for dinner tonight, I kinda wanted to change things up. I got a peacock. And will you cut it up for me. I'll take care of the salad.

Husband: Babe, where did you get this?

Wife: The neighbor's backyard. They have a couple of them. They look like pests. So I thought I was helping them.

Husband: Babe, we have to put this back.

Wife: It's already dead, we're not putting it back.

Husband: I can see that it's dead, we can just sort of. I mean.... I mean it sounds good.

Wife: Doesn't it? Healthy protein.

Husband: Yeah. I'm just a little nervous. I mean... you have a peacock recipe? We have chicken in the freezer!

Wife: I wanted to change things up! And he walked in front of my car. Wait, I'm pretty sure this is a boy right, because of the long feathers?

Husband: I don't know! Wait, you ran this thing down with your car?

You can see in this scene the husband has room to be won over if that's what the scene needs. But he's being real. The wife has a reason for her behavior that's plausible without being so reasonable it kills the fun.

The actor playing the husband has a good sense of what his character knows. He knows that he doesn't know which a male peacock is (all peacocks are male, the females are peahens—but it makes sense he wouldn't know that), but he notices when his wife said she hit it with her car.

The actors are reliable reporters of what's going on. They are engaged with the scene and using their own sensibilities. It's fun! Oh man, is it ever so good when they are allowed to play truthfully.

MARCH 22ND, 2016 at 12:16PM

"IS THIS ABOUT..."

Lots of times in scenes someone will say "Is this about...?" It's an offer. You SHOULD notice it and consider it, though you don't HAVE to accept it.

Lisa: I cut my own hair this morning. And I don't know what to do, should I... how does it look?

Gwen: I feel like when I've had bad haircuts I don't want people to lie to me when it happens, and it's not good.

Lisa: Okay, I accept the fact that it doesn't look great.

Gwen: It does NOT look great. But you're still very pretty. You have really good bone structure. I just moved to this neighborhood that has a lot of Orthodox Jews and they have a lot of wig stores.

Lisa: Let's GET a wig then! Let's get a wig!

Gwen: Yeah, let's get a wig.

Lisa: Do you have any? Do you just... happen to have some?

Gwen: Is this about Joe?

So that last sentence there is Gwen offering a justification to Lisa.

I USED to suggest you should ALWAYS accept these, unless they directly contradict something we already know. But sometimes people will offer an "is this about..." that is so far afield of what's happening it would derail the scene.

"Is this about how you really want to have sex?"

"Is this about how you resent me?"

"Is this about you hating your kids?"

If it's nowhere close to what you are thinking and feeling, it's okay to reject these offers. I'd rather you stay committed to your character and scene.

I DO think it's good form to yes-and some part of it if you can.

"In the past, this has been about sex. But right now that's not at all what I'm thinking about."

"I do sometimes resent you, but not right now."

"My kids drive me nuts, but I don't hate them."

I think you should think of these "Is this about" statements like a pass in basketball. If it's close to you, it's worth bending, even lunging, to catch it. But if it's way off, you're not doing the team any favors running all the way across the court. Your partner just threw it out of bounds. Move on.

Or maybe it's like someone offering you food at a party? Accepting it is gracious, dismissing it without even thinking about it is rude, but if you're allergic to this particular food or really full—it's okay to politely decline.

MARCH 23RD, 2016 at 3:08PM

Q: MOST HUMBLING EXPERIENCE?

Anonymous asked: What's the most humbling experience you've had doing improv?

At this very moment, which is 3pm in the afternoon on a weekday, I am sitting in the cafe of the UCB Theatre in Los Angeles with crumbs of a chocolate chip cookie on my face. Instead of writing scripts or seeing friends or exercising I'm answering questions on my improv blog. Right after I hit return I'm gonna go buy a cup of coffee and I might get another cookie.

MARCH 23RD, 2016 at 3:14PM

Q: HOW TO MAKE YOUR PARTNER LOOK FUNNY?

Anonymous asked: Hey, something I've heard people say when describing great players is that they make their partner look funny. But I have yet to hear specifically how someone can do that. Any thoughts? Thanks.

I think this is a great question BECAUSE of exactly what you said: it's one of those things that lots of people say—"make your partner look good"—but is not exactly obvious as a plan of action! Like, I had to think about it.

I think there's two main ways.

The easiest way is to make whatever your partner implies to be true. Whatever they accuse you of, you do it. Whatever they state, you see a physical example of. Whatever they confess to, you remember something from the past that verifies this confession. Make their stuff true, immediately.

Second way is to give them a fun gift. Oh god, examples. Um, ask them if they still believe they were abducted by aliens? Or ask if they are still making their own clothes? Or how their robot arm is doing? These are gifts I would like at least.

I thought of a third way! If they've given THEMSELVES a gift, they you set them up to play with it later. If they mention how they have a robot arm, then a little bit later you find a tin of oil and ask "What do you use this oil for?" and then they oil their own arm.

These examples do not sound great.

APRIL 1ST, 2016 at 10:00AM

Q: WHAT'S THE BEST WAY TO WORK ON JUSTIFICATION/ PHILOSOPHY?

Anonymous asked: What's the best way to work on justification/philosophy? I often feel like I make up facts or I'm too specific which then doesn't give me enough of a road map to make other game moves. I know I'm doing it wrong. Is there a secret to justification? I had a sub that said that Phil Jackson was a master justifier. How does one perfect that skill?

Hey, I love this question! I think this comes down to sensing the difference between an "internal" justification and an "external" one. The internal one is usually better. This is an acting thing more than a comedy thing.

Having a justification, or another way to put it is having a "why", is important. In improv, you often find yourself doing something weird first, and then having to explain yourself after.

So you are doing something that you think is fun or interesting or maybe it's something you didn't even pick. Like someone says to you:

"Roger, I see that you finished your reports on time, Unfortunately you wrote them in your own blood! Why?"

So now the actor playing Roger has to decide why. This isn't something he picked. But now he has to say yes to it and give a reason.

Almost any specific reason will do. But an internal reason is better. By "internal" I mean a philosophical one. A belief system. Something like "I wanted to show that I am dedicated to this company."

This is as opposed to an "external" reason, like circumstances that forced you. Something like "We're running so low on office supplies, I had to." That can work but it's weaker.

Another way that I do it is that I tell myself to answer truthfully. I try to internally make it true to myself—*okay, I wrote the reports in blood*—and then sort of realize what the reason is. I approach it like an actor. It helps me come up with reasons that feel less forced and more natural. And they are usually more philosophical and internal that way too.

Phil Jackson is indeed a master justifier. You cannot give him a gift too weird for him to instantly adopt it and make it as natural as can be. I saw him once play a bank robber who walks into a bank and pulls open his trenchcoat and says

"Ok, everyone as you can see I am armed with..."

And it felt like he was gonna say guns, or maybe that he had a bomb strapped to him, but his scene partner (who was feeling silly) said

"...a bunch of machetes."

And Phil, without missing a beat, said "That's right. Machetes." And then Phil started miming juggling all the machetes. "Check me out! Don't mess with this! Now hand over all your money!"

APRIL 1ST, 2016 at 12:15PM

Q: JUSTCRAIG: "YO, YO, YO, YO"

justcraig asked: In improv, what's a better way to start a rap, "My name is _____ and I'm here to say," or "yo, yo, yo, yo?"

I've heard that Del Close and Bernie Sahlins would argue about this all the time.

APRIL 5TH, 2016 at 2:06PM

Q: WHAT SHOULD MY PRACTICE GROUP DO ABOUT "THAT GUY?"

Anonymous asked: What should my practice group do about "that guy" when the person is an actor or actress only interested in socializing at practice sessions and is doing improv only because their agent told them to? They are taking up time at practice that we are paying for with a coach to socialize and go off topic. This person has no interest in taking the entire improv school's curriculum and only wants to be in a commercial. They have also failed to grasp basic concepts.

My suggestions:

   a. Wait two weeks no matter what and see if it's still bothering you.
   b. End the group and re-form with everyone but this person. Lots of people do this. If you do this and the person asks you what happened, you have two choices. Be honest with them "We wanted to try some other things. Maybe we'll all do something else some other time." That feels hard but it is respectful. Or dodge them forever, which also happens. If you do that, be cool with the idea that they'll never want to perform with you again, which you might be okay with.
   c. If this is the third or more time you've gone through this, quit improv.

(I EDITED THIS TEN MINUTES AFTER POSTING MY APOLOGIES)

APRIL 6TH, 2016 at 7:15AM

Q: "END THE GROUP AND REFORM THE GROUP" SOUNDS CHILDISH

Anonymous asked: "End the group and reform with everyone but this person." Is this really better than being direct and tossing that one person? It feels childish to me.

I'm assuming that the group matters to this person and so it'd be polite to start over with a new name. I was once in a group that kicked someone out and they were hurt badly and it seemed to me that if we had changed names, a not-that-big-deal thing to me, it would have been a gesture of respect. It's also something that I see done a lot: breaking up, reforming with most of the same people, changing names.

But these are anonymous questions and I don't know the people involved so certainly I respect that kicking them out directly may be the right move.

APRIL 21ST, 2016 at 6:23PM

Q: HOW MUCH STAGE TIME SHOULD AN IMPROVISER REALLY WANT?

Anonymous asked: How much stage time should an improviser really want? It's easy to want to do shows every night because improv is fun. Can an improviser spend too much time performing over practice with a coach or does more stage time make up for that?

A great question! Hmm, there's no formula. I think that yes, there are diminishing returns for any kind of practice. I would say that it depends on the quality of the show and/or practice. If your practice is with excellent people and a great coach, that may be more fruitful than a depressing show before very small crowds. If your show is for a great crowd with a great cast, that might be more helpful than a listless practice.

Take the quality of the performance/practice into account. What is pushing you more?

Also remember that time away from improv where you absorb real life is crucial. Be a full person. Or fake it, as I and many others have done.

MAY 3RD, 2016 at 10:38AM

Q: MY TEAM IS TOO QUICK WITH INITIATING AND WALKING ON

Anonymous asked: I think my team is a little too quick on the draw with initiating scenes or walking on. Several times this week I've been trying to walk on or initiate a scene, only to be interrupted by somebody who had to get their idea out first. In one first beat I was a son. As I'm walking out for the second beat, a teammate runs out and now he's the son. It could be funny a idea but it actually derails the scene. Anything I can do to help my team work on this?

I hear this. It's a common feeling.

It's reasonable to ask your team to practice Initiation Etiquette: whoever moves first is going to initiate and gets a few long moments to do so.

It's also reasonable to say to your team "I think our back line is getting involved too often." I call it an "oppressive" back line. Propose a compromise: no tagouts or walk-ons for the first 2 or 3 scenes. After that, people can go nuts.

Another part of this is you accepting that sometimes teammates are excited and just can't help themselves and that's part of the fun. A common problem for teams is that they are too polite and won't get involved in each other's scenes and it slows stuff down.

MAY 3RD, 2016 at 8:04PM

Q: I FIND MYSELF TRYING TO "FIX" VERY BAD IMPROV.

Anonymous asked: When I play with improvisers who I think are doing very bad improv, I find myself trying to "fix" it in ways that often don't seem to work. Example: my scene partner keeps dropping huge things that have come up and adding new crazy things. I try to tie in what they dropped while still dealing with the new stuff, because you shouldn't just drop huge stuff. But I get notes that the scene moved on and I should've just gone with it. In general, how do I "go to them" without sacrificing good improv?

My gut tells me you need to be in the moment more and not worry about fixing things. If they need fixing they'll come back up. Be in the moment, commit, react and your authentic reactions will make the good parts stick and let the bad parts dissipate and no one will miss them. More acting, less writing.

MAY 8TH, 2016 at 11:21AM

Q: HOW DO YOU GET A TEAM YOU'RE DIRECTING TO LISTEN MORE?

Anonymous asked: How do you get a team you're directing to listen more when they aren't in the scene?

Prove to them how it's hurting the scene and then tell them to listen better so that stops happening. If you can't prove that it's hurting the scene then maybe everything's fine.

MAY 9TH, 2016 at 9:56AM

CODE OF CONDUCT FOR CLASSES, FIRST DRAFT

A code of conduct for classes, first draft:

No picking each other up.

No kissing.

No miming sex.

But yes to: seduction scenes that seem to be leading up to sex, or scenes that take place after sex. But we all agree we won't get to/start with sex itself.

These are okay: hugs, holding hands, arms around each other's shoulders.

And anytime there's anything you don't want to do (lap dances? intense yoga poses? Vigorous tennis match), you tell the other person in character that you don't want to do it and they'll adjust.

(You generally shouldn't use this code of conduct to get out of acting challenges like doing an accent or straightforward conversations about uncomfortable topics.)

MAY 10TH, 2016 at 3:26PM

Q: ANY TIPS FOR GETTING OUT OF THIS RUT?

Anonymous asked: Hey there! I'm in a 401 at UCB and on an Indie Team right now and I'm finding myself really struggling. I feel like I'm pretty funny and quick in a normal setting but once I get my improv pants on all of that fizzles out and I'm not only boring but I also get stuck for any response at all! Any tips for getting out of this rut?

See "how can I get out of my head?"
http://improvnonsense.tumblr.com/head

MAY 11TH, 2016 at 11:01AM

Q: MY CLASSMATE IS NOT GREAT AT IMPROV.

Anonymous asked: Hey Will! I've been working with a classmate who is really not great at improv. Scenes just get dragged down by her choices, she steps all over everyone in scenes, and just doesn't listen. My other classmates and I have a hard time making up for it (there are only five of us to begin with). How do you compensate during rehearsal/shows for being put in a group with someone who is a relatively poor player?

http://improvnonsense.tumblr.com/thatguy

MAY 11TH, 2016 at 1:40PM

Q: MY PARTNER IS A REAL PROBLEM, HE MOVED TO LA.

kevhines asked: I do a lot of two prov, but my partner is a real problem performer. He moved to LA. It makes it real hard to do scenes, or even schedule shows. Should I say something?

Tough one. I don't know your situation specifically of course but it sounds like this guy is a real pain in the ass! Drop him, I say!

JUNE 7TH, 2016 at 8:41PM

Q: I FEEL I HAVEN'T BEEN CREATIVE OR ADDING LATELY.

Anonymous asked: Lately I feel like I haven't been doing a good enough job of being creative and adding info to a scene. My strong suit has always been finding and specifying game, but recently I've been having more moments where I think "I need to add something right now," and being at a loss for words. My usual approach is to use my personal experience, but that often runs dry. Do you have any other advice for getting better at creating information from nothing?

Commit harder. Think of what just happened before the scene started. Look at the other character and make an observation about them.

SPECIAL ESSAYS

The following essays were not actual posts on the blog. They were "pages" which meant they were like posts that were permanently listed on the side of the blog. They're each a topic I would get asked very often about.

They're usually based on a post but then heavily expanded and revised.

HOW CAN I GET OUT OF MY HEAD?

Getting out of your head refers to the desire to be doing improv without having your head full of rules and thoughts and worries. It means you want to just... play... rather than be paralyzed by all the rules your improv teachers have told you. Getting out of your head also means that you want to stop feeling stuck on stage, that you have lost your instinct of what to do next, and that you are doubting yourself and worrying constantly. You feel that way and you're tired of it: what can you do?

Closely related to this question is the "I just had a terrible class/practice/show and I'm in a rut and what should I do?"

These are very common concerns. I would say it's the number one most frequent question I hear. Part of my job is picking which classes we put up at UCB-NY. If I ever want a class to sell out in zero seconds, I call it "Get Out of Your Head!"

ZACH WOODS' ADVICE

Well the first and best set of advice I have to offer isn't even mine. It's from UCB Performer Zach Woods in an email he sent to then-UCB student (now teacher and performer) Achilles Stamatelakey about this very problem. In Achilles' words:

> In May 2006, I had no confidence in my improv. After taking classes for a year-and-a-half, I felt like I was only getting worse at performing. I sent the following e-mail to some of the teachers and coaches I'd worked closely with at the time to seek their advice.
>
> I'm not feeling great about my improv and I hope you can give me some advice.

I don't remember when I've felt this unconfident in my performance. For the past month or so, I've constantly felt indecisive in scenes (both in practices and performances). I also feel way in my head and tentative. I find myself making moves because they seem like the "right" move to make, not because they're best for the scene or the most fun. I'm making weak choices and end up in mediocre scenes because of it. In other words, I feel like I'm stuck "improvising" rather than "playing" a scene.

Part of my lack of confidence might stem from having some really great rehearsals and shows in March, then having really high expectations of myself in April during Harold team auditions and not meeting those expectations. That I got rejected from two teacher-approved performance workshops hasn't helped my confidence either. It's a vicious cycle.

What do you do when you feel like you're in a rut? I want to feel like I'm improving my skills as an improviser in some way, but I haven't felt confident in weeks. I don't see myself getting out of this slump anytime soon.

Thanks again for all your help.

—Achilles

I got a bunch of responses, all of which I am extremely grateful for. Here is one of those responses:

Hey Achilles,

I'm sorry you're feeling this way. Everyone gets in ruts from time to time, and I know how discouraging it feels. While there are some things you can do to help, I think the short (and probably disappointing) answer is you've just got to ride it out. Ruts always last longer than we want them to, but they don't last forever. So try to be patient....as impossible as that sounds.

Here's some other stuff....

– I think sometimes people who care a great deal about improv can get so wrapped up in the improv community and improv itself that their self-esteem becomes dependent on the quality of their improv. This happens to me more often than I'd like, and it's always bad news for both my improv and my self-esteem. I think it's important to remember (especially when you're in a slump) that the qualities that make you valuable as a human being have nothing to do with group games or tag-outs. Whether or not you're a worthwhile person has nothing to do with improv. If you're doing awesome shows, you could still be an asshole, if you're doing bad shows you could still be a kind, generous guy. Hopefully you're not neurotic enough to be plagued by these issues, but, I know I am, so I figured I'd mention this stuff, just in case. So....

Remind yourself that your value as a person is in no way related to, or dependent on the quality of your improv.

– Another thing that can put people in their heads is a need to "achieve."

While it's great to get some validation in the form of recognition or approval, I think it's best not to put too much stock in external recognition. The warm, mushy feeling that comes from 'achieving' (getting put on a team, class, etc.) is fleeting, and soon you're back to worrying and working and trying to improve. I think it's good to be patient and to move at your own rate. Try not to measure your progress against other people's progress. I know that's hard (maybe impossible) but I think if you allow yourself to improve at your own rate, it liberates you from the self-conscious, insecure, self-flagellation that is anathema to good improv. Put your nose to the grindstone and do the work. It's important to have goals, but I think it's also important that those goals be rooted in personal progress rather than external achievement.

– Slumps are sometimes a result of improv-overkill. If you've been watching and doing improv constantly, it's possible that you're a bit burnt out. Good improv isn't inspired by other improv, it's inspired by life. If all you do is do/watch improv, you may have a deficit of life experiences to draw from. Take time to do the non-improv activities that you enjoy— things that have absolutely nothing to do with comedy. This will allow you to recharge. It will also put you back in touch with the things that make you unique and interesting as a person. That stuff is essential to good improv. Improv isn't just about game and technique, it's also about personality. It's important to take time to do non-comedy things that make you who you are. Listen to the music you like, read a book, fly a kite, hang out with your non-improv friends, go swimming, walk a dog, do whatever you want as long as it doesn't require a coach. Just get away from improv.

In a weird way it's kind of like the game of a scene. If all you do in a scene is hit game, game, game, and you never play the reality of the scene, both the game and the scene will feel inorganic and contrived. Similarly, in life, if all you do is improv, improv, improv, and you don't do interesting, fun non-improv stuff, your improv will feel stiff, and your life won't feel so good either (in my experience).

– Get a new pair of shoes. I don't know if this works, but I was in a slump once and I asked Peter Gwinn what I should do. He told me to get new shoes and wear them during rehearsals/shows. Make sure they are significantly different from the shoes you currently wear to rehearsals/performances. This might be bullshit, but it might be a miracle cure.

– Eat healthy, sleep well, exercise. I find that this stuff makes a huge difference. Taking care of your body allows you to focus better, etc. You probably already do this, but if not, eat some soy and get 8 hours of REM.

– If you feel like a show/rehearsal went badly, don't beat yourself up. If you notice yourself moping or obsessing over the show, try to do something to take your mind off it. You are not helping your improv by mentally abusing yourself. Self-flagellation is just a way of indulging one's own insecurities and fears. Sometimes you can't help it, but try to avoid abusing yourself if you can.

– And remember, your slump is temporary. It's more in your own head than in reality.

Be patient, relax, and your slump will pass. Seriously.

You're going to be alright,

Zach

PS. I apologize if this email comes off as pedantic and/or convoluted.

Besides the great advice, my favorite part of this e-mail is that Zach apologizes at the end for having written it. Very Zach.

Yep, that's pretty good.

Here's some wordier, less helpful advice on the same subject.

WHAT I DO: REMEMBER SIMPLE MANTRAS

Expanding on Zach's "everyone gets in ruts from time to time," let me overtly state that I feel I am in my head on a fairly regular basis. I've done this for 12 years and have achieved some amount of success at least within the society of the UCB Theatre in NYC (perform on a weekly show on the weekend, am one of the senior teachers) and I'd say every 4 or 5 shows I walk off stage convinced, wholly, that I am a fraud, who snuck by everyone who is in charge of deciding who is good by keeping my head down and being quiet at signature moments.

And so here are the specific things I do when I am feeling "in my head"—and by that I mean when I am feeling doubtful, and unsure of my abilities and unfunny.

First I have a few different **mantras** I run through in my head. One is "**listen and react**." I tell myself to forget everything else and just obey that rule. This is an effort to keep it simple, but to still be participatory.

Another one is I'll tell myself "**be playful**." This was advice my brother gave me before we did a two-prov set. It was the first time we had performed at a particular theatre and we wanted to be good. He grabbed both of my shoulders and looked at me and said "be playful—you're good when you're playful" and it freed me of worrying about being "good" or doing it "right."

Another trick I will do is to **remember a particular improv class I had in which I always felt great**. For me it's my fourth improv class. For some reasons, whether it was the teacher or the people in that class I don't fully know, I always felt confident and capable in that class. When I'm backstage before a show and feeling lousy I will quietly invoke the feeling of being in the backline of that class. It helps me recall some muscle memory of that confidence.

A final trick I will do—and I bet this reveals some problem with intimacy or something but who gives a crap if it helps my show—is that I **pretend that I am performing with strangers**. Sometimes with people I know I get tentative and unsure and I will second guess myself. When playing strangers I become a nice combination of decisive but polite. I listen more but I also make bold moves. It helps. So sometimes I'll tell myself that everyone I'm playing with are strangers.

Some other thoughts to consider if you're in your head:

THE LAST SHOW

Part of this phenomenon is that you only feel as good as your very last class/practice/show. You can have 1,000 great scenes in a row, but once you have a bad one, you walk away saying "maybe I'm terrible at this." It's easy to have a short memory when assessing yourself.

The good side of that is **it only take one "good" class/practice/show to feel better again**. Often the best way to get out of your head, is simply to do more of it, and increase the odds that you will do a scene where things go your way and you walk out feeling better.

BEWARE TRYING TO PLEASE JUST ONE PERSON (WHO ISN'T YOU)

Let's get some data here: is it ONE PERSON who is making you feel in your head? Like have you started taking a class, and the teacher doesn't seem to be impressed with you, or maybe even actively seems to be unimpressed with you? Are you "in your head" trying to please this one person? It's understandable to want to please your teacher but you should know that everyone who takes even a small number of improv teachers will invariably run into a class or teacher that they simply don't jibe with.

That doesn't mean that you're bad at this, it means you're in a particular context that is making you feel a bit out of sorts. **Do not get in the habit of letting your view of yourself be dependent on what someone else thinks of you.** Especially one particular person.

If possible, try to enjoy this as a learning opportunity. It's bad to worry about someone else's opinion of you, but if that other person is a teacher there may be something to learn here.

My second level improv class was like this. The teacher was actively and evidently bored by anything I did. And watching his glassy-eyed expression when I started scenes I became painfully aware of myself as a boring performer. My first reaction was to be angry at him for not simply liking me more (mind you, I do not know what he ACTUALLY thought, this was my impression—though certainly he was not laughing or smiling).

But then I was able to shift my mindset and think of him as representing the portion of an audience that would not like me. Like, let's assume that no matter how great you become at improv, there will be people who simply do not enjoy your work. What if you could isolate that section of the audience, get them into a lab, and practice with JUST THEM until you "figure out" what it is they want? Wouldn't that be interesting to know?

I gave up on the idea of this teacher ever truly liking me, and instead started scanning for little moments of victory. I determined that this teacher liked very very small moves—and that he hated almost any big twists or fantastical elements. The smaller, the more natural the better. I abandoned the idea of being funny, or being impressive, and tried simply to say things that felt honest in the moment. I got a few smirks. I got a "good scene."

I can't say I ever "beat" this teacher. Other students got huge reactions out of him, but he never even learned my name (until years later). But I learned how to be comfortable in the environment where he wasn't cheerleading me. I learned to have a sense of accomplishment just by staying in touch with my own thoughts while in his class. I didn't need him to like me; I was learning stuff anyway.

ARE YOU PLEASING YOURSELF?

"Being in your head" often comes after you do a class or show and feel unliked by the audience: be it other classmates a teacher or an actual audience. But how do YOU feel about what you did? Rather than fall into an amorphous feeling a general self-doubt, can you pick a particular goal and measure yourself against this?

For example, do you wish to be initiating more clearly? That is something that you can do better at within the context of one session. The trick is to know that you may in fact do well at your goal, and still not have the overwhelming approval from others that you're subconsciously (or maybe consciously) looking for. Forget other people's reactions. Did you accomplish your goal?

I had a show recently in which I just wanted to "be in the moment" and not pre-plan any moves. Meaning if I was in a scene with multiple people, I didn't want to mentally leave the scene and start to think about "what would sound cool" as that is a trap I personally fall into. I wanted to just be in the scene, and react when the action of the scene headed my way. Well, I did that, and the results were … well, not great. My responses were a bit slow, and stodgy and not immediately funny. But, as I assessed myself after, they WERE natural, they were truthful, they were real. I had accomplished my goal. I was proud of it, even though it hadn't led to the amazing show I also wanted—I avoided getting in my head by being proud of hitting the goal *I* wanted to hit.

BE PATIENT
Another question: how long have you been doing improv? Is it less than a year? Then "being in your head" is just part of learning something new. You can't avoid it. You wouldn't expect to be able to sit at a piano and improvise beautiful songs after just ten months of lessons. Yet improv students seem to get frustrated if, during their first year of study, they find it difficult. You understand that to learn something means to go through a period in which you are clumsy at it, right? Well, maybe you're just in one of those necessary phases of being clumsy. Rest easy: you are growing more powerful.

DON'T COMPARE
Remember that you don't have to be the BEST to be good enough. You will see classmates and others who are better than you. There is room for you to be good even though there will ALWAYS be someone who is just... better.

AVOID HEADY CHALLENGES
Are you working on getting ideas from an opening? Are you working on "game"—meaning are you working on having clear and simple comedic ideas that define your whole scene? Those are two notoriously thinky goals. There's almost no way to practice them and not feel "in your head."

So one way to get out of your head is: take a break from working on that stuff. Find a workshop or a practice where there are no openings, and no focus on game. Focus on "saying yes" and "committing." That leads to fun scene work that is light and easy. Without game, your scenes may amble from different idea to different idea. Without an opening, they may take a while to get going. But you will feel lighter and easier.

There are workshops and teachers who specialize in this type of work. They'll often sell themselves as "get out of your head" workshops. There will be a lot of physical work—matching each other or starting with a big silly move and then justifying it. Or maybe there will be exercises where you make a big emotional choice and then immediately start heightening it. They are fun, freeing exercises. Might be just what you need to re-discover the fun of doing improv.

Mind you: these are just vacations. At some point, you're going to have to immerse yourself in the "heady" challenges of getting ideas from an opening, or minding the game of your scene. But there's nothing wrong with taking a break from that stuff to re-energize yourself with fun in the meantime.

PRACTICE BEING A FAN OF YOURSELF

I know that I'm venturing into saccharine bumper sticker-sized therapy here, but an essential skill to doing this is recalling the feeling that you are fundamentally a funny person. Not the MOST funny, not the MOST charismatic, but just—funny.

Once we like a performer, we are very forgiving of moments in which he or she falls short in a show. We barely notice them since we so surely believe that a better moment is coming down the road.

Can you simply decide to have that same attitude towards yourself?

You MUST believe that on some level you are funny or smart or charming or you wouldn't have been able to walk into that first improv class.

Somewhere in you is the belief that you are good. Make that feeling grow. When you have a good scene in class, when you are funny in a conversation with someone at work, when you write a funny email—and you know it—hold onto that feeling. Picture it like a seedling sprouting in the vast prairies of your mind and give it water and sun. Let that feeling grow. It is ultimately what will solve the problem of being in your head forever: the belief that you are good, and that when things aren't going well that you are a good person having a bad day.

WHAT DO WE DO ABOUT "THAT GUY?"

One of the most common categories of questions I get at my improv blog is the "I'm playing with someone bad. What do I do?"

EXAMPLES:

"Will, I get to play on an awesome Harold team, but there is at 1 player who seems to ask the audience what is funny in shows. They don't really ever present the swagger you mention. The worst part is that they cause a domino effect and bring other players into that insecure zone. How do you get around that/push through it?"

"I have a friend who is a great person but an absolute stage hog. It just brings down the show or jam group that she's a part of. Should I be the one to tell her this or should I just let her find out on her own?"

"Hi Will- I've been struggling with this question internally for a while, and I'd like to get your perspective on it. I recently started practicing with a group that does mostly organic improv. The issue I am having is that one individual interjects himself into every scene, mostly before a game is even established. How can I make him aware that this behavior is detrimental to the group without insulting him? Is the solution to just practice with another group?"

"I'm a beginning improviser at university, and my uni has an improv team that has some problems. The guy who runs it resists any suggestions from anyone, isn't good about encouraging improvement on any level, has been doing this for years, etc. The team also has a lot of cheap, gimmicky habits (imo, I guess). But the team performs. A lot. Is it better to play with them and get performance experience or stay away because I just wish it was a better environment? Thanks."

"I recently formed a practice group with a group of great improvisers. However, the coach they've selected—and adore—is not to my liking whatsoever. While I find this person to be a great performer, I find their coaching style low energy and extremely negative (the criticism is not constructive), and our fundamental views on improv are very different. Do you have any advice on how to navigate this situation?"

"How do I tell my teammates I think we had a bad show? I try just talking about the things I do that are bad (not listening, bailing on choices, etc.) but then that lets everyone else off the hook. No one else is open to talk about the shows that bomb. Is that how it should be? Should I just keep my mouth shut and hope that everyone gets better on their own?"

Variations include that so and so is sticking out amongst the group, or maybe is behind everyone else, or playing really broadly, or mugging at the audience, or is somehow hurting otherwise good scenes. Many varieties of "when am I allowed to tell this person they're bad" or "what do i do if I'm stuck with someone who's bad?"

A qualification: I'm not talking about people who are being jerks as human beings, like people who mistreat you or are mean. Or someone who does something straight-up inappropriate on stage, like puts you or someone in a sexual situation or who criticizes the actual humans around him/her onstage. You can and should walk away from people who are mean to you or make you feel bad. If it's in class, make sure the teacher noticed or if it's a jam, tell the host.

I'm talking about people that you think are improvisers with bad comedic or acting taste and for whatever reason you're about to do a scene or show or class with them.

YOU GO TO THEM
Without knowing the specific situation, here is my first instinct every time that question is asked: YOU GO TO THEM. You stop questioning what's wrong with the other person and you focus on what you are doing. You say "yes and" and get on that page and play. If they won't budge, you go to them and you don't even hesitate. Don't even think about what might be wrong them, you just play.

You are thinking: "No, you haven't seen this person." Not that person, no. But I have played with every kind of player, often for YEARS. And if you're asking me how to play with that person the answer is: YOU GO TO THEM. If they are literally denying their own reality each and every line, then yes-and the last thing said and change with them if need be. No excuses. This is the answer, and the sooner you learn it the sooner this will be fun.

You're thinking "Well, no, this person just needs to fix like one thing—can I say it?" Especially if you are new to this—and I'm counting new in the "less than 3 years" kinda new—then you don't really know enough. Even if you said something and the person was able to correct it, it might not have the effect you want. There might be some good behind what they're doing. The better solution is for you to adjust YOUR play, because you can control that. You know what you feel like, so keep trying different things until you enjoy the scenes.

You can still be yourself. If they are broad, then be your version of broad. If they are crazy, justify it in a way that keeps the fun of that crazy. If they are quiet and take a while to talk, then chill out. If they refuse to make eye contact, then go without eye contact. If like to make things really unusual right away, just yes-and it towards something that interests you which is what you are supposed to be doing. Assume there is a way to do it and do it. You can do it. You don't need them to change, you can connect with them whatever they do. That is your job.

Doug Moe, a UCBT improviser, talks about bringing this up to Kevin Dorff, a former Second City mainstage player and long-time writer for Conan O'Brien. "His advice was don't worry about 'the guy.' He said, you'll get rid of 'the guy' and there'll be a new 'the guy.'"

Would you rather be right or be in a great scene?

The performers MUST connect and meet else the scene does not exist. Agreement before all else. In fairness they should meet halfway, but if you find yourself in a scene with people who won't budge, then for the sake of the scene you go all the way to them.

In the second improv workshop I ever took in a black box theater on Ludlow St. in Manhattan in 1998, I did a scene with a guy who was, I can say in fairness, a terrible improviser. He contradicted facts I said, he mugged for the audience. He interrupted me and talked about sex nonstop. Problem: the audience (rest of the class) loved him. They cracked up at everything he did, laughing at his outrageousness. I sat stewing, knowing that I was doing it "right" and was getting no attention for it. I was brand new and could not get my thoughts together while playing with this jerk.

At the break I said to a friend of mine "That guy is so annoying" and my friend, who was grinning from ear to ear, shrugged his shoulders—"it's hilarious."

And he didn't mean that my frustrating predicament was hilarious. He meant this guy's outrageousness was enjoyable, and that my friend had not been paying attention to my artistic pain because who gives a shit?

And I realized I had to choose: did I want to be right, or would I prefer to be part of a fun scene?

I wish I had just said yes and made it work. That I had agreed that I was here to see the doctor for "dick pills." That my name was "Roger Roger Roger." That I was bribing him to tell my ex-wife that I was no longer on heroin. That I was "super gay." That even though I got flustered, that I amped up the fluster, so the audience could enjoy that more since they already were. I still think about it all the time. He was wrong, but by not playing, I was also wrong.

True, I didn't have to be on a team with him or even see him after that workshop. Still, my job is to make the scene work. **To play it as it is, not as I think it should be.**

You're probably thinking: I can't do that. This person is no good in any way and anything I do he/she will wreck. Maybe. I advise you at least to think of it in these terms: "I don't yet know how to make that good."

More: I asked someone who was on a great team if they ever sat down and had a big honest talk about what kind of improv they wanted to do. And this person said to me "We would never give each other notes, and even if we did, no one would take them." And that illuminated it for me. You can't worry about what the other person SHOULD do, because you don't know for sure, and you can't control it. You have to worry about your side of the street. Say yes. Add to it. You go to them. You make it work.

Even more: In some future group, you will worry that YOU are this person which everyone else dreads. At that time, you will be happy if you have discouraged the part of your brain that judges others so that it won't be so powerful when it turns in on you. I've done it to myself—judging harshly—it takes a lot of effort to undo.

WAIT, SO HOW CAN I TELL IF SOMEONE IS BEING A JERK?

Once again, if they are treating you badly as a person—either onstage or off—then you don't have to put up with it. But if just don't like their style, then you owe it your future self as an unbeatable improviser to yes-and those moves.

YOU'RE NOT GETTING IT. I HAVE TO TELL SOMEONE.

Tell your coach. If you don't have a coach, leave the group and form a new one. Or form a second group and play with both and see if that solves the problem. If this is the third time you've done this, read this whole essay again.

WHAT IF MY TEAM SAT AROUND AND GAVE EACH OTHER NOTES? YOU KNOW, JUST TO CLEAR THE AIR?

Nope. You're trying to direct the team, not play on it.

If you really need to get something off your chest, then go right to the person and be candid but polite, one-on-one. Trust them with your honest opinion, but do them the courtesy of having specific examples, worded in terms of how your felt, not what you think they should be doing. So don't say "you shouldn't walk on so much' or "you make things crazy too fast" but you can say "When you walked on to my scene in practice last week and endowed me as a member of a rap crew, it threw me off."

Many people frustrated with a teammate will go to a THIRD teammate and ask in confidence if he/she shares the opinion. "Am I crazy? Person X is bad, right?" If this helps to let go of your bad feeling, then do it. But don't make a habit of bitching behind people's back, it can be a bad habit. Also, we all have a knack of picking as our confidant someone that we believe will agree with us anyway.

Learn to play with this person and if you just can't do it, make plans to get to a new group.

WAIT, BUT, I ACTUALLY REALLY LIKE THIS PERSON BUT THEY JUST DO THIS ONE THING, COULD I GIVE THEM THE ONE NOTE?
Eyes on your own paper.

NO. I HAVE BEEN ON MY TEAM FOR YEARS AND I KNOW HOW THIS TEAM WORKS AND I NEED TO SAY SOMETHING ABOUT THE KIND OF PLAY THIS PERSON IS DOING.
Okay. If you have been doing improv for, I don't know, more than three years, minimum? And if you have been on that particular ensemble for at least three years and you are among the most senior people on that team, then, yes, you have a right to speak to the overall tone of the team. Meaning if you are a veteran in general and also a veteran on that ensemble. Here's my advice on that:

Say you want a team meeting in a BRIEF email because you need to discuss issues with shows. The meeting should be after a show when you were all going to be together. Everyone stands since that's a guaranteed way to keep the meeting short. Speak your piece in a general way and then give a specific example. "I think we've been going too crazy too fast and I want the shows to be slower, like last week when we were all fucking blow job machines in the first ten minutes—I just want to not do that." The more specific the better: "I don't like when we initiate scenes with fights. All I want to do is not fight and every initiation picks a fight. Last week I walked out and when Bob said 'Get the fuck out of my office' I couldn't even think." Or "I feel we're going for home runs every time we open our mouths and I want to go for base hits. Don't make me a Nazi before I even say what I'm doing." Or "I feel people get tagged out after one line every show." Or "Could we do a show where I don't get picked up and carried around the stage?" Bring up a show that did what you want. "The one where we were all at desks, and then we ended up rollerblading together—that one felt right."

What will probably happen is people will discuss if they see it the same way or not. They'll bring up times that the behavior you don't like actually helped. They'll point out how in the show you liked there was some of that behavior you said you didn't like, or that it was BECAUSE of that show that things happened in other shows you didn't like.

And then you'll all settle on some rule: "No tag outs for the first half of the show." Or "No going meta in the opening." Something that's simple so it doesn't restrict people too much and something that's easy to follow so there's no argument over whether it was followed or not. People will generally be cool with that in the name of the team being smoother.

My brother and I do two prov and although we weren't irritated with each other we did settle on one rule: "No fighting in the first line of the show." Sometimes we break even that easy-to-follow rule and after the show we'll say "we fought in the first line" and the other person will say "Oh right, right. Yes, we shouldn't do that." and then next time we won't. My brother and I have been doing improv for more than ten years.

In my first three years of doing improv, we had team meetings every few months. They rarely helped. I think we just didn't know enough about improv in general or our own improv preferences to really talk about them. Then they started happening once every two years. Those were helpful.

HOW CAN I GET BETTER AT GAME?

Okay, but can we first talk about what you mean by "game?" Because I find a lot of confusion with this comes from two different people thinking of the word "game" in different contexts. People will say "so and so didn't play game" and that phrase, all by itself, doesn't tell me a lot except that the person saying it didn't like a show.

ONE IDEA AT A TIME

At its very simplest, having a "game" means your scene is funny. And it has mostly just ONE funny thing that runs throughout it and probably heightens as it goes—meaning it becomes a more absurd version of itself. "Who's On First": the "game" is that Costello misunderstands that the name of the baseball players are also pronounces. That game goes throughout the scene.

So at its simplest, when you say "have a game" to improvisers, you mean for them to have their scenes settle on one idea and then stays centered around that idea.

For example, an improv scene which isn't worried about game might be about a number of ideas, only loosely related. Maybe the scene is about a couple moving into a new house, and we learn that the husband is a very nervous sort who has overly planned the move, and we spend a little time playing with that idea. Then we discover that the wife character has a very new age sensibility and has made alterations to the house to reflect her philosophy. A couple of moves there to confirm that funny bit. And along the way we learn that they had a honeymoon fraught with disasters that are funny but not really related to either of their basic personalities. There's games in here, but the improvisers aren't worried about sticking to just one, and they're not concerned with heightening any of them more than naturally happens in the flow of the scenes. This could be a rich and enjoyable scene, finding itself one step at a time. It also could be aimless and flat.

If you want to "play game," you'd stop at the first discovery that the husband was a nervous sort who had overly-planned everything—and try to expand just that idea into your whole scene. You'd learn that he alienated the realtor with questions; he booked three different sets of movers out of a fear that one would abandon them. That he is wearing a germ-resistant suit and that she had acquiesced to a honeymoon in the Arctic where diseases have trouble surviving. The scene would be more narrow in its focus, but it would heighten farther and faster. You could escalate to huge laughs, amazing your audience at how organized and pointed your scene is. You also might force it too much and get a scene that's too broad and rushed.

"Playing game" means turning "if this is true what else is true" into "if this ONE UNUSUAL THING is true, then what else is true?"

The idea of "game" turns improv from jazz explorations into tight pop songs. That can be good or bad news, depending on your goals, taste and ability.

So: is that what you mean by "getting better at game"—like just having one idea per scene? That's not really so hard to do once you've decided that what you want to do. Try to use the first funny idea you have more and more rather than switching.

HEIGHTENING

But some people, when they say "play game"—what they mean is that they want to see you hit a comedic idea several times in a way that obviously gets more absurd as you go. They want to see something REPEAT and to HEIGHTEN. If you don't do that, then to these people you did not play game.

This is where stuff starts to get confusing. Because maybe you had an improv scene that started slowly, then found something funny and then you just edited it. And then someone says "you didn't play game." But you DID, kind of, in that you arrived at a comedic idea. You just didn't stay with it.

Sticking with the "Who's on First" example—someone who prioritizes heightening wouldn't think Abbott & Costello were playing game until the conversation moved onto the subject of second base. Telling someone that the name of the first baseman is "Who"—well, that's not really playing game (to some people). But once you've revealed that the second baseman's name is "What"—ah! NOW you're playing game.

Okay, then what these people want is REPETITION and HEIGHTENING.

A CLEAR, EXPLAINABLE IDEA

And to yet ANOTHER group of people, playing "game" means that you are basing your comedy around an idea that you can explain. It's an absurd philosophy, or a clearly unusual thing as opposed to just a silly voice, or an absurd way of walking or something. If you're getting your laughs in a purely silly way, then to some people, you are not playing game.

I don't agree with this. If something is funny, it has a game. It just might not be the game you like. A silly voice is a game, it's just a silly one. The game is "say things in this silly voice." But there are people who dismiss silliness alone as being not enough.

So sometimes when people say "you're not playing game" they mean "you're just being silly."

UNUSUAL THING - REACTION - JUSTIFICATION

Finally, some people really love to break down what's funny about a scene into separate parts. A very common way to break down the comedy of a scene is the UNUSUAL THING, followed by a REACTION to that unusual thing, following soon by a JUSTIFICATION—or an explanation as to why this unusual thing and reaction is happening.

So, staying with "Who's On First"—the UNUSUAL THING is that the players have pronouns for names. The REACTION is Costello's blustery confusion. The justification is right at the top when Bud says "you know players these days have really unusual names." So I guess it's a sign of the times that baseball players have names so weird that they even have pronouns for names.

Breaking a game down into unusual thing, reaction, justification can be useful because that's the order that we generally discover our funny things in improv scenes. If you like thinking of scenes in this way, you can check to make sure you check the boxes. Do we have an unusual thing? Did someone react to it? Do we have an explanation for why this world is like this?

Another way to break this down is that the initial unusual thing is the PREMISE. And then the reaction and justification combine with that premise to give us a GAME. So the PREMISE of Who's On First is that "players on this team have pronouns for names" and the GAME is "every time we tell Costello this, he gets confused and mad."

This way is useful because it makes sure that more than one person was involved in making the game. Someone proposed a PREMISE, and then someone else reacted which gave us a GAME.

So some people will tell you that you can't play game unless you can express the comedy of your scene in these discernible parts. These people are no fun and write big long posts on their blogs about what's wrong with improv these days. Sometimes I am one of these people.

DEFINE YOUR TERMS

So if someone wants to get better at game, ask them what they mean. Or if they're trying to please a particular teacher or coach, they should ask that teacher/coach to be specific.

- Do you mean scenes should be about mostly one idea?
- Do you mean they should heighten more?
- Do you mean they should be about something that's an explainable idea and not just silly?
- Do you mean I should hit each of the separate components of a game, and in such a way that I can tell you what I consider those components to be?

GAME EQUALS TASTE

As a teacher, I don't like when I see the word "game" used simply to express disapproval of a show. "They don't play game," someone will say. That's not enough. What is it you don't like about the show? Until you've said that, I don't think you've said anything.

SAYING YOU DON'T LIKE GAME

Separately, I've seen students turn that strategy around. They'll take classes at UCB, audition for a Harold Team, not get a call back and then say "I don't like how the UCB focuses on game." Or maybe they'll have a class where the teacher doesn't think they are funny and the student will say "that teacher focuses too much on game." In both of those cases, the student has understandably had his or her feelings hurt, but these not truly disagreements about "game" or whether it's a useful philosophy. They're just upset they weren't picked.

YEAH, BUT REALLY, HOW CAN I GET BETTER AT GAME?

Ok, well, "playing game" generally means you do improv a bit more like you're writing a sketch on your feet. It should feel like your scenes come up a funny idea, and then once it finds its idea it uses that idea as the main theme.

Here some things you can work on.

1. MEMORY

So much of improv is about being in the moment and reacting to what just happened and trying not to plan ahead that it can be difficult to remember anything that happened earlier in the scene. But if you want your scenes to have a nice clean comedic shape, you have to. When someone funny happens, we are going to want to have that funny thing happen again, which means you have to remember it.

I've seen lots of players who are entertaining performers, and they have a knack for reacting to almost any move in a way that can get a laugh, but cannot seem to remember how they behaved just a few lines before. If your character gets a big laugh out of being pulled over and then telling the policeman "I don't trust cops" then it is weird if in a later scene that same character tells someone "I love cops." I would say that you are TOO in the moment, and that you need to hold onto the big moments of scenes or else your improv is going to be shapeless and rambly.

When someone funny or unusual happens, restate it. Right as you notice it.

Secondly, it helps if you are a reactive character—someone who is emotionally invested in the scene around them, and who reacts with their body and voice when something happens. If someone says "The name of the first baseman is who" and you get upset and snap back "I'm not asking you Who's on First!" you will remember that moment better than if you calmly answer in a robotic voice.

2. GIVE IT A TITLE

Games are generally simple, and if you want to show that you see the game, it helps to be able to name it. So practice naming scenes while you're watching them. Names of scenes should reflect the main funny part and be simple. Sample titles of scenes:

- "Break-up Talk With Blockbuster"
- "Dad Hates Commies"
- "Cake Equals Sex"

But I actually mean: give it a title while you're in the scene. Say a line of dialogue that summarizes the main point of what's funny.

On the backline, listen for a line of dialogue that seems to encapsulate what's funny about the scene. Generally there will be one. Something like:

- "I'll be honest, I'm using this job interview to get back together with you."
- "Oh no! That guy we pantsed is King."
- "Never trust the gym."

When I come around to a second beat, or if I'm deciding if I should enter a scene, I'll repeat that line in my head to inspire me—"never trust the gym"—and then start the second beat: "Okay, I've set up cameras in the stationary bikes. See what those bastards are up to after I leave the room."

The title—by which I mean the telltale line which summarizes the game.

3. JUSTIFY EVERYTHING

You can get laughs in an improv scene by just repeating a silly thing over and over again. But it's probably not a good game until there is a justification to explain why the character is doing that thing. Something simple, but something: The Wild And Crazy Guys are acting that way because they are from Europe. The Chicken Lady is the child of a farmer and a chicken. Penelope wants to one-up you because she is jealous in the way that we are all jealous, just more.

4. BE GOOD AT BEING WRONG

Justifying is no good if it explains away the absurdity. You must justify things so they make sense to the character but are still funny to the audience. Why is the boxing trainer advocating to stop throwing punches while in the ring? Because he read about Gandhi and now believes non-violence can beat anything.

Think about movie villains and masterminds. They have reasons for what they do, but we the audience know they are "wrong." They still have reasons, are smart and are compelling. As an improviser, it's more useful to be the bad guy. To be the Joker, not Batman. To be Alan Rickman, not Bruce Willis.

If someone says you are washing your car with a toothbrush, have a silly reason not a sensible one. That's being good at game.

5. LOOK FOR TWO THINGS

I feel like in general there's one funny thing—the unusual thing—that stands out as the funny part of a scene. But generally that one thing is only good when it's connected to something else. Like an old bit on a Conan O'Brien sketch was Mother Theresa tearing apart her hotel room in a fury over late room service. ANGRY MOTHER THERESA would stand out in your mind, but the context of TEARING APART A HOTEL ROOM is what really makes it funny. Those two things. Make sure you are taking both elements with you into second beats. Not that all the specifics have to stay the same, but remember there's two things playing off each other. So if you want to put your ANGRY MOTHER THERESA somewhere, it's got to be somewhere as mundane and everyday as a hotel room, like maybe she's having road rage at a stoplight or else screaming at a TSA agent in an airport.

Or another way to put it is think of your game having an UNUSUAL part and a particular BASE REALITY part. If it's a high school principal who seems to always mispronounce brand names—be aware that it's not just the mis-pronouncing that's funny, it's that it's coming from a principal—someone in a position of authority.

6. TAKE A SKETCH CLASS

Game tends to make your improvised scenes more like ones that were written ahead of time. So take a sketch writing class. You'll watch comedy sketches and analyze why they work. Your teacher will ask you to write sketches where there's one main idea that runs throughout your scene. You'll be working muscles that will come into play when you do improv again.

HOW DO YOU MAKE A LIVING?

I had a level 1 student in a button-down shirt who had a mortgage come up to me after class recently and say "Man, I love this. I'd really love to be paid to do comedy."

I believe he was thinking: *I'd love my current paycheck and stability in exchange for coming to this class.* That doesn't ever happen.

But it's maybe the second most common question/comment I get from people, right after "how do I get out of my head?" Some variety of "how do you make a living?" or "How could I quit my job and do improv/comedy full time?"

Short answer: You don't get paid to do improv. You can get paid to teach/coach it, making a solid notch or two below what you'd make at a cubicle job.

And "getting paid to do COMEDY," practically speaking, means living the life of a freelancer in which you hustle lots of little gigs all the time, hoping for a bigger one. And then even a bigger gig like writing for a TV show is something you get hired for just a few months at a time.

In this life, you get a lot of your time returned to you and a lot of freedom, but you get stomach-dropping insecurity when you think about: children, vacations, property, the future or even just paying rent. That's the trade-off.

Most people I know who are "doing comedy" have either a part-time job (teaching, usually), or a night-time restaurant job, or a flexible retail job, or possibly a spouse/family who bails them out once a year or so (though I hear people WISH for that more than actually having that). They sit in audition rooms and talk about real estate licenses, babysitting gigs, tutoring opportunities.

Once you make yourself available for creative stuff full-time, you WILL find a lot of small gigs some of which might lead one day to bigger gigs. Small gigs: teaching things, web videos, short films, auditions. Bigger things: TV and movie things that pay SAG rates and residuals that make your financial life temporarily easier.

CASE STUDY: ME
NOTE: The following answer is based on my experience. Everyone's is unique. I'd love to hear others, actually, if anyone cares to send theirs to me (how do you make a living, those without day jobs?). If I get enough I'll publish them (with permission, of course!. Send to whines atsign gmail dot com it you'd like).

What I did: From when I was 26 until 32 I was a full-time computer programmer making okay money. I socked a lot of it away because I was responsible and also boring.

At 33, after having done improv for 3 years I quit my full-time job and tried to do computer programming part time along with improv coaching/teaching to let me write and audition for commercials. Turns out I did very little writing/auditioning and instead ran out of money and had to get a full-time job programming again when I was 35.

I programmed computers for 1.5 more years, while teaching/coaching on the side and auditioning at lunch, i.e. not that often. I also started dabbling in stand-up where I could (not often: once every two weeks).

Then at 36 I got a job producing videos for AOL (thank you Sara Schaefer, i.e. a friend I'd made via NYC comedy world), which felt much more creative, though this was still a full-time "show up for your job" job. I learned to shoot and edit. I did that for 2 years, while teaching and auditioning on the side and writing some stuff and making web videos.

Then at 38 I got a job running the UCB school in NYC (thank you, UCB friends) which paid a small steady amount with huge time flexibility. This was essentially like having a steady part-time job. I taught more and aggressively auditioned, which I could do because I'd at this point spent several years doing it and getting known in the NYC scene.

Now I'm in LA: a "professional" improv teacher and, gulp, commercial "actor"(?) who's trying to get acting/writing work.

What I got paid for last year, very roughly in order of amount: teaching improv, residuals for two commercials, running UCB school, writing puzzles and appearing on NPR quiz show, writing for a soft-scripted reality show, acting in web videos and one TV part, plus very small computer programming gigs.

Which all added up to about as much as I made when I was 27 and wrote javascript for a computer programming company full-time. Though now I spend most of my waking hours doing fun things. I'll take that deal!

I certainly don't mean this as bragging, I hope that's obvious. Nor do I feel that this is a "poor me" situation. I am being specific because I think people who are not doing comedy seem to sometimes "flatten" the comedy world and think that "guy teaching my improv class" is very close to "person who is on SNL" and also "guy who is in this commercial playing all the time on my Hulu" is close to "guy who's been in 5 movies this year."

"Doing comedy" = "being free lance" = lots of freedom and time but less money and less consistency.

P.S. To even have a chance of this freelance life, now that you can maybe picture what it's like, you need a network of friends who know and like you. Stand-ups rely on the people they've come up with, improv people need their former fellow students and teammates. Unless you're so amazingly talented or a direct blood relation of an established person, I don't know of another way in.

P.P.S. If you're trying to get the most talented actor you personally know to be in your short film that requires several long days of shooting, try offering him/her $100!

www.ingramcontent.com/pod-product-compliance
Lightning Source LLC
Chambersburg PA
CBHW052008290426
44112CB00014B/2164